Encyclopaedia of
SWIMMING

Encyclopaedia of
SWIMMING

Compiled by
PAT BESFORD

ST MARTIN'S PRESS

First published in the United States of America 1971
by St Martin's Press, 175 Fifth Avenue,
New York, N.Y. 10010, U.S.A.

Library of Congress catalog card number
78–157521

PRINTED IN GREAT BRITAIN

Introduction

The idea behind this book was simplicity itself, to bring together, under one cover, the many facets that make up the sport of swimming. Originally, it did not seem such a difficult job. But as the weeks turned into months and the floor and every available space in my office became piled with papers and magazines, files and reference books, cuttings and copy paper, I began to wonder not so much why I had started but whether I would ever finish.

Performances and results from English-speaking nations have been given especial emphasis in this edition. Even so, many people and events that I would have liked to have included have had to be left out. Perhaps another time. . . .

Every effort has been made to be accurate but in this first attempt at a comprehensive Encyclopaedia of Swimming it would be foolish to believe that there will not be mistakes. And if readers do find errors I would be most grateful to know about them.

London   PAT BESFORD

Acknowledgements

So many people have been kind enough to help me check facts and figures and provide information. I almost need an index to refer to them. To everyone 'thank you' and especially to:

Dr. Istvan Barany (Hungary)
A. W. Barrett (New Zealand)
Alex Bulley (South Africa)
Jock Coutts (Scotland)
Mrs. Bobby Dawson (USA)
Gerald Forsberg (Long Distance Swimming)
S. B. Grange (Australia)
Hall of Fame, Fort Lauderdale (USA)

Harry Hainsworth (USA)
Margaret Jarvis
Norris and Ross McWhirter
Austin Rawlinson (GB)
R. Max Ritter (USA)
Sydney Skilton (Channel Swimming)
Nick Theirry (Canada)
Vaughan Thomas (Wales)
Miss Belle White

P. B.

Illustrations

PICTURE CREDITS

Associated Press Ltd: 1, 12, 18, 19; Tony Duffy: 2, 5, 15, 21; E. D. Lacey: 3, 4, 14; C. A. Otten, 8; Central Press: 9; Press Association: 6; *Daily Mirror:* 10; *Yorkshire Post:* 13; *Swedish Report 1921:* 16; United Press International: 20.

Key

A.S.A. – Amateur Swimming Association (of England).
F.I.N.A. – Federation Internationale de Natation Amateur.
I.O.C. – International Olympic Committee.
L.E.N. – Ligue Europeenne de Natation.

National Abbreviations

Argentina	Arg	Italy	It
Australia	Aus	Ireland	Ire
Austria	Aut	Japan	Jap
Belgium	Belg	Mexico	Mex
Brazil	Braz	Netherlands	Neth
Canada	Can	New Zealand	NZ
Cuba	Cuba	Peru	Peru
Czechoslovakia	Czech	Poland	Pol
Denmark	Den	Scotland	Scot
England	Eng	South Africa	SAf
East Germany (DDR)*	EGer	Soviet Union	USSR
Eire	Eire	Spain	Sp
Finland	Fin	Sweden	Swe
France	Fr	United States	USA
Germany*	Ger	Wales	Wales
Greece	Gre	West Germany*	WGer
Hungary	Hun	Yugoslavia	Yugo

m. – metres.
y. – yards. If used beside a time, it indicates that the performance for a metric distance was recorded over the equivalent longer yards distance.
fr. – free-style.
ba. – back-stroke.
br. – breast-stroke.

bu. – butterfly. If used beside a time under a breast-stroke heading, it indicates that the over-water arm recovery was used during some or all of the race, prior to the separation of breast-stroke and butterfly.
uw. – under-water. If used beside a time under a breast-stroke heading, it indicates that the performance included swimming long distances under water before this was prohibited (as of 1 Jan. 1957).

Times are indicated as follows: $1:01 \cdot 1 = 1$ min. $1 \cdot 1$ sec.

* East and West Germany were accepted by F.I.N.A. as separate national federations in 1950. The I.O.C., however, did not allow separate German teams in the Olympics until the 1968 Games in Mexico.

A

ADMINISTRATION. See AMATEUR SWIMMING ASSOCIATION; ENGLISH SCHOOLS SWIMMING ASSOCIATION; FEDERATION INTERNATIONALE DE NATATION AMATEUR; GREAT BRITAIN COMMITTEE; INTERNATIONAL TECHNICAL COMMITTEES; LIGUE EUROPEENNE DE NATATION.

AGE-GROUP. The United States were the pioneers of age-group swimming, a system of competition for youngsters of like age. Regarded as a development process and not an end in itself, the pioneering Americans have achieved tremendous international success through following this policy.

At the Mexico Olympics of 1968, 90 per cent of the American team, who won 58 out of a possible 90 swimming medals, were or had been age-group competitors. Altogether, the United States recognized 686 different events for their national age-group rankings.

The most common groups are 10 years and under, 11–12, 13–14 and 15–17 years, but the many countries who have followed the example of the United States choose even single year age-groups if this suits them best.

The A.S.A. have organized national age-group events on a district team basis since 1966 and in 1970 instituted open age-group competitions on an individual basis. F.I.N.A. have their own international age-group committee, as a sub-committee of their swimming committee.

AMATEURISM. The definition of amateurism of F.I.N.A. (Rule 49), which is binding on all affiliated national federations, states: 'An amateur sportsman is one who engages in sport solely for pleasure and physical, mental or social benefit he derives therefrom and to whom the sport is nothing more than recreation.'

In the modern era, when the demands upon the time of the individual for training and competition are tremendous, this simple sentence is an ideal to which few at the top can totally subscribe. Nevertheless, swimming in many countries is basically as amateur as any sport can be in the 1970s.

F.I.N.A. cite examples in which individuals cease to be amateurs by:

competing, teaching, coaching or giving exhibitions for payment, direct or indirect, in cash or kind;

taking part in a competition or exhibition with anyone he knows not to be an amateur (except in Services competitions);

accepting reimbursement for board or travelling in excess of the amount actually out of pocket (though a swimmer may accept a daily sum for petty expenses actually expended);

betting on swimming competitions;

turning into cash any prize;

capitalizing upon athletic fame;

accepting direct or indirect payment for loss of time or wages in order to train or compete.

A professional in the following sports is considered to be a professional in swimming: athletics, badminton, baseball, basketball, bowling, boxing, cricket, cycling, fencing, football, golf, gymnastics, handball, hockey, lacrosse, lawn and court tennis, rowing, shooting, skating, ski-ing, weightlifting and wrestling.

An amateur shall not lose his status if he teaches elementary swimming as part of his duties as a teacher of scholastic subjects—or by competing with professionals in baseball, basketball, cricket, football, golf, handball, hockey, lacrosse, lawn and court tennis, provided no money prize is offered or received—**or** by competing or giving exhibitions in life saving with bath or surf bathing attendants or life guards (who if paid are considered to be professionals), provided there is no monetary reward.

AMATEUR SWIMMING ASSOCIATION.

The A.S.A., the governing body for the sport in England, are accepted as having been founded on 7 Jan. 1869, though in fact were not known by this name until 17 years after this date (see Metropolitan Swimming Association).

During the intervening years, continual rows concerning amateur and professionalism caused breakaways and the formation of a rival association. Finally, on 3 Mar. 1886 the warring factions sank their differences and agreed on a set of 135 rules, based on those of the Amateur Athletic Association and the National Cyclists Union, which have been the basis of A.S.A. administration ever since and have been copied by bodies throughout the world.

Though primarily concerned with England, the A.S.A., by virtue of their greater size and number of clubs—by 1969 1,630 were affiliated—have dictated the policy of British swimming in which Scotland and Wales also participate.

After 100 years of amateur administration, the A.S.A. appointed their first professional secretary, Norman Sarsfield, in 1970 as successor to Harold Fern (see separate entry), who had been honorary secretary for 49 years.

The A.S.A. are divided into five districts, whose club memberships are approximately: Midlands (380), North (280), North-East (250), South (580) and West (160). In addition, the Royal Navy, Royal Air Force, Army, English Schools and British Universities are directly affiliated to the A.S.A.

The government of English swimming is in the hands of the A.S.A. Council, who meet once a year and the A.S.A. committee, consisting of the President (elected annually), Life Presidents (in 1970 these are Harold Fern and C. W. Plant), hon. treasurer and two representatives each from the five districts above. (See also GREAT BRITAIN COMMITTEE).

AMATEUR SWIMMING ASSOCIATION CHAMPIONSHIPS.

Although titled the A.S.A. championships (of England), these events, traditionally, have been open to the world. This has been because of the A.S.A.'s leading role in establishing organized competition and, as a result, titles have been won by competitors from Australia, Belgium, Canada, France, Hungary, New Zealand, Sweden, South Africa, the United States and, of course, Scotland, Wales Eire.

Until 1934, the events were held at varying venues and different dates around the country which often resulted in small entries, or even swim-overs, because of the time and expense involved. From then on, the bulk of the events have been held at centralized venues—though often the diving has been held separately from the swimming—and this summer 'Festival', known affectionately as 'The Nationals', has attracted more than 1,000 entries annually for what became a six-day meeting.

From 1971, the pattern is changed. There will be British closed championship in the spring which will include junior events, and an open three- or four-day summer 'Festival' for the cream of Britain's swimmers and with entries from abroad welcomed.

AMATEUR SWIMMING ASSOCIATION DIVING CHAMPIONS.

The first official championship of England, yet open to the world, was a highboard event for men in 1907. Prior to this a National Graceful Diving event for men had been organized by the Royal Life Saving Society (1895). This latter competition was handed on, in 1920, to the Amateur Diving Association—which did a great deal to foster diving from the turn of the century to the mid-thirties. It came under the auspices of the A.S.A. in 1936 following the disbandment of the A.D.A.

Since 1935, the majority of the diving

championships have been held at centralized venues as follows:

1935	New Brighton, Cheshire	
1936*	Empire Pool, Wembley	
1937*	Scarborough, Yorkshire	
1938	Empire Pool, Wembley	
1939*	Minehead, Somerset	
1940–45	No championship meetings	
1946*	New Brighton, Cheshire	
1947*	Hastings and St. Leonards, Sussex	
1948†	Hastings and St. Leonards, Sussex	
1949	Hastings and St. Leonards, Sussex	
1950	Morecambe and Hersham, Lancashire	
1951	New Brighton, Cheshire	
1952	New Brighton, Cheshire	
1953–63*	Derby Bath, Blackpool	
1964*	Crystal Palace, London	
1965–67	Crystal Palace, London	
1968	Coventry, Warwickshire	
1969	Derby Bath, Blackpool	
1970	Crystal Palace, London	
1971	Crystal Palace, London	

  * With swimming championships

  † Originally scheduled for Scarborough with the swimming championships, bad weather forced postponement and transfer of the meeting to Hastings.

MEN

Highboard diving

1907	Smyrk, Harold
1908	Smyrk, Harold
1909	Pott, Herbert
1910	Pott, Herbert
1911	Pott, Herbert
1912	Pott, Herbert
1913	Gaidzik, George (USA)
1914–19	No events
1920	Clarke, Harold
1921	Knight, Reggie
1922	Knight, Reggie
1923	Weil, R.
1924	Weil, R.
1925	Dickin, Albert
1926	Dickin, Albert
1927	Aldous, Jimmy
1928	Burne, Tommy
1929	Dickin, Albert
1930	Wild, George
1931	Tomalin, Doug
1932	Heron, Eddie
1933	Tomalin, Doug
1934	Tomalin, Doug

1935	Tomalin, Doug	
1936	Tomalin, Doug	
1937	Tomalin, Doug	
1938	Marchant, Louis	
1939	Tomalin, Doug	
1940–45	No events	
1946	Marchant, Louis	105·43
1947	Brunnhage Lennart (Swe)	101·86
1948	Ward, Gordon	87·83
1949	Heatly, Peter	140·23
1950	Heatly, Peter	147·64
1951	Heatly, Peter	142·18
1952	Turner, Tony	131·25
1953	Tarsey, David	139·59
1954	Turner, Tony	135·43
1955	Squires, Peter	135·00
1956	Tarsey, David	138·33
1957	Heatly, Peter	139·35
1958	Phelps, Brian	139·58
1959	Phelps, Brian	148·61
1960	Phelps, Brian	157·14
1961	Phelps, Brian	148·38
1962	Phelps, Brian	162·23
1963	Kitcher, Tony	161·08
1964	Phelps, Brian	165·55
1965	Phelps, Brian	161·02
1966	Phelps, Brian	165·517
1967	Priestley, David	157·30
1968	Priestley, David	153·45
1969	Gill, Andrew	426·40
1970	Drew, Philip	446·60

Springboard diving

1935	Tomalin, Doug	
1936	Hodges, Freddie	
1937	Hodges, Freddie	
1938	Hodges, Freddie	
1939	Hodges, Freddie	
1940–45	No events	
1946	Mulinghausen, Raymond (Fr)	116·30
1947	Kern, Roy	105·90
1948	Heatly, Peter	113·50
1949	Heatly, Peter	174·91
1950	Heatly, Peter	176·51
1951	Turner, Tony	160·67
1952	Turner, Tony	176·60
1953	Turner, Tony	135·14
1954	Turner, Tony	134·20
1955	Tarsey, David	133·43
1956	Tarsey, David	134·02
1957	Squires, Peter	125·14
1958	Collin, Keith	135·00

1959	Squires, Peter	150·39
1960	Phelps, Brian	152·98
1961	Phelps, Brian	154·80
1962	Phelps, Brian	152·39
1963	Collin, Keith	128·69
1964	Young, Denis	139·62
1965	Carter, Frank	135·96
1966	Carter, Frank	145·933
1967	Carter, Frank	140·20
1968	Carter, Frank	135·317
1969	Roberts, Alun	468·25
1970	Thewlis, Joe	475·60

1 m. Springboard diving

1937	Tomalin, Doug	
1938	Tomalin, Doug	
1939	Thom, Don (Can)	
1940–45	No event	
1946	Hodges, Freddie	135·85
1947	Webb, John	93·16
1948	Elliott, Peter	93·35
1949	Heatly, Peter	128·60
1950	Heatly, Peter	127·32
1951	Heatly, Peter	110·09
1952	Turner, Tony	121·94
1953	Turner, Tony	113·32
1954	Turner, Tony	102·31
1955	Mercer, Frank	110·68
1956	Raanan, Chico (Isr)	106·88
1957	Collin, Keith	120·39
1958	Squires, Peter	124·57
1959	Collin, Keith	132·53
1960	Candler, John	129·21
1961	Young, Denis	130·40
1962	Collin, Keith	125·68
1963	Young, Denis	126·88
1964	Young, Denis	127·39
1965	Young, Denis	123·58
1966	Roberts, Alun	126·03
1967	Carter, Frank	126·35
1968	Roberts, Alun	130·35
1969	Roberts, Alun	440·05
1970	Gill, Andy	425·35

Plain diving

1895	Martin, H.	
1896	Martin, H.	
1897	Sonnemans, V. (Belg)	
1898	Martin, H.	
1899	Martin, H.	
1900	Goldwell, E.	
1901	Serrano, R.	
1902	Phillips, G.	
1903	Tellander, E.	
1904	Melville Clark, Gordon	

1905	Melville Clark, Gordon	
1906	Melville Clark, Gordon	
1907	Cane, G.	
1908	Aldous, Jimmy/Johansson, Hjalmar (Swe) tie	
1909	Johansson, Hjalmar (Swe)	
1910	Johansson, Hjalmar (Swe)	
1911	Johansson, Hjalmar (Swe)	
1912	Yvon, George	
1913	Johansson, Hjalmar (Swe)	
1914–19	No events	
1920	Clarke, Harold	
1921	Clarke, Harold	
1922	Clarke, Harold	
1923	Dickin, Albert	
1924	Eve, Richmond (Aus)	
1925	Clarke, Harold	
1926	Dickin, Albert	
1927	Dickin, Albert	
1928	Burne, Tommy	
1929	Dickin, Albert	
1930	Burne, Tommy	
1931	Tomalin, Doug	
1932	Cook, Reggie/Dawsell, Harold (tie)	
1933	Marchant, Louis	
1934	Marchant, Louis	
1935	Marchant, Louis	
1936	Mather, Tommy	
1937	Tomalin, Doug	
1938	Tomalin, Doug	
1939	Redfern, Graham	
1940–45	No events	
1946	Marchant, Louis	49·30
1947	Marchant, Louis	43·70
1948	Marchant, Louis	49·72
1949	Marchant, Louis	47·92
1950	Marchant, Louis	52·81
1951	Redfern, Graham	38·75
1952	Redfern, Graham	47·60
1953	Elliot, Peter	57·28
1954	Tarsey, David	59·11
1955	Squires, Peter	55·98
1956	Squires, Peter	57·79
1957	Phelps, Brian	54·99
1958	Collin, Keith	55·98
1959	Squires, Peter	67·01
1960	Phelps, Brian	60·34
1961	Phelps, Brian	63·77
1962	Discontinued	

WOMEN

Highboard diving

| 1924 | White, Belle | |

1925	White, Belle	
1926	White, Belle	
1927	White, Belle	
1928	White, Belle	
1929	White, Belle	
1930	Leach, Dorothy	
1931	Leach, Dorothy	
1932	Leach, Dorothy	
1933	Macready, E. 'Dot'	
1934	Cousens, Cecily	
1935	Cousens, Cecily	
1936	Gilbert, Jean	
1937	Gilbert, Jean	
1938	Moulton, Madge	
1939	Slade, Betty	
1940–45	No events	
1946	Child, Edna	34·83
1947	Child, Edna	52·86
1948	Hider, Maire	61·34
1949	Child, Edna	67·55
1950	Long, Ann	52·04
1951	Cuthbert, Kay	63·59
1952	Long, Ann	67·95
1953	Long, Ann	74·48
1954	Long, Ann	76·92
1955	Welsh, Charmian	69·80
1956	Welsh, Charmian	76·06
1957	Welsh, Charmian	71·06
1958	Welsh, Charmian	83·70
1959	Long, Ann	81·17
1960	Thomas, Norma	77·18
1961	Thomas, Norma	91·03
1962	Austen, Margaret	89·13
1963	Newman, Joy	103·60
1964	Cramp, Frances	95·96
1965	Cramp, Frances	84·91
1966	Cramp, Frances	83·20
1967	Haswell, Mandi	75·233
1968	Haswell, Mandi	86·171
1969	Boys, Beverley (Can)	337·65
1970	Burrow, Shelagh	302·85

Springboard diving

1935	Larsen, Katrina	
1936	Slade, Betty	
1937	Slade, Betty	
1938	Slade, Betty	
1939	Slade, Betty	
1940–45	No events	
1946	Child, Edna	97·57
1947	Winterton, Peggy	89·01
1948	Child, Edna	102·79
1949	Child, Edna	101·15
1950	Newman, Denise	106·38

1951	Long, Ann	107·98
1952	Drew, Dorothy Ann	120·84
1953	Welsh, Charmian	117·00
1954	Welsh, Charmian	118·39
1955	Long, Ann	108·31
1956	Long, Ann	112·61
1957	Long, Ann	112·20
1958	Long, Ann	125·40
1959	Watson, Marian	128·48
1960	Ferris, Elizabeth	137·36
1961	Thomas, Norma	141·71
1962	Ferris, Elizabeth	117·18
1963	Newman, Joy	109·08
1964	Rowlatt, Kathy	122·92
1965	Stewart, Judy (Can)	131·13
1966	Dickens, Janet	118·95
1967	Rowlatt, Kathy	135·10
1968	Rowlatt, Kathy	130·917
1969	Boys, Beverley (Can)	370·30
1970	Drake, Alison	354·30

1 m. Springboard diving

1949	Child, Edna	89·12
1950	Cuthbert, Kay	68·59
1951	Long, Ann	68·20
1952	Welsh, Charmian	82·89
1953	Welsh, Charmian	84·25
1954	Welsh, Charmian	80·71
1955	Welsh, Charmian	85·38
1956	Welsh, Charmian	80·45
1957	Ferris, Elizabeth	102·56
1958	Welsh, Charmian	99·58
1959	Thomas, Norma	106·85
1960	Cramp, Frances	87·68
1961	Austen, Margaret	95·97
1962	Cramp, Frances	99·57
1963	Leiper (Thomas), Norma	100·54
1964	Francis, Susan	93·30
1965	Francis, Susan	97·11
1966	Froscher, Margo	103·65
1967	Erard (Cramp), Frances	107·667
1968	Froscher, Margo	94·933
1969	Koppell, Helen	295·05
1970	Drake, Alison	310·85

Plain diving

1953	Welsh, Charmian	51·35
1954	Long, Ann	59·85
1955	Long, Ann	52·00
1956	Welsh, Charmian	54·65
1957	Welsh, Charmian	58·71
1958	Long, Ann	59·92
1959	Ferris, Elizabeth	61·13
1960	Ferris, Elizabeth	53·99

1961	Austen, Margaret	60·95
1962	Discontinued	

AMATEUR SWIMMING ASSOCIATION PLUNGING CHAMPIONS. See under PLUNGING AMATEUR SWIMMING ASSOCIATION CHAMPIONS.

AMATEUR SWIMMING ASSOCIATION SWIMMING CHAMPIONS. The Derby Bath, Blackpool, has been the venue of 17 of the 30 A.S.A. championship meetings since centralization began in 1935. For a number of years all events over 440 yards were excluded from the main meeting, but since 1962 only the long distance event has been held separately. The venues since centralization have been:

1935 South Shore, Blackpool
1936* Empire Pool, Wembley
1937* Scarborough, Yorkshire
1938 Great Yarmouth, Norfolk
1939* Minehead, Somerset
1940–45 No championship meetings
1946* New Brighton, Cheshire
1947* Hastings and St. Leonards, Sussex
1948† Scarborough, Yorkshire
1949 Queen Street, Derby
1950 Kingsway, Lancaster
1951 Kingsway, Lancaster
1952 King Alfred, Hove, Sussex
1953–63* Derby Bath, Blackpool
1964* Crystal Palace, London
1965–70 Derby Bath, Blackpool
1971‡ Worthing, Sussex (winter)
　　　 Leeds, Yorshire (summer)
　* Diving included.
　† Diving included but bad weather forced postponement and transfer of events to Hastings.
　‡ See AMATEUR SWIMMING ASSOCIATION CHAMPIONSHIPS.

100 y. Free-style. This was the second championship to be instituted and was promoted originally by the South-East London S.C.

1878	Moore, J. S.	1:16¾
1879	Moore, J. S.	1:13¼
1880	Itter, W. R.	1:16¾
1881	Bettinson, G. R.	1:16·0
1882	Depau, C.	1:12¼
1883	Blew Jones, W.	1:11·0

1884	Mayger, J. L.	1:11·2
1885	Mayger, J. L.	1:12·0
1886	Nuttall, Joseph	1:09½
1887	Nuttall, Joseph	1:07·8
1888	Nuttall, Joseph	1:06¼
1889	Lenton, Charles	1:07·8
1890	Evans, William	1:08¾
1891	Evans, William	1:08·4
1892	Tyers, Jack	1:05·8
1893	Tyers, Jack	1:07·6
1894	Tyers, Jack	1:05·6
1895	Tyers, Jack	1:04·0
1896	Tyers, Jack	1:01·4
1897	Tyers, Jack	1:03·6
1898	Derbyshire, Rob	1:00·8
1899	Derbyshire, Rob	1:00·4
1900	Derbyshire, Rob	1:01·0
1901	Derbyshire, Rob	1:01·4
1902	Lane, Freddy (Aus)	1:00·0
1903	Derbyshire, Rob	1:01·6
1904	Derbyshire, Rob	1:00·8
1905	Halmay, Zoltan (Hun)	59·0
1906	Daniels, Charles (USA)	58·6
1907	Daniels, Charles (USA)	55·4
1908	Meyboom, Hermann (Belg)	1:00·6
1909	Radmilovic, Paul	1:01·0
1910	Beaurepaire, Frank (Aus)	59·8
1911	Hardwick, Harold (Aus)	58·6
1912	McGillivray, Peter	57·6
1913	Annison, Harold	1:00·0
1914–19	No events	
1920	Stedman, Ivan (Aus)	58·0
1921	Van Schelle, Martial (Belg)	57·6
1922	Van Schelle, Martial (Belg)	56·6
1923	Van Schelle, Martial (Belg)	57·0
1924	Henry, Ernest (Aus)	58·0
1925	Barany, Istvan (Hun)	55·8
1926	House, J. A. Jnr. (USA)	57·4
1927	Baillie, Charles	56·8
1928	Sampson, Paul	54·4
1929	Brooks, Norman	55·4
1930	Brooks, Norman	56·2
1931	Sutton, Reg	56·2
1932	Brooks, Norman	54·6
1933	Sutton, Reg	56·0
1934	Larson, Goran (Swe)	54·0
1935	Gabrielsen, R.	55·4
1936	Dove, Freddie	55·0
1937	Dove, Freddie	55·8
1938	Dove, Freddie	55·0

1939	Taylor, Mickey	54·2
1940–45	No events	
1946	Jany, Alex (Fra)	52·0
1947	Kendall, Pat	55·2
1948	Stedman, Ron	55·0
1949	Stedman, Ron	53·7
1950	Kendall, Pat	54·1
1951	Larsson, Goran (Swe)	52·1
1952	Wardrop, Jack	53·4

110 y. Free-style

1953	Roberts, Ron	59·5
1954	Baxter, Geoff	1:00·9
1955	Roberts, Ron	58·5
1956	McKechnie, Neil	58·9
1957	McKechnie, Neil	59·2
1958	Black, Ian	58·3
1959	Black, Ian	58·0
1960	Clarke, Stan	57·8
1961	Martin-Dye, John	57·2
1962	McGregor, Bobby	55·6
1963	McGregor, Bobby	54·1
1964	McGregor, Bobby	53·9
1965	Lord, Bobby	55·2
1966	McGregor, Bobby	53·5
1967	McGregor, Bobby	54·0
1968	McGregor, Bobby	53·9
1969	Windeatt, Malcolm	56·3
1970	Windeatt, Malcolm	55·2

220 y. Free-style. Instituted originally by the Swimming Association of Great Britain.

1880	Danels, Edward	3:09¾
1881	Danels, Edward	3:14½
1882	Danels, Edward	3:13¼
1883	Cairns, Tom	2:59¼
1884	Cairns, Tom	3:02¼
1885	Cairns, Tom	3:08¼
1886	Nuttall, Joseph	3:04·8
1887	Nuttall, Joseph	2:59·8
1888	Nuttall, Joseph	†3:15·6
1889	Jones, T.	2:57½
1890	Evans, William	2:51·2
1891	Evans, William	2:52·0
1892	Tyers, Jack	2:46·4
1893	Tyers, Jack	2:54·8
1894	Tyers, Jack	2:49·0
1895	Tyers, Jack	2:41·0
1896	Tyers, Jack	2:50·2
1897	Tyers, Jack	2:38·8
1898	Derbyshire, Rob	2:42·4
1899	Lane, Freddy (Aus)	2:38·2
1900	Lane, Freddy (Aus)/	
	Derbyshire, Rob	2:34·8

1901	Derbyshire, Rob	2:42·0
1902	Lane, Freddy (Aus)	2:28·6
1903	Derbyshire, Rob	2:46·0
1904	Forsyth, Eric	2:37·8
1905	Kieran, Barney (Aus)	2:37·2
1906	Healy, Charles (Fra)	2:37·4
1907	Halmay, Zoltan (Hun)	2:34·0
1908	Beaurepaire, Frank (Aus)	2:37·0
1909	Battersby, Sydney	2:32·8
1910	Beaurepaire, Frank (Aus)	2:30·0
1911	Hardwick, Harold (Aus)	2:33·6
1912	Hatfield, Jack	2:30·2
1913	Hatfield, Jack	2:30·6
1914–19	No events	
1920	Beaurepaire, Frank (Aus)	2:29·2
1921	Borg, Arne (Swe)	2:29·2
1922	Hatfield, Jack	2:32·2
1923	Borg, Arne (Swe)	2:29·6
1924	Annison, Harold	2:35·0
1925	Hatfield, Jack	2:34·4
1926	Whiteside, Joe	2:31·0
1927	Dickin, Albert	2:36·0
1928	Whiteside, Joe	2:27·2
1929	Brooks, Norman	2:28·0
1930	Brooks, Norman	2:26·0
1931	Sutton, Reg	2:22·2
1932	Sutton, Reg	2:31·5
1933	Leivers, Bobby	2:23·6
1934	Larson, Goran (Swe)	2:20·2
1935	Wainwright, Norman	2:18·6
1936	Wainwright, Norman	2:17·8
1937	Wainwright, Norman	2:18·6
1938	Wainwright, Norman	2:16·6
1939	Wainwright, Norman	2:14·4
1940–45	No events	
1946	Jany, Alex (Fra)	2:14·0
1947	Hale, Jack	2:20·1
1948	Hale, Jack	2:16·4
1949	Ostrand, Per-Ola (Swe)	2:13·6
1950	Wardrop, Jack	2:16·6
1951	Larsson, Goran (Swe)	2:12·2
1952	Wardrop, Jack	2:11·2
1953	Roberts, Ron	2:15·8
1954	Wardrop, Jack	2:11·7
1955	McKechnie, Neil	2:13·8
1956	McKechnie, Neil	2:11·3
1957	McKechnie, Neil	2:12·0
1958	Black, Ian	2:07·2
1959	Black, Ian	2:06·0
1960	Clarke, Stan	2:07·6
1961	Martin-Dye, John	2:06·9
1962	McLachlan, Murray (SAf)	2:05·5
1963	McGregor, Bobby	2:04·8
1964	Grylls, Geoff (SAf)	2:03·5

1965	Grylls, Geoff (SAf)	2:01·6
1966	McGregor, Bobby	2:02·6
1967	Jarvis, Tony	2:03·4
1968	Jarvis, Tony	2:00·1
1969	Woodroffe, Martyn	2:01·5
1970	Borrie, Mike (NZ)	2:02·4

† Race afterward declared void.

440 y. Free-style. First promoted by the Portsmouth S.C. and conducted as a salt-water championship until 1934.

1884	Cairns, Tom	6:33·0
1885	Schlotel, H.	6:48·2
1886	Schlotel, H.	6:21¼
1887	Schlotel, H.	6:21·4
1888	Nuttall, Joseph	6:16½
1889	Henry, William	6:04·0
1890	Evans, William	6:19·2
1891	Evans, William	7:15·0
1892	Evans, William	7:03·0
1893	Tyers, Jack	6:33·2
1894	Tyers, Jack	7:06·4
1895	Tyers, Jack	6:08·8
1896	Tyers, Jack	6:18·4
1897	Cavill, Percy (Aus)	4:50·4
1898	Jarvis, John	6:30·0
1899	Lane, Freddy (Aus)	6:30·8
1900	Jarvis, John	†12:55·0
1901	Billington, David	8:23·2
1902	Cavill, Richard (Aus)	5:04·8
1903	Billington, David	6:34·6
1904	Billington, David	6:19·0
1905	Kieran, Barney (Aus)	5:22·2
1906	Taylor, Henry	5:42·6
1907	Taylor, Henry	4:43·0
1908	Beaurepaire, Frank (Aus)	4:59·4
1909	Battersby, Sydney	swam over
1910	Beaurepaire, Frank (Aus)	5:38·6
1911	Hardwick, Harold (Aus)	5:40·4
1912	Hatfield, Jack	4:54·8
1913	Hatfield, Jack	5:43·0
1914–19	No events	
1920	Annison, Harold	5:41·0
1921	Peter, Percy	5:40·0
1922	Peter, Percy	5:46·8
1923	Peter, Percy	5:52·6
1924	Hatfield, Jack	5:52·6
1925	Radmilovic, Paul	5:41·2
1926	Dickin, Albert	5:44·5
1927	Hatfield, Jack	5:51·0
1928	Sampson, Paul	5:30·8
1929	Brooks, Norman	5:39·2
1930	Brooks, Norman	5:41·8
1931	Sutton, Reg	5:27·4

1932	Leivers, Bobby	5:30·4
1933	Sutton, Reg	5:28·0
1934	Leivers, Bobby	5:37·0
1935	Wainwright, Norman	5:05·8
1936	Wainwright, Norman	4:58·4
1937	Wainwright, Norman	5:03·4
1938	Wainwright, Norman	4:59·0
1939	Wainwright, Norman	4:52·6
1940–45	No events	
1946	Hale, Jack	4:56·2
1947	Hale, Jack	5:00·4
1948	Hale, Jack	5:02·4
1949	Ostrand, Per-Ola (Swe)	4:47·5
1950	Wardrop, Jack	4:54·8
1951	Wardrop, Jack	4:49·5
1952	Wardrop, Jack	4:47·2
1953	Sreenan, Bob	4:54·4
1954	Symonds, Graham	4:53·8
1955	McKechnie, Neil	4:47·0
1956	McKechnie, Neil	4:45·8
1957	Sreenan, Bob	4:53·6
1958	Black, Ian	4:28·4
1959	Black, Ian	4:32·9
1960	Martin-Dye, John	4:31·7
1961	Martin-Dye, John	4:34·2
1962	Campion, Dick	4:32·7
1963	Martin-Dye, John	4:31·3
1964	Grylls, Geoff (SAf)	4:24·9
1965	Grylls, Geoff (SAf)	4:22·2
1966	Kimber, Alan	4:24·3
1967	Kimber, Alan	4:23·5
1968	Jarvis, Tony	4:22·0
1969	Woodroffe, Martyn	4:19·6
1970	Terrell, Ray	**4:21·4**

† Against strong current.

500 y. Free-style

1878	Taylor, James (first winner)	8:07¼
	Hatfield, Jack won nine times—1912–13 and, after the war break, from 1921 to 1927.	
1934	Wainwright, Norman (last winner)	5:24·0
1934	Discontinued	

880 y. Free-style. Originally promoted by the *Sporting Life*.

1881	Ainsworth, Dave	14:31½
1882	Ainsworth, Dave	15:16¼
1883	Ainsworth, Dave	14:23½
1884	Bell, G.	14:35½
1885	Schlotel, H.	†13:04½
1886	Schlotel, H.	14:17½

1887	Nuttall, Joseph	14:44·0
1888	Bowden, H.	14:25·4
1889	Standring, J. F.	14:56·8
1890	Evans, William	14:38·0
1891	Greasley, Sam	13:42·4
1892	Greasley, Sam	14:00·8
1893	Tyers, Jack	13:41·0
1894	Tyers, Jack	13:42·4
1895	Tyers, Jack	13:56·0
1896	Not held	
1897	Derbyshire, Rob	13:38·8
1898	Jarvis, John	12:52·0
1899	Jarvis, John	12:45·6
1900	Jarvis, John	12:35·0
1901	Jarvis, John	12:42·4
1902	Cavill, Richard (Aus)	11:50·4
1903	Billington, David	13:10·6
1904	Forsyth, Eric	12:23·0
1905	Kieran, Barney (Aus)	11:28·0
1906	Taylor, Henry	11:25·4
1907	Taylor, Henry	12:16·2
1908	Beaurepaire, Frank (Aus)	12:44·0
1909	Battersby, Sydney	11:47·2
1910	Beaurepaire, Frank (Aus)	11:39·8
1911	Taylor, Henry	12:05·6
1912	Hatfield, Jack	12:21·2
1913	Hatfield, Jack	11:46·4
1914–19	No events	
1920	Annison, Harold	12:21·4
1921	Hatfield, Jack	11:46·4
1922	Hatfield, Jack	11:59·2
1923	Hatfield, Jack	12:15·2
1924	Hatfield, Jack	12:11·4
1925	Hatfield, Jack	11:51·0
1926	Radmilovic, Paul	11:57·4
1927	Peter, Percy	12:02·2
1928	White, S. W.	13:55·0
1929	Taris, Jean (Fra)	11:19·8
1930	Bramhall, Fred	swam over
1931	Taylor, Arthur	11:33·2
1932	Leivers, Bobby	11:27·4
1933	Wainwright, Norman	11:31·6
1934	Wainwright, Norman	10:57·4
1935	Wainwright, Norman	10:51·6
1936	Leivers, Bobby	10:30·0
1937	Wainwright, Norman	10:26·4
1938	Deane, Kenneth R. H.	10:47·0
1939	Wainwright, Norman	10:51·4
1940–45	No events	
1946	Hale, Jack	10:27·4
1947	Hale, Jack	10:49·6
1948	Hale, Jack	10:58·6
1949	Wardrop, Jack	10:30·3
1950	Wardrop, Jack	10:29·1

1951	Bland, Donald	10:33·1
1952	Wardrop, Jack	10:03·6
1953	Sreenan, Bob	10:24·6
1954	Symonds, Graham	10:48·4
1955	Sreenan, Bob	10:27·7
1956	McKechnie, Neil	10:12·9
1957	Sreenan, Bob	10:07·8
1958	Sreenan, Bob	10:07·8
1959	Campion, Dick	10:13·5
1960	Campion, Dick	9:56·7
1961	Kennedy, Jim	9:52·6
1962	Campion, Dick	9:47·2
1963	Kennedy, Jim	9:57·6
1964	Milton, Tony	10:13·2
1965	Grylls, Geoff (SAf)	9:15·5
1966	Kimber, Alan	9:09·3
1967	Kimber, Alan	9:13·3
1968	Kimber, Alan	9:12·7
1969	Jacks, Ron (Can)	8:58·0
1970	Treffers, Mark (NZ)	9:03·2

† Course shorter than 880 y.

One mile Free-style. This was the first official National Championship and was promoted originally by the Metropolitan Swimming Association. From 1869–1872 it was swum in the River Thames over a course from Putney Aqueduct to Hammersmith Bridge. Thereafter it was swum in still water. The first trophy was won outright by Horace Davenport in 1876. Later Davenport paid half of the cost of a replacement trophy which he won three times again. But this time it was a perpetual trophy.

1869	Morris, Tom	27:18·0
1870	Parker, Harry	26:06·4
1871	Parker, Harry	24:35·0
1872	Parker, Harry	29:03·0
1873	Ainsworth, Dave	30:38½
1874	Davenport, Horace	31:09·0
1875	Davenport, Horace	31:30·0
1876	Davenport, Horace	33:08·0
1877	Davenport, Horace	29:25½
1878	Davenport, Horace	31:15¼
1879	Davenport, Horace	34:09·0
1880	Taylor, James	30:38·0
1881	Taylor, James	35:20·0
1882	Taylor, James	32:38·0
1883	Danels, Edward	31:40·6
1884	Bell, G.	31:42¾
1885	Sargent, S.	32:11½
1886	Schlotel, H.	31:32¾
1887	Nuttall, Joseph	30:38·0

1888	Standring, J. F.	34:01½
1889	Bowden, H.	31:00·8
1890	Greasley, Sam	29:32·4
1991	Greasley, Sam	30:33·6
1892	Greasley, Sam	28:18·4
1893	Tyers, Jack	27:21·4
1894	Tyers, Jack	27:51·4
1895	Tyers, Jack	27:33·8
1896	Tyers, Jack	26:46·0
1897	Jarvis, John	32:28·6
1898	Jarvis, John	26:37·2
1899	Jarvis, John	25:13·4
1900	Jarvis, John	26:26·0
1901	Jarvis, John	25:13·8
1902	Jarvis, John	25:32·4
1903	Billington, David	24:56·4
1904	Billington, David	27:18·0
1905	Billington, David	24:42·6
1906	Taylor, Henry	27:09·0
1907	Taylor, Henry	25:04·6
1908	Beaurepaire, Frank (Aus)	25:15·4
1909	Battersby, Sydney	24:01·4
1910	Beaurepaire, Frank (Aus)	24:39·4
1911	Taylor, Henry	†23:35½
1912	Hatfield, Jack	25:02·8
1913	Hatfield, Jack	24:55·2
1914	Hatfield, Jack	24:42·4
1915–19	No events	
1920	Annison, Harold	25:25·0
1921	Hatfield, Jack	24:48·8
1922	Hatfield, Jack	26:46·8
1823	Hatfield, Jack	24:54·0
1924	Hatfield, Jack	25:22·4
1925	Radmilovic, Paul	24:27·0
1926	Radmilovic, Paul	24:27·0
1927	Radmilovic, Paul	25:39·8
1928	Lindsay, D. (NZ)	25:10·8
1929	Hatfield, Jack	25:40·6
1930	Hatfield, Jack	25:30·6
1931	Milton, Freddie	25:28·4
1932	Milton, Freddie	25:58·6
1933	Wainwright, Norman	23:20·6
1934	Wainwright, Norman	23:47·0
1935	Wainwright, Norman	23:19·0
1936	Leivers, Bobby	21:49·4
1937	Wainwright, Norman	22:31·8
1938	Leivers, Bobby	22:07·2
1939	Wainwright, Norman	21:38·8
1940–45	No events	
1946	Hale, Jack	21:47·2
1947	Hale, Jack	21:33·2
1948	Hale, Jack	21:25·2
1949	Bland, Donald	22:13·2
1950	Bland, Donald	21:54·9

1951	Bland, Donald	21:33·8
1952	Wardrop, Jack	20:53·2
1953	Sreenan, Bob	21:11·4
1954	Sreenan, Bob	22:13·2
1955	Sreenan, Bob	21:16·4
1956	Sreenan, Bob	20:57·4
1957	Sreenan, Bob	21:23·2
1958	Black, Ian	19:17·5
1959	Campion, Dick	20:48·2
1960	Campion, Dick	20:00·2
1961	Campion, Dick	19:50·6
1962	Campion, Dick	19:30·2
1963	Martin-Dye, John	20:07·5
1964	Grylls, Geoff (SAf)	19:10·1

† Course 1,755 y. 7 in.

1,650 y. Free-style (replacing one mile)

1965	Gilchrist, Sandy (Can)	17:33·9
1966	Kimber, Alan	17:52·8
1967	Kimber, Alan	17:33·9
1968	Kimber, Alan	17:48·3
1969	Jacks, Ron (Can)	17:20·8
1970	Treffers, Mark (NZ)	**17:04·4**

Long distance. Known originally as the 'Lords and Commons' Race' (1877 to 1879) the first cup having been presented by members of Parliament and which was won outright by Horace Davenport. Each man had to be accompanied by a boat and the race, a dramatic sight, was held in the River Thames, with the current, over a course of between five and six miles, until 1939. After the Second World War, the pollution of the Thames made it dangerous for swimmers, but a race was held in the Serpentine in 1947. It was then discontinued until 1962 when the British Long Distance A.S.A. became associated in the organization. The venues since then have been in the River Ouse (1962–63), River Wear (1964–65) and Trentham Park Lake, Nottingham (1966–70).

1877	Davenport, Horace	1 hr 13:27·0
1878	Davenport, Horace	1 hr 16:10·0
1879	Davenport, Horace	1 hr 22:27·0
1880	Itter, W. R.	1 hr 17:00·0
1881	Richardson, W. R.	1 hr 21:30·0
1882	Huntingdon, F. W.	1 hr 21:00·0
1883	Itter, W. R.	1 hr 15:20·0
1884	Bell, G.	1 hr 19:01.0
1885	Bell, G.	1 hr 24:42·0
1886	France, A. E.	1 hr 20:50·0
1887	France, A. E.	1 hr 18:10·0

1888	France, A. E.	1 hr 17:07·0	
1889	Bowden, H.	1 hr 25:50·0	
1890	Henry, William	1 hr 15:15·0	
1891	Ibbott, A.	1 hr 12:27·0	
1892	Drake, Mathew	1 hr 18:40·0	
1893	Tyers, Jack	1 hr 17:01·8	
1894	Tyers, Jack	1 hr 47:06·0	
1895	Race void	—	
1896	Green, W.	2 hr 33:15·0	
1897	Cavill, Percy (Aus)	1 hr 06:35·0	
1898	Jarvis, John	1 hr 07:58·0	
1899	Jarvis, John	1 hr 09:45·0	
1900	Jarvis, John	1 hr 04:17·0	
1901	Jarvis, John	1 hr 09:04·2	
1902	Jarvis, John	1 hr 13:27·0	
1903	Jarvis, John	1 hr 03:48·2	
1904	Jarvis, John	1 hr 07:32·2	
1905	Billington, David	1 hr 08:55·0	
1906	Jarvis, John	1 hr 03:40·0	
1907	Radmilovic, Paul	1 hr 09:15·2	
1908	Springfield, F. W. (Aus)	1 hr 10:57·0	
1909	Taylor, Henry	1 hr 05:24·0	
1910	Battersby, Sydney	1 hr 03:12·4	
1911	Champion, Malcom (NZ)	1 hr 06:11·4	
1912	Taylor, Henry	1 hr 04:07·4	
1913	Hatfield, Jack	1 hr 05:27·0	
1914	Hatfield, Jack	1 hr 05:04·0	
1915–19	No events		
1920	Taylor, Henry	1 hr 04:55·0	
1921	Hatfield, Jack	1 hr 08:32·0	
1922	Peter, Percy	1 hr 07:23·0	
1923	Hatfield, Jack	1 hr 16:13·0	
1924	Hatfield, Jack	1 hr 08:25·0	
1925	Radmilovic, Paul	1 hr 05:06·4	
1926	Radmilovic, Paul	1 hr 07:35·0	
1927	Pascoe, Ernie	1 hr 11:38·4	
1928	Hatfield, Jack	1 hr 04:44·0	
1929	Peter, Percy	1 hr 05:02·6	
1930	Pascoe, Ernie	1 hr 06:53·8	
1931	Hatfield, Jack	57:22·0	
1932	Milton, Freddie	53:37·4	
1933	Milton, Freddie	1 hr 08:20·0	
1934	Deane, Cecil	1 hr 08:52·6	
1935	Deane, Cecil	1 hr 03:47·4	
1936	Deane, Cecil	1 hr 04:04·8	
1937	Deane, Cecil	1 hr 02:57·6	
1938	Deane, Cecil	1 hr 05:24·2	
1939	Hale, Jack	1 hr 03:59·4	
1940–46	No events		
1947	Hale, Jack	1 hr 13:30·2	
1948–61	No events		
1962	Kennedy, Jim	1 hr 36:20·0	

1963	Milton, Tony	1 hr 35:20·0
1964	Johnson, R.	1 hr 45:57·0
1965	Milton, Tony	1 hr 40:10·0
1966	Milton, Tony	2 hr 36:10·0
1967	Wilson, Andy	2 hr 13:20·0
1968	Metcalfe, Brian	2 hr 21:09·0
1969	Kimber, Alan	2 hr 07:58·0
1970	Metcalfe, Brian	2 hr 16:05·0

150 y. Back-stroke

1903	Call, William	2:06·6
1904	Call, William	2:01·4
1905	Call, William	2:01·6
1906	Unwin, Fred	2:04·0
1907	Unwin, Fred	1:59·2
1908	Unwin, Fred	2:01·0
1909	Unwin, Fred	2:02·2
1910	Weckesser, Maurice (Belg)	1:57·2
1911	Weckesser, Maurice (Belg)	1:58·4
1912	Webster, George	2:00·0
1913	Webster, George	1:59·4
1914	Webster, George	1:54·6
1915–19	No events	
1920	Blitz, Gerard (Belg)	1:55·8
1921	Blitz, Gerard (Belg)	1:55·8
1922	Rawlinson, Austin	1:56·2
1923	Rawlinson, Austin	1:55·8
1924	Rawlinson, Austin	1:48·2
1925	Rawlinson, Austin	1:52·4
1926	Rawlinson, Austin	1:51·8
1927	Besford, John	1:50·0
1928	Besford, John	1:48·2
1929	Trippett, John	1:52·0
1930	Besford, John	1:46·2
1931	Besford, John	1:45·4
1932	Besford, John	1:45·0
1933	Francis, Willy	1:46·0
1934	Francis, Willy	1:45·0
1935	Besford, John	1:46·8
1936	Besford, John	1:48·4
1937	Taylor, Micky	1:46·4
1938	Taylor, Micky	1:46·0
1939	Tyrrell, Ian (SAf)	1:42·0
1940–45	No events	
1946	Vallery, Georges (Fr)	1:38·6

100 y. Back-stroke

1947	Kinnear, Bert	1:04·0
1948	Brockway, John	1:02·6
1949	Brockway, John	1:00·8
1950	Brockway, John	1:01·2
1951	Brockway, John	59·7
1952	Wardrop, Bert	1:00·4

110 y. Back-stroke

1953	Brockway, John	1:08·8

1954	Brockway, John	1:07·2
1955	Brockway, John	1:08·4
1956	Sykes, Graham	1:08·2
1957	Sykes, Graham	1:06·7
1958	Sykes, Graham	1:07·4
1959	Sykes, Graham	1:05·5
1960	Sykes, Graham	1:04·8
1961–63	No events	
1964	Stewart, Brian (SAf)	1:03·9
1965	Stewart, Brian (SAf)	1:03·1
1966	Jones, Roddy	1:02·2
1967	Jones, Roddy	1:03·1
1968	Jones, Roddy	1:02·4
1969	Rushton, Clive	1:02·7
1970	Richards, Mike	1:01·8

220 y. Back-stroke

1961	Sykes, Graham	2:23·9
1962	Sykes, Graham	2:21·6
1963	Jones, Roddy	2:25·0
1964	Stewart, Brian (SAf)	2:20·1
1965	Hutton, Ralph (Can)	2:16·0
1966	Jackson, Neil	2:18·5
1967	Reynolds, Peter (Aus)	2:17·9
1968	Butler, David	2:17·2
1969	Rushton, Clive	2:16·8
1970	Richards, Mike	2:15·2

110 y. Breast-stroke

1964	Nicholson, Neil	1:12·6
1965	Hotz, Basil (SAf)	1:12·3
1966	Roberts, Roger	1:11·1
1967	Roberts, Roger	1:10·3
1968	Roberts, Stuart	1:11·5
1969	Mahony, Bill (Can)	1:10·2
1970	Carty, Mark	1:12·1

200 y. Breast-stroke

1903	Robinson, William	2:49·8
1904	Robinson, William	2:52·2
1905	Robinson, William	2:49·0
1906	Naylor, F. H.	2:58·4
1907	Courtman, Percy	2:55·4
1908	Courtman, Percy	2:47·2
1909	Courtman, Percy	2:46·2
1910	Julin, Harald (Swe)	2:53·0
1911	Toldi, Odon (Hun)	2:42·0
1912	Courtman, Percy	2:47·8
1913	Courtman, Percy	2:43·0
1914–19	No events	
1920	Lassam, R. G.	2:43·2
1921	Leon, S. (Fra)	2:49·8
1922	De Combe, Joseph (Belg)	2:58·0
1923	Stoney, William	2:51·0
1924	Flint, Reg	2:51·0

1925	Flint, Reg	2:50·0
1926	Bouvier, Henri (Fra)	2:48·2
1927	Van Parys, Louis (Belg)	2:42·4
1928	Flint, Reg	2:42·4
1929	Flint, Reg	2:44·6
1930	Bell, Stanley	2:43·4
1931	Cartonnet, Jacques (Fra)	2:42·2
1932	Cartonnet, Jacques (Fra)	2:39·0
1933	Schoebel, A. (Fra)	2:38·0
1934	Hamilton, Norman	2:43·2
1935	Hamilton, Norman	2:43·6
1936	Hamilton, Norman	2:43·6
1937	Davies, John	2:41·2
1938	Davies, John	2:39·2
1939	Davies, John	2:37·8
1940–45	No events	
1946	Davies, John	2:39·6
1947	Romain, Roy	Bu 2:30·0
1948	Romain, Roy	Bu 2:30·8
1949	Romain, Roy	Bu 2:30·7
1950	Jervis, Peter	2:34·7
1951	Snelling, Deryk	Bu 2:34·0
1952	Jervis, Peter	2:29·8

220 y. Breast-stroke

1953	Jervis, Peter	2:53·0
1954	Jervis, Peter	2:51·3
1955	Walkden, Chris	2:47·3
1956	Walkden, Chris	2:46·0
1957	Day, Brian	2:50·3
1958	Walkden, Chris	2:43·9
1959	Rowlinson, Gerard	2:48·5
1960	Rowlinson, Gerard	2:46·0
1961	Wilkinson, Chris	2:43·9
1962	Wilkinson, Chris	2:43·8
1963	Nicholson, Neil	2:42·2
1964	Hotz, Basil (SAf)	2:39·2
1965	Hotz, Basil (SAf)	2:40·3
1966	Finnigan, David	2:39·4
1967	Roberts, Roger	2:36·1
1968	Roberts, Stuart	2:38·5
1969	Mahony, Bill (Can)	2:33·5
1970	Johnson, Nigel	2:36·1

110 y. Butterfly

1964	Slovin, Vincent (SAf)	1:00·4
1965	Sherry, Dan (Can)	58·1
1966	Thurley, John	1:01·7
1967	Norris, Len	1:00·3
1968	Woodroffe, Martyn	59·8
1969	Woodroffe, Martyn	59·2
1970	Woodroffe, Martyn	1:00·1

220 y. Butterfly

1953	Barnes, Brian	2:44·2

1954	Hale, Jack	2:39·5
1955	Symonds, Graham	2:36·3
1956	Dickson, Derek	2:43·8
1957	Campion, Dick	2:44·2
1958	Black, Ian	2:25·2
1959	Black, Ian	2:22·7
1960	Blyth, Ian	2:23·5
1961	Jenkins, Brian	2:19·0
1962	Jenkins, Brian	2:16·7
1963	Jenkins, Brian	2:17·6
1964	Slovin, Vincent (SAf)	2:13·6
1965	Sherry, Dan (Can)	2:13·5
1966	Thurley, John	2:15·1
1967	Woodroffe, Martyn	2:15·3
1968	Woodroffe, Martyn	2:11·0
1969	Woodroffe, Martyn	2:09·9
1970	Woodroffe, Martyn	2:10·7

220 y. Individual medley

1966	Kimber, Alan	2:21·8
1967	Reynolds, Peter (Aus)	2:19·8
1968	Woodroffe, Martyn	2:18·9
1969	Woodroffe, Martyn	2:17·6
1970	Woodroffe, Martyn	2:18·2

440 y. Individual medley

1963	Jenkins, Brian	5:16·9
1964	Lacey, Tom (SAf)	5:06·7
1965	Gilchrist, Sandy (Can)	4:55·3
1966	Kimber, Alan	5:02·0
1967	Kimber, Alan	4:54·8
1968	Woodroffe, Martyn	4:55·5
1969	Woodroffe, Martyn	4:55·1
1970	Woodroffe, Martyn	4:52·5

Team (club) relay (distances varied)

1909	Wigan
1910	Wigan
1911	Hyde Seal
1912	Hyde Seal
1913	Hyde Seal
1914	Northumberland/Otter finalists (abandoned because of outbreak of war)
1915–19	No events
1920	Hammersmith
1921	Middlesbrough
1922	Penguin
1923	Northumberland (swim over after dead-heat with Penguin)
1924	Penguin
1925	Penguin
1926	Penguin
1927	Penguin
1928	South Manchester

1929	Oldham Police
1930	Oldham Police
1931	Oldham Police
1932	Oldham Police
1933	Otter
1934	Oldham Police
1935	Otter
1936	Otter
1937	Otter
1938	Otter
1939–45	No events

Team (county) relay (distances varied)

| 1946 | Yorkshire | 10:01·0 |
| 1947 | Yorkshire | 7:57·2 |

Team (club) relay (distances varied)

1948	Otter	10:54·4
1949	Otter	11:05·4
1950	Blackpool	10:58·7
1951	Sparkhill	10:33·6
1952	Sparkhill	9:37·0
1953	Sparkhill	9:42·5
1954	Coventry	9:38·4

4 × 110 y. Free-style (club) relay

1955	Otter	4:06·5
1956	Otter	4:09·5
1957	Wallasey	4:06·1
1958	York City	4:01·4
1959	York City	4:02·6
1960	Stoke Newington	3:58·2
1961	York City	3:57·3
1962	York City	3:55·6
1963	York City	3:54·1
1964	York City	3:52·2
1965	York City	3:53·3
1966	York City	3:52·6
1967	Otter	3:49·5
1968	Southampton	3:49·9
1969	Southampton	3:48·5
1970	Southampton	3:49·1

Medley (club) relay (distances varied)

1946	Otter	3:46·4
1947	Otter	7:51·2
1948	Otter	7:53·4
1949	Otter	6:52·2
1950	Otter	7:02·0
1951	Penguin	6:56·7
1952	Penguin	7:41·6
1953	Otter	7:46·3
1954	Otter	7:32·2

4 × 110 y. Medley (club) relay

| 1955 | Otter | 4:36·5 |

1956	Stoke Newington	4:46·8
1957	Otter	4:46·4
1958	Stoke Newington	4:44·9
1959	Stoke Newington	4:38·0
1960	Stoke Newington	4:34·3
1961	Otter	4:34·5
1962	York City	4:29·4
1963	York City	4:28·0
1964	Otter	4:25·3
1965	Barracuda	4:26·4
1966	Stoke Newington	4:19·2
1967	Stoke Newington	4:18·4
1968	Southampton	4:19·3
1969	Southampton	4:20·4
1970	Southampton	4:16·0

WOMEN

100 y. Free-style

1901	Thorp, Hilda	1:30·4
1902	Scott, Maggie	1:25·2
1903	Thorp, Hilda	1:27·6
1904	Mackay, Netta	1:25·2
1905	Scott, Maggie	1:25·2
1906	Fletcher, Jennie	1:24·0
1907	Fletcher, Jennie	1:18·0
1908	Fletcher, Jennie	1:18·0
1909	Fletcher, Jennie	1:14·0
1910	Steer, Irene	1:13·6
1911	Fletcher, Jennie	1:15·6
1912	Fletcher, Jennie	1:15·2
1913	Curwen, Daisy	1:13·6
1914–18	No events	
1919	Jeans, Constance	1:11·6
1920	Jeans, Constance	1:14·0
1921	James, Hilda	1:11·0
1922	Jeans, Constance	1:09·2
1923	Jeans, Constance	1:07·4
1924	Jeans, Constance	1:07·2
1925	Jeans, Constance	1:07·2
1926	Laverty, Marion	1:07·4
1927	Hamblen, Mabel	1:08·2
1928	Tanner, Vera	1:06·2
1929	Cooper, Joyce	1:06·0
1930	King, Ellen	1:09·0
1931	Cooper, Joyce	1:05·6
1932	Cooper, Joyce	1:02·8
1933	Calderhead, Sheila	1:07·2
1934	Hughes, Edna	1:06·8
1935	Wadham, Olive	1:03·6
1936	Wadham, Olive	1:02·8
1937	Wadham, Olive	1:03·4
1938	Harrowby, Joyce	1:02·2
1939	Harrowby, Joyce	1:02·6
1940–45	No events	

1946	Riach, Nancy	1:03·0
1947	Riach, Nancy	1:02·4
1948	Wellington, Margaret	1:02·8
1949	Turner, Elizabeth	1:02·4
1950	Linton, "Pip"	1:02·9
1951	Linton, "Pip"	1:03·5
1952	Barnwell, Angela	1:02·2

110 y. Free-style

1953	Botham, Jean	1:09·7
1954	Botham, Jean	1:09·4
1955	Ewart, Fearne	1:08·3
1956	Grant, Virginia (Can)	1:07·0
1957	Wilkinson, Diana	1:05·7
1958	Grinham, Judy	1:06·8
1959	Steward, Natalie	1:05·2
1960	Steward, Natalie	1:04·9
1961	Wilkinson, Diana	1:04·9
1962	Wilkinson, Diana	1:03·3
1963	Wilkinson, Diana	1:03·3
1964	Wilkinson, Diana	1:04·4
1965	Lay, Marion (Can)	1:01·4
1966	Sillett, Pauline	1:02·9
1967	Jackson, Alex	1:02·6
1968	Jackson, Alex	1:01·7
1969	Jackson, Alex	1:03·7
1970	Jackson, Alex	1:01·2

220 y. Free-style

1912	Curwen, Daisy	3:08·8
1913	Curwen, Daisy	3:12·4
1914–18	No events	
1919	Jeans, Constance	3:04·0
1920	Jeans, Constance	3:02·6
1921	James, Hilda	3:05·2
1922	James, Hilda	3:10·0
1923	Jeans, Constance	2:54·0
1924	James, Hilda	2:58·6
1925	Jeans, Constance	2:52·8
1926	Mayne, Edith	2:57·8
1927	Cooper, Joyce	2:49·4
1928	Cooper, Joyce	2:46·4
1929	Cooper, Joyce	2:48·0
1930	Yarwood, May	3:09·0
1931	Cooper, Joyce	2:50·6
1932	Cooper, Joyce	2:42·2
1933	Wolstenholme, Beatrice	2:43·8
1934	Kenyon, Mary	2:44·8
1935	Bartle, Olive	2:45·0
1936	Morcom, Gladys	2:43·0
1937	Bartle, Olive	2:42·6
1938	Jeffery, Margaret	2:40·8
1939	Yate, Helen	2:41·6
1940–45	No events	
1946	Riach, Nancy	2:36·0

1947	Gibson, Cathie	2:29·2
1948	Gibson, Cathie	2:32·6
1949	Wellington, Margaret	2:34·2
1950	Linton, "Pip"	2:33·1
1951	Wilkinson, Daphne	2:31·1
1952	Preece, Lillian	2:32·0
1953	Preece, Lillian	2:33·7
1954	Botham, Jean	2:34·3
1955	Grant, Virginia (Can)	2:34·7
1956	Grant, Virginia (Can)	2:30·6
1957	Grinham, Judy	2:30·0
1958	Ferguson, Elizabeth	2:28·6
1959	Steward, Natalie	2:25·6
1960	Steward, Natalie	2:22·1
1961	Wilkinson, Diana	2:21·6
1962	Wilkinson, Diana	2:21·9
1963	Lonsbrough, Anita	2:19·7
1964	Long, Elizabeth	2:21·9
1965	Long, Elizabeth	2:16·1
1966	Cave, Jeanette	2:20·5
1967	Williams, Susan	2:17·2
1968	Jackson, Alex	2:17·6
1969	Ratcliffe, Shelagh	2:17·1
1970	Jackson, Alex	2:14·3

440 y. Free-style

1924	James, Hilda	6:27·0
1925	Laverty, Marion	6:18·8
1926	Laverty, Marion	6:10·6
1927	Laverty, Marion	6:11·4
1928	Cooper, Joyce	6:08·6
1929	Cooper, Joyce	6:15·4
1930	Cooper, Joyce	6:02·4
1931	Cooper, Joyce	5:58·4
1932	Cooper, Joyce	6:00·6
1933	Wolstenholme, Beatrice	6:03·0
1934	Wolstenholme, Beatrice	5:50·6
1935	Wolstenholme, Beatrice	6:00·0
1936	Morcom, Gladys	5:50·4
1937	Bartle, Olive	5:50·0
1938	Jeffery, Margaret	5:43·2
1939	Hutton, Margaret	5:49·8
1940–45	No events	
1946	Riach, Nancy	5:50·0
1947	Gibson, Cathie	5:23·2
1948	Gibson, Cathie	5:39·8
1949	Wellington, Margaret	5:36·4
1950	Wilkinson, Daphne	5:26·2
1951	Wilkinson, Daphne	5:17·6
1952	Wilkinson, Daphne	5:20·4
1953	Wilkinson, Daphne	5:29·8
1954	Brown, Christine	5:33·2
1955	Clarke, Joyce	5:34·8
1956	Girvan, Margaret	5:29·5

1957	Ferguson, Elizabeth	5:33·0
1958	Ferguson, Elizabeth	5:13·1
1959	Steward, Natalie	5:12·9
1960	Long, Elizabeth	5:05·0
1961	Rae, Nan	5:02·8
1962	Long, Elizabeth	4:53·7
1963	Long, Elizabeth	4:52·4
1964	Long, Elizabeth	4:58·5
1965	Long, Elizabeth	4:48·9
1966	Cave, Jeanette	4:52·6
1967	Williams, Susan	4:48·5
1968	Davison, Sally	4:55·8
1969	Williams, Susan	4:51·5
1970	Wright, Judith (NZ)	4:42·6

880 y. Free-style

1966	Cave, Jeanette	10:23·5
1967	Williams, Susan	9:59·8
1968	Davison, Sally	10:04·1
1969	Williams, Susan	10:06·1
1970	Wright, Judith (NZ)	9:48·5

Long Distance. (See men's long distance result for race conditions.)

1920	Jeans, Constance	1 hr 12:59·4
1921	Scott, Phyllis	1 hr 06:55·0
1922	Jeans, Constance	1 hr 07:36·0
1923	James, Hilda	1 hr 09:46·4
1924	James, Hilda	1 hr 11:24·4
1925	Scott, Phyllis	1 hr 11:47·6
1926	Hamblen, Mabel	1 hr 15:17·2
1927	Hamblen, Mabel	1 hr 11:32·0
1928	Hamblen, Mabel	1 hr 09:58·0
1929	Vine-Jackman, Gladys	1 hr 14:07·0
1930	Cooper, Joyce	1 hr 12:57·0
1931	Cooper, Joyce	1 hr 01:56·0
1932	Cooper, Joyce	59:04·2
1933	Cooper, Joyce	1 hr 06:46·8
1934	Browning, Shelagh	1 hr 11:15·8
1935	Browning, Shelagh	1 hr 11:27·4
1936	Browning, Shelagh	1 hr 10:15·0
1937	Allen, M. Y.	1 hr 15:01·0
1938	Bassett-Lowke Vivienne	1 hr 06:13·8
1939	Langer, Ruth	1 hr 14:04·0
1940–47	No events	
1948	Hill, Elizabeth	1 hr 24:56·8
1949–61	No events	
1962	Lynch, Susan	1 hr 52:30·0
1963	Gray, Elaine	1 hr 48:33·0
1964	Gray, Elaine	1 hr 50:03·0
1965	Gray, Elaine	1 hr 52:15·0
1966	Gray, Elaine	2 hr 47:16·0
1967	Gray, Elaine	2 hr 28:58·0

1968	Gray, Elaine	2 hr 33:30·0
1969	Woodall, Bridget	2 hr 35:40·0
1970	Woodall, Bridget	2 hr 40:06·0

150 y. Back-stroke

1920	Morton, Lucy	2:19·0
1921	Spencer, May	2:18·6
1922	Gilbert, Irene	2:16·0
1923	Spencer, May	2:18·4
1924	Shaw, Winifred	2:18·6
1925	King, Ellen	2:04·0
1926	King, Ellen	2:04·6
1927	Barker, M. A.	2:03·8
1928	King, Ellen	1:57·2
1929	Cooper, Joyce	1:59·2
1930	Clifford, Irene	2:05·0
1931	Cooper, Joyce	1:55·4
1932	Welsh, M.	Swim over
1933	McNulty, Margaret	2:04·8
1934	Wolstenholme, Beatrice	1:58·4
1935	Harding, Phyllis	1:56·6
1936	Harding, Phyllis	1:55·0
1937	Frampton, Lorna	1:56·4
1938	Yate, Helen	1:56·6
1939	Bassett-Lowke, Vivienne	1:54·4
1940–45	No events	
1946	Berlioux, Monique (Fr)	1:52·6

100 y. Back-stroke

1947	Gibson, Cathie	1:10·4
1948	Lane, Ngairi (NZ)	1:11·8
1949	Yate, Helen	1:10·2
1950	McDowall, Margaret	1:11·7
1951	McDowall, Margaret	1:09·2
1952	McDowall, Margaret	1:09·8

110 y. Back-stroke

1953	McDowall, Margaret	1:18·6
1954	Symons, Pat	1:16·9
1955	Grinham, Judy	1:15·3
1956	Grinham, Judy	1:04·5
1957	Hoyle, Julie	1:16·0
1958	Grinham, Judy	1:12·9
1959	Edwards, Margaret	1:12·5
1960	Steward, Natalie	1:11·0
1961	Edwards, Margaret	1:13·8
1962	Ludgrove, Linda	1:10·9
1963	Ludgrove, Linda	1:11·7
1964	Ludgrove, Linda	1:09·9
1965	Fairlie, Ann (SAf)	1:08·9
1966	Ludgrove, Linda	1:09·1
1967	Ludgrove, Linda	1:09·5
1968	Burrell, Wendy	1:11·2
1969	Gurr, Donna-Marie (Can)	1:09·1
1970	Stirling, Glenda (NZ)	1:08·7

220 y. Back-stroke

1964	Ludgrove, Linda	2:31·3
1965	Fairlie, Ann (SAf)	2:30·2
1966	Ludgrove, Linda	2:29·0
1967	Ludgrove, Linda	2:29·8
1968	Burrell, Wendy	2:32·8
1969	Gurr, Donna-Marie (Can)	2:28·8
1970	Burrell, Wendy	2:28·9

110 y. Breast-stroke

1964	Slattery, Jill	1:20·6
1965	Harris, Diana	1:19·2
1966	Harris, Diana	1:19·2
1967	Radnage, Amanda	1:19·1
1968	Harris, Diana	1:18·8
1969	O'Connor, Anne (Eire)	1:19·9
1970	Radnage, Amanda	1:19·5

200 y. Breast-stroke

1920	Morton, Lucy	3:10·0
1921	Carson, Gladys	3:12·4
1922	Hart, Doris	3:02·8
1923	Hart, Doris	3:03·8
1924	Harrison, Marion	3:07·6
1925	Gilbert, Irene	3:05·0
1926	Morris, E. M.	3:11·2
1927	King, Ellen	3:06·4
1928	King, Ellen	3:10·0
1929	Hinton, Margery	3:08·0
1930	Wolstenholme, Celia	2:56·8
1931	Hinton, Margery	2:56·6
1932	Hinton, Margery	2:56·6
1933	Hinton, Margery	2:58·6
1934	Hinton, Margery	2:57·4
1935	Kingston, Vera	2:53·6
1936	Storey, Doris	2:53·6
1937	Storey, Doris	2:53·8
1938	Storey, Doris	2:49·2
1939	Storey, Doris	2:43·6
1940–45	No events	
1946	Caplin, Jean	3:01·2
1947	Church, Elizabeth	2:52·8
1948	Church, Elizabeth	2:54·2
1949	Caspers, Jennie (Neth)	2:47·1
1950	Gordon, Elenor	2:46·0
1951	Gordon, Elenor	2:45·5
1952	Gordon, Elenor	2:43·0

220 y. Breast-stroke

1953	Grundy, Margaret	3:07·9
1954	Grundy, Margaret	3:03·8
1955	Gordon, Elenor	3:00·1
1956	Gordon, Elenor	2:59·2
1957	Gosden, Christine	2:56·5
1958	Lonsbrough, Anita	2:55·8

1959	Lonsbrough, Anita	2:54·0
1960	Lonsbrough, Anita	2:56·1
1961	Lonsbrough, Anita	2:53·7
1962	Lonsbrough, Anita	2:52·2
1963	Mitchell, Stella	2:52·6
1964	Mitchell, Stella	2:50·5
1965	Mitchell, Stella	2:49·2
1966	Mitchell, Stella	2:49·3
1967	Slattery, Jill	2:49·2
1968	Slattery, Jill	2:49·3
1969	Harrison, Dorothy	2:50·0
1970	Harrison, Dorothy	2:48·8

110 y. Butterfly

1953	Ivinson, Margaret	1:24·2
1954	Webb, Fenella	1:24·0
1955	Macadam, Cathy	1:17·7
1956	Morton, Anne	1:17·4
1957	Gosden, Christine	1:16·9
1958	Watt, Sheila	1:14·5
1959	Watt, Sheila	1:13·9
1960	Watt, Sheila	1:12·4
1961	Green, Lesley	1:12·7
1962	Baines, Pat	1:11·3
1963	Stewart, Mary (Can)	1:08·6
1964	Cotterill, Anne	1:10·2
1965	Tanner, Elaine (Can)	1:08·1
1966	Barner, Ann	1:08·8
1967	Barner, Ann	1:08·0
1968	Auton, Margaret	1:08·1
1969	Auton, Margaret	1:08·1
1970	Whiting, Cathy (NZ)	1:08·0

220 y. Butterfly

1966	Barner, Ann	2:34·7
1967	Barner, Ann	2:36·4
1968	Auton, Margaret	2:32·7
1969	Smith, Vicki (Eire)	2:33·1
1970	Smith, Vicki (Eire)	2:33·7

220 y. Individual medley

1966	Turnbull, Judith	2:37·6
1967	Ratcliffe, Shelagh	2:34·6
1968	Ratcliffe, Shelagh	2:34·7
1969	Ratcliffe, Shelagh	2:34·2
1970	Ratcliffe, Shelagh	2:30·7

440 y. Individual medley

1963	Lonsbrough, Anita	5:37·0
1964	Lonsbrough, Anita	5:39·4
1965	Hounsell, Barbara (Can)	5:35·0
1966	Williams, Susan	5:37·0
1967	Ratcliffe, Shelagh	5:27·7
1968	Ratcliffe, Shelagh	5:31·3
1969	Ratcliffe, Shelagh	5:28·0
1970	Ratcliffe, Shelagh	5:19·1

Free-style (club) relay (various distances)

1948	Beckenham Ladies	4:38·0
1949	Weston-super-Mare	4:36·6
1950	Croydon Ladies	4:40·7
1951	Croydon Ladies	4:39·5

4 × 110 y. Free-style (club) relay

1952	Mermaid	4:57·0
1953	Mermaid	5:01·8
1954	Mermaid	4:59·4
1955	Leander	5:02·3
1956	Mermaid	4:53·3
1957	Kingston Ladies	4:53·0
1958	Kingston Ladies	4:49·8
1959	Beckenham Ladies	4:45·3
1960	Mermaid	4:40·5
1961	Hampstead Ladies	4:40·0
1962	Hampstead Ladies	4:34·3
1963	Hampstead Ladies	4:30·3
1964	Stoke Newington	4:33·2
1965	Hampstead Ladies	4:31·6
1966	Kingston Ladies	4:29·1
1967	Beckenham Ladies	4:26·2
1968	Beckenham Ladies	4:31·8
1969	Beckenham Ladies	4:28·8
1970	Hornchurch	4:25·3

Medley (club) relay (various distances)

1935	Coventry Three Spires	
1936	Bournemouth	
1937	Bournemouth	
1938	Leicester United Ladies	
1939	Armley Ladies	
1940–45	No events	
1946	Mermaid	5:59·2
1947	Beckenham Ladies	5:38·1
1948	Mermaid	5:27·4
1949	Northampton	4:55·2
1950	Hampstead Ladies	4:56·9
1951	Croydon Ladies	4:56·6
1952	Mermaid	5:26·4

4 × 110 y. Medley (club) relay

1953	Mermaid	5:19·0
1954	Mermaid	5:22·7
1955	Mermaid	5:15·0
1956	Leander	5:24·7
1957	Heston	5:21·7
1958	Heston	5:14·5
1959	Heston	5:04·9
1960	Heston	5:09·2
1961	Heston	5:04·9
1962	Hampstead Ladies	5:05·5
1963	Hampstead Ladies	4:58·0
1964	Beckenham Ladies	4:51·7
1965	Beckenham Ladies	4:52·2

1966	Beckenham Ladies	4:50·5
1967	Beckenham Ladies	4:48·9
1968	York City	4:55·5
1969	Hartlepool	4:50·4
1970	Beckenham Ladies	4:53·1

AMATEUR SWIMMING ASSOCIATION WATER POLO CHAMPIONS.

See under WATER POLO, AMATEUR SWIMMING ASSOCIATION CHAMPIONS

AMERICAN CHAMPIONS. See UNITED STATES CHAMPIONS.

ANDERSEN, Greta (Denmark, 1928–). As an Olympic champion and also a conqueror of the English Channel, Miss Andersen claims a double place in swimming history. At 20, in the Games of 1948, she won the 100 m. free-style in 66·3, having equalled the Olympic record of 65·9 in a heat. Later she collapsed and had to be dragged from the water during a heat of the 400 m., but recovered in time to help Denmark to silver medals in the free-style relay. The Dane also won the European 400 m. title in 1950 (5:30·9) and placed third in the 100 m. in 1947 and 1950. In addition, she was a member of Danish relay teams who placed first in the 1947 Europeans and second in 1950.

Miss Andersen, at this time recognized as a sprinter and middle-distance competitor, then turned her talents to long distance events and between 1957 and 1964, as a professional, she made the hazardous Channel crossing six times. The first was during a Butlin-sponsored race in 1957 when only two out of 24 starters got across and Greta finished two hours ahead of her male rival.

She holds the record for England to France (the more difficult crossing) with 13 hours 14 minutes in 1964. Strangely, despite her Olympic success, she broke only one world record, for 100 y. (58·2) in 1949. She married an American and now lives in California.

AUSTRALIA, AMATEUR SWIMMING UNION OF. The A.S.U.A. was formed in Sydney on 22 Feb. 1909, at a meeting chaired by the late James Taylor and attended by representatives from the state associations of New South Wales, Victoria and South Australia, who became founder members, and of Queensland and Western Australia, who, with Tasmania, became members in 1913.

Although from 1894 to 1909 there was no central controlling authority, Australasian championships took place under an agreement between New South Wales, Victoria, Queensland, Western Australia and the A.S.A. of New Zealand.

Combined Australasian teams were entered for the 1908 and 1912 Olympic Games in London and Stockholm. At the latter, a team of three Australians (Healy, Bordman and Hardwick) and one New Zealander (Champion) won the 4 × 200 m. relay gold medals.

AUSTRALIAN CHAMPIONS. Australian championships organized under the auspices of the A.S.U.A. have been held since 1910 (see also AUSTRALIA, AMATEUR SWIMMING UNION OF). No championships were held between 1915–19, because of the First World War, nor from 1941–45. The winners since the Second World War are:

MEN

100 m. Free-style (instituted for 100 y. 1894)

1946*	O'Neill, Frank	1:02·6
1947*	O'Neill, Frank	1:02·2
1948*	Boyd, Warren	1:00·0
1949	Marshall, John	1:00·3
1950*	O'Neill, Frank	59·6
1951*	O'Neill, Frank	1:00·8
1952*	Aubrey, Rex	59·2
1953*	Henricks, Jon	57·2
1954*	Henricks, Jon	56·8
1955*	Henricks, Jon	57·2
1956*	Henricks, Jon	55·5
1957*	Devitt, John	56·6
1958*	Devitt, John	55·9
1959*	Konrads, John	55·9
1960*	Devitt, John	55·4
1961	Dickson, David	56·2
1962*	Staples, Charles	56·3
1963*	Dickson, David	55·5
1964	Dickson, David	55·1
1965*	Dickson, David	55·6

1966	Wenden, Michael	54·6
1967*	Doak, Peter	56·7
1968	Wenden, Michael	53·8
1969	Rogers, Greg	54·9
1970	Wenden, Michael	54·0
	* = 110 y.	

200 m. Free-style (instituted 1894)

1946*	Beard, Arthur	2:22·4
1947*	Marshall, John	2:20·3
1948	Marshall, John	2:16·8
1949*	Marshall, John	2:14·3
1950*	O'Neill, Frank	2:14·6
1951*	O'Neill, Frank	2:17·6
1952*	O'Neill, Frank	2:17·2
1953*	Henricks, Jon	2:09·8
1954*	Henricks, Jon	2:09·9
1955*	Rose, Murray	2:11·6
1956*	Chapman, Gary	2:05·8
1957*	Garretty, Murray	2:11·6
1958*	Konrads, John	2:05·1
1959*	Konrads, John	2:03·3
1960	Konrads, John	2:01·6
1961	Konrads, John	2:04·5
1962*	Windle, Bobby	2:02·9
1963*	Windle, Bobby	2:02·8
1964	Windle, Bobby	2:00·0
1965*	Dickson, David	2:04·7
1966	Wenden, Michael	2:00·5
1967*	Wenden, Michael	2:02·2
1968	Wenden, Michael	1:57·9
1969	Rogers, Greg	1:59·2
1970	Wenden, Michael	1:59·4
	* = 220 y.	

400 m. Free-style (instituted 1894)

1946*	Beard, Arthur	5:04·6
1947*	Marshall, John	5:02·0
1948*	Marshall, John	4:52·2
1949	Marshall, John	4:50·5
1950*	Agnew, David	4:53·3
1951*	Kelleway, Brian	4:54·3
1952*	Beard, John	5:02·2
1953*	Chapman, Gary	4:42·6
1954*	Chapman, Gary	4:39·3
1955*	Rose, Murray	4:47·3
1956*	Rose, Murray	4:33·0
1957*	Garretty, Murray	4:40·6
1958*	Konrads, John	4:21·8
1959*	Konrads, John	4:31·2
1960*	Konrads, John	4:15·9
1961	Konrads, John	4:25·1
1962*	Windle, Bobby	4:25·0
1963*	Windle, Bobby	4:23·0
1964	Windle, Bobby	4:17·6

1965*	Pick, John	4:24·7
1966	Bennett, John	4:23·6
1967*	Bennett, John	4:18·3
1968	Brough, Greg	4:13·6
1969	Brough, Greg	4:13·3
1970	Brough, Greg	4:10·0
	* = 440 y.	

1,500 m. Free-style (instituted 1937)

1946*	Sever, Ken	21:05·0
1947*	Marshall, John	20:23·4
1948	Marshall, John	20:35·5
1949	Marshall, John	19:35·2
1950*	Kelleway, Brian	20:32·7
1951*	Darke, Barry	21:05·7
1952*	McCormick, James	20:41·4
1953*	Mortenson, Brian	19:47·1
1954*	Donohue, James	19:47·1
1955*	Winram, Gary	19:14·8
1956*	Garretty, Murray	18:33·5
1957*	Garretty, Murray	19:04·4
1958*	Konrads, John	17:28·7
1959*	Konrads, John	18:24·2
1960*	Konrads, John	17:11·0
1961	Windle, Bobby	17:37·7
1962*	Windle, Bobby	17:53·3
1963*	Windle, Bobby	17:59·6
1964	Windle, Bobby	17:09·4
1965*	Pick, John	17:40·4
1966	Jackson, Ron	17:37·3
1967*	Bennett, John	17:23·6
1968	Brough, Greg	16:51·9
1969	Brough, Greg	16:43·6
1970	Windeatt, Graham	16:23·1
	* = 1,650 y.	

100 m. Back-stroke (instituted 1921 for 100 y.)

1946*	Milgate, Rodney	1:15·0
1947*	Bourke, Bruce	1:13·4
1948*	Bourke, Bruce	1:11·0
1949	Bourke, Bruce	1:11·5
1950*	Bourke, Bruce	1:11·9
1951*	O'Keefe, Leslie	1:14·5
1952*	Barry, Robert	1:10·6
1953*	Barry, Robert	1:09·7
1954*	Weld, Cyrus	1:08·3
1955*	Theile, David	1:07·4
1956*	Theile, David	1:05·5
1957*	Monckton, John	1:03·9
1958*	Monckton, John	1:01·5
1959*	Theile, David	1:04·0
1960*	Theile, David	1:03·0
1961	Fingleton, Tony	1:05·4
1962*	Carroll, Julian	1:05·8

1963*	Fingleton, Alan	1:05·4
1964	Byrom, John	1:04·2
1965*	Reynolds, Peter	1:02·6
1966	Reynolds, Peter	1:03·7
1967*	Reynolds, Peter	1:05·0
1968	Byrom, Karl	1:02·1
1969	Byrom, Karl	1:03·0
1970	Rogers, Neil	1:03·6
	* = 110 y.	

200 m. Back-stroke (instituted 1957)

1957*	Monckton, John	2:23·5
1958*	Monckton, John	2:18·8
1959*	Hayres, John	2:26·9
1960*	Carroll, Julian	2:19·7
1961	Carroll, Julian	2:24·9
1962*	Carroll, Julian	2:22·1
1963*	Fingleton, Tony	2:23·5
1964	Reynolds, Peter	2:19·1
1965*	Reynolds, Peter	2:18·1
1966*	Reynolds, Peter	2:14·6
1967*	Byrom, Karl	2:19·9
1968	Byrom, Karl	2:14·8
1969	Byrom, Karl	2:15·4
1970	Rogers, Neil	2:17·1
	* = 220 y.	

100 m. Breast-stroke (instituted 1957)

1957*	Gathercole, Terry	1:14·8
1958*	Hunt, Maxwell	1:15·0
1959*	Gathercole, Terry	1:14·1
1960*	Gathercole, Terry	1:15·4
1961	Burton, William	1:14·3
1962*	Burton, William	1:13·9
1963*	O'Brien, Ian	1:11·3
1964	O'Brien, Ian	1:08·1
1965*	O'Brien, Ian	1:11·1
1966	O'Brien, Ian	1:11·8
1967*	Oxer, David	1:15·6
1968	Tonkin, Peter	1:11·2
1969	Jarvie, Peter	1:11·8
1970	Jalmaani, Amman (Phil)	1:10·7
	* = 110 y.	

200 m. Breast-stroke (instituted 1908)

1946	Johnson, John	3:00·8
1947*	Davies, John	Bu2:58·2
1948*	Davies, John	Bu2:45·9
1949	Shanahan, James	2:53·0
1950*	Hallet, Kevin	2:58·1
1951*	Hawkins, David	2:49·7
1952*	Hawkins, David	2:42·3
1953*	Stott, Graeme	3:02·0
1954*	Gathercole, Terry	2:56·2
1955*	Gathercole, Terry	2:47·0
1956*	Gathercole, Terry	2:45·4

1957*	Gathercole, Terry	2:40·9
1958*	Gathercole, Terry	2:44·7
1959*	Gathercole, Terry	2:47·1
1960*	Gathercole, Terry	2:43·0
1961	Burton, William	2:42·6
1962*	O'Brien, Ian	2:41·8
1963*	O'Brien, Ian	2:37·4
1964	O'Brien, Ian	2:32·6
1965*	O'Brien, Ian	2:38·9
1966	O'Brien, Ian	2:41·6
1967*	Edwards, Gregory	2:41·5
1968	Oxer, David	2:38·9
1969	Gynther, Neil	2:41·7
1970	Gynther, Neil	2:37·0
	* = 220 y.	

100 m. Butterfly (instituted 1957)

1957*	Wilkinson, Brian	1:03·8
1958*	Wilkinson, Brian	1:04·4
1959*	Wilkinson, Brian	1:04·3
1960*	Hayes, Neville	1:03·0
1961	Hayes, Neville	1:01·6
1962*	Berry, Kevin	1:00·1
1963*	Berry, Kevin	59·9
1964	Berry, Kevin	58·8
1965*	Stark, John	1:01·8
1966	Reynolds, Peter	1:00·1
1967*	Dunn, Graham	1:00·9
1968	Cusack, Bob	59·1
1969	Scott, Ken	1:01·3
1970	Rogers, Neil	59·7
	* = 110 y.	

200 m. Butterfly (instituted 1953)

1953*	Fitzpatrick, Ken	2:56·8
1954*	Sharpe, Ken	2:50·0
1955*	Middleton, Graeme	2:47·6
1956*	Middleton, Graeme	2:36·5
1957*	Wilkinson, Brian	2:33·2
1958*	Wilkinson, Brian	2:27·0
1959*	Wilkinson, Brian	2:24·9
1960*	Hayes, Neville	2:17·9
1961	Hayes, Neville	2:14·7
1962*	Berry, Kevin	2:12·5
1963*	Berry, Kevin	2:13·4
1964	Berry, Kevin	2:06·9
1965*	Stark, John	2:13·4
1966	Stark, John	2:11·7
1967*	Hill, Brett	2:13·7
1968	Hill, Brett	2:13·5
1969	Wilkinson, Rick	2:13·3
1970	Findlay, James	2:10·2
	* = 220 y.	

200 m. Individual medley (instituted 1964)

| 1964 | Buck, Terry | 2:22·0 |

1965*	Reynolds, Peter	2:22·3
1966	Reynolds, Peter	2:19·6
1967*	Reid, Peter	2:22·4
1968	Reid, Peter	2:19·8
1969	Findlay, James	2:20·4
1970	Findlay, James	2:18·0
	* = 220 y.	

400 m. Individual medley (instituted 1953)

1953*	O'Neill, Frank	5:43·0
1954*	Barry, Robert	4:48·6
1955*	Henricks, Jon	5:55·0
1956*	Weld, Cyrus	5:40·9
1957*	Garretty, Murray	5:37·5
1958*	Wilkinson, Brian	5:27·4
1959*	Kable, Anthony	5:45·4
1960*	Kable, Anthony	5:33·6
1961	Burton, William	5:29·0
1962*	Alexander, Alex	5:23·3
1963*	Ebsary, Bill	5:18·8
1964	Buck, Terry	5:04·0
1965*	Reynolds, Peter	5:03·7
1966	Reynolds, Peter	4:54·0
1967*	Reynolds, Peter	5:06·2
1968	Byrom, Karl	4:58·7
1969	Findlay, James	4:57·4
1970	Findlay, James	4:49·6
	* = 440 y.	

WOMEN

100 m. Free-style (instituted 1930 for 100 y.)

1946*	West, Dawn	1:12·6
1947*	Davies, Judy-Joy	1:11·9
1948*	Spencer, Denise	1:10·1
1949	McQuade, Marjorie	1:09·9
1950*	McQuade, Marjorie	1:08·5
1951*	McQuade, Marjorie	1:09·0
1952*	McQuade, Marjorie	1:09·5
1953*	McQuade, Marjorie	1:08·4
1954*	Crapp, Lorraine	1:08·2
1955*	Leech, Faith	1:07·6
1956*	Fraser, Dawn	1:04·5
1957*	Morgan, Sandra	1:07·8
1958*	Fraser, Dawn	1:01·5
1959*	Fraser, Dawn	1:01·7
1960*	Fraser, Dawn	1:00·2
1961	Fraser, Dawn	1:01·0
1962*	Fraser, Dawn	1:00·6
1963*	Turner, Jan	1:04·4
1964	Fraser, Dawn	58·9
1965*	Murphy, Janice	1:03·1
1966	Bell, Lynn	1:03·0
1967*	Steinbeck, Jenny	1:03·4

1968	Watson, Lynn	1:01·8
1969	Steinbeck, Jenny	1:02·5
1970	Watson, Lynn	1:01·7
	* = 110 y.	

200 m. Free-style (instituted 1930)

1946*	Spencer, Denise	2:39·4
1947*	Spencer, Denise	2:37·6
1948*	Spencer, Denise	2:35·0
1949	McQuade, Marjorie	2:35·0
1950*	Davies, Judy-Joy	2:33·3
1951*	Davies, Judy-Joy	2:33·1
1953*	McQuade, Marjorie	2:36·0
1953*	McQuade, Marjorie	2:29·6
1954*	Crapp, Lorraine	2:30·9
1955*	Fraser, Dawn	2:29·3
1956*	Fraser, Dawn	2:21·2
1957*	Morgan, Sandra	2:29·3
1958*	Fraser, Dawn	2:14·7
1959*	Fraser, Dawn	2:15·3
1960*	Fraser, Dawn	2:11·6
1961	Fraser, Dawn	2:15·5
1962*	Fraser, Dawn	2:21·1
1963*	Konrads, Ilsa	2:18·6
1964	Fraser, Dawn	2:13·1
1965*	Herford, Kim	2:19·3
1966	Bell, Lynn	2:17·5
1967*	McDonald, Julie	2:18·0
1968	McDonald, Julie	2:14·2
1969	Rillie, Faye	2:15·4
1970	Moras, Karen	2:09·8
	* = 220 y.	

400 m. Free-style (instituted 1930)

1946*	Spencer, Denise	5:48·2
1947*	Spencer, Denise	5:47·0
1948*	Spencer, Denise	5:31·5
1949	Spencer, Denise	5:39·2
1950*	Davies, Judy-Joy	5:23·5
1951*	Davies, Judy-Joy	5:26·8
1952*	Norton, Denise	5:29·4
1953*	Davies, Judy-Joy	5:29·6
1954*	Crapp, Lorraine	5:19·0
1955*	Crapp, Lorraine	5:30·2
1956*	Crapp, Lorraine	5:05·9
1957*	Morgan, Sandra	5:21·6
1958*	Fraser, Dawn	4:55·7
1959*	Konrads, Ilsa	4:50·2
1960*	Fraser, Dawn	4:47·4
1961	Fraser, Dawn	4:49·7
1962*	Fraser, Dawn	4:58·7
1963*	Konrads, Ilsa	4:56·7
1964	Fraser, Dawn	4:50·6
1965*	Duncan, Nan	4:54·9
1966	Wainwright, Kathy	4:49·2

1967*	Thorn, Jenny	4:52·7
1968	Moras, Karen	4:39·9
1969	Moras, Karen	4:34·5
1970	Moras, Karen	4:26·3
	* = 440 y.	

800 m. Free-style (instituted 1933)

1946*	Spencer, Denise	12:11·2
1947	Not held	
1948	Davies, Judy-Joy	12:08·5
1949	Spencer, Denise	11:46·9
1950*	Norton, Denise	11:29·8
1951*	Norton, Denise	11:36·5
1952*	Norton, Denise	11:40·9
1953*	Davies, Judy-Joy	11:14·2
1954*	Davies, Judy-Joy	11:30·2
1955*	Munro, Jan	11:28·8
1956*	Munro, Jan	11:07·4
1957*	Giles, Maureen	11:21·8
1958*	Konrads, Ilsa	10:16·2
1959*	Konrads, Ilsa	10:11·4
1960*	Konrads, Ilsa	10:17·9
1961	Paine, Yvonne	10:29·8
1962*	Paine, Yvonne	10:37·0
1963*	Holley, Dawn	10:33·1
1964	Wainwright, Kathy	10:11·1
1965*	Wainwright, Kathy	9:58·2
1966	Wainwright, Kathy	10:06·4
1967*	Wainwright, Kathy	9:54·1
1968	Moras, Karen	9:36·9
1969	Deakes, Christine	9:42·5
1970	Moras, Karen	9:09·1
	* = 880 y.	

100 m. Back-stroke (instituted 1930 for 100 y.)

1946*	Davies, Judy-Joy	1:24·4
1947*	Davies, Judy-Joy	1:21·5
1948*	Davies, Judy-Joy	1:18·2
1949	Davies, Judy-Joy	1:20·2
1950*	Davies, Judy-Joy	1:16·6
1951*	Davies, Judy-Joy	1:17·9
1952*	Davies, Judy-Joy	1:18·0
1953*	Pascall, Margaret	1:18·1
1954*	Knight, Dianne	1:18·2
1955*	Huntingford, Pat	1:18·8
1956*	Beckett, Gergaynia	1:17·5
1957*	Jackson, Barbara	1:18·1
1958*	Beckett, Gergaynia	1:14·0
1959*	Nelson, Ann	1:15·8
1960*	Wilson, Marilyn	1:13·7
1961	Costin, Sue	1:13·2
1962	Nelson, Ann	1:13·5
1963*	Woosley, Belinda	1:12·9
1964	Woosley, Belinda	1:12·3

1965*	Mabb, Allyson	1:13·7
1966	Mabb, Allyson	1:11·8
1967*	Watson, Lyn	1:12·1
1968	Watson, Lyn	1:09·1
1969	Watson, Lyn	1:09·4
1970	Watson, Lyn	1:09·2
	* = 110 y.	

200 m. Back-stroke (instituted 1957)

1957*	Jackson, Barbara	2:50·5
1958*	Beckett, Gergaynia	2:45·1
1959*	Nelson, Ann	2:45·8
1960*	Wilson, Marilyn	2:39·0
1961	Wilson, Marilyn	2:39·6
1962*	Costin, Sue	2:41·7
1963	Woosley, Belinda	2:38·7
1964*	Woosley, Belinda	2:34·5
1965*	Cooper, Vivian	2:37·2
1966	Mabb, Allyson	2:35·0
1967*	Mabb, Allyson	2:34·8
1968	Watson, Lyn	2:28·9
1969	Watson, Lyn	2:31·4
1970	Watson, Lyn	2:28·9
	* = 220 y.	

100 m. Breast-stroke (instituted 1956)

1956*	Whillier, Lynette	1:26·7
1957*	Evans, Barbara	1:26·0
1958*	Lassig, Rosemary	1:25·9
1959*	Lassig, Rosemary	1:23·3
1960*	Lassig, Rosemary	1:22·2
1961	Hogan, Jan	1:25·2
1962*	Hogan, Jan	1:25·2
1963*	Ruygrok, Marguerite	1:22·0
1964	Ruygrok, Marguerite	1:22·8
1965*	Saville, Heather	1:20·1
1966	Saville, Heather	1:18·3
1967*	Saville, Heather	1:21·1
1968	Playfair, Judy	1:17·9
1969	Barnes, Joanne	1:18·1
1970	Whitfield, Beverley	1:18·5
	* = 110 y.	

200 m. Breast-stroke (instituted 1930)

1946*	Lyons, Nancy	3:14·0
1947*	Lyons, Nancy	3:17·8
1948*	Lyons, Nancy	3:09·9
1949	Lyons, Nancy	3:09·8
1950*	Lyons, Nancy	3:09·5
1951*	Uren, Joan	3:12·3
1952*	Lyons, Nancy	3:03·0
1953*	Fehr, Jenny	3:10·6
1954*	Grier, Jane	3:08·3
1955*	Whillier, Lynette	3:08·3
1956*	Evans, Barbara	3:05·4

1957*	Evans, Barbara	3:04·0
1958*	Evans, Barbara	3:02·4
1959*	Lassig, Rosemary	3:00·8
1960*	Lassig, Rosemary	2:57·7
1961	Hogan, Jane	3:02·1
1962*	Hogan, Jane	3:02·3
1963*	Ruygrok, Marguerite	2:54·2
1964	McGill, Linda	2:57·0
1965*	Saville, Heather	2:52·2
1966	Saville, Heather	2:50·8
1967*	Saville, Heather	2:54·6
1968	McKenzie, Sue	2:48·3
1969	Barnes, Joanne	2:49·4
1970	Whitfield, Beverley	2:48·0
	* = 220 y.	

100 m. Butterfly (instituted 1955)

1955*	Munro, Jan	1:25·3
1956*	Bainbridge, Beverley	1:16·8
1957*	Bainbridge, Beverley	1:16·0
1958*	Bainbridge, Beverley	1:15·5
1959*	Andrew, Jan	1:15·2
1960*	Fraser, Dawn	1:10·8
1961	Andrew, Jan	1:10·7
1962*	Fraser, Dawn	1:12·8
1963*	McGill, Linda	1:12·8
1964	McGill, Linda	1:11·2
1965*	Groeger, Jill	1:12·3
1966	Groeger, Jill	1:10·4
1967*	George, Lynette	1:11·8
1968	McClements, Lynn	1:09·4
1969	McClements, Lynn	1:08·7
1970	Mabb, Allyson	1:07·2
	* = 110 y.	

200 m. Butterfly (instituted 1960)

1960*	Andrew, Jan	2:44·1
1961	Andrew, Jan	2:40·5
1962*	McGill, Linda	2:46·0
1963*	McGill, Linda	2:41·5

1964	McGill, Linda	2:37·3
1965*	George, Lynette	2:43·9
1966	Groeger, Jill	2:40·4
1967*	Turner, Cecily	2:39·8
1968	Byrnes, Anne	2:33·3
1969	McClements, Lynn	2:31·1
1970	Robinson, Maree	2:27·0
	* = 220 y.	

200 m. Individual medley (instituted 1953)

1953*	Davies, Judy-Joy	3:06·4
1954*	Munro, Jan	3:06·0
1955*	Munro, Jan	3:05·6
1956*	Bainbridge, Beverley	2:50·2
1957*	Bainbridge, Beverley	2:54·4
1958*	Lassig, Rosemary	2:52·2
1959*	Fraser, Dawn	2:44·2
1960–63	Not held	
1964	McGill, Linda	2:40·7
1965*	Murphy, Jan	2:40·8
1966	Murphy, Jan	2:39·3
1967*	Murphy, Jan	2:40·4
1968	Watson, Lyn	2:35·6
1969	Rickard, Diana	2:36·2
1970	Rickard, Diana	2:31·3
	* = 220 y.	

400 m. Individual medley (instituted 1960)

1960*	Colquhoun, Alva	5:54·5
1961	McGill, Linda	5:59·1
1962*	McGill, Linda	5:50·8
1963*	McGill, Linda	5:41·2
1964	McGill, Linda	5:36·4
1965*	Murphy, Jan	5:51·1
1966	Murphy, Jan	5:41·5
1967*	Murphy, Jan	5:41·2
1968	Rickard, Diana	5:32·2
1969	Eddy, Sue	5:31·3
1970	Langford, Denise	5:17·8
	* = 440 y.	

B

BACK-STROKE. The third of the recognized strokes, back-stroke was put in the Olympic programme in 1908 (for men) and in 1924 (for women). The first A.S.A. championship for this style was won in 1903 by William Call.

The early swimmers used an inverted breast-stroke technique with a double arm swing and a frog-leg kick. With the development of front crawl, it was soon realized that an alternating arm action and a flutter leg kick could be as effective on the back as on the front.

It is the only one of the four modern styles in which the competitor starts in the water. He must stay on his back throughout the race, except at the turns. There, having touched on his back, he may move from this position to make a somersault turn provided he has returned on to his back before his feet leave the wall.

Three men have won the A.S.A. back-stroke title seven times each. John Besford of Manchester, 1927–28, 1930–32 and 1935–36, John Brockway of Maindee 1948–51 and 1953–54 and Graham Sykes of Coventry successively from 1956–60 (over 110 y.) and 1961–62 (for 220 y.).

BALL, Catie (United States, 30 Sep. 1951–). Holder of all four world breast-stroke records before the 1968 Olympic Games in Mexico City, Miss Ball, from Jacksonville, Florida, was taken ill with a virus infection and failed to win either of the individual golds.

She staved off collapse on the first days of the swimming to take a gold in the United States medley relay team and to struggle into fifth place in the final of the 100 metres. Normally 5 ft. 7 in. and 128 lb, Miss Ball lost 10 lb in weight and was too ill even to start in the heats of the 200 m.

Pan American 100 and 200 m. champion in 1967 and double winner of the United States outdoor titles in 1967 and 1968, Miss Ball broke ten world breast-stroke records between December 1966 and August 1968. These include five successive 100 m. marks from 1:15·6 to 1:14·2. Her other best times were 1:17·0 (110 y.), 2:38·5 (200 m.) and 2:46·9 (220 y.)

BARANY, Istvan (Hungary, 20 Dec. 1907–). A great competitor in the era when Johnny Weissmuller bestrode the world swimming scene, Dr. Barany ('Pista' to his friends) became the first European to break the minute for 100 m. (59·8) in coming second to Weissmuller in the 1928 Olympics. He also won a silver in the 4 × 200 m. relay in 1932.

Barany, a man of many talents, is a doctor of law and political science, worked as a town clerk, journalist, was secretary of the Hungarian Swimming Federation (1957–59) and organized the 1958 European championships in Budapest. He has written 18 books about swimming and is editor of the Hungarian S.F. official bulletin *Uszosport*.

Winner of seven European championship medals—100 m., gold (1926 and 1931); silver (1927); 400 m. gold (1931); 4 × 200 m. silver (1926), bronze (1927) and gold (1931)—his best times were 100 m. (58·4), 200 m. (2:16·0), both European records, and 5:04·0 for 400 m.

BEAUREPAIRE, Sir Frank (Australia, 1891–May 1956). In a swimming career which stretched from 1903 to 1928, Beaurepaire competed in four Olympics —1908, 1912, 1920 and 1924—in which he won three silver and three bronze medals, the last of these at the age of 33, for 400, 1,500 and 4 × 200 m. free-style. He set eight world records.

And he did this despite three warnings that swimming was dangerous to him as a result of rheumatic fever in childhood. In fact, Beaurepaire swam himself back to health and became one of Australia's outstanding distance free-stylers.

He was Lord Mayor of Melbourne from 1940 to 1942, and knighted at the end of his term of office. Business success made him a millionaire and he was a noted philanthropist, but his great dream of seeing the Olympics in his city was never fulfilled.

Melbourne was awarded the 1956 Games and Beaurepaire was elected Lord Mayor again to host the event. But he died of a heart attack seven months before the opening.

He made many trips to Europe, during which he won ten A.S.A. titles from 220 y. to one mile. His best performances were 200 m. in 2:30·0, 440 y. in 5:23·0 and 1,000 m. in 14:28·0—a mark he set on the way to another world record for one mile, at the age of 30.

BENJAMIN, HENRY, NATIONAL MEMORIAL TROPHY.

Awarded to the top men's club in England, this trophy was presented to the A.S.A. by the five district associations in 1909 to perpetuate the memory of the late Henry Benjamin, a noted administrator, who was president of the A.S.A. in 1900. Points are awarded for success in A.S.A. championships as follows:

Swimming (individual)—winner 4, second 3, third 2, unplaced standard time 1.

Swimming (team)—winner 5, second 3, third 2, other competing teams 1 (only one team from each club).

Water polo—each match won 2.

Not more than three entries from any one club in each individual event may score.

Otter S.C. have the most wins (13). They were joint holders, with Plaistow United (1933) and Hull Kingston (1947) and won outright in 1935, 1938, 1948–50, 1953, 1955, 1962 and 1963–64. Until 1951, when a trophy was awarded for the top diving club (see MELVILLE CLARK, G., National Memorial Trophy) success in diving championships also counted. The winners have been:

Year	Club	Points
1910	Wigan	29
1911	Hyde Seal	33
1912	Hyde Seal/Middlesbrough	23
1913	Middlesbrough	30
1914–19	Not awarded	
1920	Hammersmith	27
1921	Middlesbrough	32
1922	Penguin	36
1923	Penguin	34
1924	Penguin	23
1925	Weston-super-Mare	28
1926	Penguin	22
1927	Penguin	19
1928	South Manchester	25
1929	Oldham Police	27
1930	Oldham Police	28
1931	Plaistow United	32
1932	Plaistow United	32
1933	Otter/Plaistow United	20
1934	Oldham Police	22
1935	Otter	25
1936	Penguin	23
1937	Otter	27
1938	Otter	34
1939	Hanley	19
1940–46	Not awarded	
1947	Hull Kingston/Otter	24
1948	Otter	20
1949	Otter	27
1950	Otter	15
1951	Penguin	18
1952	Penguin	22
1953	Otter	17
1954	Coventry	17
1955	Otter	19
1956	Wallasey	22
1957	Wallasey	18
1958	Stoke Newington/Wallasey	21
1959	Stoke Newington	30
1960	Stoke Newington	36
1961	York City	31
1962	Otter	41
1963	York City	48
1964	Otter	49
1965	Otter	27
1966	Southampton	49
1967	Southampton	55
1968	Southampton	53

| 1969 | Southampton | 29 |
| 1970 | Southampton | 33 |

BERRY, Kevin (Australia, 10 Apr. 1945–
). The career of butterflyer Kevin
Berry was short and successful. In
three years, from 1962 to 1964, he won
an Olympic title and a relay bronze,
three Commonwealth golds and broke
12 world records.

Berry, from Marrickville, Sydney, was
15 in 1960 when he made his first Olympic appearance as Australia's second
string in the 200 m. in Rome and did well
to place sixth in 2:18·5. Four years later,
Berry was world record-holder with
2:06·9 and favourite for the Tokyo title.
This he duly won, 0·9 ahead of America's
Carl Robie, in a new world mark of
2:06·6—a time which took three years
to better.

Commonwealth 110 and 220 y.
butterfly champion in Perth (Aus) in
1962, Berry, who won six Australian
titles, improved the world 200 m. time
by 5·9 seconds in 21 months, yet never
broke the 100 m. mark, nor was he a
member of a world record-breaking relay squad. His best times, all world
marks, were 59·0 (110 y.), 2:06·6 (200 m.)
and 2:08·4 (220 y.). The last performance, on 12 Jan. 1963, stayed on the
record books until the event was discontinued in December 1968.

BESFORD, John C. P. (Great Britain,
30 Jan. 1911–). Seven times English
back-stroke champion between 1927–36,
Besford's memorable feat was to win the
1934 European 100 m. title in Magdeburg. For this he received the Hitler
trophy, a magnificent bronze eagle,
mounted on a bronze globe, surmount-
ing a marble plinth and weighing a
hundredweight, a prize which Germany,
the host nation, had confidently expected would go to their Ernst Kuppers.

Besford, from the South Manchester
club, swam in the Olympics in Antwerp
in 1928, when he was sixth in the 100 m.
back-stroke and in Berlin in 1936 having
had to miss the 1932 Games because of
his dentistry finals at Manchester University.

He won the back-stroke bronze in the
first Empire Games in Hamilton in 1930
and a silver, plus a medley relay bronze
at the second Games at the Empire Pool,
Wembley, four years later. He now has
a dental practice in Tokyo, and during
the 1964 Olympics in Japan helped with
the welfare arrangements for the British
swimming team.

BJEDOV, Djurdjica (Yugoslavia, 5 Apr.
1947–). A shock winner of the 100 m.
breast-stroke at the 1968 Games—
Yugoslavia's first and only Olympic
swimming champion—Djurdjica Bjedov
almost did not go to Mexico. She was
chosen only to make up a medley relay
squad. Ironically the team were disqualified for a faulty take-over and did
not even reach the final.

Bjedov had no claims to fame. Third
in her 200 m. heat in the 1966 European
championships was her only commen-
dation. But in Mexico, fit and apparently
unaffected by the altitude, she improved
as more famous swimmers wilted. She
was the fifth fastest qualifier for the 100
m. final and she came through in lane 2
to snatch the gold by one-tenth in an
Olympic record of 1:15·8 from Russia's
Galina Prosumenschikova, the only
European to have won an Olympic
swimming title at the 1964 Games.

The slim, pale, dark-haired student
from Split, swam from an even more
unfavoured position—as seventh qualifier for the final she was in an outside
lane—to win the silver for 200 m. in
2:46·4. This was three seconds better
than she had done before, only 2 sec.
behind the winner Sharon Wichman
(United States) and she beat the Russian
again, this time by six-tenths.

BLACK, Ian M. (Great Britain, 27 June
1941–). World renown came to Ian
Black of Aberdeen in 1958 when, at 17,
he won three European titles—two in
the space of 40 minutes—in Budapest.
He first took the 400 m. free-style,
almost without seeming to exert himself,
by eight metres. With barely time to dry
off, he was back in the water for the
200 m. butterfly. And three days later,

he captured the 1,500 m. for a hat-trick of individual golds only once achieved before in these championships, by Arne Borg of Sweden in 1927.

Black's time at the top was short, from 1958 to 1960. But he packed a lot into these three years. He won the 220 y. butterfly gold, and silvers in the 440 y. free-style and 4 × 220 y. relay in the 1958 Empire Games in Cardiff.

The same year, he set European free-style records for 400 m. (4:28·4), 800 m. (9:25·5) and 1,500 m. (18:05·8).

For these achievements he was voted Britain's Sportsman of the Year of 1968 in three national polls.

The fair-haired Scot's only world mark came in 1959 when he became the first holder of the 440 y. medley (5:08·8). The following year he dead-heated with John Konrads of Australia for the bronze medal in the 400 m. free-style in the Rome Olympics, but was judged into fourth place on a technicality. His 4:21·8 then was a European record and he helped Britain to fourth place and to another European record in the 4 × 200 m. free-style relay.

In the A.S.A. championships Black won four titles at each of the meetings of 1958 and 1959—110, 220 and 440 y. free-style and 220 y. butterfly. He also won the mile, a distance he detested, in 1958 and 18 Scottish titles. And one time he held nine of the 18 British records.

BOITEUX, Jean (France,   ). A suprise Olympic 400 m. winner in Helsinki in 1952, the tall dark-haired Boiteux was close to being disqualified after his victory, for his father leapt into the water to embrace his son before some of the other swimmers had finished. Papa Boiteux's excitement was understand-able, for in beating America's Ford Konno by six-tenths in 4:30·7—more than ten seconds faster than the 1948 winning time—his son Jean had become France's first individual Olympic swim-ming champion.

Boiteux, who two years before had won silver medals for 400 and 1,500 m. in the European championship in Vienna,

later failed to qualify for the final of the Helsinki 1,500 m. He won a slow heat in 19:12·3, missed the final by two seconds and the very real chance of a second medal for France.

BOLOGNA TROPHY. This huge, handsome cup was awarded to the British women's relay team for winning the 4 × 100 m. at the 1927 European championships, the first in which women participated, in Bologna, Italy. The team consisted of Joyce Cooper and Marion Laverty of England, Ellen King of Scotland and Valerie Davies of Wales.

It was decided by the three countries that the trophy should be put up for an Inter-Country Speed Swimming team contest. Between 1920 and 1955 the match was held annually, except in Olympic years. Since 1956 it has been held every year. Of the 31 meetings, England have won 29 and Scotland two.

Year	Venue	Eng-land	Scot-land	Wales
1929	Paisley	19	17	—
1930	Nelson	34	24	14
1931	Rhyl	36	23	13
1933	Dunfermline	32	27	13
1934	Hastings	28	25	17
1935	Newport	35	22	14
1937	Renfrew	35	22	15
1938	Wembley	34	20	18
1939	Barry	36	20	16
1947	Aberdeen	30	28	14
1949	Birmingham	32	25	15
1950	Aberdare	26	30	16
1951	Kilmarnock	24	32	16
1953	Birmingham	33	24	15
1954	Newport	28	27	17
1955	Aberdeen	34	24	14
1956	Gateshead	40	28	16
1957	Newport	39	30	15
1958	Kilmarnock	37	25	19
1959	Liverpool	38	29	17
1960	Newport	40	29	15
1961	Coatbridge	39	25	20
1962	Blackburn	39	25	20
1963	Cardiff	40	25	19
1964	Dumfries	36	28	20
1965	Liverpool	41	21	22
1966	Aberavon	42	20	22
1967	Wishaw	41	21	22
1968	Grimsby	38	21	25

Year	Venue	Eng-land	Scot-land	Wales
1969	Aberavon	40	25	19
1970	Edinburgh	56	36	28

BORG, Arne (Sweden, 1901–   ). A giant of his time, Borg's theme song could have been wine, women and water, for he always did what he felt like doing and, among other things, he liked to swim.

His first Olympic appearance was in the 1924 Games where after heats and semi-finals—unheard of these days—he lost the 1,500 m. final to Boy Charlton (Australia) by 34·8 seconds though he was himself 1:41·8 inside the 1920 Olympic record with 20:41·4. But he finished ahead of Charlton, though behind Johnny Weissmuller, in the 400 m. and, such was his versatility, placed fourth in the 100 m.

At the 1928 Games he beat Charlton in the 1,500 m. but was third, behind Alberto Zorilla, the Argentine's only Olympic gold medal swimmer and the Australian in the 400 m. Borg won the 400 and 1,500 m. at the first European championships in 1926 and was second in the 100 m. The following year, he took all three gold medals at the second European meeting. His astonishing 1,500 m. winning time of 19:07·2 was a world record that stood for 11 years—and Borg did this only hours after playing for Sweden, the silver medal winners, in a water-polo match in which he had two teeth knocked out.

Borg set 32 world records between 1921–29 for every free-style distance, from 300 y. up to one mile. As well as his 1,500 m. marks, he swam 400 m. in 4:50·3 in 1925, a time that was not beaten until 1931.

A great patriot, Borg nevertheless did not allow things he thought a waste of time to interfere with his pleasures. Called up for national service during peace time, just as he was setting off on a holiday tour of Spain, he chose Spain. This time even his tremendous popularity did not prevent him being sent to prison. Yet his time in cell 306 in Gota prison seems to have been one long round of visits from friends, food and drink were sent in to him to such a degree that he was 8 kilograms heavier on his release.

BOYS, Beverley (Canada, 4 July 1951–   ). Double diving gold medallist at the 1970 Commonwealth Games, Beverley Boys, from Pickering, Ontario, has a notable diving record. Her overwhelming highboard and springboard victories in Edinburgh were despite perforating an ear drum on her first practice dive after flying into Scotland.

Four years earlier, then only 15, this fair-haired girl had won the silver from the highboard and bronze from the springboard in the 1966 Commonwealth Games in Jamaica. And in between these successes she had been the runner-up in the 1967 Pan-American highboard diving in Winnipeg, placed fourth in this event in the 1968 Olympics in Mexico and become the first foreign diver to win an American national title, the indoor highboard crown in 1969, beating in the process Olympic champion Milena Duchkova of Czechoslovakia.

BREAST-STROKE. The first of the competitive strokes and the only one in which a prescribed style is laid down, the breast-stroke probably has caused more legislating and officiating trouble than the rest of swimming's problems put together.

The F.I.N.A. Rule 65 states:

(a) both hands must be pushed forward together from the breast on or under the surface of the water and brought backward simultaneously and symmetrically with lateral extension.

(b) the body must be kept perfectly on the breast, and both shoulders in line with the surface of the water.

(c) the feet shall be drawn up together, the knees bent and open. The movement shall be continued with a rounded and outward sweep of the feet, bringing the legs together. All movements of the legs and feet shall be simultaneous, symmetrical and in the same lateral plane. Up and down movements of the legs in the vertical plane are prohibited.

Further, the rules say that swimming under the surface of the water is prohibited, except for one arm stroke and one leg kick after start and turn.

Arguments have ranged from how perfect the movements of the arms and legs must be; whether a swimmer ducking his head into his own bow-wave is swimming under water; to the time, in the early 1930s, when some bright people realized there was nothing in the current rules to prevent the arms being recovered over instead of under the water (see BUTTERFLY).

The interim time (1934–52) during which swimmers could use the over or under water arm technique played havoc with the world records for the butterfly style proved to be the faster.

From 1952–56, the Japanese in particular exploited another loophole in the rules and began to swim great distances under the water. This was immeasurably faster than on the surface and again the world record picture became distorted.

In the present day, the sprinting technique, developed especially by the Soviet Union, is causing problems. In order to speed the stroke, it is necessary to shorten both arm and leg actions. As a result, many competitors come perilously close to vertical instead of the lateral movements of this classic style so much beloved by traditionalists.

BRITISH COMMONWEALTH GAMES. See COMMONWEALTH GAMES.

BRITISH EMPIRE GAMES. See COMMONWEALTH GAMES.

BRITISH EMPIRE AND COMMONWEALTH GAMES. See COMMONWEALTH GAMES.

BRITISH MEDALLISTS, EUROPEAN CHAMPIONSHIPS. The following swimmers and divers, listed in alphabetical order, have won European medals while representing Great Britain. g = gold (1st), s = silver (2nd), and b = bronze (3rd).

Amos, Linda, 1962, 4 × 100 m. fr. (s).

Bartle, Olive, 1934, 4 × 100 m. fr. (b).

Besford, John, 1934, 100 m. ba (g).

Black, Ian, 1958, 400 and 1,500 m. fr. and 200 m. bu. (g).

Brenner, Adrienne, 1962, 4 × 100 m. fr. (s).

Brockway, John, 1954, 100 m. ba. (b).

Campion, Dick, 1962, 1,500 m. fr. (b).

Child, Edna, 1938, springboard (b).

Clarke, Stan, 1962, 4 × 100 m. fr. (s).

Cooper, Joyce, 1927, 4 × 100 m. fr. (g), 100 m. fr. (s); 1931, 400 and 4 × 100 m. fr. and 100 m. ba. (s), 100 m. fr. (b).

Cotterill, Anne, 1962, 4 × 100 m. med. (b).

Davies, Valerie, 1927, 4 × 100 m. fr. (g); 1931 4 × 100 m. fr. (s).

Deane, Kenneth, 1938, 4 × 200 m. fr. (b).

Dove, Freddie, 1938, 100 m. fr. (s), 4 × 200 m. fr. (b).

Edwards, Margaret, 1958, 100 m. ba. (s).

Ferguson, Elspeth, 1958, 4 × 100 m. fr. (s).

Gegan, Judy, 1966, 4 × 100 m. med. (b).

Gibson, Cathie, 1947, 400 m. fr. and 100 m. ba. (s), 4 × 100 m. fr. (b).

Girvan, Margaret, 1947, 4 × 100 m. fr. (b).

Gosden, Christine, 1958, 4 × 100 m. med. (b).

Grant, Zilpha, 1938, 4 × 100 m. fr. (b).

Grinham, Judy, 1958, 100 m. ba. (g), 4 × 100 m. fr. (s), 100 m. fr., 4 × 100 m. med. (b).

Harding, Phyllis, 1927, 100 m. ba. (b); 1931, 4 × 100 m. fr. (s), 100 m. ba. (b).

Harris, Diana, 1966, 4 × 100 m. med. (b).

Harrison, Dorothy, 1970, 200 m. br. (b).

Harrowby, Joyce, 1938, 4 × 100 m. fr. (b).

Heatly, Peter, 1954, highboard (b).

Hinton, Margery, 1931, 200 m. br. (b); 1934, 4 × 100 m. fr. (b); 1938, 4 × 100 m. fr. (b).

Hodges, Freddie, 1938, springboard (b).

Hughes, Edna, 1934, 4 × 100 m. fr. (b).

Jackson, Alex, 1970, 100 m. fr. (b).

Jenkins, Brian, 1962, 200 m. bu. (s).

Kendrew, Peter, 1962, 4 × 100 m. fr. (s).

Kimber, Alan, 1966, 1,500 m. fr. (s).

King, Ellen, 1927, 4 × 100 m. fr. (s).

Knight, Albert, 1926, highboard, (b).

Larsen, Katinka, 1934, springboard (s).

Laverty, Marion, 1927, 4 × 100 m. fr. (g), 400 m. fr. (s).

Leivers, Bobby, 1938, 1,500 m. fr. (s), 4 × 200 m. fr. (b).

Lonsbrough, Anita, 1958, 200 m. br. (s), 4 × 100 m. med. (b); 1962, 200 m. br. (g), 400 m. med. (s), 4 × 100 m. med. (b).

Ludgrove, Linda, 1962, 4 × 100 m. med. (b); 1966, 100 m. ba. (s), 4 × 100 m. med. (b).

McDowall, Jean, 1931, 4 × 100 m. fr. (s).

McGregor, Bobby, 1962, 4 × 100 m. fr. (s); 1966, 100 m. fr. (g).

Marchant, Louis, 1947, highboard (b).

Martin-Dye, John, 1962, 4 × 100 m. fr. (s).

Phelps, Brian, 1958, highboard (g); 1962, highboard (g); 1966, highboard (s).

Preece, Lillian, 1947, 4 × 100 m. fr. (b).

Rae, Nan, 1958, 400 m. fr. (b).

Ratcliffe, Shelagh, 1970, 200 and 400 m. med. (b).

Romain, Roy, 1947, 200 m. br. (g).

Samuel, Judy, 1958, 4 × 100 m. fr. (s).

Sillett, Pauline, 100 m. fr. and 4 × 100 m. med. (b).

Slade, Berry, 1938, springboard (g).

Slattery, Jill, 1966, 200 m. br. (b).

Storey, Doris, 1938, 200 m. br. (s).

Symonds, Graham, 1958, 200 m. bu. (b).

Symons, Pat, 1954, 100 m. ba. (b).

Thompson, Jenny, 1962, 4 × 100 m. fr. (s).

Wadham, Olive, 1938, 4 × 100 m. fr. (b).

Wainwright, Norman, 1934, 1,500 m. fr. (b); 1938, 400 m. and 4 × 200 m. fr. (b).

Wellington, Margaret, 1947, 4 × 100 m. fr. (b).

Welsh, Charmian, 1958, springboard (s).

White, Belle, 1927, highboard (g).

Wilkinson, Diana, 1958, 4 × 100 m. fr. (s), 4 × 100 m. med. (b); 1962, 100 and 4 × 100 m. fr. (s), 4 × 100 m. med. (b).

Wolstenholme, Beatrice, 1934, 4 × 100 m. fr. (b).

Wolstenholme, Celia, 1931, 200 m. br. (g).

BRITISH MEDALLISTS, OLYMPIC GAMES. The following swimmers, divers and water-polo players listed in alphabetical order, have won Olympic medals while representing Great Britain g = gold (1st), s = silver (2nd) and b = bronze (3rd).

Annison, Harold, 1920, 4 × 200 m. fr. (b).

Armstrong, Eileen, 1920, springboard (s).

Barker, Florence, 1924, 4 × 100 m. fr. (s).

Battersby, Sydney, 1908, 1,500 m. fr. (s), 4 × 200 m. fr. (b).

Bentham, Isaac, 1912, wp. (g).

Bugbee, Charles, 1912, wp. (g); 1920, wp. (g).

Carson, Gladys, 1924, 200 m. br. (b).

Clarke, Harold, 1924, highboard (b).

Coe, Thomas, 1900, wp. (g).

Cooper, Joyce, 1928, 4 × 100 m. fr. (s), 100 m. fr. and 100 m. ba. (b); 1932, 4 × 100 m. fr. (b).

Cornet, George, 1908, wp. (g); 1912, wp. (g).

Courtman, Percy, 1912, 400 m. br. (b).

Davies, Valerie, 1932, 100 m. ba. and 4 × 100 m. fr. (b).

Dean, William, 1920, wp. (g).

Derbyshire, J. H. (Rob.), 1900, wp. (g); 1906, 4 × 250 m. fr. (b); 1908, 4 × 200 m. fr. (g).

Edwards, Margaret, 1956, 100 m. ba. (b).

Ferris, Elizabeth, 1960, springboard (b).

Fletcher, Jennie, 1912, 4 × 100 m. fr. (g), 100 m. fr. (b).

Forsyth, Eric, 1908, wp. (g).

Foster, William, 1908, 4 × 200 m. fr. (g); 1912, 4 × 200 m. fr. (b).

Gibson, Cathie, 1948, 400 m. fr. (b).

Gordon, Elenor, 1952, 200 m. br. (b).

Grinham, Judy, 1956, 100 m. ba. (g).

Harding, Phyllis, 1924, 100 m. ba. (s).

Haresnape, Herbert, 1908, 100 m. ba. (b).

Hatfield, Jack, 1912, 400 and 1,500 m. fr. (s), 4 × 200 m. fr. (b).

Henry, William, 1906, 4 × 250 m. fr. (b).

Hill, Arthur, 1912, wp. (g).

Holman, Frederick, 1908, 200 m. br. (g).

Hughes, Edna, 1832, 4 × 100 m. fr. (b).

James, Hilda, 1920, 4 × 100 m. fr. (s).

Jarvis, John, 1900, 1,000 and 4,00 m. fr.

(g); 1906, One mile (s), 400 m. and 4 × 250 m. fr. (b).

Jeans, Constance, 1920, 4 × 100 m. fr. (s); 1924, 4 × 100 m. fr. (s).

Jones, Christopher, 1920, wp. (g).

Kemp, Peter, 1900, wp. (g), 200 m. obstacle (b).

King, Ellen, 1928, 100 m. ba. and 4 × 100 m. fr. (s).

Lister, William, 1900, wp. (g).

Lonsbrough, Anita, 1960, 200 m. br. (g).

McGregor, Bobby, 1964, 100 m. fr. (s).

McKenzie, Grace, 1920, 4 × 100 m. fr. (s); 1924, 4 × 100 m. fr. (s).

Moore, Bella, 1912, 4 × 100 m. fr. (g).

Morton, Lucy, 1924, 200 m. br. (g).

Nevinson, George, 1908, wp. (g).

Peacock, William, 1920, wp. (g).

Peter, Percy, 1920, 4 × 200 m. fr. (b).

Phelps, Brian, 1960, highboard (b).

Purcell, Norman, 1920, wp. (g).

Radcliffe, Charlotte, 1920, 4 × 100 m. fr. (s).

Radmilovic, Paul, 1908, 4 × 200 m. fr.

and wp. (g); 1912, wp. (g); 1920, wp. (g).

Robertson, Arthur, 1900, wp. (g).

Robinson, Eric, 1900, wp. (g).

Robinson, William, 1908, 200 m. br. (s).

Savage, Leslie, 1920, 4 × 200 m. fr. (b).

Smith, Charles, 1908, wp. (g); 1912, wp. (g); 1920, wp. (g).

Spiers, Annie, 1912, 4 × 100 m. fr. (g).

Steer, Irene, 1912, 4 × 100 m. fr. (g).

Steward, Natalie, 1960, 100 m. ba. (s), 100 m. fr. (b).

Stewart, Cissie, 1928, 4 × 100 m. fr. (s).

Tanner, Vera, 1924, 4 × 100 m. fr. (s); 1928, 4 × 100 m. fr. (s).

Taylor, Henry, 1906, One mile (g), 400 m. fr. (s), 4 × 250 m. fr. (b); 1908, 400 and 1,500 m. fr. and 4 × 200 m. fr. (g); 1912, 4 × 200 m. fr. (b); 1920, 4 × 200 m. fr. (b).

Thould, Thomas, 1908, wp. (g).

Varcoe, Helen, 1932, 4 × 100 m. fr. (b).

White, Belle, 1912, highboard (b).

Wilkinson, George, 1900, wp. (g); 1908, wp. (g); 1912, wp. (g).

Woodroffe, Martyn, 1968, 200 m. bu. (s).

BRITISH RECORDS

MEN

Free-style

100 m.	53·4	McGregor, Bobby (Scot)	Tokyo	29 Aug. 1967
200 m.	2:00·1y	Jarvis, Tony (Eng)	Blackpool	9 Aug. 1968
400 m.	4:19·6y	Woodroffe, Martyn (Wal)	Blackpool	6 Aug. 1969
800 m.	9:05·4	Kimber, Alan (Eng)	Utrecht	27 Aug. 1966
	9:05·4y	Woodroffe, Martyn (Wal)	Blackpool	6 Aug. 1969
1,500 m.	17:13·2	Kimber, Alan (Eng)	Utrecht	27 Aug. 1966

Back-stroke

100 m.	1:00·9	Richards, Mike (Wal)	Barcelona	9 Sept. 1970
200 m.	2:14·5	Richards, Mike (Wal)	Edinburgh	20 July 1970

Breast-stroke

100 m.	1:09·9y	Roberts, Roger (Eng)	London	4 May 1968
200 m.	2:32·5	Wilkie, David (Sco)	Edinburgh	17 July 1970

Butterfly

100 m.	58·8	Woodroffe, Martyn (Wal)	Santa Clara	11 July 1969
200 m.	2:07·8	Woodroffe, Martyn (Wal)	Santa Clara	13 July 1969

Medley

200 m.	2:16·6	Woodroffe, Martyn (Wal)	Edinburgh	21 July 1970
400 m.	4:49·5	Woodroffe, Martyn (Wal)	Santa Clara	12 July 1969

WOMEN

Free-style

100 m.	1:00·5	Jackson, Alex (Eng)	Mexico	18 Oct. 1968
200 m.	2:13·5	Jackson, Alex (Eng)	Edinburgh	21 July 1970
400 m.	4:45·6y	Williams, Sue (Eng)	Coventry	22 July 1967
800 m.	9:58·4	Hogg (Davison), Sally (Sco)	Edinburgh	18 July 1970
1,500 m.	19:40·0	Standard time		

Back-stroke

100 m.	1:08·7y	Ludgrove, Linda (Eng)	Coventry	22 July 1967
200 m.	2:26·2	Burrell, Wendy (Eng)	Barcelona	9 Sept. 1970

Breast-stroke

100 m.	1:17·0	Harrison, Dorothy (Eng)	Barcelona	7 Sept. 1970
200 m.	2:45·6	Harrison, Dorothy (Eng)	Barcelona	11 Sept. 1970

Butterfly

100 m.	1:07·4y	Auton, Margaret (Eng)	Coventry	14 June 1968
200 m.	2:31·6y	Lansley, Diane (Eng)	Blackpool	13 June 1970

Medley

200 m.	2:29·5	Ratcliffe, Shelagh (Eng)	Kecskemet	4 Apr. 1970
400 m.	5:17·9	Ratcliffe, Shelagh (Eng)	Edinburgh	23 July 1970

BROCKWAY, W. John (Great Britain, 8 Oct. 1928–). Empire back-stroke champion in 1954 and a bronze medallist in the European championships the same year. Brockway from Wales, dominated British dorsal swimming for eight years. He held the A.S.A. title seven times— over 100 y. from 1948 to 1951 (second in 1952) and over 110 y. from 1953–55.

Brockway swam in three Olympics— in 1948 when he came seventh, in 1952 when he missed the final by four-tenths and in 1956 where he had his best 100 m. time of 67·7 but failed to get into even the semi-finals.

He also took part in three Empire Games and as well as his 66·5 for the 110 y. gold medal in 1954, he took the silver four years earlier. His last big Games appearance was at the European championships in 1958 when he finished sixth.

BURRELL, Wendy (Great Britain, 16 May 1952–). Quiet but amazingly determined, Wendy Burrell came out of nowhere to win a place in Britain's team for the 1968 Olympics and in Mexico she came fifth in the 200 m. back-stroke.

A.S.A. 110 and 220 y. champion in 1968' Wendy does much of her training in an 18-yard school bath near her Carlisle home under the supervision of her father-coach.

In 1970, Wendy broke the British 200 m. back-stroke record (2:28·4) at the Commonwealth Games, though she did not win a medal, and retained the A.S.A. 220 y. title two weeks later. She closed the year by setting a European 200 m. record (2:26·2) in a heat of the European championships but could not repeat this in the final and was fourth.

BURTON, Mike (United States, 3 June 1947–). "Mr. Machine" Burton made tremendous inroads into the world figures for the distance free-style events. In less than three years, from Sept. 1966 to Aug. 1969, he improved the 1,500 m. record four times, from 16:41·6 to 16:08·5 and twice, on the way, set world marks for 800 m.

Burton took his 1,500 m. time under 16 min. (15:57·3) in the U.S.A. championships in August, 1970, but was beaten into second place by John Kinsella, whose 15:57·1 was a world record. Severely injured in a cycling crash with a lorry at 13 which ended his athletics ambitions, Burton has never allowed anything to divert him in his swimming career, He was suffering badly from a stomach complaint in 1967 when he won the World Student 1,500 m. title in Tokyo in only a fraction outside his world record. "Montezuma's revenge" attacked him again during the 1968 Olympics, yet he survived this handicap and that of altitude to win without difficulty, the 400 m. (4:09·0) and 1,500 m. (16:38·9).

Burton, Pan American 1,500 champion and third in the 400 m. in 1967, is a powerful 5 ft. 9 in. and 153 lb. He was born in Des Moines, Iowa, but has done most of his swimming in California as a member of the Arden Hills club, coached by Sherman Chavoor. In training, he is a demon to his team-mates for he swims on and on and in competition he is perpetual motion.

BUTTERFLY. Butterfly was separated from breast-stroke and became the fourth swimming style in 1952. This was twenty years after enterprising swimmers in the United States had realized there was nothing in the rules to stop them recovering their arms over instead of under the water (see BREAST-STROKE).

At the beginning, butterflyers used the frog-leg kick of breast-stroke with the flying arms technique. It was a tiring style and few were able to do it throughout a 200 m. race. Experiments at the University of Iowa, with a dolphin fish-like kick in 1935, though illegal for competitions, threatened the total extinction of classic breast-stroke.

But when the strokes were divided, up and down leg movement in the vertical plane were permitted. The only breast-stroke similarities now are the simultaneous movements of arms and legs and the rule that the competitor may not swim under water, except for one stroke after the start and at turns.

F.I.N.A. (Rule 66) states:

(a) Both arms must be brought forward together over the water and brought backward simultaneously and symmetrically;

(b) The body must be kept perfectly on the breast and both shoulders in line with the surface of the water.

(c) All movements of the feet must be executed in a simultaneous and symmetirical manner. Simultaneous up and down movements of the legs and feet in the vertical plane are permitted.

C

CANADIAN AMATEUR SWIMMING ASSOCIATION.

The C.A.S.A. was founded in Montreal in 1909 and consists of ten provincial sections—Alberta, British Columbia, Manitoba, New Brunswick, Newfoundland, Nova Scotia, Ontario, Prince Edward Island (affiliated 1970), Quebec and Saskatchewan.

Montreal had many active swimming organizations at this time though none have survived. The oldest known club still in existence is the Vancouver Amateur Swimming Club (1903). In 1969 an overall umbrella organization, the Canadian Federation of Amateur Aquatics was formed. The work of the C.A.S.A., which previously had embraced all aspects of the sport, became confined specifically to swimming and seperate associations were set up for diving, synchronized swimming and water-polo.

The Canadian National Department of Health and Welfare, through its office for Fitness and Amateur Sport has assisted financially since 1963 with increasing annual grants. This money is used for travel for competitors' costs to the National championships, training camps and international travel.

It is intended in the near future to set up a National Aquatics Administration with a headquarters in Ottawa with a paid administrator whose salary will come from the office for Fitness and Amateur Sport.

CANADIAN SWIMMING CHAMPIONS.

There has been some difficulty in obtaining the full list of winners of Canadian swimming championships since World War II. The results as known are listed here in the hope that the spaces may be filled in due time.

The centralized venues and lengths of pools are:

Year	Venue	Course
1947	Victoria, B.C.	50 y.
1948	Verdun, Quebec	25 y.
1949	Vancouver, B.C.	25 y.
1950		
1951		
1952	Toronto, Ontario	25 y.
1953	Winnipeg, Manitoba	25 y.
1954	Vancouver, B.C.	55 y.
1955	Montreal, Quebec	25 y.
1956	Toronto, Ontario	50 y.
1957	Vancouver, B.C.	55 y.
1958	Vancouver, B.C.	55 y.
1959	Brantford, Ontario	55 y.
1960	Winnipeg, Manitoba	25 m.
1961	Dorval, Quebec	25 y.
1962	Vancouver, B.C.	55 y.
1963	Montreal, Quebec	50 m.
1964	Vancouver, B.C.	55 y.
1965	Red Deer, Alberta	50 m.
1966	Hamilton, Ontario	55 y.
1967	Winnipeg, Manitoba	50 m.
1968	Winnipeg, Manitoba	50 m.
1969	Pointe Claire, Quebec	50 m.
1970	Winnipeg, Manitoba	50 m.

The winners are:

MEN

100 m. Free-style

1947*	Rowlinson, P. (USA)	53·6
1948*	Salmon, Peter	54·8
1949*	Salmon, Peter	53·2
1950		
1951*	McNamee, Gerry	55·8
1952*	Salmon, Peter	52·6
1953*	McNamee, Gerry	54·1
1954†		
1955*	Park, George	52·0
1956*	Park, George	52·8
1957†		
1958†	Williams, Ken	59·5
1959†	Grout, Cameron	58·8
1960	Pound, Dick	56·9

1961*	Pound, Dick	50·3
1962†	Pound, Dick	57·0
1963	Sherry, Dan	55·6
1964†	Gilchrist, Sandy	56·5
1965	Sherry, Dan	55·9
1966†	Gilchrist, Sandy	56·0
1967	Kasting, Bob	55·4
1968	Finch, Glen	54·8
1969	Kasting, Bob	55·0
1970	Kasting, Bob	54·8

* = 100 y.   † = 110 y.

200 m. Free-style

1947–48	Event not held	
1949*	Gilchrist, Allen	2:01·8
1950		
1951*	McNamee, Gerry	2:02·1
1952*	McNamee, Gerry	2:00·4
1953	Event not held	
1954		
1955	Event not held	
1956†	McNamee, Gerry	2:14·7
1957		
1958†	Slater, Bill	2:14·6
1959†	Rounds, Fred (USA)	2:13·8
1960	Grout, Cameron	2:06·9
1961*	Pound, Dick	1:53·4
1962†	Verth, Tom	2:08·1
1963	Gilchrist, Sandy	2:03·2
1964†	Rose, Murray (Aus)	2:01·9
1965	Hutton, Ralph	2:03·2
1966†	Gilchrist, Sandy	2:02·0
1967	Jacks, Ron	2:03·3
1968	Hutton, Ralph	1:58·9
1969	Kasting, Bob	2:00·7
1970	Bello, Juan (Peru)	2:00·5

* = 200 y.   † = 220 y.

400 m. Free-style

1947*	Rowlinson, P. (USA)	4:32·8
1948*	Gilchrist, Allen	4:44·3
1949*	Gilchrist, Allen	4:42·7
1950		
1951*	McNamee, Gerry	4:26·4
1952*	McNamee, Gerry	4:18·9
1953*	McNamee, Gerry	4:24·8
1954†		
1955†	Stagman, Charles (USA)	4:48·8
1956†	Slater, Bill	4:49·8
1957		
1958†	Slater, Bill	4:46·4
1959†	Rounds, Fred (USA)	4:46·1
1960	Verth, Tom	4:31·5
1961*	Gilchrist, Sandy	4:35·5
1963	Gilchrist, Sandy	4:26·0

1964†	Rose, Murray (Aus)	4:16·6
1965	Gilchrist, Sandy	4:26·6
1966†	Hutton, Ralph	4:19·0
1967	Hutton, Ralph	4:19·6
1968	Hutton, Ralph	4:15·7
1969	Smith, George	4:17·5
1970	Kasting, Bob	4:19·7

* = 400 y.   † = 440 y.

1,500 m. Free-style

1947	Event not held	
1948*	Gibson, D.	18:52·8
1949*	Portelance, Jim	18:30·8
1950		
1951*	McNamee, Gerry	18:31·9
1952*	McNamee, Gerry	18:03·1
1953*	McNamee, Gerry	18:21·6
1954†		
1955†	Stagman, Charles (USA)	19:42·3
1956†	Slater, Bill	19:24·4
1957†		
1958†		
1959†	Brackett, Dick (USA)	19:24·9
1960	Slater, Bill	18:59·6
1961†	Gilchrist, Sandy	18:24·7
1962†	Webb, Ken (USA)	18:13·9
1963	Gilchrist, Sandy	18:00·6
1964†	Rose, Murray (Aus)	17:14·1
1965	Gilchrist, Sandy	17:48·1
1966†	Hutton, Ralph	17:25·5
1967	Hutton, Ralph	17:14·8
1968	Hutton, Ralph	16:51·5
1969	Jacks, Ron	17:34·8
1970	Roxborough, Steve	17:36·0

* = 1,500 y.   † = 1,650 y.

100 m. Backstroke

1947*	Buckboro, Kel	1:09·2
1948*	Mingie, Peter	1:05·0
1949†	Salmon, Peter	1:03·0
1950		
1951†	Mingie, Peter	1:03·6
1952*	Salmon, Peter	1:01·7
1953†	Mcnamee, Gerry	1:04·5
1954†		
1955*	Dolbey, Jerry (USA)	58·8
1956*	Miller, Don	1:05·0
1957†		
1958†	Wheaton, Bob	1:07·6
1959†	Verth, Tom	1:10·4
1960	Wheaton, Bob	1:04·3
1961†	Blanchette, Yvon	1:01·8
1962†	Richards, Charles (USA)	1:08·3
1963	Stratten, Gaye	1:06·9
1964†	Stratten, Gaye	1:04·6

1965	Shaw, Jim	1:04·2
1966†	Hutton, Ralph	1:03·5
1967	Shaw, Jim	1:02·0
1968	Shaw, Jim	1:01·6
1969	Shaw, Jim	1:03·5
1970	Kennedy, Bill	1:02·0
	† = 100 y. * = 110 y.	

200 m. Back-stroke

1947–56	Event not held	
1957		
1958†	Wheaton, Bob	2:30·7
1959†	Fisher, Robert	2:35·5
1960	Wheaton, Bob,	2:26·6
1961*	Blanchette, Yvon	2:17·4
1962†	Richards, Charles (USA)	2:29·5
1963	Hutton, Ralph	2:21·3
1964†	Jacks, Ron	2:20·4
1965	Stratten, Gaye	2:22·5
1966†	Hutton, Ralph	2:16·2
1967	Shaw, Jim	2:16·4
1968	Shaw, Jim	2:14·9
1969	Hawes, John	2:17·4
1970	Crichton, George	2:18·5
	* = 200 y. † = 220 y.	

100 m. Breast-stroke

1957*	Jubb, Eric	1:11·3
1948	Event not held	
1949*	Salmon, Peter	1:02·1
1950		
1951*	Ross, B. (USA)	1:08·2
1952*	Salmon, Peter	1:03·5
1953*	Crane, R.	1:07·0
1954		
1955–56	Event not held	
1957		
1958†	Rumpel, Norbert (WGer)	1:17·0
1959	Rabinovitch, Steve	1:15·8
1960	Rabinovitch, Steve	1:13·3
1961†	Nelson, Richard (USA)	1:03·4
1962†	Rabinovitch, Steve	1:14·0
1963	Rabinovitch, Steve	1:11·2
1964†	Kelso, Jack	1:12·8
1965	Chase, Marvin	1:13·5
1966†	Chase, Marvin	1:13·6
1967	Mahony, Bill	1:10·8
1968	Mahony, Bill	1:09·3
1969	Mahony, Bill	1:08·7
1970	Fiolo, Jose (Braz)	1:10·7
	* = 100 y. † = 110 y.	

200 m. Breast-stroke

1947*	Salmon, Peter	2:47·8
1948*	Salmon, Peter	2:35·0
1949*	Ross, Bill (USA)	Bu2:27·9

1950		
1951*	Ross, Bill (USA)	Bu2:34·6
1952*	Portelance, Leo	Bu2:23·4
1953	Gair, Bob	Bu2:36·7
1954		
1955*	Bell, Peter	2:35·8
1956	Bell, Peter	2:52·4
1957		
1958†	Rumpel, Norbert (WGer)	2:49·0
1959†	Rabinovitch, Steve	2:53·5
1960	Rabinovitch, Steve	2:42·3
1961*	Nelson, Richard (USA)	2:23·0
1962†	Rabinovitch, Steve	2:44·4
1963	Rabinovitch, Steve	2:43·3
1964†	Chase, Marvin	2:42·0
1965	Chase, Marvin	2:41·3
1966†	Mahony, Bill	2:38·8
1967	Mahony, Bill	2:33·9
1968	Mahony, Bill	2:31·0
1969	Mahony, Bill	2:30·3
1970	Fowler, K.	2:40·9
	* = 200 y. † = 220 y.	

100 m. Butterfly

1956 and before	Event not held	
1957		
1958†	Corrigan, M. (USA)	1:06·4
1959†	Grout, Cameron	1:06·6
1960	Grout, Cameron	2:01·5
1961*	Pound, Dick	56·9
1962†	Richards, Charles (USA)	1:03·3
1963	Sherry, Dan	59·3
1964†	Sherry, Dan	59·5
1965	Sherry, Dan	59·1
1966†	Jacks, Ron	1:00·1
1967	Arusoo, Tom	59·5
1968	Jacks, Ron	58·4
1969	Jacks, Ron	59·4
1970	MacDonald, Byron	57·4
	* = 100 y. † = 110 y.	

200 m. Butterfly

1954		
1955*	Stagman, Charles	2:21·7
1956†	Rutherford, Peter	2:51·3
1957		
1958†	Jacobs, Lorne	2:43·6
1959†	Kitchell, Dick (USA)	2:33·5
1960	Grout, Cameron	2:20·2
1961*	Gretzinger, Richard	
	(USA)	2:13·1
1962†	Richards, Charles (USA)	2:26·8
1963	Sherry, Dan	2:17·8
1964†	Sherry, Dan	2:16·4
1965	Sherry, Dan	2:14·9

1966†	Hutton, Ralph	2:15·3
1967	Arusoo, Tom	2:14·3
1968	Arusoo, Tom	2:11·3
1969	Jacks, Ron	2:12·2
1970	MacDonald, Byron	2:14·4
	* = 200 y. † = 220 y.	

200 m. Individual medley

1964–63	Event not held	
1964†	Leovich, Ted (USA)	2:24·7
1965	Gilchrist, Sandy	2:21·1
1966†	Gilchrist, Sandy	2:20·5
1967	Smith, George	2:20·8
1968	Smith, George	2:16·4
1969	Smith, George	2:13·4
1970	Bello, Juan (Peru)	2:16·7
	† = 220 y.	

400 m. Individual medley

1954		
1955*	Brunell, Frank (USA)	4:54·4
1956*	Slater, Bill	5:11·6
1957		
1958†	Slater, Bill	5:35·1
1959†	Grout, Cameron	5:43·5
1960	Grout, Cameron	5:25·6
1961*	Gretzinger, Richard	
	(USA)	4:49·9
1962†	Webb, Ken (USA)	5:08·3
1963	Gilchrist, Sandy	5:08·8
1964†	Gilchrist, Sandy	4:59·2
1965	Hutton, Ralph	5:00·4
1966†	Gilchrist, Sandy	4:58·1
1967	Gilchrist, Sandy	5:01·4
1968	Gilchrist, Sandy	4:51·8
1969	Smith, George	4:48·0
1970	Bello, Juan (Peru)	4:56·3
	* = 400 y. † = 440 y.	

WOMEN

100 m. Free-style

1947*	King, Vivian	1:06·3
1948*	Strong, Irene	1:03·0
1949*	Kerr, Catherine	1:04·1
1950		
1951*	McNamee, Kay	1:04·7
1952*	McNamee, Kay	1:03·6
1953*	Wittall, Beth	1:04·3
1954†		
1955*	Mann, Shelley (USA)	58·9
1956*	Grant, Virginia	58·6
1957†		
1958†	Ordogh, Susan (Hun)	1:07·5
1959†	Rhoads, Deirdre (USA)	1:07·6
1960	Stewart, Mary	1:05·5

1961*	Stewart, Mary	57·2
1962†	Wood, Carolyn (USA)	1:04·4
1963	Stewart, Mary	1:04·3
1964†	Lay, Marion	1:02·6
1965	Lay, Marion	1:02·2
1966†	Lay, Marion	1:02·5
1967	Lay, Marion	1:01·1
1968	Coughlan, Angela	1:01·8
1969	Coughlan, Angela	1:01·8
1970	Coughlan, Angela	1:01·4
	* = 100 y. † = 110 y.	

200 m. Free-style

1947–50	Event not held	
1951*	McNamee, Kay	2:32·2
1952*	McNamee, Kay	2:18·5
1953	Event not held	
1954		
1955	Event not held	
1956	Event not held	
1957		
1958†	Ramey, Nancy (USA)	2:31·6
1959†	Rhoads, Deidre (USA)	2:31·5
1960	Iwasaki, Margaret	2:27·6
1961*	Campbell, Katy	2:09·1
1962†	Wood, Carolyn (USA)	2:21·7
1963	Stewart, Mary	2:23·9
1964†	Lay, Marion	2:19·6
1965	Lay, Marion	2:18·5
1966†	Kennedy, Louise	2:17·9
1967	Coughlan, Angela	2:16·6
1968	Coughlan, Angela	2:13·2
1969	Coughlan, Angela	2:13·2
1970	Coughlan, Angela	2:13·4
	* = 200 y. † = 220 y.	

400 m. Free-style

1947*	King, Vivian	5:29·8
1948*	King, Vivian	5:19·4
1949*	McNamee, Kay	5:03·4
1950		
1951		
1952	McNamee, Kay	5:13·8
1953	Whittall, Beth	5:07·8
1954		
1955*	Gray, Dougie (USA)	5:09·5
1956†	Wittall, Beth	5:22·2
1957		
1958†	Ramey, Nancy (USA)	5:32·2
1959†	Rhoads, Deidre (USA)	5:21·4
1960	Campbell, Katy	5:13·4
1961*	Campbell, Katy	4:37·1
1962†	Thompson, Patty	5:09·7
1963	Pomfret, Lynne	5:03·5
1964†	Hounsell, Barbara	4:56·2

1965	Kennedy, Louise	4:52·5
1966†	Tanner, Elaine	4:46·4
1967†	Tanner, Elaine	4:45·6
1968	Coughlan, Angela	4:39·8
1969	Coughlan, Angela	4:37·3
1970	Coughlan, Angela	4:45·1

* = 400 y.   † = 440 y.

1,500 m. Free-style

| 1965 | Hughes, Jane | 19:35·8 |
| 1966† | Hughes, Jane | 19:28·8 |

† = 1,650 y.

800 m. Free-style

1967	Warren, Jeanne	10:01·9
1968	Coughlan, Angela	9:52·3
1969	Coughlan, Angela	9:30·8
1970	Coughlan, Angela	9:51·2

100 m. Back-stroke

1947*	Geldard, D.	1:17·6
1948*	Court, Joyce	1:15·3
1949*	Strong, Irene	1:13·3
1950		
1951*	Morgan, J.	1:15·1
1952*	Fisher, Lenore	1:12·0
1953*	Fisher, Lenore	1:09·8
1954		
1955*	Fisher, Lenore	1:07·2
1956*	Fisher, Lenore	1:10·8
1957		
1958†	Barber, Sara	1:15·3
1959†	Barber, Sara	1:15·3
1960	Barber, Sara	1:11·2
1961*	Stewart, Mary	1:05·6
1962†	Barber, Sara	1:13·4
1963	Weir, Eileen	1:13·1
1964†	Weir, Eileen	1:11·2
1965	Weir, Eileen	1:11·0
1966†	Tanner, Elaine	1:09·8
1967	Tanner, Elaine	1:08·6
1968	Tanner, Elaine	1:06·7
1969	Gurr, Donna-Marie	1:10·0
1970	Goshi, Yuikiko (Jap)	1:07·7

* = 100 y.   † = 110 y.

200 m. Back-stroke

1958†	Barber, Sara	2:49·5
1959†	Barber, Sara	2:46·2
1960	Barber, Sara	2:42·6
1961*	Conklin, Donna	2:31·7
1962†	Gabie, Noel (USA)	2:46·9
1963	Weir, Eileen	2:40·1
1964†	Weir, Eileen	2:37·7
1965	Tanner, Elaine	2:36·7
1966†	Tanner, Elaine	2:34·1

1967	Tanner, Elaine	2:33·3
1968	Tanner, Elaine	2:26·7
1969	Gurr, Donna-Marie	2:29·2
1970	Gurr, Donna-Marie	2:27·1

* = 200 y.   † = 220 y.

100 m. Breast-stroke

1949*	Strong, Irene	1:13·4
1949*	Strong, Irene	Bu1:13·4
1950		
1951*	Stewart, N.	Bu1:17·6
1952*	Strong, Irene	Bu1:14·0
1953*	Stewart, Helen	1:24·2
1954†		
1955	Event not held	
1956*	Stewart, Helen	1:21·9
1957		
1958†	Ordogh, Susan (Hun)	1:25·2
1959†	Benson, Bonnie	1:26·7
1960	McHale, Judy	1:24·0
1961*	Benson, Bonnie	1:15·0
1962†	Glendenning, Alison	1:22·3
1963	Glendenning, Alison	1:22·6
1964†	Colella, Lynn (USA)	1:23·7
1965	Wilmink, Marjon	1:23·6
1966†	Ross, Donna	1:23·1
1967	Lay, Marion	1:22·6
1968	Dockerill, Sylvia	1:20·5
1969	Wright, Jane	1:19·1
1970	Wright, Jane	1:20·0

* = 100 y.   † = 110 y.

200 m. Breast-stroke

1947*	Strong, Irene	2:55·7
1948*	Strong, Irene	2:51·0
1949*	Strong, Irene	2:48·1
1950		
1951*	Stewart, N.	2:58·4
1952*	Strong, Irene	2:44·3
1953*	Peebles, Margaret	3:09·8
1954		
1955*	Sears, Mary Jane (USA)	2:39·8
1956†	Peebles, Margaret	3:21·5
1957		
1958†	Ordogh, Susan (Hun)	3:01·6
1959†	Schmidlin, Suzette	3:06·0
1960	McHale, Judy	3:01·6
1961*	Wilson, Pam	2:43·7
1962†	Glendenning, Alison	2:57·2
1963	Wilmink, Marjon	2:56·6
1964†	Wilmink, Marjon	2:59·0
1963	Wilmink, Marjon	2:57·6
1966†	Ross, Donna	3:01·1
1967	Pumfrey, Mary Pat	2:59·4
1968	Smith, Susan	2:57·5

1969	Dockerill, Sylvia	2:54·4
1970	Nishigawa, Yoshima (Jap)	2:48·6

* = 200 y.   † = 220 y.

100 m. Butterfly

1954		
1955*	Sears, Mary Jane (USA)	1:05·6
1956*	Wittall, Beth	1:10·0
1957		
1958†	Ramey, Nancy (USA)	1:13·4
1959†	Doerr, Susan (USA)	1:17·8
1960	Stewart, Mary	1:13·0
1961*	Stewart, Mary	1:02·0
1962†	Wood, Carolyn (USA)	1:09·9
1963	Stewart, Mary	1:08·1
1964†	Stewart, Mary	1:08·8
1965	Tanner, Elaine	1:09·6
1966†	Tanner, Elaine	1:06·2
1967	Tanner, Elaine	1:05·9
1968	Tanner, Elaine	1:06·7
1969	Smith, Susan	1:07·5
1970	Aoki, Mayumi (Jap)	1:07·5

* = 100 y.   † = 110 y.

200 m. Butterfly

1965	Humeniuk, Marianne	2:40·2
1966†	Tanner, Elaine	2:33·1
1967	Corson, Marilyn	2:31·9
1968	Warren, Jeanne	2:31·6
1969	Warren, Jeanne	2:30·2
1970	Asano, Noriko (Jap)	2:28·4

† = 220 y.

200 m. Individual medley

1954		
1955*	Mann, Shelley (USA)	2:26·4
1956*	Stewart, Helen	2:41·2
1957		
1958–63	Event not held	
1964†	Hounsell, Barbara	2:40·9
1965	Hounsell, Barabara	2:38·5
1966†	Dowler, Sandra	2:41·1
1967	Dowler, Sandra	2:36·7
1968	Tanner, Elaine	2:31·8
1969	Smith, Susan	2:31·7
1970	Nishigawa, Yoshima (Jap)	2:25·8

* = 200 y.   † = 220 y.

400 m. Individual medley

1958†	Barber, Sara	6:14·1
1959†	Rhoads, Deidre (USA)	6:03·5
1960	Barber, Sara	5:53·7
1961*	Campbell, Katy	5:19·1
1962†	Stewart, Mary	5:59·9
1963	Pomfret, Lynne	5:46·9
1964†	Hounsell, Barbara	5:33·0
1965	Hounsell, Barbara	5:37·9

1966†	Tanner, Elaine	5:27·2
1967	Tanner, Elaine	5:29·2
1968	Corson, Marilyn	5:30·8
1969	Warren, Jeanne	5:24·9
1970	Nishigawa, Yoshima (Jap)	5:11·8

* = 400 y.   † = 440 y.

CAPILLA, Joaquin (Mexico). Mexico's only Olympic diving champion, Joaquin Capilla earned his gold the hard way by working up from the lesser honours. He was third in the highboard at the London Games of 1948. In Helsinki he was second. Finally, in Melbourne, Capilla achieved his golden ambition, by almost the narrowest possible margin, beating Gary Tobian (USA) by three-hundredths of a point. The American, incidentally, also lost the 1960 highboard title by a fraction—0·31 of a point to his team mate Robert Webster. Joaquin, largely trained in the United States, additionally took third place in the springboard in 1956 while his brother Alberto competed for Mexico in the 1952 and '56 Games but won no medals.

CARON, Christine (France, 10 July 1948–). Parisienne 'Kiki' Caron, the darling of French swimming, was one of a long line of world-class back-strokers from France. She broke the European 100 m. record six successive times between 1963–64, of which her 1:08·6 on 14 June 1964 also was a world mark. From 1963–66 she also set five European marks for 200 m. and it was not until April 1970 that her fastest time of 2:27·9 was beaten. At the 1964 Tokyo Olympics, Kiki won the silver medal for the 100 m. (67·9, her best). She swam too at the 1968 Games but failed to reach either back-stroke final. She was champion of European in 1966 (100 m. in 68·1).

CHANNEL SWIMMING. Since 25 August 1875, when Captain Matthew Webb made the historic first swimming crossing of the English Channel, from Dover to Calais, this battle of brawn and brain against tides and temperature, has remained the high point in the life of any long distance swimmer (see WEBB, MATTHEW).

It took forty-eight years, until 1923, for Webb's feat to be emulated, by Londoner Tom Burgess, who was successful at his thirteenth attempt. And the proportion of successes to failures is less than 7 per cent. More than 3,000 men and women from thirty-five countries have attempted the Channel marathon, either from France to England—the easier way—or England to France. Of these, only about 135 have shared around 200 successful attempts. These figures are not completely correct, despite the formation, in 1927, of the Channel Swimming Association to control and authenticate claims. Some crossings were not made under the supervision of official C.S.A. observers and certain records were lost during the London blitz of World War II, including details of some of the twenty-five successes up to that time.

The first woman to cross was America's Gertrude Ederle, an Olympic swimming medallist, who went from France to England in 14 hr. 34 min. in 1926. Then came the two-way swims. The first man was Britain's Olympic water-polo player Ted Temme who followed his France to England success in 1927 with an England to France safe landing in 1934. America's Florence Chadwick showed that a woman could do it too by crossing from France in 1950 and from England in 1951.

Not for thirty years was Temme's double achievement recognized by the C.S.A. who, in 1964, after irrefutable evidence, ratified his performance of 1934. In Miss Chadwick's case, her first swim was not officially observed and does not appear in the C.S.A. lists.

The next stage was the two-way crossing. Antonio Abertondo of Argentine, who once swam 262 miles down the Mississippi, achieved this in 1961—swimming from England to France in 18 hr. 50 min., taking a five-minute rest on French soil and then returning to England in 24 hr. 10 min. for an aggregate time of 43 hr. 5 min.

England to France		Hr., min.	Year
First man	Matthew Webb (GB)	21:45	1875
First woman	Florence Chadwick (USA)	16:19	1951
Fastest man	Nitindra Narayan Ray (Ind)	10:21	1967
Fastest woman	Greta Anderson (Den/USA)	13:40	1964
Slowest man	Henry Sullivan (USA)	26:50	1923
Slowest woman	Rosemary George (GB)	21:35	1961

France to England			
First man	Enrico Tiraboschi (Arg)	16:33	1923
First woman	Gertrude Ederle (USA)	14:34	1926
Fastest man	Barry Watson (GB)	9:35	1964
Fastest woman	Linda McGill (Aus)	9:59	1967
Slowest man	Philip Mickman (GB)	23:48	1949
Slowest woman	Dorothy Perkins (GB)	20:26	1961

Both ways				
First man	Ted Temme (GB)	Fr–Eng		1927
		Eng–Fr		1934
First woman	Florence Chadwick (USA)	Fr–Eng		1950
		Eng- Fr		1951

Two-way crossings			
First man	Antonio Abertondo (Arg)	43:05	1961
Fastest man	Ted Erickson (USA)	30:03	1965
First Briton	Kevin Murphy	35:10	1970

Youngest Conquerors				
Boy	Jon Erikson (USA)	14	Fr–Eng	11:23	1969
Girl	Leonore Modell (USA)	14	Fr–Eng	15:27	1964

AUSTRALIAN CHAMPIONS. Free-style world record breakers all. From left to right: Ilsa Konrads, Sandra Morgan, Lorraine Crapp and Dawn Fraser. Miss Konrads set twelve distance world records; Miss Morgan was a member of two Australian record-breaking relay teams; Miss Crapp was the first woman to break five minutes for 400m; and Miss Fraser won the 100m title at three successive Olympic Games

BREAST-STROKE. (*Above*) Galina Stepanova, formerly Miss Prosumen-schikova, of the Soviet Union, winner of the Olympic breast-stroke title in 1964 and European crowns in 1966 and 1970. (*Below*) World record breaker America's Catie Ball

The first Briton to make the two-way crossing was Kevin Murphy, a 21-year-old reporter on a Hemel Hempstead newspaper, who on 5/6 August 1970 made the double trip in 35 hr. 10 min. He left from Shakespeare Beach on the Kent coast and reached land west of Calais after 15 hr. 35 min. After a 10-min. rest and a cup of coffee, he swam back, to land near Folkestone after 19 hr. 25 min. His first thought after walking ashore was to telephone a story of his swim to his newspaper.

The distance as the crow flies is not what makes a crossing so difficult. The shortest distance—Dover to Cap Gris Nez—is only 20½ land (17¾ nautical) miles and racing swimmers will cover half of this, at speed, in training daily. It is the tides and currents that can double the distance actually swum, and bad weather, battering waves, stinging jelly fish, sea-sickness, wind, fog and the cold are additional hazards.

The crucial factor is timing. There are two complete tidal streams or four ebb and flow tides of six hours in a day. So the aim is to start on an out-going tide and land on the opposite shore on an in-going one. Swimming too slowly—or too fast—can catch a swimmer on the wrong tide and throw him miles off course and lose the right homeward tide.

The cost of an attempt can be high. There is up to £120 for the accompanying boat and pilot plus extras for food, lanolin—and swimmers must be well greased to keep out the cold—the C.S.A. official observer's fee etc. And as much again can be spent on living at the coast, maybe for weeks, waiting for favourable sea and weather conditions. These days many swims are sponsored and many aspirants professionals.

Great swimming prowess is not the main attribute for the Channel swimmer. Tenacity and grit are far more important. In 1964 American John Starrett, a spastic, and Canadian Robert Cossette, a polio victim, swam from France in 12 hr. 45 min. and 12 hr. 5 min. respectively.

There have been sponsored races—

by the *Daily Mail* and later by Butlin holiday camps. There are relay races with teams of six who must each stay at least one hour at a time in the water. And there is the continuing personal pride of anyone, fast or slow, who can simply say: 'I have swum the Channel.'

Among the successful crossings have been:

CHARLTON, 'Boy' (Australia, 1908–). The first great Australian swimmer of the 1920s, Andrew 'Boy' Charlton won five Olympic middle- and long-distance medals and set five world records between 1923 and 1928. He came from a poor part of Sydney and his talent was recognized by Tom Adrian, himself a noted swimmer, who adopted 'Boy', clothed and fed him and coached him to world fame.

A child prodigy, Charlton won his first race at five and broke his first world record, for 880 y. at 15. By the time of the Paris Olympics of 1924, he was a sturdy 12½ stone and totally dedicated to his sport. But there was near-disaster on the way by boat to Europe. His stepfather had a nervous breakdown and and threw himself from the liner into the sea. Fortunately Adrian was rescued though he was never a really fit man again.

Nevertheless, in Paris Charlton won the 1,500 m. (20:06·6), was in the Australian 4 × 200 m. silver medal team and took third place in the 400 m. (5:06·6), behind Johnny Weissmuller (USA) and Arne Borg (Swe). In Amsterdam, four years later he was second in the 400 and 1,500 m.

Charlton's three world 880 y. records included a 10:32·0 on 8 January 1927. He also set a mark for 1,000 m. in 13:19·6 on the way to a 20:06·6 world record in winning his 1924 Olympic gold—an improvement of 1:04·8 on the previous figures of Borg. Except when sprinting, Charlton's style had all the external appearance of a classic trudgeon of a decade earlier while incorporating the fundamentals of the crawl of the future.

CHILD, Edna (Great Britain, 10 Oct. 1922–). The diving career of Edna

D

Child, from Romford, Essex, spanned World War II. At 16 she was third in the European springboard championship in London. At 28, in 1950, she was the highboard and springboard gold medallist at the Commonwealth Games in Auckland, New Zealand. Edna was seven times A.S.A. champion, from the highboard (1946, '47, '49), springboard (1946, '49 and '49) and was the first winner of the 1 m. springboard title.

CLARK, Steve (United States, 17 June 1943–). One of the fastest movers in the water, Steve Clark's special talent was short course racing. He was the first man to swim 50 y. in 21·0, 100 y. in 46·0, 100 m. in 53·0, 200 y. in 1:50·0 and 200 m. in 2:00·0 in a 25 y. pool. Split-second turns—he was there and then he wasn't— were the recipe for Clark's success.

United States representative at the 1960 and 1964 Olympics, Clark from Oakland, California, who competed for Yale University and the Santa Clara club, never swam in an Olympic individual event though he won the Pan American 100 m. title in 1963.

But in the 1964 Tokyo Games he won three relay golds in world record-breaking American squads. On the first leg of the 4 × 100 m. free-style he clocked 52·9 to equal the world record. On the anchor leg of the medley relay—a berth he won from Don Schollander, later to become the 100 m. champion—he was given a split of 52·4. He was also lead-off swimmer in the 4 × 200 m. relay. Clark's only official world record was 54·4 for 100 m. in 1961.

COLEMAN, Georgia (United States, 12 Jan. 1912–41). The first woman to do a 2½ forward somersault in competition, Georgia Coleman, according to her coach Fred Cady, was: 'a girl who could dive like a man'. After only six months in competitive diving, she won the silver for highboard and the bronze for springboard at the 1928 Olympics. Four years later, at the Los Angeles Games, she won the springboard and was second again in the highboard. Between 1929–32 Georgia, from St. Maries, Idaho, was beaten only once—and that from the 1 m. board—in United States championships. Always smiling, she was only 29 when she died.

COMMONWEALTH GAMES. The idea of holding a four-yearly English Speaking Festival, including sport, was first mooted by the Rev. Ashley Cooper in *The Times* (London) in October 1891. But the concept did not come into being until 1911 when 'Inter-Empire championships', mainly at the Crystal Palace, London, were organized as part of the Festival of Empire to mark the Coronation of King George V. Teams from Australasia, Canada, South Africa and the United Kingdom took part.

The first practical steps to organize a British Empire Games were taken during the Olympics of 1928 when Mr. M. M. (Bobby) Robinson of Canada called a meeting of Empire representatives in Amsterdam. He was able, through the efforts of Mr. J. H. Crocker, to promise full support, financial and otherwise, from the Hamilton Civic Authorities to hold a Games in Canada in 1930.

The Hamilton Games—based on the ideal that 'they shall be merrier and less stern, and will substitute the stimulus of novel adventure for the pressure of international rivalry'—are regarded as the true starting points of the present series of Games of which those in Edinburgh in July 1970 were the ninth.

As a result of the changing nature of the British Empire and the development of the Commonwealth, the title of this multi-sports occasion has changed a number of times. But the ideals of the first Games in Hamilton remain.

COMMONWEALTH GAMES

No.	Title	Venue	Dates
I	British Empire Games	Hamilton, Canada	16–23 Aug., 1930
II	British Empire Games	London, England	4–11 Aug., 1934

No.	Title	Venue	Dates
III	British Empire Games	Sydney, Australia	5–12 Feb., 1938
IV	British Empire Games	Auckland, New Zealand	4–11 Feb., 1950
V	British Empire and Commonwealth Games	Vancouver, Canada	30 July–7 Aug., 1954
VI	British Empire and Commonwealth Games	Cardiff, Wales	18–26 July, 1958
VII	British Empire and Commonwealth Games	Perth, Australia	22 Nov.–1 Dec., 1962
VIII	British Empire and Commonwealth Games	Kingston, Jamaica	4–13 Aug., 1966
IX	British Commonwealth Games	Edinburgh, Scotland	16–25 July, 1970
X	British Commonwealth Games	Christchurch, New Zealand	February 1974

COMMONWEALTH GAMES CHAMPIONS. Because of the different titles under which the Games of the Empire and Commonwealth have been conducted (see COMMONWEALTH GAMES), throughout this book the words 'Commonwealth Games' or 'Commonwealth champion' etc., will refer to the British Empire Games, British Empire and Commonwealth Games and British Commonwealth Games and the champions and medal winners of these Games.

MEN

100 y. Free-style
1930   Bourne, Munro (Can)   56·0
1934   Burleigh, George (Can)   55·0

110 y. Free-style
1938   Pirie, Robert (Can)   59·6
1950   Salmon, Peter (Can)   1:00·4
1954   Henricks, Jon (Aus)   56·6
1958   Devitt, John (Aus)   56·6
1962   Pound, Dick (Can)   55·8
1966   Wenden, Mike (Aus)   54·0

100 m. Free-style
1970   Wenden, Mike (Aus)   53·1

200 m. Free-style
1970   Wenden, Mike (Aus)   1:56·7

400 y. Free-style
1930   Ryan, Noel (Aus)   4:39·8

440 y. Free-style
1934   Ryan, Noel (Aus)   5:03·0
1938   Pirie, Robert (Can)   4:54·6
1950   Agnew, David (Aus)   4:49·4
1954   Chapman, Gary (Aus)   4:39·8

1958   Konrads, John (Aus)   4:25·9
1962   Rose, Murray (Aus)   4:20·0
1966   Windle, Robert (Aus)   4:15·0

400 m. Free-style
1970   White, Graham (Aus)   4:08·5

1,500 y. Free-style
1930   Ryan, Noel (Aus)   18:55·0
1934   Ryan, Noel (Aus)   18:25·4

1,650 y. Free-style
1938   Leivers, Bobby (Eng)   19:46·4
1950   Johnston, Graham (SAf)   19:55·7
1954   Johnston, Graham (SAf)   19:01·4
1958   Konrads, John (Aus)   17:45·4
1962   Rose, Murray (Aus)   17:18·1
1966   Jackson, Ron (Aus)   17:25·1

1,500 m. Free-style
1970   Windeatt, Graham (Aus)   16:23·8

100 y. Back-stroke
1930   Trippett, John (Eng)   1:05·4
1934   Francis, Willy (Scot)   1:05·2

110 y. Back-stroke
1938   Oliver, Percy (Aus)   1:07·9
1950   Wiid, Jackie (SAf)   1:07·7
1954   Brockway, John (Wales)   1:06·5
1958   Monckton, John (Aus)   1:01·7
1962   Sykes, Graham (Eng)   1:04·5
1966   Reynolds, Peter (Aus)   1:02·4

100 m. Back-stroke
1970   Kennedy, Bill (Can)   1:01·6

220 y. Back-stroke
1962   Carroll, John (Aus)   2:20·9
1966   Reynolds, Peter (Aus)   2:12·0

200 m. Back-stroke
1970 Richards, Mike (Wal)   2:14·5

110 y. Breast-stroke
1962 O'Brien, Ian (Aus)   1:11·4
1966 O'Brien, Ian (Aus)   1:08·2

100 m. Breast-stroke
1970 Mahoney, Bill (Can)   1:09·0

200 y. Breast-stroke
1930 Aubin, Jack (Can)   2:35·4
1934 Hamilton, Norman (Scot) 2:41·6

220 y. Breast-stroke
1938 Davies, John (Eng) Bu2:51·9
1950 Hawkins, David (Aus) Bu2:54·1
1954 Doms, John (NZ)   2:52·6
1958 Gathercole, Terry (Aus) 2:41·6
1962 O'Brien, Ian (Aus)   2:38·2
1966 O'Brien, Ian (Aus)   2:29·3

200 m. Breast-stroke
1970 Mahony, Bill (Can)   2:30·3

110 y. Butterfly
1962 Berry, Kevin (Aus)   59·5
1966 Jacks, Ron (Can)   1:00·3

100 m. Butterfly
1970 MacDonald, Byron (Can) 58·4

220 y. Butterfly
1958 Black, Ian (Scot)   2:22·6
1962 Berry, Kevin (Aus)   2:10·8
1966 Gerrard, David (NZ)   2:12·7

200 m. Butterfly
1970 Arusoo, Tom (Can)   2:09·0

200 m. Individual medley
1970 Smith, George (Can)   2:13·7

440 y. Individual medley
1962 Alexander, Alex (Aus)   5:15·3
1966 Reynolds, Peter (Aus)   4:50·8

400 m. Individual medley
1970 Smith, George (Can)   4:48·9

4 × 110 y. Free-style relay
1962 Australia   3:43·9
(Phelps, Peter; Rose, Murray; Doak, Peter; Dickson, David)
1966 Australia   3:35·6
(Wenden, Mike; Ryan, John; Dickson, David; Windle, Robert)

4 × 100 m. Free-style relay
1970 Australia   3:36·0

(Rogers, Greg; Devenish, Bill; White, Graham; Wenden, Mike)

4 × 200 y. Free-style relay
1930 Canada   8:42·4
1934 Canada   8:40·6
(Larsen, George; Hooper, Robert; Pirie, Bob; Burleigh, George)

4 × 220 y. Free-style relay
1938 England   9:19·0
(Dove, Freddie; Ffrench-Williams, Micky; Leivers, Bobby; Wainwright, Norman)
1950 New Zealand   9:27·7
(Amos, Michael; Barry, Lyall; Chambers, Noel; Lucas, Frederick)
1954 Australia   8:47·6
(Chapman, Gary; Aubrey, Rex; Hawkins, David; Henricks, Jon)
1958 Australia   8:33·4
(Konrads, John; Wilkinson, Brian; Devitt, John; Chapman, Gary)
1962 Australia   8:13·5
(Rose, Murray; Wood, Alan; Strahan, Anthony; Windle, Robert)
1966 Australia   7:59·5
(Wenden, Mike; Reynolds, Peter; Dickson, David; Windle, Robert)

4 × 200 m. Free-style relay
1970 Australia   7:50·8
(Rogers, Greg; Devenish, Bill; White, Graham; Wenden, Mike)

3 × 100 y. Medley relay
1934 Canada   3:11·4
(Gazell, Ben; Puddy, William; Burleigh, George)

3 × 110 y. Medley relay
1938 England   3:28·2
(Taylor, Micky; Davies, John; Dove, Freddie)
1950 England   3:26·6
(Hale, Jack; Romain, Roy; Kendall, Pat)
1954 Australia   3:22·0
(Weld, Cyrus; Hawkins, David; Hendicks, Jon)

4 × 110 y. Medley relay
1958 Australia   4:14·2
(Monckton, John; Gathercole, Terry; Wilkinson, Brian; Devitt, John)
1962 Australia   4:12·4

(Carroll, Julian; O'Brien, Ian; Berry, Kevin; Dickson, David)

1966 Canada   4:10·5
(Hutton, Ralph; Chase, Marvin; Jacks, Ron; Gilchrist, Sandy)

4 × 100 m. Medley relay
1970 Canada   4:01·1
(Kennedy, Bill; Mahony, Bill; Macdonald, Byron; Kasting, Bob)

Springboard diving

1930	Phillips, Al (Can)	—
1934	Ray, J. Briscoe (Eng)	117·12
1938	Masters, Ray (Aus)	126·36
1950	Athans, George (Can)	169·21
1954	Heatly, Peter (Scot)	146·76
1958	Collin, Keith (Eng)	126·78
1962	Phelps, Brian (Eng)	154·14
1966	Phelps, Brian (Eng)	154·55
1970	Wagstaff, Don (Aus)	557·73

Highboard diving

1930	Phillips, Al (Can)	—
1934	Mather, Tommy (Eng)	83·83
1938	Tomalin, Doug (Eng)	108·74
1950	Heatly, Peter (Scot)	156·07
1954	Patrick, William (Can)	142·70
1958	Heatly, Peter (Scot)	147·79
1962	Phelps, Brian (Eng)	168·35
1966	Phelps, Brian (Eng)	164·57
1970	Wagstaff, Don (Aus)	485·73

WOMEN

100 y. Free-style

1930	Cooper, Joyce (Eng)	1:07·0
1934	Dewar, Phyl (Can)	1:03·0

110 y. Free-style

1938	De Lacey, Evelyn (Aus)	1:10·1
1950	McQuade, Marjory (Aus)	1:09·1
1954	Crapp, Lorraine (Aus)	1:05·8
1958	Fraser, Dawn (Aus)	1:01·4
1962	Fraser, Dawn (Aus)	59·5
1966	Lay, Marion (Can)	1:02·3

100 m. Free-style
1970 Coughlan, Angela (Can)   1:01·2

200 m. Free-style
1970 Moras, Karen (Aus)   2:09·8

400 y. Free-style
1930 Cooper, Joyce (Eng)   5:25·4

440 y. Free-style

1934	Dewar, Phyl (Can)	5:45·6
1938	Green, Dorothy (Aus)	5:39·9

1950	Harrison, Joan (SAf)	5:26·4
1954	Crapp, Lorraine (Aus)	5:11·4
1958	Konrads, Ilsa (Aus)	4:49·4
1962	Fraser, Dawn (Aus)	4:51·4
1966	Wainwright, Kathy (Aus)	4:38·8

400 m. Free-style
1970 Moras, Karen (Aus)   4:27·4

800 m. Free-style
1970 Moras, Karen (Aus)   9:02·4

100 y. Back-stroke

1930	Cooper, Joyce (Eng)	1:15·0
1934	Harding Phyl (Eng)	1:13·8

110 y. Back-stroke

1938	Norton, Patricia (Aus)	1:19·5
1950	Davies, Judy-Joy (Aus)	1:18·6
1954	Harrison, Joan (SAf)	1:15·2
1958	Grinham, Judy (Eng)	1:11·9
1962	Ludgrove, Linda (Eng)	1:11·1
1966	Ludgrove, Linda (Eng)	1:09·2

100 m. Back-stroke
1970 Watson, Lynn (Aus)   1:07·1

220 y. Back-stroke

1962	Ludgrove, Linda (Eng)	2:35·2
1966	Ludgrove, Linda (Eng)	2:28·5

200 m. Back-stroke
1970 Watson, Lynn (Aus)   2:22·9

110 y. Breast-stroke

1962	Lonsbrough, Anita (Eng)	1:21·3
1966	Harris, Diana (Eng)	1:19·7

100 m. Breast-stroke
1970 Whitfield, Beverley (Aus)   1:17·4

200 y. Breast-stroke
1930 Wolstenholme, Celia (Eng)   2:54·6
1934 Dennis, Clare (Aus)   2:50·2

220 y. Breast-stroke

1938	Storey, Doris (Eng)	3:06·3
1950	Gordon, Elenor (Scot)	3:01·7
1954	Gordon, Elenor (Scot)	2:59·2
1958	Lonsbrough, Anita (Eng)	2:53·5
1962	Lonsbrough, Anita (Eng)	2:51·7
1966	Slattery, Jill (Eng)	2:50·3

200 m. Breast-stroke
1970 Whitfield, Beverley (Aus)   2:44·1

110 y. Butterfly
1958 Bainbridge, Beverley (Aus) 1:13·5

| 1962 | Stewart, Mary (Can) | 1:10·1 |
| 1966 | Tanner, Elaine (Can) | 1:06·8 |

100 m. Butterfly

| 1970 | Lansley, Diane (Eng) | 1:07·9 |

220 y. Butterfly

| 1966 | Tanner, Elaine (Can) | 2:29·9 |

200 m. Butterfly

| 1970 | Robinson, Maree (Aus) | 2:24·7 |

200 m. Individual medley

| 1970 | Langford, Denise (Aus) | 2:28·9 |

440 y. Individual medley

| 1962 | Lonsbrough, Anita (Eng) | 5:38·6 |
| 1966 | Tanner, Elaine (Can) | 5:26·3 |

400 m. Individual medley

| 1970 | Langford, Denise (Aus) | 5:10·7 |

4 × 100 y. Free-style relay

1930 England   4:32·8
(Joynes (Wadham), Olive; Harding,
Phyl; Cooper, Doreen; Cooper, Joyce)
1934 Canada   4:21·8
(Dewar, Phyl; Humble, F.; Hutton,
Margaret; Pirie, Irene)

4 × 110 y. Free-style relay

1938 Canada   4:48·3
(Dewar, Phyl; Lyon, Dorothy; Bagga-
ley, M.; Dobson, D.)
1950 Australia   4:44·9
(Spencer, Denise, Norton, Denise;
Davies, Judy-Joy; McQuade, Marjory)
1954 South Africa   4:33·9
(Loveday, Felicity; Petzer, Machduldt;
Myburgh, Natalie; Harrison, Joan)
1958 Australia   4:17·4
(Colquhoun, Alva; Morgan, Sandra;
Crapp, Lorraine; Fraser, Dawn)
1962 Australia   4:11·1
(Bell, Lyn; Thorn, Robyn; Everuss,
Ruth; Fraser, Dawn)
1966 Canada   4:10·8
(Tanner, Elaine; Hughes, Jane; Ken-
nedy, Louise; Lay, Marion)

4 × 100 m. Free-style relay

1970 Australia   4:06·4
(Cain, Debbie; Watson, Lynn; Watts,
Jenny; Langford, Denise)

3 × 100 y. Medley relay

1934 Canada   3:42·0
(Hutton, Margaret; Haslam, Phyllis;
Dewar, Phyl)

3 × 110 y. Medley relay

1938 England   3:57·7
(Frampton, Lorna; Storey, Doris;
Hinton, Margery)
1950 Australia   3:53·8
(Davies, Judy-Joy; Lyons, Nancy;
McQuade, Marjory)
1954 Scotland   3:51·0
(McDowall, Margaret; Gordon,
Elenor; Girvan, Margaret)

4 × 110 y. Medley relay

1958 England   4:54·0
(Grinham, Judy; Lonsbrough, Anita;
Gosden, Chris; Wilkinson, Diana)
1962 Australia   4:45·9
(Sargeant, Pam; Ruygrok, Marguerite;
McGill, Linda; Fraser, Dawn)
1966 England   4:40·6
(Ludgrove, Linda; Harris, Diana;
Gegan, Judy; Sillett, Pauline)

4 × 100 m. Medley relay

1970 Australia   4:30·7
(Watson, Lynn; Whitfield, Beverley;
Mabb, Allyson; Langford, Denise)

Springboard diving

1930	Whitsett, Oonagh (SAf)	—
1934	Moss, Judith (Can)	62·27
1938	Donnett, Irene (Aus)	91·18
1950	Child, Edna (Eng)	126·58
1954	Long, Ann (Eng)	128·27
1958	Welsh, Charmian (Eng)	118·81
1962	Knight, Susan (Aus)	134·72
1966	Rowlatt, Kathy (Eng)	147·10
1970	Boys, Beverley (Can)	432·87

Highboard diving

1930	Stonebrugh, Marjorie (Can)	—
1934	Macready, E. 'Dot' (Eng)	30·74
1938	Hook, Lurline (Aus)	36·47
1950	Child, Edna (Eng)	70·89
1954	McAulay, Barbara (Aus)	86·55
1958	Welsh, Charmian (Eng)	77·23
1962	Knight, Susan (Aus)	101·35
1966	Newman, Joy (Eng)	98·87
1970	Boys, Beverley (Can)	361·95

**COMMONWEALTH GAMES FED-
ERATION.** A meeting of Empire repre-
sentatives in Los Angeles on Sunday, 7
Aug. 1932, during the Olympic Games
of that year, decided to form a British
Empire Games Federation. This was two
years after the first British Empire
Games had been held in Hamilton,

Canada, and the decision was confirmed later in London after British Empire Games Associations had been set up in Australia, Bermuda, Canada, England, India, Newfoundland, New Zealand, Rhodesia, Scotland, South Africa and Wales.

As the character of the Empire changed so did the name of the Federation—to 'The British Empire and Commonwealth Games Federation' on 20 July 1952 and to 'The British Commonwealth Games Federation on 7 Aug. 1966. By the time of the Edinburgh Games in July 1970, there was a membership of forty-seven national associations.

COMMONWEALTH RECORDS

MEN

Free-style

100 m.	52·2	Wenden, Mike (Aus)	Mexico	10 Oct. 1968
200 m.	1:55·2	Wenden, Mike (Aus)	Mexico	24 Oct. 1968
400 m.	4:06·5	Hutton, Ralph (Can)	Lincoln, USA	2 Aug. 1970
800 m.	8:36·2	Windeatt, Graham (Aus)	Edinburgh	23 July 1970
1,500 m.	16:23·1	Windeatt, Graham (Aus)	Sydney	1 Mar. 1970
4 × 100 m.	3:34·7	National team (Aus)	Mexico	17 Oct. 1968
		(Rogers, Greg; Cusack, Bob; Windle, Bob; Wenden, Mike)		
4 × 200 m.	7:50·8	National team (Aus)	Edinburgh	24 July 1970
		(Rogers, Greg; Devenish, Bill; White, Graham; Wenden, Mike)		

Back-stroke

100 m.	1:00·9	Richards, Mike (Wal)	Barcelona	9 Sept. 1970
200 m.	2:12·0y	Reynolds, Peter (Aus)	Kingston, Jam.	9 Aug. 1970

Breast-stroke

100 m.	1:07·6	O'Brien, Ian (Aus)	Sydney	13 Jan. 1964
200 m.	2:27·8	O'Brien, Ian (Aus)	Tokyo	15 Oct. 1964

Butterfly

100 m.	57·4	MacDonald, Byron (Can)	Winnipeg	Aug 1970
200 m.	2:06·6	Berry, Kevin (Aus)	Tokyo	18 Oct. 1964

Medley

200 m.	2:13·4	Smith, George (Can)	Pointe Claire	14 Aug. 1969
400 m.	4:48·0	Smith, George (Can)	Pointe Claire	12 Aug. 1969
4 × 100 m.	4:00·8	National team (Aus)	Mexico	17 Oct. 1968
		(Byrom, Karl; O'Brien, Ian; Cusack, Bob; Wenden, Mike)		

WOMEN

Free-style

100 m.	58·9	Fraser, Dawn (Aus)	Sydney	26 Aug. 1964
200 m.	2:09·8	Moras, Karen (Aus)	Sydney	1 Mar. 1970
			Edinburgh	21 July 1970
400 m.	4:24·8	Moras, Karen (Aus)	Edinburgh	23 July 1970
800 m.	9:02·4	Moras, Karen (Aus)	Edinburgh	18 July 1970
1,500 m.	17:58·5	Risson, Robyn (Aus)	Sydney	28 Feb. 1970
4 × 100 m.	4:06·4	National team (Aus)	Edinburgh	23 July 1970
		(Cain, Debbie; Watson, Lynn; Langford, Denise; Watts, Jenny)		

Back-stroke

100 m.	1:06·7	Tanner, Elaine (Can)	Winnipeg	29 July 1967
200 m.	2:22·9	Watson, Lynn (Aus)	Edinburgh	21 July 1970

Breast-stroke

| 100 m. | 1:16·8 | Playfair, Judy (Aus) | Brisbane | 18 Aug. 1968 |
| 200 m. | 2:44·1 | Whitfield, Beverley (Aus) | Edinburgh | 21 July 1970 |

Butterfly

| 100 m. | 1:05·4 | Tanner, Elaine (Can) | Winnipeg | 29 July 1967 |
| 200 m. | 2:24·7 | Robinson, Maree (Aus) | Edinburgh | 24 July 1970 |

Medley

200 m.	2:28·9	Langford, Denise (Aus)	Edinburgh	18 July 1970
400 m.	5:10·7	Langford, Denise (Aus)	Edinburgh	23 July 1970
4 × 100 m.	4:30·0	National team (Aus)	Mexico	17 Oct. 1968

(Watson, Lynn; Playfair, Judy; McClements, Lyn; Steinbeck, Jenny)

COOPER, Joyce (Great Britain, 18 Apr. 1909–). A member of the Mermaid club of London, Joyce Cooper's swimming talent embraced almost the whole range of women's events from 1927 to 1933. In fact, the only style at which she did not excel was breast-stroke on which she said: 'I go backwards.'

She was third in the Olympic 100 m. free-style and back-stroke in 1928 and won a silver in the 4 × 100 m. relay. Four years later, in Los Angeles, she was a member of the British relay squad who came third and she also reached the finals of the 400 m. free-style and 100 m. back-stroke.

In European events Joyce won a silver for 100 m. free-style in 1927 and shared the Bologna Trophy (see BOLOGNA TROPHY) with her team-mates who took the relay gold that year. In the 1931 Europeans she was second in the 400 m. free-style, 100 m. back-stroke and the relay and was third in the 100 m. free-style.

Miss Cooper, who was born in Ceylon, represented England at the first Empire Games in 1930 when she took three of the four individual titles—100 and 400 y. free-style and 100 y. back-stroke—and a fourth gold in the relay with her sister Doreen also a member of this squad.

She won nineteen A.S.A. titles—100 y. (1929, '31, '32), 220 y. (1927–29 and 1931–32), 440 y. (1928–32), long distance (1930–33) and the 150y. back-stroke (1929 and '31). Miss Cooper married Olympic rowing gold medallist John Badcock and has two sons, the elder of whom rowed in the English eight at the 1958 Empire Games.

COUGHLAN, Angela (Canada, 4 Oct. 1952–). Olympic free-style relay bronze medallist in Mexico, Angela Coughlan from Toronto was also a 400 and 800 m. finalist at 15. Her rise from obscurity was meteoric since she joined the University Settlement Aquatic Club, coached by Nick Thierry, only in 1966.

Her first international appearance was at the 1967 Pan-American Games in Winnipeg where she won free-style bronze medals for 200 (2:15·7), 400 (4:48·9) and 800 (9:48·6) metres and a silver in the 4 × 100 m. relay. The next year she broke the world 1,650 y. record with 18:47·8—the last holder for the distance which was discontinued at the end of 1968.

Angela's first Canadian title came in 1967 when she took the 200 m. free-style. The next year she won all four free-style crowns (100, 200, 400 and 800 m.) and repeated this performance in 1969 and again in the winter championships of 1970.

In the 1970 Commonwealth Games, despite the powerful challenge from Australia, the Toronto student won the 100 m. and took the silver, 1·0 sec. behind Karen Moras (Aus), in the 200 m. in a National record of 2:10·8. And in the Canadian championships immediately following, she won all four free-style titles for the third successive year.

CRABBE, Buster (United States, 2 Feb. 1908–). Successor to Johnny Weissmuller as the screen Tarzan, Clarence 'Buster' Crabbe was Olympic 400 m. champion in 1932 (4:48·4) having taken third place in the 1,500 m. four years earlier in Amsterdam in 20:28·8, a time he improved to 20:02·7 in placing fifth in 1932. Crabbe's only world record was 10:20·4 for 880 y. (1930) but he won eleven American outdoor titles including the one mile five years in succession (1927–31).

Crabbe's film and television roles—and he appeared in nearly 170 pictures—were all in heroic mould. He was space idol Buck Rogers, legionnaire Captain Gallant, conquering the Sahara Desert, Flash Gordon and he was seventh in a long line of Tarzans.

Born in Oakland, California, his family moved when he was eighteen months to the Hawaiian Islands, where his father became overseer of a pineapple plantation. Crabbe learned to swim at five and later, at Puna Hou High School in Honolulu, he was also an outstanding footballer, basketball player and track athlete.

He returned to the mainland to the University of Southern California and as a first-year law student there won a place in the 1928 Olympic team. He starred in the World's Fair Aquacade in New York before World War II. His present interests include the Buster Crabbe Swim Pools and a summer camp for boys.

CRAPP, Lorraine (Australia, 1938–). The first girl to break five minutes for 400 m. free-style is Lorraine Crapp's special claim to fame. Sixteen years after Ragnhild Hveger had set the world mark of 5:00·1, the blonde Miss Crapp from Sydney in one swim on 15 Aug. 1956, set four world marks for 200 m., 220 y., 400 m., and 440 y. with times of 2:19·3, 2:20·5, 4:50·8 and 4:52·4. She repeated this four-records-in-one-swim effort two months later with 2:18·5, 2:19·1, 4:47·2 and 4:48·6 which are her best times. And as a side-line to her achievements, Miss Hveger's 1940 record was in a 25 m. pool, with a time advantage through the extra turns of about 5·6 sec. compared with Miss Crapp's 55 y. bath achievement.

Miss Crapp won the 1956 Olympic 400 m. title, beating her team-mate Dawn Fraser by more than 10 y., took the silver, behind Miss Fraser, in the 100 m. and a second gold in the 4 × 100 m. relay.

A style perfectionist and coached by Frank Gutherie, Miss Crapp had to train with men because she was too speedy for the girls, yet she had been written off as a swimmer in 1955, within a few months of winning the 110 and 440 y. titles at the 1954 Commonwealth Games. A severe ear infection brought fears she would never recover her medal-winning form. But recover she did to set 16 individual world records (including 10:30·9 for 800 m. and 10:34·6 for 880 y.) and help the Australian national team to seven more. Her career ended at the 1960 Olympics with a silver in the free-style relay.

CSIK, Ferenc (Hungary, 12 Dec. 1913–29 Mar. 1945). A doctor of medicine, Csik, was the shock winner of the Olympic 100 m. free-style in Berlin in 1936 when he succeeded despite the handicap of an outside lane. European and champion and record holder for 100 m. in 1934 and winner of thirteen Hungarian individual titles, Csik was killed during an air raid in 1945 while working as a Hungarian army surgeon.

CURTIS, Ann (United States, 6 Mar. 1926–). The graceful lady of American swimming after World War II, Ann Curtis—now Mrs. Cuneo—crowned her career by winning the Olympic 400 m. title in London in 5:17·8 and placing second in the 100 m. (66·5) behind Denmark's Greta Andersen. Despite these competitive successes and winning eighteen United States outdoor titles between 1943–48, the only world marks by this tall girl from the San Francisco, Crystal Plunge Club were for yards distances—440 y. in 5:07·9 (25 y. bath) in 1947 and 880 y. in 11:08·6 in 1944.

D

DANIELS, Charles (United States, b. 24 March, 1885). America's first great swimmer, Daniels, who won five medals at the 1904 Olympics in St. Louis and two more at the London Games of 1908, was considered to be a wonder of his age.

The swimming arrangements in St. Louis, where the competitions took place in a lake in the grounds of the World Fair, were somewhat chaotic. Starts were from a raft which often submerged under the weight of the competitors, the turn markers tended to drift and the swimmers found it difficult to keep straight because the lake had no parallel banks for them to follow.

Yet Daniels, then 19, managed to win the 220 and 440 y. and a third gold in the relay, and placed second in the 100 y. and third in the 50 y. dash—the only time this last event was in the Olympic programme. Four years later, he took the 100 m., a race which he had also won at the 1906 Interim Games, and a relay bronze.

He set seven world records between 1907–11 and his best times were 55·8 (100 y.), 62·8 (100 m.), 2:25·4 (200 m.), 2:25·4 (220 y.), 3:57·6 (300 m.) and 7:03·4 (500 m.).

Daniels, an early exponent of the American crawl, had a great influence on the development of the stroke in Britain. He twice won the A.S.A. 100 y. title (1906, '07) and his first world record for this distance (55·4) was set during the 1907 championship race in Manchester.

DAVENPORT, Horace (Great Britain). This great gentleman of early English swimming was not only a champion in the pool but also out of it. He won the A.S.A. mile championship six times from 1874–79 and the Long Distance, or as it was known then 'The Lords and Commons Race' (see AMATEUR SWIMMING ASSOCIATION MILE and LONG DISTANCE CHAMPIONSHIPS), three times (1877–79). The record he set in winning the mile title in still water in the Welsh Harp in 1977 (29:25½) stood until 1892.

Davenport, a member of the now defunct Ilex and Surbiton Club, also played a vital part in smoothing the troubled waters of the early days of formal swimming administration in England. He was president of the Swimming Association of Great Britain from 1880–83 and of the re-named Amateur Swimming Association from 1890 to 1894.

DAVIES, Judy-Joy (Australia, 21 Feb. 1926–). Judith Davies, generally known as Judy-Joy, was an Olympic medallist in the days before Australia made a habit of winning Games medals. She took the bronze for 100 m. back-stroke in London in 1948 and followed this with a Commonwealth gold for 100 y. back-stroke in 1950 and relay golds in the free-style and medley events. By the time of the 1952 Olympics, Judy-Joy from Victoria, had turned again to free-style, and she reached the semi-finals of the 400 m., missing the final by 4½ seconds.

Her first competitive success was at 13, in 1940 when she took the Australian junior 110 y. free-style title which she retained in 1941–42, before World War II halted competitive swimming. Judy-Joy won seventeen national championships between 1946 and 1954. Nine were for free-style—110 y. (1947), 220 y. (1950–51), 440 y. (1950, '51, '53), 880 y. (1948, '53, '54). She was seven successive times 110 y. back-stroke champion (1946–52) and won the first 220 y. medley event in 1953.

Judy-Joy later became a sports journalist and has covered all the Olympic and Commonwealth Games since her retirement from swimming.

DENNIS, Clare (Australia). Olympic 200 m. breast-stroke champion in 1932 in a Games record of 3:06·3, Clare Dennis, from New South Wales, also won the Commonwealth 200 y. title in 1934. She set two world marks, both short course—100 m. in 1:24·6 in 1933 and 200 m. in 3:08·4 in 1932. This latter mark was broken twice, by Miss Rocke (Germany) and Else Jacobsen (Denmark), before the Berlin Olympics but in the Games, the Dane was only third and the German did not reach the final. Miss Dennis was Australian 200 y. breast-stroke champion in 1931 and from 1933–35, the 1932 event having been cancelled.

DEN OUDEN, Willy (Netherlands, 1918–   ). The darling of Dutch swimming before World War II, Willy den Ouden was femininity personified out of the water, and a flashing mermaid in it. At 13, at the 1931 European championships, she was second in the 100 m. and won a gold in the 4 × 100 m. relay. At the Olympic Games the following year she was again second in the 100 m. and a member of Holland's silver medal relay squad. Her great year was 1934 when she became champion of Europe for her favourite 100 m. distance, was second in the 400 m. (though her 5:27·4 was the same as for her team-mate winner Rie Mastenbroek) and helped Holland retain the relay title.

Willy's only disappointing big occasion was the 1936 Olympics. In February of that year she had set a world 100 m. record of 64·6 (which stood for twenty years). But she was three seconds slower in the Berlin Games and placed fourth. There was consolation with a relay gold. And she won a third European relay medal, a silver, in the 1938 championships.

Her thirteen individual world records included these best times—59·8 (100 y.— the first girl under the minute), 64·6 (100 m.), 2:25·3 (200 m.), 2:27·6 (220 y.),

3:27·0 (300 y.), 3:50·4 (300 m.), 5:16·0 (400 m.), and 6:48·4 (500 m.).

DERBYSHIRE, Rob(Great Britain, 29 Nov. 1878–1938). John Henry Derbyshire, from Manchester, was always known as 'Rob'—an abbreviation of his childhood pet name. In the years at the turn of the twentieth century, when British swimmers were supreme, Derbyshire won a gold medal in the 1900 Olympic water-polo tournament, a silver in the 4 × 250 m. relay in the Interim Games in 1906 and another gold in 1908 for the 4 × 200 m. relay at the London Games.

Like most swimmers of his generation, he raced a wide range of distances and won ten A.S.A. titles, including the 100 y. six times from 1898–1901 and 1903–04. He became a baths manager in the north of England and later at Lime Grove Baths, London, where a lane was always set aside, even in busy public time, for the serious swimmers to train without hindrance.

DESJARDINS, Pete (United States, 12 Apr. 1907–   ). The 'Little Bronze statue from Florida', Peter was born in Manitoba, Canada, but at an early age moved with his family to Miami Beach where he has lived ever since and eventually became an American citizen.

Double diving medallist in the 1928 Games, he made history then by being the only Olympic competitor to get 10 out of 10 for a dive. This was in the springboard and, in fact, he got the maximum for two dives and his aggregate of judges' marks over the whole test was an amazing 9·2. Not surprisingly, he won this event (by 11 marks) in which he had been second four years earlier, and also took the highboard title.

A compact athlete, standing 5 ft. 3 in., Desjardins, an economics graduate from Stanford University, turned professional and among many notable exhibition tours made four trips to Britain between 1935 and 1938. He travelled always with a typewriter, and his first chore on the train on the way to his next stop was to write a letter of thanks to his last hosts.

He dived in every part of the United Kingdom and in August 1936 alone covered 4,570 miles—an average of 150 miles a day—between engagements, which often involved a thirty-minute solo show of straight and comic diving from plank-like springboards into shallow water.

DEVITT, John (Australia, 4 Feb. 1937–). Winner of the Olympic 100 m. in 1960, Devitt is best remembered for the row his victory in Rome caused. And, inevitably, his name always will be linked with American Lance Larson, the man who many thought won this blue riband race.

The Rome Games were staged in the days before automatic timing and judging. And in the closing stages of this race, Larson, in an adjacent lane to Devitt, had surged forward with amazing speed. Two of the three first place judges gave Devitt their vote. Two of the second place judges put Devitt second. Thus, of the six officials, three, by implication thought the Australian had won and three favoured the American.

The timekeepers had no doubt. They gave Larson 55·0, 55·1 and 55·1 (for an Olympic record of 55·1) against the 55·2, 55·2 and 55·2 for Devitt. And the unofficial manually-operated judging machine, which recorded the touch on three paper tapes, made Larson the clear winner.

Despite all this evidence, Devitt was awarded the gold in an Olympic record of 55·2, thanks to a judging casting vote by the referee, who technically did not have a vote! Larson got the silver and his time changed to 55·2. Poor Larson was the subject of protests on his behalf for four years. And poor Devitt had to grin and bear it.

The career of Devitt from Sydney started in earnest at the 1956 Melbourne Olympics where he was second to his team-mate Jon Henricks in the 100 m. and won a gold in Australia's winning 4 × 200 m. relay team. As well as his disputed Roman gold, he gained a bronze in the 4 × 200 m. relay in 1960. Essentially a sprinter, he was Com-

monwealth 100 m. and relay champion in Cardiff in 1958, broke four world records, for 100 m. (55·2 and 54·6) and 110 y. (55·2 and 55·1) and helped Australian relay teams to ten world marks.

DEWAR, Phyllis (Canada). Tipped as an 'also ran' even by her own country's swimming experts, Phyl Dewar returned from the London Commonwealth Games of 1934 with two individual golds in the 100 and 440 y. free-style and two more golds in the free-style and medley relays. To emphasize the poor judgment of the critics, Miss Dewar's winning 100 y. time of 63·0 was four seconds faster than the championship record set by England's Joyce Cooper at the first Games in 1930. Phyl also swam in the 1936 Olympics and was a member of the Canadian squad who were fifth in the free-style relay.

DIBIASI, Klaus (Italy, 6 Oct. 1947–). The only Italian to win an individual Olympic gold medal in the pool, Dibiasi became highboard diving champion in Mexico City in 1968, winning by more than 10 points from Alvaro Gaxiola (Mex). Dibiasi, runner-up in this event in Tokyo in 1964, also took the silver medal for springboard diving in Mexico.

This tall 5 ft. 11 in. fair-haired man was born in Austria, but in his childhood his Italian parents went to live in Bolzano, in northern Italy. His father Carlo was springboard champion of Italy from 1933 to 1936 and later coached his son to the top of world diving.

Early on Dibiasi had to train outdoors, which in the Italian Dolomites was a chilly business in winter. After his silver success in 1964, an indoor diving tank with a 10 m. board was built for him by the town of Bolzano.

As well as his Olympic successes, Dibiasi won the European highboard title in Utrecht in 1966. Four years later, in Barcelona, he was second in both the highboard and springboard.

DIVER OF THE YEAR. (See MELVILLE, CLARKE G., NATIONAL MEMORIAL TROPHY.)

DIVING. This complicated sport demands acrobatic ability, the grace of a ballet dancer, iron nerve and a liking for heights.

Competitions are divided into springboard and highboard events (see SPRING-BOARD DIVING, HIGHBOARD DIVING) with prescribed tests. There are five directional groups of dives on the international springboard table and six groups for highboard, as follows:

Group 1. Forward. Starting forward and entering forward.

Group 2. Back. Starting backward and entering backward.

Group 3. Reverse. Starting forward with a backward rotation.

Group 4. Inward. Starting backward with a forward rotation.

Group 5. Twist. Starting forward or backward, making from $\frac{1}{2}$ to $2\frac{1}{2}$ twists during straight or somersaulting dives from the groups 1–4 above.

Group 6. Armstand. (Highboard only.) Starting with an arm balance (handstand) which must be held steadily before the start of the dive or somersault.

There are also four positions in which movements may be performed:

Position (a) Straight. Not bent at knees or hips.

Position (b) Piked. Bent at hips but with knees straight.

Position (c) Tucked. Bunched with hands on knees.

Position (d) Free. Any body position but only applicable to certain more difficult dives with twists.

All dives on the international table have tariff values according to their degree of difficulty. The judge marks the dive without reference to its difficulty and this mark is multiplied by the degree of difficulty to produce the score for the dive (see DIVING JUDGING). Degrees of difficulty range from 1·1 (inward dive (c) from 5 or 10 m.) to 3·0 (forward $3\frac{1}{2}$ somersault (b) from 3 m.).

DIVING CLUB OF THE YEAR. (See HEARN, GEORGE, CUP.)

DIVING JUDGING. Marks in diving are awarded from 0 to 10 on the following basis: completely failed = 0; unsatisfactory = $\frac{1}{2}$–2; deficient = $2\frac{1}{2}$–$4\frac{1}{2}$; satisfactory = 5–6; good = $6\frac{1}{2}$–8 and very good = $8\frac{1}{2}$–10.

There are normally five judges, but in events like the Olympic Games there are seven and the dive is marked solely on merit without considering the difficulty of the dive. One highest and one lowest mark are eliminated and the remainder are added together and multiplied by the degree of difficulty (see DIVING). If there are five scoring judges the points are reduced to three judges by dividing by five and multiplying by three. And the final product is the mark for the dive.

The recorders do not have to do lightning calculations in their heads. There are tables to deal with this elaborate procedure from which the score can be extracted within seconds to two decimal points.

DRAVES, Vickie (United States). The first woman to win the Olympic springboard and highboard titles at the same Games—she did it in London in 1948—Victoria Manalo Draves, a twin, had a Filipino father and an English mother. Born in San Francisco, her Filipino parentage caused her many difficulties before World War II and at one time her club on Nob Hill demanded that she drop her father's surname of Manalo in favour of her mother's maiden name of Taylor. A talented diver before the war, at 16, Vickie's first United States outdoor title success was in 1946 when she won the highboard crown and retained it in 1947 and '48. She never won an outdoor springboard title, but did take the indoor 3 m. championship in 1948.

In the early part of her career, Vickie was coached by Phil Patterson and Jimmy McHugh. But her greatest successes came after she had joined the Lyle Draves squad at the Athens club in Oakland. She married Draves in 1946 and he was with her, though not as the team coach, in 1948 when, diving as America's second string, she achieved her historic double at the London Olympics.

DUCHKOVA, Milena (Czechoslovakia, 25 Apr. 1952–). The first Czechoslovakian to win any kind of medal in Olympic pool competitions. Milena had to survive the tensions of occupation of her country by the Soviet Union as well as beat the history of failure. And she did both to win the highboard title in Mexico City.

Only 16 in August 1968, when the Soviet troops occupied Prague, she had to cross the River Vitava over bridges guarded by soldiers with machine guns to do her training and did not know for sure if she could go to the Olympics a week before the team left for Mexico.

But at the Games, the pool crowds were solidly behind her, clapping her every appearance on the board as well as each dive. She won by 4½ marks from Natalia Lobanova (U.S.S.R.) and Duchkova's greatest thrill was to see the Czech flag hoisted above the Russian hammer and sickle at her victory ceremony. Two years after, Milena confirmed her supremacy from the 10 m. platform by winning the European title.

A tiny child—and in Mexico she was only 5 ft. 2¼ in. and 8 st. lb.—she had been coached since she was seven by Maria Cermakova, who at first was reluctant to give Milena a test because she did not want to take such a little girl as a pupil.

DURACK, Fanny (Australia). The first woman Olympic swimming champion, Fanny Durack achieved that honour in 1912 when she won the 100 m. free-style, the only individual event for women, in the Stockholm Games. Racing in an open-air, 100 m. long, specially-built pool in Stockholm harbour, she clipped eight-tenths of a second off the world record, held by Daisy Curwen of England, in winning her heat in 1:19·8 and she beat her team-mate Mina Wylie by 3·2 in 1:22·2 in the final.

In the swimming sense, Fanny was before her time and World War I, which caused the cancellation of the 1916 Games, robbed her of further Olympic honours. She broke nine world records between 1912–18, from 100 yards (by 6·6 seconds) to one mile and was the first to put her name in the record book for 220 and 500 y. and one mile.

She started her career as a breast-stroke swimmer—the only style for which there was an Australian championships for women at that time. In fact, Fanny never held a national title though she won the first New South Wales 100 m. breast-stroke championship in 1906. Later she swam the trudgen and crawl and her demonstrations around the world did a great deal to promote women's swimming.

Her best times were 66·0 (100 y.), 1:16·2 (100 m.), 2:56·0 (220 y.), 4:43·6 (300 m.), 8:08·2 (500 y.) and 26:08·0 (one mile). It was many years before her standards were equalled.

E

EDERLE, Gertrude (United States). Trudy Ederle has two claims to swimming fame, as an Olympic medallist and a conqueror of the English Channel. Her Olympic successes were in 1924 when she won bronze medals in the 100 and 400 m. free-style and a gold in America's winning free-style relay team. In her amateur swimming days she also broke nine world records—from 100 to 500 m., her times being: 72·8 (100 m.), 2:45·2 (200 m. s/c), 2:46·8 (220 y. s/c), 3:58·4 (300 y. s/c), 5:53·2 (400 m.), 5:54·6 (440 y.), 6:45·2 (500 y.), 7:22·2 (500 m.) and 13:19·0 (880 y.).

Gertrude turned professional in 1925 —after winning six United States outdoor titles—and a year later became the first woman to swim the English Channel. Her 14 hr. 34 min. from France to England, fifty-one years after Matthew Webb had made the first crossing, was faster than any man before her.

EDWARDS, Margaret (Great Britain, 25 Mar. 1939–). Unlucky is the word to describe Margaret Edwards from Heston, whose years among the top back-strokers in the world coincided with the era of an even greater British back-stroke swimmer Judy Grinham (see GRINHAM, JUDY).

Petite, dark-haired Margaret was overshadowed physically by her Middlesex county team-mate Judy, yet she broke four world records and won Olympic, European and Commonwealth medals. She was third behind Judy in the 1956 Olympic 100 m. only months after being in a plaster cast because of a slipped disc. And she was second to her great rival in the 1958 Commonwealth Games in Cardiff and European championships in Budapest.

Blue-eyed Margaret set her first world mark for 110 y. (1:13·5) in Blackpool in 1957 and, swimming again ten minutes later in a relay, lost her record to Gretje Kraan of Holland. Margaret set new figures in a heat at the Cardiff Games (1:12·3), then watching from the bathside, saw Judy clip this to 1:11·9 in the final.

The best tribute to Margaret comes from her old rival Judy, who says: 'I could never have achieved the things I did if Margaret had not been there to challenge all the time.'

ENGLISH MEDALLISTS, COMMONWEALTH GAMES. The following swimmers and divers, listed in alphabetical order, have won Commonwealth medals while representing England. g = gold (1st), s = silver (2nd) and b = bronze (3rd).

Allardice, Lesley, 1970, 4 × 100 m. fr. (b).

Amos, Linda, 1962, 4 × 110 y. fr (b).

Austen, Margaret, 1962, highboard (s).

Barner, Ann, 1966, 110 y. bu (b), 220 y. bu (b).

Bartle, Olive, 1934, 4 × 100 y. fr (b).

Bell, Stanley, 1930, 200 y. br (s).

Besford, John, 1930, 100 y. ba (b); 1934, 100 y. ba (s), 3 × 100 y. med (b).

Bewley, Keith, 1966, 110 y. bu (b), 4 × 110 y. med (s), 4 × 220 y. fr (b).

Bland, Donald, 1950, 4 × 220 y. fr (b).

Botham, Jean, 1954, 4 × 110 y. fr (b).

Brooks, Norman, 1930, 100 y. fr (s), 4 × 200 y. fr (s).

Burrow, Shelagh, 1970, highboard (b).

Campion, Dick, 1962, 4 × 220 y. fr (b).

Cave, Jeanette, 1966, 4 × 110 y. fr (b).

Child, Edna, 1950, highboard (g), springboard (g).

Church, Elizabeth, 1950, 220 y. br (b) 3 × 110 y. med (s).

Clarke, Stan, 1962, 4 × 110 y. fr (b), 4 × 220 y. fr (b).

Collin, Keith, 1958, springboard (g).

Cooper, Doreen, 1930, 4 × 100 y. fr (g).

Cooper, Joyce, 1930, 100 y. fr (g), 400 y. fr (g), 100 y. ba (g), 4 × 100 y. fr (g).

Cope, Sue, 1966, 4 × 110 y. fr (b).

Cotterill, Anne, 1962, 110 y. by (s), 4 × 110 y. med (s).

Cousens, Cecily, 1934, highboard (b).

Davies, John, 1938, 220 y. br (g), 3 × 110 y. med (g)

Dove, Freddy, 1938, 4 × 220 y. fr (g), 3 × 110 y. med (g).

Drew, Philip, 1970, highboard (s).

Dyson, Jackie, 1958, 220 y. br (s).

Edwards, Margaret, 1958, 110 y. ba (s).

Enfield, Jackie, 1962, 220 y. br (s).

Ewart, Fearne, 1954, 4 × 110 y. fr (b).

Ferris, Elizabeth, 1958, springboard (b); 1962, springboard (s).

Flint, Reggie, 1930, 220 y. br (b).

Frampton, Lorna, 1938, 3 × 110 y. med (g).

Franklin, Janet, 1966, 110 y. ba (b).

Fraser, Dorinda, 1962, 110 y. br (b).

Ffrench-Williams, Micky, 1934, 4 × 200 y. fr (s), 3 × 100 y. med (b); 1938, 4 × 220 y. fr (g).

Gegan, Judy, 1966, 110 y. bu (s), 4 × 110 y. med (g)

Gill, Andy, 1970, highboard (b).

Glenville, Terry, 1962, 4 × 110 y. med (s).

Gosden, Christine, 1958, 220 y. br (b), 4 × 110 y. med (g).

Grant, Zilpha, 1938, 4 × 110 y. fr (b).

Grinham, Judy, 1958, 110 y. ba (g), 4 × 110 y. med (g), 4 × 110 y. fr (b).

Grundy, Margaret, 1954, 220 y. br (b).

Hale, Jack, 1950, 4 × 220 y. fr (b), 3 × 110 y. med (g).

Harding, Phyllis, 1930, 100 y. ba (b), 4 × 100 y. fr (g); 1934, 100 y. ba (g), 3 × 100 y. med (s).

Harris, Diana, 1966, 110 y. br (g), 4 × 110 y. med (g).

Harrison, Dorothy, 1970, 100, 200 m. br. and 4 × 100 m. med. (s).

Harrowby, Joyce, 1938, 4 × 110 y. fr (b).

Hime, Alan, 1954, 220 y. br (b).

Hinton, Margery, 1930, 200 y. br (s); 1934, 200 y. br (b), 4 × 100 y. fr (b);

1938, 4 × 110 y. fr (b), 3 × 110 y. med (g).

Hughes, Edna, 1934, 4 × 110 y. fr (b), 3 × 110 y. med (s); 1938, 4 × 110 y. fr (b).

Jackson, Neil, 1966, 110 y. ba (b), 4 × 110 y. med (s)

Jarvis, Christine, 1970, 100 m. br (b).

Jarvis, Tony, 1966, 4 × 110 y. fr (b), 4 × 220 y. fr (b); 1970, 4 × 100 and 4 × 200 m. (b).

Jeffrey, Margaret, 1938, 440 y. fr (s).

Jervis, Peter, 1954, 220 y. br (s).

Joynes, Olive (Mrs. Wadham), 1930, 4 × 100 y. fr (g).

Keen, Sandra, 1962, 4 × 110 y. fr (b).

Kendall, Pat, 1950, 110 y. fr (b), 4 × 220 y. fr (b), 3 × 110 y. med (g).

Kendrew, Peter, 1962, 4 × 110 y. fr (b), 4 × 220 y. fr (b), 4 × 110 y. med (s).

Kingston, Vera, 1934, 3 × 100 y. med (s).

Kitcher, Tony, 1962, highboard (b).

Lansley, Diane, 1970, 100 m. bu (g), 4 × 100 m. med (s).

Legg, Ray, 1950, 4 × 220 y. fr (b).

Leivers, Bobby, 1934, 4 × 200 y. fr (s); 1938, 440 y. fr (s), 1,650 y. fr (g), 4 × 220 y. fr (g).

Lewis, Sylvia, 1962, 110 y. ba (b), 220 y. ba (s).

Long, Ann, 1954, highboard (b), springboard (g); 1958, highboard (s).

Long, Elizabeth, 1962, 440 y. fr (b), 4 × 110 y. fr (b).

Lonsbrough, Anita, 1958, 220 y. br (g), 4 × 110 y. med (g); 1962, 110 y. br (g), 220 y. br (g), 440 y. IM (g), 4 × 110 y. fr (s).

Lord, Bobby, 1966, 4 × 110 y. fr (b).

Ludgrove, Linda, 1962, 110 y. ba (g), 220 y. ba (g), 4 × 110 y. med (s); 1966, 110 y. ba (g), 220 y. ba (g), 4 × 110 y. med (g).

McKechnie, Neil, 1958, 4 × 110 y. med (b).

Macready, 'Dot', 1934, highboard (g).

Marshall, Anne, 1958, 4 × 110 y. fr (b).

Martin-Dye, John, 1962, 4 × 110 y. fr (b), 4 × 220 y. fr (b); 1966, 4 × 110 y. (b).

Mather, Tommy, 1934, highboard (g).

Millar, Eunice, 1954, highboard (s).

BUTTERFLY. (*Above*) Mark Spitz (USA) the world record holder. (*Below*) Martyn Woodroffe (GB), surprise silver medallist in the 200m butterfly at the 1968 Olympics, in which he finished only three-tenths of a second behind champion Carl Robie and 4½ seconds ahead of Spitz, who was eighth and last in this final

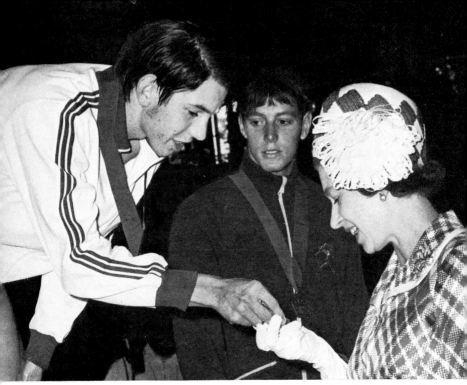

CANADIAN SWIMMING CHAMPION. Canada's double Commonwealth breast-stroke champion, Bill Mahony, at the 1970 Games in Edinburgh, giving his team badge to the Queen after Her Majesty had presented him with his second gold medal

DEVITT, JOHN. The controversial Australian winner of the Olympic 100m free-style title in Rome in 1960. He is here with Lance Larson the man many thought had won, and bronze medallist Manuel dos Santos (Brazil)

Mills, John, 1970, 4 × 200 m. fr (b).

Milton, Freddie, 1930, 4 × 200 y. fr (s).

Mitchell, Stella, 1966, 220 y. br (s).

Myall, Ivan, 1970, 4 × 100 and 4 × 200 m. fr (b).

Nares-Pillow, Valerie, 1954, 4 × 110 y. fr (b).

Newman, Joy, 1966, highboard (g)

Nicholson, Neil, 1962, 220 y. br (b), 4 × 110 y. med (s).

Noakes, Beryl, 1958, 4 × 110 y. fr (b).

Phelps, Brian, 1958, highboard (s); 1962, highboard (g), springboard (g); 1966, highboard (g), springboard (g).

Pickering, Sally, 1970, 4 × 100 m. fr (b).

Platt, Sylvia, 1970, 4 × 100 m. med (s).

Preece, Lillian, 1952, 4 × 110 y. fr (b).

Radnage, Amanda, 1970, 200 m. br (b).

Ratcliffe, Shelagh, 1970, 200 m. IM (s), 400 m. IM (b)

Ray, J. Briscoe, 1934, springboard (g).

Romain, Roy, 1950, 220 y. br (s), 3 × 110 y. med (g).

Rowlatt, Kathy, 1966, springboard (g).

Scott, Terry, 1930, highboard (b).

Sillett, Pauline, 1966, 4 × 110 y. fr (b), 4 × 110 y. med (g).

Slattery, Jill, 1966, 220 y. br (g), 110 y. br (s).

Smith, Katie, 1970, 4 × 100 m. med (s), 4 × 100 m. fr (b)

Storey, Doris, 1938, 220 y. br (g), 3 × 110 y. med (g).

Summers, Alan, 1934, 3 × 110 y. med (b).

Sutherland, Diana, 1970, 4 × 100 m.fr (b).

Sutton, Reg, 1934, 4 × 200 y. fr (s).

Sykes, Graham, 1958, 4 × 110 y. med (b); 1962, 110 y. ba (g), 4 × 110 y. med (s).

Symonds, Graham, 1958, 220 y. bu (s), 4 × 110 y. med (b).

Symons, Pat, 1954, 110 y. ba (s).

Tarsey, David, 1958, springboard (b).

Taylor, Micky, 1938, 110 y. ba (b), 3 × 110 y. med (g).

Terrell, Ray, 1970, 200 m. ba and 400 m. IM (s), 4 × 100, 4 × 200 m. fr (b).

Thurley, John, 1966, 4 × 220 y. fr (b).

Tomalin, Doug, 1934, highboard (s), springboard (s); 1938, highboard (g), springboard (s).

Trippett, John, 1930, 100 y. ba (g).

Tucker, Malcolm, 1966, 110 y. br (b), 4 × 110 y. med (s).

Turner, Mike, 1966, 4 × 110 y. fr (b), 4 × 220 y. fr (b), 4 × 110 y. med (s).

Turner, Tony, 1954, springboard (s).

Wainwright, Norman, 1934, 440 y. fr (s), 1,500 y. (b), 4 × 200 y. fr (s); 1938, 1,650 y. fr (b), 4 × 220 y. (g).

Walkden, Chris, 1958, 220 y. br (b), 4 × 110 y. med (b).

Watts, A. G., 1930, 4 × 200 y. fr (s).

Weiland, Molly, 1958, highboard (b).

Wellington, Margaret, 1950, 110 y. fr (s), 440 y. fr (s), 4 × 110 y. fr (g), 3 × 110 y. med (s).

Welsh, Charmian, 1958, highboard (g), springboard (g).

Whiteside, Joe, 1930, 4 × 200 y. fr (s).

Wilkinson, Daphne, 1954, 4 × 110 y. fr (b).

Wilkinson, Diana, 1958, 4 × 110 y. med (g), 4 × 110 y. fr (b); 1962, 4 × 110 y. med (s), 4 × 110 y. fr (b); 1966, 4 × 110 y. fr (b).

Windeatt, Malcolm, 1970, 4 × 100 m. fr (b).

Wolstenholme, Celia, 1930, 200 y. br (g).

Wolstenholme, Beatrice, 1934, 4 × 100 y. fr (b).

Wood, Grace, 1950, 4 × 110 y. fr (b).

Yate, Helen, 1950, 110 y. ba (b), 4 × 110 y. fr (b), 3 × 110 y. med (s).

ELECTRICAL TIMING. See TIMING.

EMPIRE GAMES. See COMMONWEALTH GAMES.

EMPIRE GAMES CHAMPIONS. See COMMONWEALTH GAMES CHAMPIONS.

ENGLISH DIVER OF THE YEAR. See HEARN, GEORGE, CUP.

ENGLISH DIVING CHAMPIONS. See AMATEUR SWIMMING ASSOCIATION DIVING CHAMPIONS.

ENGLISH DIVING CLUB OF THE YEAR. See MELVILLE, CLARK G., NATIONAL MEMORIAL TROPHY.

ENGLISH PLUNGING CHAMPIONS. See PLUNGING, AMATEUR SWIMMING ASSOCIATION CHAMPIONS.

ENGLISH SCHOOLS SWIMMING ASSOCIATION. The E.S.S.A. was inaugurated in May 1949 through the efforts of Harry Finch of the Great Yarmouth S.S.A., who became the association's first honorary secretary. By the time the first annual meeting was held in Great Yarmouth the following April, the energetic Finch had succeeded in affiliating more than 200 schools swimming associations.

The first English Schools championships were held in Bethnal Green, London, in 1950 with teams from the then 12 division who were able to enter one competitor or team for each of the events for boys and girls on a junior (13–15 years) and senior (15–18) basis.

Sadly, Harry Finch was killed in a motor accident on his way to the championships meeting at Bristol in 1952 , but the excellent foundation he laid down for his brain child has enabled the E.S.S.A. to grow from strength to strength.

The E.S.S.A. became affiliated to the A.S.A. in 1951, added a thirteenth division to their list in 1955 when Dorset, Devonshire and Cornwall joined and, in 1968, split the age groupings of the championships into three—for juniors (12–14), intermediate (14–16) and senior (16–19).

ENGLISH SWIMMER OF THE YEAR. See YEADEN, T. M., MEMORIAL TROPHY.

ENGLISH SWIMMING CHAMPIONS. See AMATEUR SWIMMING ASSOCIATION SWIMMING CHAMPIONS.

ENGLISH SWIMMING CLUB OF THE YEAR—MEN. See BENJAMIN, HENRY, NATIONAL MEMORIAL TROPHY.

ENGLISH SWIMMING CLUB OF THE YEAR—WOMEN. See FERN, HAROLD, NATIONAL TROPHY.

ENGLISH WATER-POLO CHAMPIONS. See WATER-POLO, AMATEUR SWIMMING ASSOCIATION CHAMPIONS.

EUROPEAN CHAMPIONSHIPS. The first European championships were held in Budapest in 1926 through the initiative of Hungary, who had pressed for the inauguration of such a Continental event before the First World War. At that time no official European body existed to give title to the competitions. But as a result of this first meeting a European Swimming League was founded (see LIGUE EUROPENNE DE NATATION). The venues and dates of the European championships are:

No.	Venue	Dates
I	Budapest, Hungary	18 Aug.–22 Aug., 1926
II	Bologna, Italy	31 Aug.–4 Sept., 1927
III	Paris, France	23 Aug.–30 Aug., 1931
IV	Magdeburg, Germany	12 Aug.–19 Aug., 1934
V	London, England	6 Aug.–13 Aug., 1938
VI	Monte Carlo, Monaco	10 Sept.–14 Sept., 1947
VII	Vienna, Austria	20 Aug.–27 Aug., 1950
VIII	Turin, Italy	31 Aug.–5 Sept., 1954
IX	Budapest, Hungary	31 Aug.–6 Sept , 1958
X	Leipzig, East Germany	18 Aug.–25 Aug., 1962
XI	Utrecht, Netherlands	20 Aug.–27 Aug., 1966
XII	Barcelona, Spain	5 Sept.–12 Sept., 1970
XIII	Vienna, Austria	To be decided, 1974

EUROPEAN CHAMPIONSHIP WINNERS

MEN

100 m. Free-style

1926	Barany, Istvan (Hun)	1:01·0
1927	Borg, Arne (Swe)	1:00·0
1931	Barany, Istvan (Hun)	59·8
1934	Csik, Ferenc (Hun)	59·7
1938	Hoving, Karl (Neth)	59·8
1947	Jany, Alex (Fr)	56·9
1950	Jany, Alex (Fr)	57·7
1954	Nyeki, Imre (Hun)	57·8
1958	Pucci, Paolo (It)	56·3

1962	Gottvalles, Alain (Fr)	55·0
1966	McGregor, Bobby (GB)	53·7
1970	Rousseau, Michael (Fr)	52·9

200 m. Free-style
| 1970 | Fassnacht, Hans (WGer) | 1:55·2 |

400 m. Free-style
1926	Borg, Arne (Swe)	5:14·2
1927	Borg, Arne (Swe)	5:08·6
1931	Barany, Istvan (Hun)	5:04·0
1934	Taris, Jean (Fr)	4:55·5
1938	Borg, Bjorn (Swe)	4:51·6
1947	Jany, Alex (Fr)	4:35·2
1950	Jany, Alex (Fr)	4:48·0
1954	Csordas, Gyorgy (Hun)	4:38·8
1958	Black, Ian (GB)	4:31·3
1962	Bontekoe, Johan (Neth)	4:25·6
1966	Wiegand, Frank (EGer)	4:11·1
1970	Larsson, Gunnar (Swe)	4:02·6

1,500 m. Free-style
1926	Borg, Arne (Swe)	21:29·2
1927	Borg, Arne (Swe)	19:07·2
1931	Halassy, Oliver (Hun)	20:49·0
1934	Taris, Jean (Fr)	20:01·5
1938	Borg, Bjorn (Swe)	19:55·6
1947	Mitro, Gyorgy (Hun)	19:28·0
1950	Lehmann, Heinz (Ger)	19:48·2
1954	Csordas, Gyorgy (Hun)	18:57·8
1958	Black, Ian (GB)	18:05·8
1962	Katona, Jozsef (Hun)	17:49·5
1966	Belits-Geiman, Semyon (USSR)	16:58·5
1970	Fassnacht, Hans (WGer)	16:19·2

100 m. Back-stroke
1926	Frohlich, Gustav (Ger)	1:16·0
1927	Lundahl, Eksil (Swe)	1:17·4
1931	Deutsch, Gerhard (Ger)	1:14·8
1934	Besford, John (GB)	1:11·7
1938	Schlauch, Hans (Ger)	1:09·0
1947	Vallerey, Georges (Fr)	1:07·6
1950	Larsson, Goran (Swe)	1:09·4
1954	Bozon, Gilbert (Fr)	1:05·1
1958	Christophe, Robert (Fr)	1:03·1
1962	No event	
1966	No event	
1970	Matthes, Roland (EGer)	58·9

200 m. Back-stroke
1962	Barbier, Leonid (USSR)	2:16·6
1966	Gromak, Yuri (USSR)	2:12·9
1970	Matthes, Roland (EGer)	2:08·8

100 m. Breast-stroke
| 1970 | Pankin, Nicolai (USSR) | 1:06·8 |

200 m. Breast-stroke
1926	Rademacher, Erich (Ger)	2:52·6
1927	Rademacher, Erich (Ger)	2:55·2
1931	Reingoldt, Toivo (Fin)	2:52·2
1934	Sietas, Erwin (Ger)	2:49·0
1938	Balke, Joachim (Ger)	2:45·8
1947	Romain, Roy (GB)	Bu2:40·1
1950	Klein, Herbert (WGer)	Bu2:38·6
1954	Bodinger, Klaus (EGer)	2:40·9
1958	Kolesnikov, Leonid (USSR)	2:41·1
1962	Prokopenko, Georgy (USSR)	2:32·8
1966	Prokopenko, Georgy (USSR)	2:30·0
1970	Katzur, Klaus (EGer)	2:26·0

Bu = won on butterfly before the separation of breast-stroke and butterfly in 1954

100 m. Butterfly
| 1970 | Lampe, Hans (WGer) | 57·6 |

200 m. Butterfly
1954	Tumpek, Gyorgy (Hun)	2:32·2
1958	Black, Ian (GB)	2:21·9
1962	Kuzmin, Valentin (USSR)	2:14·2
1966	Kuzmin, Valentin (USSR)	2:10·2
1970	Poser, Udo (EGer)	2:08·4

200 m. Individual medley
| 1970 | Larsson, Gunnar (Swe) | 2:09·3 |

400 m. Individual medley
1962	Androssov, Gennadi (USSR)	5:01·5
1966	Wiegand, Frank (EGer)	4:47·9
1970	Larsson, Gunnar (Swe)	4:36·2

4 × 100m . Free-style relay
| 1962 | France | 3:43·7 |

(Gropaiz, Gerard; Christophe, Robert; Curtillet, Jean-Pasqual; Gottvalles, Alain)

| 1966 | East Germany | 3:36·8 |

(Wiegand, Frank; Poser, Udo; Gregor, Horst; Sommer, Peter)

| 1970 | USSR | 3:32·3 |

(Bure, Vladimir; Mazanov, Victor; Kulikov, Georgi; Ilichev, Leonid)

4 × 200 m. Free-style relay
| 1926 | Germany | 9:57·2 |

(Heitmann, August; Berges, Friedel; Rademacher, Joachim; Heinrich, Herbert)

1927 Germany   9:49·6
  (Heitmann, August; Berges, Friedel;
  Rademacher, Joachim; Heinrich, Her-
  bert)
1930 Hungary   9:34·0
  (Szabados, Laszlo; Szekely, Andras;
  Wanie, Andras; Barany, Istvan)
1934 Hungary   9:30·2
  (Grof, Odon; Csik, Ferenc; Marothy,
  Andras; Lengyel, Arpad)
1938 Germany   9:17·6
  (Birr, Werner; Plath, Werner; Heim-
  lich, Arthur; Freese, Hans)
1947 Sweden   9:00·5
  (Olsson, Per Olaf; Ostrand, Per Olaf;
  Lunden, Martin; Johansson, Olle)
1950 Sweden   9:06·5
  (Synnerholm, Tore; Larsson, Goran;
  Ostrand, Per Olaf; Johansson, Olle)
1954 Hungary   8:47·8
  (Till, Laszlo; Kadas, Geza; Domotor,
  Zoltan, Nyeki, Imre)
1958 USSR   8:33·7
  (Nikolaev, Gennadi; Luzkovski, Joz-
  sef; Struzanov, Vladimir; Nikitin,
  Boris)
1962 Sweden   8:14·8
  (Rosendhal, Hans; Svensson, Mats;
  Bengtsson, Lars-Erik; Lindberg, Per
  Ole)
1966 USSR   8:00·2
  (Ilichev, Leonid; Belits-Geiman,
  Semyon; Pletnev; Novikov, Eugeny)
1970 West Germany   7:49·5
  (Lampe, Werner; von Schilling, Olaf;
  Meeuw, Folkert; Fassnacht, Hans)

4 × 100 m. Medley relay
1958 USSR   4:16·5
  (Barbier, Leonid; Minaschkin, Vladi-
  mir; Semjenkov, Vitali; Polevoi, Vik-
  tor)
1962 East Germany   4:09·0
  (Dietze; Henninger, Egon; Gregor,
  Horst; Wiegand, Frank)
1966 USSR   4:02·4
  (Mazanov, Victor; Prokopenko,
  Georgy; Kuzmin, Valentin; Ilichev,
  Leonid)
1970 East Germany   3:54·4
  (Matthes, Roland; Katzur, Klaus;
  Poser, Udo; Unger, Lutz)

Springboard diving
1926 Mundt, Arthur (Ger)   186·42

1927 Riebschlager, Ewald (Ger) 173·86
1931 Riebschlager, Ewald (Ger) 136·22
1934 Esser, Leon (Ger)   137·74
1938 Weiss, Erhard (Ger)   148·02
1947 Heinkele, Roger (Fr)   126·71
1950 Aderhold, Hans (WGer)   183·60
1954 Brener, Roman (USSR)   144·01
1958 Ujvari, Laszlo (Hun)   141·17
1962 Mrkwicka, Kurt (Aut)   147·21
1966 Safonov, Mikhail (USSR)   155·27
1970 Cagnotto, Giorgio (It)   555·21

Highboard diving
1926 Luber, Hans (Ger)   110·80
1927 Luber, Hans (Ger)   114·86
1931 Staudinger Josef (Aut)   111·82
1934 Stork, Hermann (Ger)   98·99
1938 Weiss, Erhard (Ger)   124·67
1947 Christiansen, Thomas
                          (Den) 105·55
1950 Haase, Gunther (WGer)   158·13
1954 Brener, Roman (USSR)   153·25
1958 Phelps, Brian (GB)   143·74
1962 Phelps, Brian (GB)   150·81
1966 Dibiasi, Klaus (It)   162·92
1970 Matthes, Lothar (EGer)   454·74

Water-polo
1926 Hungary
  (Barta, Istvan; Fazekas, Tibor; Hom-
  monai, Marton; Kesseru, Alajos;
  Kesseru, Ferenc; Vertesy, Josef;
  Wenk, Janos)
1927 Hungary
  (Barta, Istvan; Fazekas, Tibor; Hom-
  monai, Marton; Kesseru, Alajos;
  Kesseru, Ferenc; Vertesy, Josef;
  Wenk, Janos; Czelle, Laszlo)
1931 Hungary
  (Brody, Gyorgy; Ivady, Sandor;
  Hommonai, Marton, Halassy, Oliver;
  Vertesy, Josef; Nemeth, Janos; Kes-
  seru, Alajos; Barta, Istvan; Sarkany,
  Miklos; Kesseru, Ferenc; Bozsi,
  Mihaly)
1934 Hungary
  (Brody, Gorgy; Sarkany, Miklos;
  Hommonai, Marton; Halassy, Oliver;
  Brandi, Jeno; Ivadi, Sandor; Kesseru,
  Alajos, Nemeth, Janos, Vertesy, Josef;
  Kusinzky, Gyorgy; Boszi, Miholy)
1938 Hungary
  (Mezei, Ferenc; Mezey, Istvan; Sar-
  kany, Miklos; Molnar, Istvan; Tolnai,
  Josef; Halassy, Oliver; Kanasy, Gyula;

Kidleghy, Kalman; Brandi, Jeno;
Bozsi, Mihaly; Nemeth, Janos)
1947 Italy
(Buonocore, Pasquale; Bulgarelli,
Emilio; Maioni, Mario; Ognio,
Geminio; Arena, Gildo; Ghira, Aldo;
Signori, Giacomo; Soracco, Hugo;
Pandolfini, Tullo, Pandolfini, Gian-
franco; Gaorsi, Giovanni)
1950 Netherlands
(Van Gelder, Max; Brassem, Cor;
Keetelaar, Henni; Bijslma, Gerrit;
Koorevaar, Nijs; Van Feggelen, Rudi;
Smol, Fritz)
1954 Hungary
(Jeney, Laszlo; Gyarmati, Dezso;
Hevesi, Istvan; Markovits, Kalman;
Bolvari, Antal; Martin, Miklos; Kar-
pati, Gyorgy; Boros, Otto; Szabo,
Aladar; Szivos, Istvan; Vizvari,
Gyorgy)
1958 Hungary
(Boros, Otto; Molnar, Endre; Hevesi,
Istvan; Markovits, Kalman; Kanizsa,
Tivadar; Domotor, Zoltan; Karpaty,
Gyorgy; Jeney, Laszlo; Mayer, Mi-
haly; Csillay, Gyorgy; Katona, A.)
1962 Hungary
(Boros, Otto; Mayer, Mihaly; Gyar-
mati, Dezso; Markovits, Kalman;
Karpati, Gyorgy; Domotor, Zoltan;
Felkai, Laszlo; Tanizsa, Tivadar;
Konrad II, Janos; Pocsik, Denes;
Ambrus, Miklos)
1966 Hungary
(Ambrus, Miklos; Bodnar, Andras;
Domotor, Zoltan; Felkai, Laszlo;
Karpati, Gyorgy; Konrad, Janos;
Konrad, Ferenc; Molnar, Endre;
Pocsik, Denes; Rusoran, Peter;
Szivos, Istvan)
1970 USSR
(Bovin, Oleg; Guliaev, Vadim;
Akimov, Anatoli; Dreval, Aleksandr;
Dolgushin, Aleksandr; Semenov,
Vladimir; Shidlovski, Aledsandr;
Barkalov, Aleksei; Osipov, Leonid;
Skok, Viacheslav)

WOMEN

100 m. Free-style
1927 Vierdag, Marie (Neth)   1:15·0
1931 Godard, Yvonne (Fr)   1:10·0
1934 Den Ouden, Willy (Neth) 1:07·1

1938 Hveger, Ragnhild (Den)   1:06·2
1947 Nathansen, Fritze (Den)   1:07·8
1950 Schumacher, Irma (Neth)   1:06·4
1954 Szoke, Katalin (Hun)   1:05·8
1958 Jobson, Kate (Swe)   1:04·7
1962 Pechstein, Heidi (EGer)   1:03·3
1966 Grunert, Martine (EGer)   1:01·2
1970 Wetzko, Gabriele (EGer)   59·6

200 m. Free-style
1970 Wetzko, Gabriele (EGer)   2:08·2

400 m. Free-style
1927 Braun, Marie (Neth)   6:11·8
1931 Braun, Marie (Neth)   5:42·0
1934 Mastenbroek, Rie (Neth)   5:27·4
1938 Hveger, Ranghild (Den)   5:09·0
1947 Harup, Karen (Den)   5:18·2
1950 Andersen, Greta (Den)   5:30·9
1954 Sebo, Agota (Hun)   5:14·4
1958 Koster, Jan (Neth)   5:02·6
1962 Lasterie, Adrie (Neth)   4:52·4
1966 Mandonnaud, Claude (Fr) 4:48·2
1970 Sehmisch, Elke (EGer)   4:32·9

800 m. Free-style
1970 Neugebauer, Karin (EGer) 9:29·1

100 m. Back-stroke
1927 Den Turk, Willy (Neth)   1:24·6
1931 Braun, Marie (Neth)   1:22·8
1934 Mastenbroek, Rie (Neth)   1:20·3
1938 Kint, Cor (Neth)   1:15·0
1947 Harup, Karen (Den)   1:15·9
1950 Van der Horst, Ria (Neth) 1:17·1
1954 Wielema, Geertje (Neth)   1:13·2
1958 Grinham, Judy (GB)   1:12·6
1962 Van Velsen, Ria (Neth)   1:10·5
1966 Caron, Christine (Fr)   1;08·1
1970 Lekveishvili, Tina
                       (USSR) 1:07·8

200 m. Back-stroke
1970 Gyarmati, Andrea (Hun)   2:25·5

100 m. Breast-stroke
1970 Stepanova, Galina
                       (USSR) 1:15·6

200 m. Breast-stroke
1927 Schrader, Hilda (Ger)   3:20·4
1931 Wolstenholme, Celia
                         (GB)   3:16·2
1934 Genenger, Martha (Ger)   3:09·1
1938 Sorensen, Inge (Den)   3:05·4
1947 Van Vliet, Nel (Neth)   2:56·6
1950 Vergauwen, Raymonde
                       (Belg)   3:00·1

1954	Happe, Ursula (WGer)	2:54·9
1958	Den Haan, Ada (Neth)	2:52·0
1962	Lonsbrough, Anita (GB)	2:50·2
1966	Prosumenschikova, Galina	
	(USSR)	2:40·8
1970	Stepanova (Prosumenschikova), Galina (USSR)	2:40·7

100 m. Butterfly

1954	Langenau, Jutta (EGer)	1:16·6
1958	Lagerberg, Tineke (Neth)	1:11·9
1962	Kok, Ada (Neth)	1:09·0
1966	Kok, Ada (Neth)	1:05·6
1970	Gyarmati, Andrea (Hun)	1:05·0

200 m. Butterfly

| 1970 | Lindner, Helga (EGer) | 2:20·2 |

200 m. Individual medley

| 1970 | Grunert, Martine (EGer) | 2:27·6 |

400 m. Individual medley

1962	Lasterie, Adrie (Neth)	5:27·8
1966	Heukels, Betty (Neth)	5:25·0
1970	Stoltze, Evelyn (EGer)	5:07·9

4 × 100 m. Free-style relay

1927 Great Britain 5:11·6
(Laverty, Marion; King, Ellen; Davies, Valerie; Cooper, Joyce)
1931 Netherlands 4:55·0
(Baumeister, Truus; Den Ouden, Willy; Vierdag, Marie; Braun, Marie)
1934 Netherlands 4:41·5
(Selbach, Jopie; Den Ouden, Willy; Timmermann, Ans; Mastenbroek, Rie)
1938 Denmark 4:31·4
(Arndt, Eva; Ove-Petersen, Birte; Kraft, Gunvor; Hveger, Ragnhild)
1947 Denmark 4:32·3
(Andersen, Greta; Harup, Karen; Svendsen, Eva; Nathansen, Fritze)
1950 Netherlands 4:33·9
(Mauser, Ann; Vaessen, Marie-Louise; Termeulen, Hannie; Schumacher, Irma)
1954 Hungary 4:30·6
(Gyenge, Valeria; Temes, Judit; Sebo, Agota; Szoke, Katalin)
1958 Netherlands 4:22·9
(Schimmel, Corrie; Kraan, Gretje; Lagerberg, Tinke; Gastelaars, Cockie)
1962 Netherlands 4:15·1
(Gastelaars, Cockie; Lasterie, Adrie; Terpstra, Erica; Tigelaar, Ineke)
1966 U.S.S.R. 4:11·3

(Sipchenko, Natalia; Rudenka, Antonia; Ustinova, Natalia; Sosnova, Tamara)
1970 East Germany 4:00·8
(Wetzko, Gabriele; Komor, Iris; Sehmisch, Elke; Schulze, Carola)

4 × 100 m. Medley relay

1958 Netherlands 4:52·9
(De Nijs, Lennie; Den Haan, Ada; Voorbij, Atie; Gastelaars, Cockie)
1962 East Germany 4:40·1
(Schmidt, Ingrid; Goebel, Barbara; Noack, Ute; Pechstein, Heidi)
1966 Netherlands 4:36·4
(Sikkens, Coby; Kok, Gretta; Kok, Ada; Beumer, Toos)
1970 East Germany 4:30·1
(Hofmeister, Barbara; Schuchardt, Brigitte; Lindner, Helga; Wetzko, Gabriele)

Springboard diving

1927	Bornett, Clara (Aut)	103·32
1931	Jordan, Olga (Ger)	77·00
1934	Jensch-Jordan, Olga (Ger)	74·78
1938	Slade, Betty (GB)	103·60
1947	Moreau, Mady (Fr)	100·43
1950	Moreau, Mady (Fr)	155·58
1954	Tchumitcheva, Valentyina (USSR)	129·45
1958	Krutova, Ninel (USSR)	124·22
1962	Kramer, Ingrid (EGer)	153·57
1966	Baklanova, Vera (USSR)	136·59
1970	Becker, Heidi (EGer)	420·63

Highboard diving

1927	White, Belle (GB)	36·04
1931	Epply, Madie (Aut)	34·28
1934	Schieche, Hertha (Ger)	35·43
1938	Becken, Inge (Den)	37·09
1947	Pélissard, Nicole (Fr)	60·03
1950	Pélissard, Nicole (Fr)	85·67
1954	Karakasjanz, Tatjana (USSR)	79·86
1958	Karezkaite, Aldona (USSR)	81·14
1962	Kramer, Ingrid (EGer)	107·96
1966	Kuznetsova, Natalia (USSR)	100·93
1970	Duchkova, Milena (Czech)	336·33

NATIONAL PLACINGS

Europa Cup (Best nation in men's events)
1926 Germany 132 points

1927	Germany	111	points
1931	Hungary	114	points
1934	Germany	118	points
1938	Germany	145	points
1947	Hungary	79	points
1950	France	87	points
1954	Hungary	140	points
1958	U.S.S.R.	135	points
1962	U.S.S.R.	116	points
1966	U.S.S.R.	212	points
1970	East Germany	168	points

Bredius Cup (Best nation in women's events)

1934	Netherlands	88½	points
1938	Denmark	100	points
1947	Denmark	72	points
1950	Netherlands	92	points
1954	Hungary	87	points
1958	Netherlands	123	points
1962	Netherlands	137	points
1966	U.S.S.R.	112	points
1970	East Germany	230	points

EUROPEAN CUPS. Instituted in 1969, the European Cup competitions are for men's and women's swimming teams. (There is a separate event for diving instituted in 1963.) Sixteen countries are split into 'A' and 'B' divisions and the competitions are over the full Olympic programme. One competitor per country is allowed in each individual event and one team each in the relays. The two nations who finish bottom in group 'A' are relegated and the top two in 'B' promoted.

East Germany won the men's cup (in Wurtzburg) and the women's (in Budapest(with the Soviety Union runners-up in both. Britain's men did disastrously in fihinishing 7th and were relegated along with Holland. The British women were fourth behind third-placed Hungary.

Spain won the men's 'B' contest and go up in 1971, when the cup competitions are held again, with Poland. Promoted from the women's section are Yugoslavia and Czechoslovakia who replace France and Sweden, relegated from group 'A'.

EUROPEAN RECORDS

MEN

Free-style

100 m.	52·8	Rousseau, Michael (Fra)	Barcelona	5 Sept. 1970
200 m.	1:55·2	Fassnacht, Hans (WGer)	Barcelona	9 Sept. 1970
400 m.	4:02·6	Larsson, Gunnar (Swe)	Barcelona	7 Sept. 1970
800 m.	8:41·4	Fassnacht, Hans (WGer)	Barcelona	11 Sept. 1970
1,500 m.	16:19·9	Fassnacht, Hans (WGer)	Barcelona	11 Sept. 1970
4 × 100 m.	3:32·3	National team (USSR) (Bure, Vladimir; Mazanov, Victor; Kulikov, Georgi; Ilichev, Leonid)	Barcelona	10 Sept. 1970
4 × 200 m.	7:49·5	National team (WGer) (Lampe, Werner; von Schilling, Olaf; Meeuw, Folkert; Fassnacht, Hans)	Barcelona	12 Sept. 1970

Back-stroke

| 100 m. | 56·9 | Matthes, Roland (EGer) | Barcelona | 8 Sept. 1970 |
| 200 m. | 2:06·1 | Matthes, Roland (EGer) | Barcelona | 11 Sept. 1970 |

Breast-stroke

| 100 m. | 1:05·8 | Pankin, Nicolai (USSR) | Magdeburg | 20 Apr. 1969 |
| 200 m. | 2:25·4 | Pankin, Nicolai (USSR) | Magdeburg | 19 Apr. 1969 |

Butterfly

| 100 m. | 57·5 | Lampe, Hans (WGer) | Barcelona | 7 Sept. 1970 |
| 200 m. | 2:06·9 | Fassnacht, Hans (WGer) | Los Angeles | 22 Aug. 1970 |

Medley

200m.	2:09·3	Larsson, Gunnar (Swe)	Barcelona	12 Sept. 1970
400 m.	4:36·2	Larsson, Gunnar (Swe)	Barcelona	8 Sept. 1970
4 × 100 m.	3:54·4	National team (EGer) (Matthes, Roland; Katzur, Klaus; Poser, Udo; Unger, Lutz)	Barcelona	8 Sept. 1970

WOMEN

Free-style

100 m.	59·3	Wetzko, Gabriele (EGer)	Barcelona	11 Sept. 1970
200 m.	2:08·2	Wetzko, Gabriele (EGer)	Barcelona	10 Sept. 1970
400 m.	4:32·9	Sehmisch, Elke (EGer)	Barcelona	8 Sept. 1970
800 m.	9:29·1	Neugebauer, Karin (EGer)	Barcelona	12 Sept. 1970
1,500 m.	18:11·6	Calligaris, Novella (It)	Rome	10 Sept. 1969
4 × 100 m.	4:00·8	National team (EGer) (Wetzko, Gabriele; Komor, Iris; Sehmisch, Elke; Schulze, Carola)	Barcelona	11 Sept. 1970

Back-stroke

100 m.	1:07·8	Lekveishvili, Tina (USSR)	Barcelona	6 Sept. 1970
200 m.	2:25·5	Gyarmati, Andrea (Hun)	Barcelona	10 Sept. 1970

Breast-stroke

100 m.	1:15·4	Prosumenschikova (Stepanova), Galina (USSR)	Tallin	3 Apr. 1968
200 m.	2:40·7	Stepanova, Galina (USSR)	Barcelona	11 Sept. 1970

Butterfly

100 m.	1:04·5	Kok, Ada (Neth)	Budapest	14 Aug. 1965
200 m.	2:20·2	Lindner, Helga (EGer)	Barcelona	12 Sept. 1970

Medley

200 m.	2:27·5	Grunert, Martine (EGer)	Budapest	23 Aug. 1969
400 m.	5:07·9	Stolze, Evelyn (EGer)	Barcelona	6 Sept. 1970
4 × 100 m.	4:30·1	National team (EGer) (Hofmeister, Barbara; Schuchardt, Brigitte; Lindner, Helga; Wetzko, Gabriele)	Barcelona	9 Sept. 1970

EUROPEAN SWIMMING LEAGUE. See LIGUE EUROPEENNE DE NATATION.

EUROPEAN YOUTH CHAMPION-SHIPS. European championships for boys and girls of 15 years or under were instituted in 1967. The first meeting in Linkoping, Sweden (15–15 Aug.) attracted twenty-five nations but Britain was not among them. There was a British team at the second championships in Vienna from 14–17 Aug. 1969 but the disappointing party did not win any medals. Winners:

BOYS

100 m. Free-style
1967 Grivennikov, Igor (USSR)   56·3
1969 Comas, Jorge (Sp)   55·6

400 m. Free-style
1967 Borloi, Matyas (Hun)   4:28·1
1969 Hamburg, Roger van (Neth)   4:24·7

1,500 m. Free-style
1967 Esteva, Santiago (Spa)   17:49·8
1969 Hamburg, Roger van (Neth)   17:31·1

100 m. Back-stroke
1967 Davidov, Grigory (USSR) 1:03·0
1969 Milos, Predrag (Yugo)   1:04·9

200 m. Back-stroke
1967 Davidov, Grigory (USSR) 2:16·2
1969 Nistri, Massimo (Ita)   2:19·0

100 m. Breast-stroke
1967 Ivanov, Sergei (USSR)   1:13·5
1969 Poljakov, Alexander
                       (USSR)   1:12·0

200 m. Breast-stroke
1967 Turpe, Bertram (EGer)   2:37·6
1969 Hargittai, Andras (Hun)   2:38·2

100 m. Butterfly
1967 Cseh, Laszlo (Hun)   1:01·9
1969 Lenarczyk, Udo (WGer)   1:01·0

200 m. Butterfly
1967 Freygang, Roland (EGer) 2:22·1
1969 Shestopalov, Vladimir
                       (USSR)   2:18·9

200 m. Individual medley
1967 Davidov, Grigory (USSR) 2:19·2
1969 Hargittai, Andras (Hun)   2:21·5

Springboard diving
1969 Lieberum, Hans (EGer)   334·20

GIRLS

100 m. Free-style
1967 Grebets, Lidia (USSR)   1:02·6
1969 Wetzko, Gabriele (EGer)   1:00·1

400 m. Free-style
1967 Kock, Vera (Swe)   4:55·2
1969 Wetzko, Gabriele (EGer)   4:36·1

800 m. Free-style
1967 Kock, Vera (Swe)   10:13·4
1969 Neugebauer, Karin (EGer) 9:30·8

100 m. Back-stroke
1967 Steinbach, Sabine (EGer) 1:11·1
1969 Gyarmati, Andrea (Hun)   1:09·1

200 m. Back-stroke
1967 Hammarsten, Britt-Marie
                       (Swe)   2:34·4
1969 Hofmeister, Barbara
                       (EGer)   2:28·1

100 m. Breast-stroke
1967 Pozdnyakova, Irina
                       (USSR)   1:19·4
1969 Rusanova, Lydia (USSR)   1:19·1

200 m. Breast-stroke
1967 Pozdnyakova, Irina
                       (USSR)   2:47·0
1969 Rusanova Lydia (USSR)   2:50·5

100 m. Butterfly
1967 Gyarmati, Andrea (Hun)   1:10·1
1969 Gyarmati, Andrea (Hun)   1:06·1

200 m. Butterfly
1967 Steinbach, Sabine (EGer) 2:31.0
1969 Stolze, Evelyn (EGer)   2:33·7

200 m. Individual medley
1967 Steinbach, Sabine (EGer) 2:32·0
1969 Schuchardt, Brigitte
                       (EGer)   2:32·3

Springboard diving
1969 Semina, Alla (USSR)   313·47

F

FARRELL, Jeff (United States, 28 Feb. 1937–). An appendicectomy six days before the American Olympic trials of 1960 should have ended Jeff Farrell's medal ambitions. But this naval officer did not give up. He was out of bed within twenty-four hours, training within three days, competed in the trials, and though he 'failed' to win an individual event place he was picked for the relays.

In Rome he swam as anchor man in the 4 × 200 m. free-style and 4 × 100 m. medley and brought his squad home first in world record times of 8:10·2 and 4:05·4. The 1959 Pan American 100 m. champion (56·3), the Olympic sprint gold could well have been Farrell's had not fate intervened. His medley relay split was an unpressed 54·9 as the Americans beat Australia by 6.6 seconds, as against John Devitt's 100 m. winning time of 55·2.

FASSNACHT, Hans (West Germany, 28 Nov. 1950–). One of the new breed of American-trained Europeans, Hans Fassnacht stepped from relative obscurity to a world record-breaker in a matter of eight months . . . from a seventh place in the 1968 Olympic 400 m. (4:18·1) to a world record 4:04·0 in Louisville on 14 Aug. 1969. This stood until the following August, when John Kinsella (USA) clocked 2:02·8.

As a member of the Don Gambril squad at California State College, Fassnacht trains on what he calls 'hard sprints', but which, in fact are 15 × 400 m. repetitions with 10 seconds' rest, or 5 × 1,500 m., finishing with his fastest time on his fifth swim. He did 12–15 kilometres a day, seven days a week. In 1969 this work brought him, as well as his world record, European free-style

records for 200 m. (1:56·5), 1,500 m. (16:32·1) and for 400 m. medley (4:42·5). Despite collapsing during an air flight in 1970, when he had difficulty in breathing, Fassnacht was soon back in the water . . . covering 18 kilometres a day!

In the 1966 European championships in Utrecht, the West German was fifth in the 1,500 m. (17:28·6). At the 1970 Europeans in Barcelona Fassnacht was considerably more successful.

His medal tally was three golds and three silvers. He won the 200 m. free-style in 1:55·2 and the 1,500 m. in 16:19·9—both European records—and, en route for the longer distance, he also broke the European record for 800 m. with 8:41·4. And he helped West Germany to a European record-breaking victory in the 4 × 200 m. free-style relay with a remarkable anchor leg 'split' of 1:54·4.

Fassnacht's silvers came in the 400 m. free-style (in which he lost his European record to Gunnar Larsson of Sweden but, in clocking 4:03·0, put up the third best time of all time), the 400 m. medley and the 4 × 100 m. free-style.

Two weeks before these European championships in Barcelona, Fassnacht had shown his tremendous versatility by breaking the European record for 200 m. butterfly in clocking 2:06·9 in the American championships.

FEDERATION INTERNATIONALE DE NATATION AMATEUR. F.I.N.A., the world governing body for swimming, were founded in London, during the 1908 Olympic Games, by accident rather than design. The initiative came from an Englishman, George W. Hearn (see HEARN, GEORGE W.), then President of the A.S.A., who thought this was a good opportunity to talk over the problems of the sport, particularly about amateurism. What resulted was an official world federation.

Eight nations were represented at the historic founding-day meeting at the Manchester Hotel, on 14 July—Belgium, Denmark, Finland, France, Germany, Great Britain and Ireland, Hungary and Sweden. Of those present, R. Max Ritter, now an American citizen but at that time representing Germany, was still actively concerned with swimming administration in 1970. The first aims of F.I.N.A. were to draw up rules for the conduct of swimming, diving and water-polo events, to set up world record lists and to take on the responsibility for the organization of the swimming events at Olympic Games.

Now the influence and power that F.I.N.A. exert over swimming are un-challenged and no international contests can be organized except under the laws of the Federation. From eight, the F.I.N.A. membership has grown to almost 100 affiliated countries, the only world power not included being Com-munist China. The official languages of the Federation are English and French but in the case of interpretation of rules the English text is accepted. Yet the Federation is known by its French title and not the English version of the Inter-national Amateur Swimming Federation. (See INTERNATIONAL TECHNICAL COM-MITTEES.)

The F.I.N.A. officers elected in Mexico, in 1968, to serve for four years, are: President: Lic. J. Ostos (Mexico); Hon. Secretary: Dr. Harold Henning (USA); Hon. Treasurer: Ante Lambasa (Yugoslavia).

FERGUSON, Cathy Jean (United States, 17 July 1948–). There were six world record-breakers in the line-up for the final of the 1964 Olympic 100 m. back-stroke in Tokyo, but after a world record-breaking 67·7 seconds, the freckle-faced Californian Cathy Ferguson emerged as Olympic champion. The beaten record-breakers were Christine Caron (France), Ginny Duenkel (USA), Sato Tanaka (Japan) and Linda Lud-grove and Jill Norfolk (GB). The sixth was Miss Ferguson.

That individual performance gave the tall (5 ft 8 in.) and slim high school girl from Burbank the back-stroke berth in the United States medley relay squad— and another gold.

A product of the United States age-group competitive system, Miss Fer-guson's career took in age-group records from 11 years upwards. In four seasons she improved her 100 m. back-stroke by 8·4 seconds to her Tokyo world record and her 200 m. time came down by 7·6 to a world record 2:27·4 in a single year.

FERN, Harold E. (Great Britain, Apr. 1881–). The end of an era probably unparalleled in sports administration came in March, 1970 when Harold Fern retired after 49 years as honorary secre-tary of the A.S.A. No sports governing body in the world has received service to approach the length and quality given to swimming by Alderman Fern.

Honorary secretary of the Southern District in 1905, at 24, he held this office until his election as England's top administrator in 1921. Fern was elected President of F.I.N.A. in 1936 and held this office through World War II until 1948. Between 1940 and 1946 he was also honorary secretary and treasurer and he was treasurer again from 1948–60. He is now the only life president of F.I.N.A. and also of the L.E.N.

The number of affiliated clubs in-creased almost 100 per cent—from 875 to 1,629—during his years in office, and the financial assets from £339 18s. 2d. in 1921 to more than £140,000, making the A.S.A. one of the wealthiest amateur governing bodies in Britain.

For his services to swimming and to the Hertfordshire County Council, of which he was a member for fifty years, Fern has been honoured with both an O.B.E. and a C.B.E., but his real acco-lade is the healthy state of his association as he left it.

FERN, Harold, National Trophy. This trophy was presented to the A.S.A. in 1961 by Alderman Harold Fern (see

FERN, HAROLD) to enable a national award for women's clubs to be instituted on similar lines to the top men's club award (see BENJAMIN, HENRY, MEMORIAL TROPHY) which had been in existence since 1910.

Points are awarded for success in A.S.A. swimming championships— individual events, winner 4, second 3, third 2, unplaced standard time 1 and relays, 5, 3, 2 and other competing teams 1. Not more than three entries or one team in each event from any one club may score and the award is open to English women's clubs or women's sections of mixed clubs. Winners:

1962	Hampstead Ladies	21 points
1963	Hampstead Ladies	27 points
1964	Beckenham Ladies/	
	Stoke Newington (tie)	24 points
1965	Beckenham Ladies	26 points
1966	Beckenham Ladies	33 points
1967	York City Bath	31 points
1968	Beckenham Ladies	24 points
1969	Beckenham Ladies	21 points
1970	Beckenham Ladies	21 points

FERRIS, Elizabeth (Great Britain, 19 Nov. 1940–). The first Briton to win an Olympic diving medal in thirty-six years, Elizabeth Ferris of London took the bronze for springboard diving at the 1960 Rome Games. It was a somewhat unexpected success for Liz was not renowned for her consistency. But on that sunny day in the beautiful outdoor Stadio del Nuoto in Rome, she survived even a hold up before her vital last dive to win third place by just over one mark.

Runner-up to Australia's Sue Knight in the 1962 Commonwealth springboard, Elizabeth won five A.S.A. titles —3 m. springboard 1960 and '62, 1 m. springboard 1957, highboard plain 1959/60. A doctor of medicine and after a short spell in hospital work, Dr. Ferris became scientific adviser to television and documentary film companies.

FLETCHER, Jennie (Great Britain, 1890–1967). Miss Fletcher from Leicester was Britain's first woman Olympic medallist. She won the bronze behind two Australians in the 100 m. in Stock-

holm in 1912 (1:27·0)—the first time events for women had been included— and was a member of the British squad who won the relay by 12 sec. from Germany. She was six times A.S.A. 100 y. champion, from 1906–09 and 1911–12, her fastest time being in 1909 (1:14·0).

FRASER, Dawn (Australia, Sept. 1937–). It would take a book—and she has written one—to do justice to Dawn Fraser, the queen of swimming and the only pool competitor to win the same Olympic title—100 m. free-style—at three successive Games. An independent stormy petrel, who had more than one clash with officialdom, her final punishment of ten years' suspension for misbehaviour during the 1964 Olympics was hardly the reward Australian swimming circles owed their greatest champion. The high-handed undemocratic way in which the Australian A.S.U. treated Miss Fraser in 1964 shocked the sporting world. It came shortly after the 27-year-old star had been named 'Australian of the Year' and been honoured with a ceremonial drive around Melbourne race-course on one of the big race days. Two of the incidents in which she was involved were appearing in the parade at the opening cremony against orders, because of her early races, and being involved in a Japanese flag-purloining prank, but she, along with the other three disciplined swimmers, was not allowed to appear in her own defence.

Miss Fraser, sprinter extraordinary, won her first Olympic 100 m. gold in 1956 when she beat her team-mate Lorraine Crapp by 0·3 in a world record 62·0. Superb form in Rome, four years later, enabled her to keep her crown, clocking 61·2, finishing 3 yards ahead of America's Christ von Saltza. And she wrote her final piece of history in Tokyo on 13 Oct. 1964, when she came home 0·4 ahead of Sharon Stouder (USA) in 59·5.

She reached the 400 m. final in each of these Games, coming second to Miss Crapp in 1956 (5:02·5), fifth in 1960 (4:58·3) and fourth in 1964 in her fastest

4:47·6. And she collected four relay medals—free-style gold in Melbourne, free-style and medley silvers in Rome and a free-style silver in Tokyo.

Dawn, originally from Adelaide, was the first woman to break the minute for 100 m. and 110 y. and her twenty-seven individual world records included nine successive marks for 100 m. In her remarkable ten-year career, Miss Fraser won eight Commonwealth medals, six of them gold—110 y. (1958/62), 440 y. (1962), 4 × 110 y. free-style (1958/62) and medley relay (1962)—plus two silvers in the 440 y. and medley relay in 1958.

She won twenty-three Australian titles—the 100 m. (7 times) and 200 m. (8), 400 m. (5), 100 m. butterfly (2) and 200 m. medley (1). The best of her many world record times were: 100 y. (56·9), 100 m. (58·9), 110 y. (59·5), 200 m. and 220 y. (2:11·6).

FREE-STYLE. There are no special rules for free-style swimming, in fact, the words mean exactly what they say—that the style is the free choice of the competitor, But in modern usage, the free choice in free-style is almost always front crawl, the fastest stroke in the water. Only in the context of medley races, individual and relay, is there a special regulation concerning free-style. And it is a negative ruling. It says that free-style is any style other than butterfly, breast-stroke or back-stroke; which, again, means that free-style is front crawl.

FRONT CRAWL. The fastest means of swimming propulsion, the front crawl, is not mentioned in the rule book of F.I.N.A. This is a strange anomaly for there are more races and records for front crawl swimmers than for any other style, but they all come under the heading of free-style (see FREE-STYLE).

The have been many stages in the development of the front crawl, with its alternating arm stroke and six-beat leg kick. There was side stroke and then the English overarm or side over arm which were developments from the breast-stroke. By changing position from prone to side the swimmer could lift one arm out over the water on recovery thus speeding his action. The leg movement changed too, the principles of prone frog kick becoming a side-on scissor blades action.

The trudgen, demonstrated by John Trudgen in London in 1873, was the first style in which both arms were re-covered over the water. There were many faults in Trudgen's technique, but the Australians refined this style and their Richard Cavill, using a vertical leg action, bending from the knee, pioneered the Australian crawl. The United States improved the leg kick—after experiment-ing with eight- and even twelve-beat actions, they settled for the six-beat—and breathing techniques and the em-bryo of the 'modern' American crawl, now used the world over, was born.

FURUHASHI, Hironashin (Japan, 16 Sept. 1928–). Japan's Hironashin Furuhashi was known as the 'Flying Fish' not, as most people thought, be-cause of his undoubted speed in the water but because he belonged to the Tobiuo swimming club in Tokyo and 'Tobiuo' means 'Flying Fish' in Japanese. The world's greatest middle and long distance free-styler in 1948/49, Furu-hashi never won an Olympic medal. The reason was that Japan, not yet admitted to re-membership of F.I.N.A. after World War II, were excluded from the 1948 Games.

The Japanese had their own way of dealing with this situation. Within minutes of America's Jimmy McLane winning the Olympic 1,500 m. gold medal in London in 19:18·5, news came that Furuhashi had taken 21·8 seconds off the ten-year-old world record of his compatriot Tomikatsu Amano with a time of 18:37·0. Another 'flash' brought the news that Furuhashi had clipped 2·2 from the world 400 m. mark with 4:33·0 which was eight seconds better than the winning time of Bill Smith (USA) in London.

A most unorthodox swimmer, with a deep, rolling style and trailing one leg, Furuhashi's 1948 world best times were not ratified because Japan were not in good standing with F.I.N.A. But he went on to break six official world records—two for 400 m. (best 4:33·3), three for 800 m. (finally 9:35·5) and 1,500 m. (18:19·0). This last mark stood for seven years.

Although Japan were allowed to take part in the 1952 Olympics, Furuhashi, now 24, was past his peak and eighth and last in the 400 m. final was his lone claim to Olympic fame. A graduate of Nihon University in Tokyo, Furuhashi is an assistant professor of athletics at the university and a member of the Japanese Olympic Committee and the F.I.N.A.

FURUKAWA, Masaru (Japan, 6 Jan. 1936–   ). Furukawa's career at the top of the world breast-stroke rankings (1954–56) coincided with the brief era when swimming long distances under-water—pioneered by the Japanese—was permitted. And a change of the F.I.N.A. rules prohibiting under-water swimming swept this Nihon University student out of the world rankings almost as quickly as he had gone into them.

Breast-stroke and butterfly were made separate strokes in 1952. Then, in search for speed, some breast-stroke swimmers discovered the advantages of racing great distances under water. Furukawa, with his big lung capacity, exploited this loop-hole in the laws brilliantly.

Twice on the same day he broke the world 200 m. record (10 April 1954). But his remarkable day was 1 October 1955 when he broke all four world records in two swims in one afternoon. In Tokyo, Furukawa set new figures for 200 m. and 220 y. (2:31·0 and 2:31·9) by taking his first breath at the 25 m. turn, breathing again just before the second turn and taking only three breaths on each of his other six laps. Later he swam 100 y. and 100 m. in 61·4 and 68·2 taking only five breaths during the whole of the race.

His only long course world record was in August 1955 when he swam 200 m. in 2:33·7. It took six years for a competitor (Chet Jastremski, USA) swimming on the surface to better this time by a tenth.

Furukawa won the Olympic 200 m. title in 1956 but at the end of the Melbourne Games F.I.N.A. put an end to the under-water era and an end, too, to Furukawa's time at the top.

G

GATHERCOLE, Terry (Australia, 1935 –). Gathercole, from Sydney, was the world's best for breast-stroke in the years immediately following the separation of butterfly from breast-stroke and the ruling out of under-water swimming (see BREAST-STROKE). His effective time at the top covered two months, June and July of 1958 when, at 23, he set six world records, won the Commonwealth 220 y. title and a second gold in the medley relay in the Cardiff Games.

His best times set on 28 June 1958—1:12·4 (110 y.) and 2:35·5 (200 m. and 220 y.)—stood in the world record book until 1961 when America's Chet Jastremski made substantial inroads into the Australian's times.

Gathercole swam in two Olympics. In 1956 he was fourth in the 200 m. breast-stroke in 2:38·7, four seconds behind the winner, under-water expert Masaru Furukawa. In Rome in 1960 he was sixth (2:40·2), but won a silver medal in the medley relay which was in the Olympic programme for the first time.

A former plumber, Gathercole turned to coaching and was the Australian women's team coach at the 1964 Olympics and 1966 Commonwealth Games.

GERRARD, David (New Zealand, 3 Apr. 1945–). Gerrard, from Otago, was New Zealand's only swimming gold medallist at the 1966 Commonwealth Games where he was a surprise first in the 220 y. butterfly in 2:12·7. His butterfly leg also helped his team to the bronze medals in the medley relay and he was sixth (62·1) in the 110 y. Four years earlier Gerrard had been a medalless finalist in both butterfly events at the Perth Commonwealth Games.

In his only Olympic appearance—

Tokyo, 1964—the New Zealander did well to reach the semi-finals of the 200 m. butterfly. He won his first national 220 y. title in 1960 when only 14 and retained it for nine successive years until his retirement in 1969. He was also six times sprint butterfly champion.

GESTRING, Marjorie (United States, 18 Nov. 1922–). The youngest competitor to win an Olympic title in the pool, Marjorie Gestring was only 13 years and 9 months in early August 1936 when she came first in the springboard diving in Berlin. A tall, slim and graceful girl, Marjorie, from Los Angeles, beat her team mate Katherine Rawls, four years her senior, by less than one point. Now Mrs. Bowman, she lives in Honolulu.

GIBSON, Cathy (Great Britain, 25 Mar. 1931–). Winner of Britain's only swimming medal, a bronze for 400 m. free-style, at the 1948 Olympics, Cathy Gibson was also a talented back-stroker. In fact, she only missed the final of the London Games back-stroke by two-tenths and was a member of the British 4 × 100 m. free-style squad who were fourth.

Cathy was 16, in 1947, when she came second in the European 400 m. free-style (5:19·0) and 100 m. back-stroke (1:16·5) in Monte Carlo, losing narrowly each time to Denmark's 1948 Olympic back-stroke champion Karen Harup. Strangely, the Motherwell girl never swam in a Commonwealth Games.

She won five A.S.A. titles—220 and 440 y. (1947/48) and 100 y. back-stroke (1947)—and sixteen Scottish ones, including the 200 y. free-style six times

79

between 1946–52. Her best Scottish record times were 60·9 (100 y.), 2:31·5 (220 y.), 5:29·9 (440 y.), 12:5·2 (880 y.), 24:55·6 (one mile), and 1:09·5 (100 y. back-stroke). Long course she clocked 2:29·2 (220 y.), 5:23·2 (440 y.) and 1:10·4 (100 y. back-stroke).

GORDON, Elenor (Great Britain, 10 May 1934–). Helen Orr Gordon, known as Elenor, from Hamilton was one of Scotland's outstanding women swimmers in the 1950s' Her bronze medal in the 200 m. breast-stroke (2:57·6) at the 1952 Olympics was the highlight of her career but she also won the Commonwealth 220 y. titles in 1950 and '54, a medley relay bronze in 1950 and an unexpected medley relay gold in 1954—the first and only time a Scottish squad had won a relay title.

She first swam for Britain, age 13, at the 1947 European championship, appeared in three Olympics (1948, '52, 56), placing sixth in the 200 m. breast-stroke in Melbourne, and in two Commonwealth Games. She would have had one more European badge had not Britain decided not to enter the 1950 championships in Austria because of Russian occupation of Vienna.

This pretty and petite, dark-haired girl won five A.S.A. breast-stroke titles between 1950–56 and was undefeated in the Scottish championships from 1947–57 (eleven years). She was able to stay at the top for such a long time because she insisted on an annual holiday away from swimming, turning down, if necessary, exciting invitations abroad. Her best British records, all short course, were 1:24·5 (110 y.), 2:38·2 (200 y.) and 2:58·8 (220 y.).

GOULD, Phillipa (New Zealand). New Zealand's only world record-breaker, Phillipa Gould was the first holder of the 220 y. back-stroke mark with her 2:39·9 on 16 Jan. 1957, set within days of this distance coming into the record book. This time, which only stood for five months, was also a world record for 200 m. For a brief spell, one month and one

week in fact, she also held the 100 m. and 110 y. marks with 1:12·5.

Phillipa was one of six New Zealand swimmers at the 1956 Olympic Games, but failed to reach the back-stroke final. Two years later, at the Cardiff Commonwealth Games, she came third, behind Olympic gold and and bronze medal winners Judy Grinham and Margaret Edwards of England, in the 110 y. back-stroke.

Essentially a back-stroke swimmer, the Auckland girl's short career took in five New Zealand titles—110 y. (1957/58) and 220 y. (1956–58).

GREAT BRITAIN COMMITTEE. The major part of the organization and administration of swimming in Britain is the autonomous responsibility of the separate amateur associations of England, Scotland and Wales. The responsibility for British affairs, almost exclusively the participation of Great Britain teams in the Olympic Games, European championships and other international contests, is in the hands of a Great Britain committee on which sit representatives of the three home A.S.A.s, with England, the largest, having the majority.

This 'House of Lords' set-up, without any real system of reference back to the 'Commons' of the three Associations, has caused a great deal of discontent, but abortive efforts over many years to create a better system of British swimming government have not been particularly successful.

The Great Britain Committee have no funds of their own, the expenses being shared pro-rata by the three associations according to their individual participation. Again, it is England, who provide the bulk of the swimmers in British teams, bearing the brunt of the cost.

GRINHAM, Judy (Great Britain, 5 Mar. 1939–). The first Briton to win an Olympic swimming gold medal for thirty-two years, Judith Brenda Grinham—but always known as Judy—stepped into a new world on 5 Dec. 1956 when, at 17, she won the 100 m. back-stroke in Melbourne. Lucy Morton had been the last British Olympic champion, way back in 1924, and Judy's Melbourne victory ended starvation time and opened up a new era for her country.

This win, in fact, was just the beginning of an amazing career for this unsophisticated but determined girl from Neasden, who went on to take the back-stroke golds at the 1958 Commonwealth Games and European championships—the first time this kind of hat-trick had been achieved. That year Judy also won a gold in England's world record-breaking medley relay team and a bronze in the free-style relay in Cardiff. And in the Budapest European championships, she added to her medal store with a 100 m. free-style bronze—one of her proudest achievements—and a silver and bronze in the free-style and medley relays respectively.

Her Olympic winning time of 1:12·9 became the first long course world record for 100 m. back-stroke. Later she cut this to 1:11·9, a time which was also a world mark for the two feet longer 110 y.

Judy won three A.S.A. back-stroke titles (1955, '56, '58) while her brief excursion into the free-style field, because she was sick of back-stroke, brought her the National 220 y. title in 1957 and the 110 y. crown in 1958.

For her Melbourne achievements, Judy was voted Britain's sportswoman of 1956. Many thought her swimming achievements were worthy also of a place in a Royal honours list. Unfortunately her era was just before awards to sports stars became commonplace.

Judy Grinham retired from competition on her twentieth birthday, already a legend and one that will remain for ever in British, if not world, swimming history.

GYARMATI FAMILY (Hungary).
Dezso (24 Oct. 1927), Eva (3 Apr. 1927) and their daughter Andrea (15 May 1954) are perhaps the most remarkable swimming family in the world.

Father Dezso ranks among the

greatest of water-polo players. He won medals at five Olympics—golds in 1952, 1956 and 1964, a silver in 1948 and a bronze in 1960. He was a member of Hungary's European champion teams of 1954 and 1962. He could play as well with his right hand as his left, and at back as well as forward.

Mother Eva Szekely (always known in the swimming world by her maiden name) was in the 1948, '52 and '56 Games. She was Olympic breast-stroke champion (using the over water arm recovery before the division of butterfly) and sixth in the 400 m. free-style in 1952. Four years later, using the orthodox underwater arm recovery, she came second in the 200 m. breast-stroke. Runner-up in the European 200 m. breast-stroke in 1947, world record-holder for 100 m. breast-stroke (1:16·9—using butterfly) and 400 m. medley (5:40·8), versatile Eva won twenty-nine Hungarian titles.

Daughter Andrea has taken the best from each of her parents. She has her father's passionate love for the water. Her mother, who is her coach, has handed down determination and application.

Andrea's first success came at 13, when she won the European Youth 100 m. butterfly title. A year later, at the 1968 Olympic Games she was fifth in the 100 m. back-stroke and butterfly. And a year after this, she retained her Youth butterfly title and was also first in the 100 m. back-stroke.

The year of 1970 brought the third Gyarmati swimmer gold medals in her own right. In the European championships in Barcelona, this delightful daughter of charming and successful parents won the 200 m. back-stroke in a European record of 2:25·5 and the 100 m. butterfly in 65·0. She was also second in the 100 m. back-stroke and swam the first leg (60·3) in Hungary's 4 × 100 m. silver medal free-style relay team.

GUNDLING, Beulah (United States).
The high priestess of synchronized swimming and Pan American solo champion

F

in 1955, Mrs. Gundling and her husband Henry, founders of the International Academy of Aquatic Art, played a most important part in popularising this artistic branch of water sport. They travelled the world giving lectures and demonstrations and their efforts were rewarded in 1952 when F.I.N.A. accepted synchronized swimming as one of their official activities.

H

HADDON, Vivien (New Zealand, 14 Aug. 1945–). Many people believe that Vivien Haddon and not England's Anita Lonsbrough won the 110 y. breast-stroke title at the 1962 Commonwealth Games. The judges thought otherwise and awarded the gold to the Briton, though the girls were given the same time (1:21·3). The student teacher from Auckland also won the bronze in the 220 y. (2:56·3) in this her first major competition.

Miss Haddon's luck was out again at the 1964 Olympics in Tokyo where, as half of the NZ one man/one woman team, she narrowly missed qualifying for the 200 m. final. And it was third time unfortunate in Jamaica in 1966. The New Zealander set a Commonwealth Games record of 1:19·7 in a heat of the 110 y. and though England's Diana Harris only equalled this mark in winning the final, Miss Haddon came fourth in 1:21·9. She was third, again, in the 220 y.

The Kiwi won eight New Zealand titles, the 110 y. and 220 y. in each of 1962–64 and '66 (she did not swim in 1965). Her best furlong time was 2:51·9 in 1964.

HAJOS, Alfred (Hungary, 1 Feb. 1878– 12 Nov. 1955). The first Olympic swimming champion, Alfred Hajos won two out of the three golds (100 and 1,200 m.) at the Athens Games of 1896. Born Arnold Guttmann, in Budapest, his swimming pseudonym eventually became his legal name. A noted architect, Hajos designed the indoor pool on Margaret Island in the Danube, dividing Buda and Pest, and many other stadia and hydrophatic installations. Twice a member of the Hungarian national soccer team, Hajos won the silver medal for sports architecture at the 1924 Olympics (the first prize was not awarded) and was elected to the Fort Lauderdale Hall of Fame in 1966.

No world records were ratified in his day and Hajos's Olympic winning time of 1:22·2 for 100 m. did not compare with the 61·4 of England's Jack Tyers (who did not swim in Athens) in taking the A.S.A. 100 y. title that year. But the Hungarian's 18:22·2 for 1,200 m., in beating Antoine Papanos of Greece by 1:41·2, was infinitely superior to the performances by English distance swimmers.

HALASY, Oliver (Hungary, 31 July 1909–10 Sept. 1946). Born Haltmayer, in Ujpest, just north of Budapest, Halasy lost his left foot in a childhood tramway accident, yet became the world's best water-polo half-back of the 1930s' An auditor by profession, Halasy was a member of the Hungarian gold medal teams at the 1932 and '36 Olympics, having won a water-polo silver in 1928, and won more golds at the European championships of 1931, '34 and '38. He also took the European 1,500 m. free-style in 1931 (20:49·0) and twenty-five Hungarian individual swimming titles. Halasy was shot dead while returning to his home by taxi late at night when only 37.

HALE, Jack (Great Britain, 1923–). Jack Hale from Hull was originally a free-styler, but his chief contribution to swimming and his best racing success came at the end of his career with his peioneering experiments with the butterfly dolphin leg kick. Though Hale's undulating style did not stay in vogue very long, it was an important development towards the stroke as it is swum to-day. Using the dolphin, Hale was fourth in the European 200 m. butterfly in 1954, fifteen years after he had won his first A.S.A. title—the free-style long distance five mile race in the River Thames. He took the long distance title again in 1947, was 440 and 880 y. and one mile champion from 1946–48 and 220 y. winner in 1947/48, and 220 y. butterfly gold medallist in 1954. His best times were: 2:16·4 (220 y.), 4:56·2 (440 y.), 10:27·4 (880 y.), 21:25·2 (one mile) and 2:39·5 (220 y. butterfly).

He also demonstrated his versatility by swimming the back-stroke leg in England's winning medley relay team at the 1950 Commonwealth Games.

HALL, Gary (United States, 7 Aug. 1951–). World record breaking is always a surprise but in relation to Gary Hall's decimation of the 400 m. medley figures in 1969, astonishment was a mild word. The Californian took three-tenths off the year-old mark of his fellow America, Olympic champion Charles Hickcox and in clocking 4:38·7 was ten seconds faster than his own silver medal time in Mexico. Five weeks later he improved 4·8 secs to 4:33·9. The same summer Hall broke the world records for 200 m. back-stroke and medley with 2:06·6 and 2:09·6 respectively.

Hall's versatile talent takes in a 4:08·5 for 400 m. free-style and 1,500 m. in 16:32·8—both in the world's top ten of all time.

In August, 1970, Hall demonstrated his all-round swimming ability further, by breaking the world record for 200 m. butterfly, in the American championships, with 2:05·0. At the same meeting he reduced his 200 m. medley time to 2:09·5 (but this world mark was beaten two weeks later by Sweden's Gunnar Larsson in the European championships) and the 400 m. medley world record to 4:31·0.

HALL OF FAME. Founded in 1965 to further the interests of all aquatic activities and to honour outstanding personalities in swimming, the Hall of Fame is a non profit-making educational corporation. The citizens of Fort Lauder-

dale, Florida, collected $1,190,000 to pay for the building of the vast hall and the 50 m. swimming pool. There is an annual festival at Christmas when the Hall of Fame is visited by many of the world's greatest competitors and enthusiasts. It is at this time that the honour ceremonies take place.

Many Americans, of course, have been elected to the Hall of Fame, but those honoured from other countries include:
1965—Austalian swimmers Dawn Fraser and Murray Rose.
1966—Swimmers Alfred Hajos (Hungary), Ragnhild Hveger (Denmark) and Arne Borg (Sweden).
1967—Britain's Olympic swimming and water-polo gold medallist, Paul Radmilovic and Australia's Frank Beaurepaire and Fanny Durack.
1968—Canada's George Hodgson, John Jarvis of Britain and David Theile, all Olympic swimming champions.
1969—Swimmers Freddy Lane and Barney Kieran (Australia) and Henry Taylor (Great Britain).

HALMAY, Zoltan (Hungary, 18 June 1881–20 May 1956). Wrongly listed in many history books as de Halmay or von Halmay, Zoltan Halmay's swimming talents covered the whole range of events from 50 y. to 4,000 m. Between 1900 and 1908 he won seven Olympic medals at three Games—two silvers (200 and 4,000 m.) and a bronze (1,000 m.) in 1900, two golds (50 and 100 y.) in 1904 and two silvers (100 and 4 × 200 m.) in 1908. He also won the silver for 100 m. at the 1906 Interim Games and was the first world record-holder for this distance. His 65·8 set on 3 Dec. 1905 stood for 4½ years.

Halmay, a factory manager from Budapest, was involved in a row and an historic swim-off before being acclaimed winner of the Olympic 50 y. in St. Louis. In the final, he appeared to have beaten his American rival Scott Leary by a foot, but the judges were split on who was first. A bath-side brawl involving everyone in sight was resolved by the chairman of the jury who ruled the two men

would race again. This time Halmay
made no mistake and won by 0·6 in 28·0
sec.

His Olympic medal-winning times—
100 y. 62·8, 200 m. 2:31·0, 1,000 m.
15:16·4 and 4,000 68:55·4—were miracu-
lous in their era. And he did all. this
swimming with arms only and without
any leg movements.

HARDING, Phyllis (Great Britain, 15
Dec. 1907–). An outstanding back-
stroker, Phyl Harding is the only woman
swimmer to have competed at four
Olympic Games. She was second in the
100 m. (1:27·4) in 1924 at 17. She was
unplaced in 1928, but four years later
came fourth behind Britain's bronze
medal winner Valerie Davies. And in
1936, in Berlin, she was seventh in the
final in her fastest 1:21·5.

Her three European championship
appearances included bronzes in 1927—
the first year women's events were in the
programme—and 1931 and fourth in
1934. The Commonwealth Games did
not begin until Miss Harding's seventh
international season. At the 1930 first
meeting she was third in the 100 y. and
in 1934, at 26, she won a gold in 1:13·8
and also a silver in the medley relay.

Miss Harding's astonishing career
brought her only two A.S.A. titles
(1935/36) but, of course, her twelve years
at the top were also those of three other
great British swimmers—Joyce Cooper,
Valerie Davies and Ellen King—who
themselves were Olympic back-stroke
medallists.

HARRIS, Diana (Great Britain, 14 Aug.
1948–). Commonwealth 110 y. breast-
stroke champion in 1966 and winner of
the World Student 100 m. title in 1967—
the only non-American to gain a gold in
the Tokyo pool—the talented but erratic
Miss Harris was three times A.S.A. 110
y. champion (1965, '66, '68).

Art student Diana was one of the three
Beckenham Club members who were in
the England medley relay team who
broke the world 4 × 110 y. y. record in
winning the Commonwealth title in 1966.
(The others were Linda Ludgrove and

Judy Gegan). Her best times were
1:17·3 (100 m.), 1:17·6 (110 y.), 2:50·0
(200 m.) and 2:51·3 (220 y.). An Olympic
representative in 1968, she had the fastest
time of the three British competitors in
the 100 m. semi-finals, but did not
qualify for the final. And she did not
qualify for the final again in defence of
her Commonwealth title in Edinburgh
in 1970 having been disqualified for
taking more than the permitted one
under-water stroke at the turn.

HARRISON, Dorothy (Great Britain, 16
Mar. 1950–). In this sport in which
kids are kings, quiet Dorothy Harrison,
from Hartlepool, could be considered to
be a late developer. It was something of
a surprise in 1968 when she won her
place, at 18, in the British team for the
Mexico Olympics and her 100 and 200
m. breast-stroke times (1:19·6 and
2:55·1) did not get her past the heats.
But the next year she won the A.S.A.
220 y. title in 2:50·0 and early in 1970
broke the British 200 m. record with
2:46·8 in Bussum, Holland.

In the 1970 Commonwealth Games,
Dorothy won two silver medals for the
100 and 200 m. breast-stroke, behind
Australia's Beverley Whitfield. But her
big success in 1970 was in the European
championships, in Barcelona, where she
reduced her British record to 2:45·6 in
winning the bronze medal for 200 m.
She was fourth in the 100 m., also in a
British record of 1:17·0.

HARRISON, Joan (South Africa, 1947–
). South Africa's only Olympic swimming champion, Joan Harrison's win in
the 100 m. back-stroke (1:14·3—a
Games record) in 1952 so excited her
team manager Alex Bulley that he collapsed as she touched first. And in that
Helsinki Olympics she came close to a
second gold medal for free-style. This
100 m. final was a dramatic affair with
the South Africa one of three different
leaders in the last 10 m. In the end, Joan
was placed fourth in 67·1, a time also
given to the third and fifth swimmers,
only three-tenths behind Hungarian
winner Katalin Szoke.

Joan was only 13, in 1950, when she took the Commonwealth 440 y. title in 5:26·4, more than seven seconds ahead of England's Margaret Wellington and came third in the 110 y. (70·7) in Auckland. Her final successes came in the 1954 Commonwealth Games in Vancouver where she won two golds (110 y. back-stroke and free-style relay) a silver (medley relay) and a bronze (110 y. free-style). But like many great racers, Joan Harrison never broke a world record.

HATFIELD, Jack (Great Britain, 15 Aug. 1893–1965). John Gatenby Hatfield, but known as Jack in the swimming world, won forty A.S.A. titles during his amazing 20-year career from 1912 to 1931. He was silver medallist behind Canada's George Hodgson in the 1912 Olympic 400 and 1,500 m. free-style and was fifth and fourth respectively in these events in the Olympics of 1924 when he was 31 years old. Hatfield was also a member of Britain's bronze medal 4 × 200 m. relay squad in 1912 in Stockholm.

His English championship successes and best times in each were: 220 y. (1912—2:30·2, 1913, '22, '25); 440 y. (1912—4:54·8, 1913, '24, '27); 500 y. (1912, '13, '21, '22—6:11·4, 1923–27); 880 y. (1912, '13—11:46·4, 1921–25); one mile (1912, '13, '14—24:42·4, 1921–24, 1929–30); long distance (1913–14, 1921, '23, '24, '28, '31—57:22·0 sec).

Hatfield broke four world records: 300 y. in 3:26·4 (1913), 400 m. in 5:21·6 (1912), 500 y. 6:02·8 (1913), 500 m. 6:56·8 (1912).

HEARN, George (Great Britain, d. 10 Dec. 1949). The father of organized world swimming, George Hearn from England's West Country was President of the A.S.A. in 1908 when he called a meeting of nations taking part in the London Olympics to discuss their mutual problems. At this meeting it was decided to found the International Amateur Swimming Federation (see F.I.N.A.). Hearn, who had been hon. secretary of the A.S.A. from 1903–07, became the first secretary/treasurer of the new world organization and held those offices until 1928. He was then made a life honorary president.

HEARN, George, Memorial Trophy (English 'Diver of the Year'). This trophy was purchased from the widow of George Hearn (see previous entry) by Mr. T. E. H. Tanton and presented, through the *Swimming Times* to the A.S.A. in 1954. It is awarded to the English diver whose performance is judged the best of the year. Winners:

1954	Long, Ann (Ilford)
1955	Welsh Charmian (Durham City)
1956	Tarsey, David (Ealing)
1957	Welsh, Charmian (Durham City)
1955	Welsh, Charmian (Durham City)
1958	Phelps, Brian (Highgate)
1959	Phelps, Brian (Highgate)
1960	Phelps, Brian (Highgate)
1961	Ferris, Elizabeth (Mermaid)
1962	Phelps, Brian (Highgate)
1963	Austen, Margaret (Isleworth)/ Newman, Joy (Isander) (tie)
1964	Phelps Brian (Highgate)
1965	Rowlatt, Kathy (Leyton)
1966	Phelps, Brian (Highgate)
1967	Rowlatt, Kathy (Leyton)
1968	Rowlatt, Kathy (Leyton)
1969	Wetheridge, Brian (Metropolitan)
1970	Thewlis, Joe (Luton)

HEATLY, Peter (Great Britain, 9 June 1924–). Scotland's only home-produced diver of real class, Heatly coached himself to medal successes at three Commonwealth Games and a European championship and to participation in two Olympics.

Swimming was his first love. He won Scottish 440 and 880 y. titles in 1946 and might have earned a place in the British swimming team for the 1948 Olympics. But Heatly decided he had better long term prospects in diving and a fifth place from the highboard at the London Games was his first reward.

In the Commonwealth Games, he won the highboard in 1950 and was second in the springboard; won the springboard and was third in the highboard in 1954 and regained his highboard crown in

1958. But his finest fighting effort was in the European championships of 1954 when he just got into the final as twelfth and last qualifier and then pulled back to take the bronze medal on his final dive. Unaccountably, he was left out of the British team for the 1956 Olympics which caused a small storm at the time.

Two engineering degrees, his own engineering and contracting firm, membership of the Edinburgh Town Council and the Vice-Chairmanship of the Organizing Committee for the 1970 Commonwealth Games in Edinburgh are among Heatley's other achievements. He won twenty-eight diving Scottish titles, ten A.S.A. titles and is Britain's representative on the F.I.N.A. international diving committee.

HENNE, Jan (United States, 11 Aug. 1947–). A breast-stroke swimmer of no great repute, Jan Henne turned to front crawl and in 1968 was a surprise winner of the Olympic 100 m. free-style title, the silver medallist in the 200 m. and a member of the winning American team in the free-style relay. Yet she had never won a national free-style title in her own country. Her Mexico Games times, at altitude, were 60·0 and 2:11·0. Her best times, also in 1968, were 59·1 (only Australia's world record-breaker Dawn Fraser and Jan's countrywoman Sue Pedersen had ever swum faster) and 2:07·9 (beaten only by America's Debbie Meyer).

HENRICKS, Jon (Australia, 6 June 1935–). One of the world's great sprinters, Jon Henricks from Sydney proved this in winning the 1956 Olympic 100 m. in 55·4 and taking a second gold in the Australian 4 × 200 m. team. Yet, strangely, the 6 ft. and 12 st. fair-haired Henricks was trained as a distance swimmer in the early days, though against his own inclinations.

He missed the 1952 Olympic because of ear trouble and, on the way to Rome in 1960, an illness which hit many of the Australian team robbed him of a possible second 100 m. gold. He was, in fact, one of the favourites, but did not get through

the semi-finals and was not well enough to swim at all in the relay.

Henricks was a triple gold medallist (110 y., 4 × 200 free-style and 3 × 110 y. medley) in the 1954 Commonwealth Games in Vancouver and won six Australian titles—110 y. from 1953–56 and 220 y. in 1952–54. His 1956 Olympic winning time was later ratified as the first long course world record and he also helped to set four world relay marks.

HENRY, William (Great Britain, b. 29 June 1859). First co-honorary secretary, with Archibald Sinclair, of the Royal Life Saving Society, William Henry of London worked hard and long to encourage the teaching of life saving and resuscitation. He was also co-author, with Sinclair, of the Badminton Library *Book of Swimming*, published first in June 1893 and revised in December 1894 which gives, to those lucky enough to have a copy now, an encyclopaedic and fascinating picture of the sport in the last century.

This remarkable, dapper gentleman, with his neat military moustache, was a practicing as well as a theoretical swimming enthusiast. He won the A.S.A. quarter-mile salt water amateur championship in 1889, the long distance in 1890 and was 100 m. champion of Europe in 1896. A water-polo internationa, he played for England against Scotland in 1890 and 1892, captaining the team on the latter occasion. He was also one of Britain's finest scientific swimmers.

In 1900, Henry, a member of the Amateur and Zephyr clubs, was in the British team for the 1900 Olympic Games in Paris where he came sixth in the 200 m. obstacle race at the age of 41.

HICKCOX, Charles (United States, 6 Feb. 1947–). A talented medley man with a leaning towards back-stroke, Hickcox from Pheonix, Arizona, won three golds and a silver at the 1968 Olympics. His medley racing stint in Mexico, with all the problems of altitude, was tremendously hard. Yet Hickcox took the 200 and 400 m. titles in 2:12·0, one second ahead of Greg Buckingham (USA) and 4:48·4, three-tenths in front of his other medley team-mate Gary Hall. The presentation ceremony for the 200 m. medley was most dramatic, for Hickcox had to support his bronze medal-winning team-mate John Ferris, suffering from the effects of altitude, who finally collapsed at the foot of the rostrum and had to be given oxygen.

Hickcox was also second to East Germany's great Roland Matthes in the 100 m. back-stroke (60·2 to the 58·7 of Matthes) and he led off the United States medley relay team to victory and a world record of 3:54·9.

His five individual world marks (set between 28 Aug. 1967 and 30 Aug. 1968) included three for back-stroke—100 m. 59·3 and 59·1 and 300 m. 2:09·4, all set during his three gold medal winning appearance in the 1967 World Student Games in Tokyo. His third gold came in the medley relay.

Two months before Mexico, Hickcox set world medley marks for 200 m. (2:10·6) and 400 m. (4:39·0). He was Pan-American 100 m. back-stroke champion in 1967, runner-up in the 200 m. and a member of the United States 4 × 200 m. free-style gold medal team. He won four United States outdoor titles—100 and 200 m. back-stroke in both 1966 and '67.

HIGHBOARD DIVING. The high-boards, which are rigid platforms, are 5, 7½ and 10 m. above the water level, but in major competitions only the highest platform is used. The international test for men consists of six voluntary dives, with the total degree of difficulty not exceeding 11·2 and four voluntary dives without any limit. In each section each dive shall be slected from a different group. If there are sixteen or more competitors there are preliminary and final rounds. The preliminary round consists of the six dives with tariff limit, plus one dive without limit. The top twelve compete in the final round of three dives without limit.

The women's test is four required dives and four voluntary from different groups. The required dives are forward, back, reverse and inward, performd in either (a), (b) or (c) positions. With more than twelve competitors there is a preliminary contest consisting of the four required dives in the order above, plus one voluntary dive. The top twelve compete in the final round of three dives. The winners, of course, are those with the highest scores for the whole test. (See DIVING.)

HISTORY OF SWIMMING. Swimming was not in the programme of the Ancient Olympic Games, though the sport of swimming was not unknown to the Greeks and races took place in Japan in 36 B.C., during the reign of Emperor Suigiu.

Japan was the first country to organize swimming nationally and an Imperial edict in 1603 made it compulsory in schools; there were even inter-college competitions and a three-day swimming meeting was organized in 1810. But Japan was a closed country and it was left to the Anglo-Saxon countries to lead the world in modern swimming development.

The first swimming organization in England was the National Swimming Society, founded in London by John Strachan in 1837 when the metropolis had six indoor baths, all of which, surprisingly, had diving boards. The first indoor bath in England was built in Liverpool in 1828 at St. George's Pier-head.

It was in Australia that the first modern swimming championship was organized—in 1846, at the Robinson baths in Sydney where the 440 y. event was won by W. Redman in 8:43·0. In Australia, too, a so-called 'world championship' 100 y. race was held at St. Kilda, a suburb of Melbourne, on 9 Feb. 1858. This was won by Australia's Jo Bennett from Sydney, who beat Charles Stedman of England.

There was no amateur or professional distinction about swimming competitions prior to 1869. But there were a great number of aquatic activities in Britain . . . races for money prizes or side bets and ornamental and trick swimming demonstrations. Harold Kenworthy beat Indians of the Ojibbeway tribe at the Holborn baths in 1844 and Fred Beckwith, English professional champion defeated Deerfoot, a Seneca Indian, in 1861.

The Amateur Swimming Association, founded on 7 Jan. 1869 under the then title of the Metropolitan Swimming Club Association (see separate entries) is considered to be the first national swimming association. And on 11 Feb. 1869, the M.S.C.A. defined an 'amateur' and established rules for competition. The first National amateur champion was Tom Morris, who won a mile race, downstream, between Putney Aqueduct and Hammersmith Bridge in 1969. The first official record approved by the M.S.C.A. was Winston Cole's 100 y. in 1:15·0 in 1871.

The German Federation was founded in 1882, the Hungarian in 1896 and the French in 1899. The New Zealand A.S.A. (1890) preceded by one year, the formation of the A.S.A. of New South Wales. These two associations co-operated in the organization of Australasian championships until the Australian Amateur Swimming Union was founded in 1909. Combined Australasian teams, in fact, took part in the Olympics up to 1912.

The United States held their first championships in 1877, the distance was one mile and it was won by R. Weissenboth. Until 1888, American championships were organized by the New York Athletic Club. Events for women were not introduced in the United States until 1916. Scotland anticipated American, and indeed English action, by holding their first national championship for women in 1892—a 200 y. event won by E. Dobbie of Glasgow in 4:25·0.

In 1889, the Erste Wiener Amateur Swim Club of Vienna held two races (60 and 500 m.) under the title of European championships and these continued annually until 1903. In 1896, at the first Olympic Games in Athens, three swimming races were held in the bay of Zea, near Piraeus. Around 1900, events described as world championships were also organized.

The Federation Internationale de Natation Amateur was founded in London on 19 July 1908 and established that year the first list of official world swimming records. In 1912 women's events were added to the Olympic programme and Fanny Durack of Australia and Greta Johansson of Sweden became the first swimming and diving champions.

European championships were first held in 1926 (for men) and the following year women's races were added and the European Swimming League (see LIGUE EUROPEENNE NATATION) was founded. The first Commonwealth Games (known then as the British Empire Games) took place in 1930.

HINTON, Margery (Great Britain, 25 June 1915–   ). An outstanding British breast-stroke and free-style swimmer in the 1930s, Margery Hinton from Manchester was a European 200 m. breast-stroke bronze medallist in Paris in 1931 and a bronze medal winner again in the 4 × 100 m. free-style relay in 1934 and 1938. She also swam in two Olympics— in 1932 when she was fourth in the 200 m. breast-stroke and in 1936 when she failed to reach the final.

Miss Hinton also swam in three Commonwealth Games. In the first, in 1930 she was second to her England team-mate Cecilia Wolstenholme in the 200 y. breast-stroke . . . in 1934 she was third in the breast-stroke and a bronze medallist in the 4 × 100 y. free-style relay . . . and in 1938, at 23 years old, she was not in the breast-stroke medals but won a gold as the free-style anchor swimmer in the 3 × 110 y. medley relay and bronze medallist again in the free-style relay.

Five times A.S.A. breast-stroke champion (1929 and 1931–34), Miss Hinton held the world 200 y. record (3:00·0) for three months in 1929—at 14—and the world 200 m. mark (3:10·6) for six months in 1931/32. She was the all-round team swimmer that any country would be proud to claim.

HODGSON, George (Canada, b. 1894). Canada's only Olympic swimming champion, George Ritchie Hodgson was undefeated in his three years of racing culminating in his 400 and 1,500 m. world record-breaking victories in the Stockholm Games of 1912.

Hodgson, who learned to swim in the Laurentian Mountain Lakes, never had a swimming lesson or a coach . . . being in 'good physical shape' was his way to success. In Stockholm he set world records for 1,000 y. and m. on the way to his gold medal. And having beaten Britain's Jack Hatfield by 39 sec., Hodgson swam on a further 109 m. to break the world record for one mile.

A day later, the Canadian beat Hatfield again, by 1·4 sec. to win the 400 m. championship. His world record of 5:24·4 in the 100 m. salt-water pool in Stockholm harbour fell to the Briton three months later in an indoor, 100 ft. bath swim. But Hodgson's 1,500 m. mark of 22:00·0 remained on the books for eleven years.

Hodgson won the one mile in the Inter-Empire championships of 1911 to celebrate the coronation of King George V. The course at London's old Crystal Palace, as he recalls, was: 'without lanes or guiding lines on the bottom and the turn was on a log boom across one end'. The Canadian retired at 18, after his Stockholm golden double, the undisputed, undefeated champion of the world.

HOLM-JARRETT, Eleanor (United States, 6 Dec. 1913–   ). Eleanor Holm, later Mrs. Jarrett, qualified for American teams at three Olympics and swam at two. In 1928, at 14, she was fifth in the 100 m. back-stroke in Amsterdam. Four years later she won this event (1:19·4) at the Los Angeles Games. Picked for the 1936 Olympics, she was disciplined for her behaviour on the boat to Europe and was sent home without setting even a toe in the Berlin pool.

Eleanor Holm won twenty-nine American championships and broke seven world back-stroke records. Her best times were 1:16·3 (100 m. s/c), 1:52·0 (150 y. l/c) and 2:48·7 (200 m. s/c). Her American 100 and 220 y. back-stroke records stood for more than sixteen years and she was also an outstanding individual medley competitor.

After her Berlin disappointment, she turned professional and starred with Johnny Weissmuller and Buster Crabbe in Aquacades and films having been born not only with an exceptional swimming talent but also the glamour to succeed in show business.

HUTTON, Ralph (Canda, 6 Mar. 1948– They call Ralph Hutton the 'Iron Man' and his non-stop stint at the 1966 Commonwealth Games in Jamaica supports this nickname. He competed in thirteen races, swam 3½ miles in six days and collected one gold, five silver and two bronze medals from his marathon effort. The versatile Hutton from Ocean Falls, but who has done much of his swimming in the United States, was in the Canadian winning medley team (swimming back-stroke), was second in the 110 and 220 y. back-stroke, 440 y. medley and 4 × 110 and 4 × 220 y. free-style relays. He was third in the 440 y. and 1,650 y. free-style.

But it was for free-style that he made his world mark—with a 400 m. world record of 4:06·5 on 1 Aug. 1968. But at the Mexico Olympics two months later the Canadian had to bow to America's Mike Burton, who took the gold in 4:09·0 to Hutton's 4:11·7.

Multiple racing seems to be Hutton's forte. In the 1964 Olympics, at 16, he took part in eight of the ten events (100/400 m. free-style, 200 m. back-stroke and butterfly, 400 m. medley and all three relays). He only skipped the 1,500 m. and 200 m. breast-stroke.

In the 1967 Pan-American championships he was the 200 m. back-stroke champion, free-style silver medallist in the 200 m. (behind Olympic champion Don Schollander), 400 and 1,500 m. and the two relays.

As an indication of Hutton's talent—he won his first Canadian title in 1963 for 200 m. back-stroke (2:21·3) at 15. His tally before the start of the Edinburgh Commonwealth Games in 1970 was sixteen titles—from 200 to 1,500 m. free-style, back-stroke, butterfly and medley and he ranked among the top six in ten of Canada's best-of-all-time lists and was the fastest in four.

In Edinburgh, the jinx on Hutton winning an individual Commonwealth title continued. He almost did take the gold in the 400 m. free-style, but was passed in the last yards by Australia's Graham White who beat the Canadian by 0·3. Hutton won three more silvers (200, 4 × 100 and 4 × 200 m. free-style) but missed even a relay gold with Canada's winning medley squad having lost the free-style leg trial to Bob Kasting. Even so, in two Games, he took 12 medals—including nine silvers—to be the champion runner-up.

HVEGER, Ragnhild (Denmark, 10 Dec. 1920–). 'The greatest swimmer who never won an Olympic title' is not an extravagant tag to tie around the fame of Ragnhild Hveger. Denmark's 'Golden Torpedo' broke forty-two individual world records for fifteen different free-style distances plus three for back-stroke between 1936 and 1942. Ten years later, after seven years in retirement and at the age of 32, Hveger was still good enough

to place fifth in the 1952 Olympic 400 m. final only 4·8 seconds behind the winner.

She showed her budding talent at 13 when the Danish championships took place in her home town of Elsinore. Unknown Ragnhild had never been in a race before, yet she won the 400 m. title. World War II cost her an Olympic crown. In September, 1940, about the time the cancelled XIIth Games should have taken place, Hveger at the peak of her brilliance set her eighth 400 m. world mark with 5:00·1. It took sixteen years for a girl to break five minutes.

The Dane, at 15, won the 400 m. silver medal at the 1936 Berlin Olympics. At the 1938 European championships she took three golds—an unforgettable half a length of the 50 m. pool victory in the 400 m. (clearly her favourite distance), the 100 and 4 × 100 m. free-style.

Hveger's world record list include 59·7 (100 y.), 2:21·7 (200 m.), 2:22·6 (220 y.), 3:25·6 (300 y.), 3:42·5 (300 m.), 5:00·1 (400 m.), 5:11·5 (440 y.), 5:53·0 (500 y.), 6:27·4 (500 m.), 10:52·5 (800 m.), 11:08·7 (880 y.), 12:36·0 (1,000 y.), 13:54·4 (1,000 m.), 20:57·0 (1,500 m.) and 23:11·5 (one mile) and for back-stroke 2:41·3 and 5:38·2 for 200 and 400 m. respectively.

INTER-COUNTRY SPEED SWIM-MING CONTEST. See BOLOGNA TROPHY.

INTER-SERVICES CHAMPION-SHIP. The winners since World War II of this triangular swimming and diving contest for the W. A. H. Buller Trophy have been:

1948	Royal Air Force
1949–50	Army (2)
1951–62	Royal Air Force (12)
1963	Army
1964	Royal Navy
1965–68	Royal Air Force (4)
1969	Royal Navy
1970	Royal Navy

INTERIM GAMES. See OLYMPIC CHAMPIONS.

INTERNATIONAL TECHNICAL COMMITTEES. The I.T.C.s of F.I.N.A. are made up of twelve members from different countries who normally serve for four years—between Olympics—and must be amateurs. The committees in offce for 1968–72 are:

International Technical Swimming Committee (I.T.S.C.)—Chairman: N. W. Sarsfield (GB); Secretary: W. A. Lippman (USA).

International Water-Polo Committee (I.W.P.C.)—Chairman: J. Mahoney (USA); Secretary: C. W. Plant (GB).

International Diving Committee (I.D.C.)—Chairman: R. Smith (USA); Secretary: L. van de Ven (Belg).

International Synchronized Swimming Committee (I.S.S.C.)— Chairman: J. Armbrust (Neth); Secretary: Mrs. D. Smith (Can).

International Sports Medicine Committee (I.S.M.C.)—Chairman: Dr. S. Firsov (USSR); Secretary: Dr. E. Gebhardt (WGer).

The committees are responsible for recommending rule changes affecting their special interest, interpreting rules, advising on standard equipment and pool specifications and, in co-operation with the F.I.N.A. Bureau, for the daily organization of their special events at Olympic Games or World Championships.

INTERNATIONAL AMATEUR SWIMMING FEDERATION. See FEDERATION INTERNATIONALE DE NATATION AMATEUR.

J

JACKS, Ron (Canada, 23 Jan. 1948–). Another of Canada's versatile American-trained stars, Ron Jacks won the 110 y. butterfly (60·3) at the 1966 Commonwealth Games, beating the more favoured Graham Dunn, of Australia. Jacks swam in two Olympics (1964/68) without any medals to show for his efforts, but in the 1967 Pan-American championships he was in all three Canadian silver medal relay teams.

As well as winning seven Canadian titles from 1966, Jacks, born in Winnipeg but a member of the Canadian Dolphin Club of Vancouver, made two trips to Britain to swim in the A.S.A. championships at Blackpool. In 1965 he was second in the 110 y. butterfly behind his team-mate Dan Sherry, who set a world record then of 58·1. In 1969 he reached six finals, won three (440, 880 and 1,650 y. free-style), was second to Olympic silver medallist Martyn Woodroffe in the 220 y. butterfly and third in the 110 y. butterfly and 220 y. free-style.

His best times prior to the 1970 Commonwealth Games in Edinburgh (all ranking in the top ten of all time Canadian lists) were: free-style: 100 m., 56·2; 200 m., 2:00·2; 400 m., 4:17·2; f,500 m., 17:20·8. Back-stroke: 200 m., 2:19·5. Butterfly: 100 m., 58·4; 200 m., 2:12·2.

Canada made a clean sweep of the medals in the 100 m. butterfly in Edinburgh but defending champion Jacks was third although his 59·0 was equivalently 0·9 faster than his winning time in 1966. He also won two free-style relay silvers.

JACKSON, Alex (Great Britain, 10 June 1952–). Born in Dublin, Eire, of English-born parents, Alexandra Elizabeth Jackson—but do not dare call her anything but Alex—has lived most of her life in the Isle of Man. She broke her first British record, the junior 110 y. in 1967 (62·6) and the following year came sixth in the Olympic 100 m. final in 61·0m having set a national record of 60·5 in a semi-final.

Winner of the A.S.A. 110 y. title in 1967, '68, '69 and the 220 y. in 1968, she opened the 1970 season by breaking the British 200 m. record (2:14·3). An English international and record-holder, tall, fair-haired Alex opted to swim for the Isle of Man in the Commonwealth Games in Edinburgh.

But she did not win the expected first swimming gold for the Island. In the 100 m., although she had the fastest heat time (60·9), she was 0·9 slower in the final—won by Angela Coughlan of Canada in 61·2—and dropped to fourth place. Alex took a bronze in the 200 m. in a British record of 2:13·5 but officials had to go to the third decimal point in order to separate the Briton and Australia's Helen Gray by 0·003 of a second.

In the European championships, in September 1970, Alex was third in the 100 m. free-style but failed, surprisingly. to qualify for the final of the 200 m.

JANY, Alex (France, 1929–). Heralded as the best swimming prospect in the world in 1947, Alex Jany, son of a baths superintendent in Toulouse, failed to live up to his reputation at the 1948 Olympics. This 6 ft. 2 in. and 16 st. giant, was only fifth in the 100 m. (58·3, 1 sec. behind American winner Wally Ris) having been head and shoulders in front at 60 m. He was only sixth in the 400 m. though he pulled France into third place in the relay.

But the London Games was one of

Jany's few swimming failures. The year before, in the European championships in Monte Carlo, he won the 100 m. by 2·4 in 57·3 and the 400 m. by 15·2 in 4:35·2—a world record. And he swam his heart out for France in the 4 × 200 m. relay. As anchorman, he took over a 10 m. deficit behind Sweden and though he closed the gap inexorably he lost the gold by 0·2 at the touch. When he realized he had 'failed', he clung to the bath end and wept. Jany retained his 100 and 400 m. European titles in Vienna in 1950, but France had to be satisfied with second place in the relay, again behind Sweden.

Jany broke five world records: 100 m. (55·8 s/c 1947), 200 m. (2:05·4 s/c 1946), 300 y. (3:03·0 s/c 1948), 300 m. (3:21·0 1947), 400 m. (4:25·2 1947). In 1946 he competed in the A.S.A. championships at New Brighton and won the 100 and 220 y. titles.

JARVIS, John (Great Britain, 24 Feb. 1872–9 May 1933). John Arthur Jarvis— Arthur to his family, but John to the swimming world—called himself the 'Amateur Swimming Champion of the World' and he won 108 titles to justify his claim.

In the 1900 Olympics in Paris he won the 1,000 and 4,000 m. gold medals and is credited in the F.I.N.A. records with having also won the 100 m., though in every other Olympic book of reference this event does not appear to have taken place, certainly within the official swimming programme. At any rate, swimming in the River Seine, Jarvis, from Leicester, took the 1,000 m. in 13:40·2 finishing an astonishing 1:13·2 ahead of Austria's Otto Wahle. But his 4,000 m. victory was even more amazing. Jarvis was timed in 58:24·0—more than 10½ minutes ahead of Hungary's Zoltan Halmay.

There were no British competitors at the 1904 Games in Los Angeles, but at the 1906 Interim Games Jarvis was second in the 1,500 m. and third in the 400 m.

Jarvis, a non-smoker and virtual teetotaller, and his professional rival Joey Nuttall used the right overarm sidestroke and developed a special kick which became known as the Jarvis-Nuttall kick. Using it Jarvis set many world bests though he was never credited with an official record. His efficient technique won for him twenty-four A.S.A. titles—440 y. (1898, 1900), 500 and 880 y. (1898, '99, 1900, '01), mile (1897–1902 = 6), long distance (1898–1904 and 1906 = 8). He was also plunging champion in 1904.

His international and national successes included winning the Queen Victoria Diamond Jubilee one mile championship (1897), the German Kaiser's championship of Europe, the Emperor of Austria's world championship (in Vienna), the King of Italy's world distance championship, the Queen of the Netherlands' world 4,000 m. championship, the King Edward VII Coronation Cup one mile (handed to him by the King) and two gold cups for 15-mile River Thames swims, open to the world.

Jarvis, later referred to as Professor Jarvis, did a great deal to promote lifesaving. He saved many lives, once rescuing twin sisters, and he introduced life-saving techniques to Italy on one of his many international tours. He was an English water-polo international from 1894 to 1904, though he did not play for Britain in the Olympic Games. Three of his daughters became swimming teachers and one was chaperone to the British women's team who won the relay gold medals at the 1912 Stockholm Olympics. Jarvis was honoured by the Hall of Fame in 1968.

JASTREMSKI, Chet (United States, 12 Jan. 1941–). A great breast-stroke swimmer of his time, Chester Jastremski was also one of the unluckiest. A pioneer of the modern fast-stroking sprint style, he made devastating inroads into the world records lists, yet missed selection for the 1960 Olympics owing to a rule misinterpretation and was only third in the 1964 Games 200 m. though at that time he was the world record holder.

In six weeks from 2 July–20 Aug 1961,

the stocky student (5 ft 9 in, 11 st. 11 lb.) who lived in Giant Street, Toledo, broke the world 100 m. mark six times—from 1:11·1 to astonishing 1:07·8 and 1:07·5 on the same day. He also took the 200 m. world record from 2:33·6 to 2:28·2 in three bites.

Jastremski, of Polish extraction, then a medical student at Indiana University and a pupil of Doc Jim Counsilman, became the first man to break the minute for 100 y. breast-stroke (s/c) with 59·6 in April 1961 and the same week he swam 220 y. in 2:26·7 (equal to 66·3 and 2:29·2 for 100/200 m. l/c).

JENKINS, Brian (Great Britain, 20 June 1943–). An apprentice plumber from Swindon, Brian Jenkins schemed and sacrificed to win his silver medal for 200 m. butterfly in the 1962 European championships. His home pool was closed for repairs that summer. So in order to train properly for Leipzig, Jenkins gave up his holiday for the following year and spent two weeks travelling 40 miles a day to the next-nearest bath. It was a bad summer and it rained the whole of the fortnight, but, with his fiancée holding the stopwatch, Jenkins trained three times a day, spending his rest time in cinemas or cafés. His determination was rewarded with a 2:15·6, only 1·4 behind Russian winner Valentin Kuzmin.

Later the same year, Jenkins was fourth for Wales in the 220 y. butterfly (2:21·0) at the Perth Commonwealth Games. He also swam in the 1964 Olympics, but was only seventh in a semi-final of the 200 m. (2:15·5). Discouraged because of his inability to 'train as the Americans' do, Jenkins then retired from swimming.

He was Welsh butterfly champion in 1962/63, won the A.S.A. title in 1961, '62, '63 and had a fastest 220 y. (l/c) time of 2:14·7.

JOHANSSON, Hjalmar (Sweden, b. about 1873). A pioneer of diving, in and out of the water, Hjalmar Johansson won the Olympic high plain championships in 1908 at the age of 35. His speciality was the forward dive which he performed with arms held wide in flight instead of stretching them above his head as in the English header. This variation, known as the 'Swedish swallow' is the only version of the plain dive used in modern competition. The Swede won the silver medal in this event in 1912 and was fourth in the high fancy event while his wife, Greta Johansson became the first woman Olympic diving champion (for plain diving).

Johansson had been champion of Sweden since 1897 except for the two years he spent in London prior to the 1908 Games. And during those years, he helped to draw up the Olympic code of conduct for diving competitions, the prototype of the modern international diving regulations.

JONES, Alice (United States, 1952–). Seventh in the American outdoor 100 m. butterfly in 1969 (66·7) and not through at all to the final of the 200 m. (2:30·0). Alice Jones from Cincinnati shot to the top at the 1970 national championships in Los Angeles.

This fair-haired, 5 ft. 7 in., and 139 pound 'flyer' took the 100 m. in 64·1. breaking the five-year-old world record of Holland's Ada Kok. Later, this second year student at the University of Cincinnati won the 200 m. in 2:19·3. again a world record, breaking the month-old mark of Karen Moe. Miss Jones turned third at 100 m. in 67·9, was just in the lead at 150 m. and held off a tremendous challenge to win by 0·19 of a second. The next three girls (Lynn Colella, Karen Moe and Ellie Daniel) were also inside the old world record of 2:20·7.

K

KAHANAMOKU, Duke (United States, 14 Aug. 1890–22 Jan. 19). Duke was his christian name and ducal was Kahanamoku's swimming talent. He came out of the Hawaiian Islands in 1911, a superbly conditioned athlete who could plane on the surface of the water as no man of his size had ever done before.

An island king in many movies, Kahanamoku had Hawaiian royal blood. He was born in Princess Ruth's palace in Honolulu during a visit of the Duke of Edinburgh, second son of Queen Victoria. And his father Captain Kahanamoku christened him Duke to celebrate the occasion.

He swam in four Olympics and it would have been five had not the 1916 meeting been cancelled. In 1912 he won the 100 m. free-style (63·4) and a silver in America's relay team. He retained his sprint title in 1920 in a world record 60·4, after the final had been re-swum following Austalian protests that their man, William Harold, had been boxed in . . . there were no lane ropes in those days. It was Duke's 30th birthday. And he anchored America to world record-breaking golds in the relay. Duke missed an historic hat-trick of sprint golds in 1924, when Johnny Weissmuller the American heir to his swimming kingdom, beat him into second place, by 2·4, with the first sub-minute Games record (59·0). Despite this confirmation of his form, Duke did not swim in America's winning relay squad. But he was back in the team again in 1928, at 38, though this time he went home medalless. He was also on the American water-polo team strength at the 1932 Olympics, but did not play.

Essentially a sprinter, Duke's first world record came just after he had won his first Olympic gold, when on 20 July 1912 he clocked 61·6 for 100 m. on a straight course. He followed this with four 100 y. marks (54·5, 53·8, 53·2 and 53·0) between 5 July 1913 and 5 Sept. 1917. He clipped his four-year-old 100 m. time to 61·4 in 1918 and finally to 60·4 in retaining his Olympic crown in Antwerp.

KIEFER, Adolph (United States, 27 June 1918–). Olympic 100 m. backstroke champion in 1936, Kiefer's winning time (65·9) in Berlin stood until 1952 when America's Yoshinobu Oyakawa trimmed it by 0·2 in Helsinki. Chicago-born Kiefer broke seventeen world marks from 100 y. to 400 m. in his long career at the top from 1935–44. These included cutting the 100 m. time from 67·0 to 64·8 in four record swims in three months (20 Oct. 1935–18 Jan. 1936). His other best times were 56·8 (100 y., 1944), 1:30·4 (150 y., 1941), 2:19·3 (200 m. 1944) and 5:10·9 (400 m., 1941). During World War II, young Lt. Kiefer was officer in charge of swimming for the entire U.S. Navy and revamped the instruction programme for the training or re-training of 11,000 Navy swimming instructors.

KIERAN, Barney (Australia, 1887–22 Sept. 1905). One of the first great trudgen (double over-arm) swimmers, Bernard Bede Kieran's death at 19, following an appendicectomy, was a tragedy for swimming. His performances in his short, three-year racing life, were phenomenal. They included world best times for almost all the free-style distances, though only one, for 500 y. in 6:07·2—which stood for eight years—was ratified retrospectively as a world record when, in 1908, F.I.N.A. was founded and created the first official world list.

Despite the suspicions in Europe and in England in particular, there is little doubt of the authenticity of Kieran's times. His Australian records included 2:28·4 (220 y.) in 1905 which beat the ratified world mark of his compatriot Freddy Lane by 0·2 and was 3·2 faster than the first world record for the four feet shorter 200 m. by Otto Scheff in 1908. Technically, the first man to swim 200 m. faster than Kieran was Charles Daniels (USA) in 1911. (See WORLD RECORDS, introduction).

Kieran from New South Wales did 5:19·0 for 440 y. (1905), which was 17·8 better than the first ratified world 400 m. record in 1908 and 7.4 faster than the first official 440 y. mark. Also in 1905, he clocked 11:11·6 for 880 y., an Australian record, yet the year after Kieran's death, the first world mark was awarded to England's Henry Taylor with 11:25·4. And Kieran's 23:16·8 for one mile the same year was 2:07·6 faster than the first official world mark and it was not until 1924 that Arne Borg put up a better performance.

Kieran won nine Australian titles—220, 440 y. and one mile twice each and the 880 y. three times. He died during the Australian championships in Brisbane soon after a most successful visit to England. Although out of training, after months on a ship, he won the A.S.A. 220, 440, 500 and 880 y. titles.

Without any Olympic medals to his credit—he was only coming to the fore in 1904 and was dead before the 1906 Interim Games—and only one world record to mark his passing in the F.I.N.A. lists, Kieran's name and fame were recorded for posterity by his election to the Hall of Fame in 1969.

KING, Ellen (Great Britain, 16 Jan. 1909–). A tremendously versatile swimmer, Ellen King of Scotland competed in the era from 1924–31 when Britain's women competitors challenged the world. Her Olympic medal successes were for back-stroke and free-style

relay, but she was also more than competent on breast-stroke.

Ellen, from Edinburgh, swam in her first Games in 1924, at 15, when she was sixth in the 100 m. back-stroke final. Four years later, she was second in 1:22·2, only 0·2 behind the winner Marie Braun, of Holland. In Amsterdam Ellen also won a silver in the relay.

She was the Scottish member of the British quartette—the others were Joyce Cooper and Marion Laverty of England and Valerie Davies of Wales—who won the first European 4 × 100 m. free-style title in 1927 in Italy and their prize was the Bologna Trophy (see BOLOGNA TROPHY). And she swam in the first Commonwealth Games in Hamilton and came second in the 100 y. free-style, third in the 200 m. breast-stroke and free-style relay.

Ellen King won sixteen Scottish titles: Free-style—100 y. (1925, '26, '28), 200 y. (1924, '25, '26), 440 y. (1931); back-stroke—150 y. (1924, '25, '26, '29, '30, '31); breast-stroke—200 y. (1925, '26, '27). In A.S.A. championships she was first in the 150 y. back-stroke in 1923, '26 and second in 1927, '29; won the 200 y. breast-stroke in 1927 and was third in the 100 y. free-style in 1923, '26 and '29. Her fifteen Scottish records included: Free-style—30·2 (50 y.), 67·4 (100 y.), 3:03·4 (220 y.), 6:50·6 (440 y.); breast-stroke 1:24·4 (100 y.), 3:02·0 (200 y.); back-stroke 1:16·0 (100 y., broke record five times).

KINSELLA, John (United States, 26 Aug. 1952–). Silver medallist for 1,500 m. (16:57·3) at the 1968 Olympic Games, Kinsella, a towering 6 ft. 5 in. and powerful 190 pounds, had to wait two more years to win his first American title. But when the time came, he won in no uncertain fashion.

This he did in Los Angeles in August, 1970 by gaining his first victory over Olympic champion Mike Burton (see Burton, Mike) in the 400 m. free-style in a world record 4:02·8. And he followed this by taking the 1,500 m. in 15:57·1, a world mark, of course, and the first man to break sixteen minutes. Burton also broke this minute barrier with 15:57·3 and except in the middle of the race when Kinsella tried, unsuccessfully, to break the world 800 m. record, never more than half a second divided the men.

Kinsella, a talented American footballer as well as a brilliant swimmer, entered the University of Indiana in the autumn of 1970.

KIPHUTH, Bob (United States, 17 Nov. 1890–7 Jan. 1967). The most highly honoured of all America's great coaches, Robert John Herman Kiphuth, born in Tonawanda, New York, gave his entire life to swimming. And his life's work was crowned with the 'Medal of Freedom', America's highest civilian award. The citation speaks for itself . . . 'He has inspired generations of athletes with high ideals of achievement and sportsmanship.' Bob Kiphuth received his medal from President Johnson at the White House on 6 Dec. 1963.

His physical education teaching career began in 1914 when, at 23, he went to Yale University as an instructor and he stayed there until his death in 1967. He was head coach from 1918 until mandatory retirement in 1959 when he became Professor Emeritus of Physical Education and Director Emeritus of the University's Payne Whitney Gymnasium.

Professor Kiphuth attended every Olympic Games from 1924–64, at four of which (1928–48) he was coach to the American team. He preached his gospel of swimming around the world—in France, Germany, Holland, Sweden, Britain, Japan, Austria, Hungary, Cuba, Hawaii, Mexico, Iceland, Israel, Hong Kong, Thailand, India, Turkey, Greece, Italy, Spain . . . you name it, Bob went to it.

An honorary Master of Arts and Doctor of Law, honoured by the Emperor of Japan with the order of the Sacred Treasure, member of the United States National Olympic and Swimming Committees, Bob Kiphuth, non-smoker and teetotaller, a quiet, kindly man with a great sense of humour, believed ferociously in amateurism. Any swimming stars who went to Yale on scholarships got them for academic and not sporting merit.

The successes of his Yale University swimming teams, who were beaten only ten times in inter-collegiate matches in forty-two years, is tremendous testimony to his swimming knowledge. Yale, in this time, won the Eastern Intercollegiate league thirty-eight times. Between 1949 and 1957, Yale were high point team at seven National indoor championships meetings (1949, 1951–55, 1957) while the New Haven Swim Club (Yale's summer season club title) were top at five outdoor championships (1950–51, '53, '55–56).

His epitaph, in the words of President Kingman Brewster of Yale, could not be more fitting: 'To Bob Kiphuth athletics was an integral part of learning and all learning was an exercise in self-fulfilment and self-discipline. Generations of students and colleagues have outdone themselves because of the values he inspired and the standards he set.'

KITAMURA, Kuoso (Japan, 1918–). The youngest man to win an Olympic swimming title, Kitamura was only 14 in 1932 when he took the 1,500 m. in Los Angeles. He was the first in the trend towards younger and younger champions and his success, like those who have followed, was the result of careful nutrition, training and stroke mechanics.

His 19:12·4, in beating his team-mate Shozo Makino by 1·7 and Jim Christy, the best from the United States, by 17·1, was 5·2 outside the 1927 world record of Sweden's Arne Borg—a world mark which stood for another six years. But Kitamura's was a remarkable performance and stood as a Games record until 1952.

Kitamura, in fact, only broke one world mark, for 1,000 m. (12:42·6) in 1933. He became Chairman of the Foreign Relations committee of the Japanese Swimming Federation and was one of the first foreign swimmers to be honoured by the Hall of Fame (1965).

KOK, Ada (Netherlands, 6 June 1947–). This gentle giant, Ada Kok, over-shadowed Dutch and world butterfly swimming in the 1960s. And though she retired in 1968, after winning an Olympic gold for 200 m. in Mexico City, the records she set between 1963–67 remained unchallenged as swimming went into the 1970s.

The 6 ft. 0 in., 13 st. Dutch girl from the Hague won her first golds in the 1962 European championships, in the 100 m. (69·0) and medley relay. She retained her 100 m. title four years later in Utrecht (65·6), swam the vital leg in Holland's medley relay win and for the first—and last—time showed her freestyle power by taking the 400 m. silver medal (4:48·7).

Between these European successes, there had been disappointment in Ada's silver—which all Holland had hoped would be a gold—in the 100 m. butterfly at the 1964 Tokyo Olympics. She was world record-holder at the time with the 65·1 for 110 y. (equal to 64·4 for 100 m.) set at Blackpool four months before the Games. But in the big race she could do only 65·6 in finishing 0·9 behind Sharon Stouder (USA). Ada out-swam the American on the butterfly leg of the medley relay (65·0 to Stouder's 66·1), but the superior strength of the rest of the United States squad left Holland again with the silvers.

After seven years at the top of butterfly swimming, Mexico seemed the last chance for Holland's popular Ada to win that elusive Olympic title. So the despondency was extreme as she finished fourth in the 100 m. But, three days later, she fought back to take the new 200 m. title in 2:24·7, having been 1·4 behind runner-up Helga Lindner (East Germany) at half distance.

Ada broke nine individual world butterfly records between September 1963 and August 1967: 100 m. 66·1, 65·1, 64·5; 110 y. 65·1; 200 m. 2:25·8, 2:25·3, 2:22·5, 2:21·0 (the last time was also a record for 220 y.) In medley relay swimming she was magnificent and Holland were seldom beaten in this event in all the years that Ada, who could turn impossible deficits into winning leads, was in the team.

KOLB, Claudia (United States, 19 Dec. 1949–). At 14, swimming in the 200 m. breast-stroke, Claudia Kolb won an unexpected silver medal in the 1964 Olympics. It was a courageous effort, for she had qualified for the final only as fifth best and with 25 m. to go she was in fourth place. Suddenly Claudia abandoned all caution, put her head down and sprinted like mad for 10 m. to swim into second place (2:47·6) splitting the mighty Russian pair Prosumenschikova (2:46·4) and Babanina (2:48·6).

Four years later, at the Mexico Games, Claudia was the best in the world for the medley individual and she won the 200 and 400 m. gold medals with almost contemptuous ease—the former (2:24·7) by 4·1 from her team-mate Sue Pedersen and the latter by a huge 13·7 from another American Lynn Vidali.

She was the first holder of the world record for 200 m. medley with her 2:27·8 on 21 Aug. 1966. Two years and four world records later, she had brought her time down to 2:23·5. She broke the 400 m. world record four times, taking it from 5:11·7 in July 1967 to 5:04·7 in Aug. 1968.

Claudia, from the George Haines stable at Santa Clara, twice (1964, '65) won the United States outdoor 100 and 200 m. breast-stroke titles (best winning times 1:17·1 and 2:48·6 in dead-heating with Cynthia Goyette in 1965). She won the 200 m. medley four times (1965–68) and the 400 m. medley twice (1966–67).

KONRADS, John (Australia, 21 May 1942–) and **KONRADS, Ilsa** (Australia, 29 Mar. 1944–). Born in Riga, Latvia, John and Ilsa Konrads fled with their parents to Germany (1944) before emigrating to Australia (in 1949) where their extraordinary swimming talents came to full bloom. Their ability and the expert coaching of Don Talbot brought them a total of thirty-seven world records between Jan. 1958 and

Feb. 1960, most of them metric-linear marks with times taken for the longer yards distances.

John contracted polio while the family were living in a refugee camp near Stutgart before going to Sydney. Despite the illness he became more successful than his sister, though it was Ilsa, at 13, who first put the name of Konrads into the world record book. On 9 Jan. 1958 she set new figures for 800 m. and 880 y.

Two days later, John broke the men's world records for the same distance and in two more swims in the next seven days added the 200 m., 220 y., 400 m., and 440 y. Altogether he set twenty-five world marks, won three Olympic medals in 1960—a gold for 1,500 m., and bronzes in the 400 and 4 × 200 m.—and was a triple gold medal winner at the Cardiff Commonwealth Games (440, 1,650 and 4 × 220 y.) in 1958.

Ilsa won the 440 y. in Cardiff to make the Konrads the only brother–sister individual champions in the history of the Games and she came second to Dawn Fraser in this event in Perth in 1962. She also gained an Olympic relay silver in 1960.

John was a member of Australia's Olympic teams for the 1956, '60 and '64 Games, though he was only a stand-by at the first and past his peak for the third. Ilsa swam in the 1960 and 1964 Games, but a fourth place in the 400 m.

on her first appearance was her best individual Olympic effort.

Their best times were—John: 2:02·2 (200 m.), 2:01·6 (220 y.), 4:15·9 (400 m. and 440 y.), 8:59·6 (the first man under nine minutes for 800 m. and 880 y.), 17:11·0 (1,500 m. and 1,650 y.); Ilsa: 4:45·4 (400 m./440 y.), 10:11·4 (800 m./ 880 y.), 19:25·7 (1,500 m./1,650 y.).

KRÄMER, Ingrid (East Germany, 29 July 1943–). Dresden's diving star Ingrid competed in three Olympics under three different names. In 1960, as Miss Krämer she won the golden double beating America's Paula Jean Pope in both the highboard and springboard by 2·34 and 14·57 points respectively.

In Tokyo in 1964, as Mrs. Engel-Krämer, the German retained her springboard title by nearly seven points from Jeanne Collier (USA), but lost the highboard narrowly to America's Lesley Bush. Divorced and re-married, Ingrid Gulbin-Krämer was only fifth in the springboard in Mexico and did not dive in the highboard.

Ingrid's first big diving occasion was, at 15, in the 1958 European championships. A slim child, with beautiful feet, she came fourth in the springboard and eighth in the highboard. Four years later she had two sweeping wins, taking the springboard by 14·79 and the highboard by 12·04 point margins.

L

LANE, Freddy (Australia, 1877–29 May 1969). The only Australian swimmer in the 1900 Olympics, Freddy Lane won the 200 m. title (2:25·2), by 5·8 seconds from Hungary's Zoltan Halmay, and also the 200 m. obstacle gold medal (the only time this event was in the programme) in the River Seine in Paris. He swam a double over-arm stroke, similar to the trudgen but with a narrow kick, which was considered to be too strenuous for distance racing until Lane won the New South Wales mile title, using this style throughout, in 1899. The fact that the rugged Lane, all 9½ stone of him, who died at the ripe old age of 92, was exhausted after some of his longer races, caused considerable concern and there were strong warnings 'never to use the trudgen except for short distance races'.

Lane, from Sydney, swam three seasons in English championships. In 1899 he won the 220 and 440 y. titles. In 1900 he dead-heated with his compatriot Frank Beaurepaire in the 220 y. in a world best 2:34·8. In July 1902, in Manchester, he took the 100 y., beating Australia's Dick Cavill and England's Rob Derbyshire, to become the first man to clock one minute flat, and he won the 220 y. in 2:28·6 (later ratified as the first world record). In October of that year, in Leicester, he astounded the swimming world by breaking the minute for 100 y. (59·6).

In fact, Lane won more English titles than Australian ones—the 100 y. (in 1898 and 1902) and the 220 y. (1902), plus two national 100 y. records of 67·6 (1898) and 60·6 (1902) were his only claims to fame at home. He belonged, of course, to the era before the world-wide system of record ratification had been regularised—thus his minute-breaking 100 y. in Leicester does not appear in the Australia record book. Had F.I.N.A., in establishing their first world record list in 1908, been able to carry out an accurate retrospective investigation of performances and had there not been suspicion in Europe of the veracity of Australian times in those days, the names of Lane and his compatriot Barney Kieran (see KIERAN, BARNEY) would have had an even more important place in the history of the sport. As it is, Lane was honoured in the Hall of Fame in 1969.

LANGFORD, Denise (Australia, 31 Dec. 1955–). This fair-haired student from Newtown, New South Wales, was one of the outstanding competitors at the 1970 Commonwealth Games in Edinburgh where she won more medals than any other woman swimmer—four golds and a silver.

She took the 200 and 400 m. medley in Commonwealth records of 2:28·9 and 5:10·7 and was in the Australian winning free-style and medley relay teams. And she was second in the 400 m. free-style in 4:31·4, four seconds behind her team mate Karen Moras. Yet, despite these successes, her only Australian championship win prior going to Scotland was in the 400 m. medley in 1970.

LANSLEY, Diane (Great Britain, 16 Feb. 1953–). Commonwealth 100 m. butterfly champion in 1970, England's only swimming gold medallist and a shock one at that, Diane Lansley from Southampton had only one national medal to her credit before she went to Edinburgh—and that was a bronze in the girls 110 y. event in 1968. And after the Games, her appearance in the A.S.A. championships at Blackpool was disappointing. She was second in the 110 y. in 68·6, seven tenths slower than her gold medal winning time, and, after swallowing water, came only fifth in the 220 y.

LARSON, Lance (United States). See DEVITT, JOHN.

LARSSON, Gunnar (Sweden, 12 May, 1951–). Karl Gunnar Larsson, born in Malmo, appeared to be in with a chance of gold medals in four events at the European championships in Barcelona in September, 1970. But the standard of his successes was quite astonishing.

In fact, this fair-haired man, a student at the California State College, at Long Beach (USA) and coached by Don Gambril, won three golds and a silver and broke two world records plus a European one.

Larsson had three tremendous battles with West Germany's Hans Fassnacht (see Fassnacht, Hans), also coached by Gambril, winning two and losing one. The Swede beat his training partner and rival in the 400 m. free-style by 0·4 and his 4:02·6 was a world record, two tenths faster than the time returned the month before by America's John Kinsella (see Kinsella, John).

The second clash, in the 400 m. medley, also ended in Larsson's favour with a European mark of 4:36·2. The German took the 200 m. free-style (1:55·2) but the Swede with 1:55·7 was also inside Fassnacht's European record set in a heat.

Larsson's fourth medal and third gold was in the 200 m. medley which, in the absence of Fassnacht, he won with ease in a world mark of 2:09·3.

The benefit of his American training is underlined by the Swede's non-success at the Mexico Olympics two years earlier. He did not reach the final of any individual event and was only in the final of the 4 × 200 m. relay in which Sweden were last. Larsson clocked 2:04·9 in the 200 m. (4th in his heat), was eliminated from the 400 and 1,500 m. with 4:25·0 and 17:57·0 and was not good enough to be chosen for the medley races.

LEE, Sammy (United States, 1 Aug. 1920–). A little man but with colossal diving talent, Sammy Lee won the Olympic highboard title and a bronze medal in the springboard at the 1948 Olympics. Four years later, now Doctor Lee, he retained his highboard crown in Helsinki—the first man to win this event at successive Games.

Born in Fresno, California, of Korean parents, Lee graduated top of his class at the Benjamin Franklin High School in Los Angeles, where he was chosen as the school's top athlete in 1939. He won his first American titles (highboard and springboard) in 1942 and, after giving up diving upon entering medical college in 1943. he returned to win the highboard crown again in 1946.

The first American-born Oriental to win an Olympic gold medal for the United States, Dr. Lee received the Sullivan Award as America's outstanding amateur athlete in 1953. He was coach to the American diving team at the Rome Olympics where his pupil Bob Webster won the highboard title (which he retained in 1964). Dr. Lee's professional specialization is in diseases of the ear—very much an occupational hazard of divers.

LEIVERS, Bobby (Great Britain, 27 Dec. 1941–28 Aug. 1964). Robert Hanford Leivers from Longton, and his Staffordshire rival from Hanley Norman Wainwright, the elder by five months, were Britain's outstanding middle and distance swimmers of the 1930s (see WAINWRIGHT, NORMAN). Leivers swam in the 1932 and '36 Olympics. He was a member of the relay squads who were fifth and sixth respectively and he was also sixth in the 1,500 m. in Berlin—in clocking 19:57·4, he was the first Briton to break twenty minutes.

In European championships, Leivers, a butcher by trade, was unplaced in 1934, but in 1938, in London, took the silver in the 1,500 m.—losing the gold to Sweden's Bjorn Borg only because of bad turns—and a relay bronze. He was a relay silver medallist at the 1934 Commonwealth Games and won two golds—for 1,650 y. (19:46·4) and the relay—and a silver in the 440 y. (4:55·4) in 1938.

Leivers won nine A.S.A. titles—220 y. (1933), 440 y. (1932, '34), 500 y. (1932, '33), 880 y. (1932, '36), mile (1936, '38). After suffering from heart trouble for many years, Leivers died four months before his fiftieth birthday.

LIFE SAVING, See ROYAL LIFE SAVING SOCIETY.

LIGUE EUROPEENNE DE NATATION. The European Swimming League, known internationally by the abbreviation of its French title, L.E.N., was founded in 1927 in order to control and manage the European championships which had been held for the first time, experimentally, in Budapest the previous year.

The L.E.N. now has twenty-eight member countries, recognizes its own regional list of records and has international technical committees similar to those of the F.I.N.A. (see INTERNATIONAL TECHNICAL COMMITTEES). As well as the European championships, held normally every four years, L.E.N. also organizes Youth Championships (instituted 1967), a club water-polo championship and international team swimming and diving cup competitions.

LINTON, Pip (Great Britain, 9 June 1929–). Phyllis Margaret Linton from Maindee, Newport, won twenty-three Welsh free-style titles between 1947–55 and was also A.S.A. 100 y. (1950, '51) and 220 y. (1950) champion. She and back-stroker John Brockway were the only swimmers in the Welsh team at the 1954 Commonwealth Games in Vancouver. Pip was in the British relay team that came fifth in the 1952 Olympics.

LONG, Ann (Great Britain, 6 July 1936–). Winner of fourteen A.S.A. diving titles, Ann Long from Ilford competed in three Olympics and reached the last eight for springboard and highboard on each occasion. Her respective placings were: 1952, eighth and fifth; 1956, sixth and seventh; 1960, seventh and eighth.

She competed in two European championships—placing fifth in the highboard in 1954 and sixth in 1958—and two Commonwealth Games, winning the springboard and finishing third in the highboard in 1954 and second in the highboard in 1958.

Ann's A.S.A. diving championship wins were: highboard (5)—1950, '52, '53, '54, '59; springboard (5)—1951, '55, '56, '57, '58; high plain (3)—1954, '55, '58 and 1 m. springboard (1)—1951.

LONG, Elizabeth (Great Britain, 30 July 1947–). Free-styler Liz Long from Ilford—no relation to Ann Long (see LONG, ANN)—twice broke the European 200 m. record with times set over the four feet longer 220 y. during the 1965 A.S.A. championships. She clocked 2:16·2 in a heat, to improve the old record by 1·8 (or equivalently by 2·7 for metres) and returned 2:16·1 in the final. She won seven A.S.A. titles: 220 y. 1964, '65 and 440 y. 1960, '62, '63, '64, '65.

The Essex girl was sixth in the 1964 Olympic 400 m. (4:52·0) and anchored the medley relay squad who were fifth. She won bronzes in the Commonwealth 440 y. in 1962 (5:00·4) and free-style relay. She also represented England at the 1966 Games but without medal success.

Elizabeth missed another bronze in the European 400 m. in 1962 by 0·1 and her fifth place 4:58·2 was only 1·1 outside the silver medal time. Her best British record times were: 220 y. 2:16·1; 440 y. 4:47·8; 880 y. 10:19·0 and mile 20:56·9.

LONG COURSE. The term 'long course' is used to distinguish performances set in international-size pools of 50 m. or 55 y., from those swum in shorter baths. The distinction is necessary because the extra turns in a 'short course' pool give a time advantage (see

TURNS). All World, European, Commonwealth and British records now have to be set long course and all major swimming competitions are held in 50 m. pools.

LONG DISTANCE SWIMMING. This branch of swimming demands the same arduous training as all other branches of aquatics. It further demands the physical ability to maintain effort and to withstand cold, and sometimes rough water, for prolonged periods—and the mental ability to persevere where currents, tidal streams and wind drifts seem to have stopped progress altogether. Finally, long distance swimming requires courage, for example, to go through a pitch black night, fog, weed, flotsam, occasional oil fuel patches, swarms of jellyfish and maritime traffic.

There are two organisations in Britain primarily concerned with long distance swimming—the British Long Distance Swimming Association and the Channel Swimming Association, (see Channel Swimming).

The BLDSA organise the following annual British championships (the mile distances are given in brackets): Trentham Gardens Lake (3), Lake Bala (6), Torbay (7½) and Windermere (10¼). The Association also hold, periodically, an event in Loch Lomond (22) and a quadrennial international championship in Windermere (16). Clubs and associations affiliated to the BLDSA stage some 40 other open championships over distances between 2 and 20 miles. These range over the British Isles from the Shannon to the Tay and from Rathlin Sound to Clacton. Apart from these races, there are two BLDSA junior events over 2 and 3 miles and a 3½-mile veterans event.

The CSA observes (or investigates) and ratifies all successful swims across the Straits of Dover. Similarly, many local clubs and associations issue certificates in their own locality e.g. the Morecambe Cross Bay Swimming Association, the Solent Swimming club, the Essex Long distance S.A. Where no local sponsoring authority exists, the BLDSA will ratify and award certificates for legitimately observed and timed swims of more than 5 miles.

Long distance swimming was probably first chronicled in the legend of Leander swimming nightly across the Hellespont to meet Hero—1¼ miles each way. Much later, the Sicilians boasted a local athlete said to have swum for five days and five nights i.e. for 120 hours. Nowadays, the best endurance record is 105 hours by Luis Ruiz in the Argentine.

In the early nineteenth century, Lord Byron gave the sport some impetus by several distance swims. But modern marathon history dates from Matthew Webb's 1875 Channel swim (see WEBB, MATTHEW). In 1884, Horace Davenport (see DAVENPORT, HORACE) swam from Southsea to Ryde; in 1907 'Professor' Stearne crossed Morecambe Bay and in 1911 James Foster was the first man to conquer Windermere. This last achievement is a good basis for comparing modern standards with those of the past.

In common with sprint swimming— and these days the longest Olympic event 1,500 m., has almost become a sprint— distance norms have improved enormously over the years. The records for Lake Windermere, which is non-tidal and minimally affected by weather, form an excellent yardstick to measure these great improvements. They show a most interesting and regular trend resulting, in turn, from better stroke techniques, virtual abolition of feeding stops, fiercer competition and expert attendance from qualified BLDSA pilot-lifesavers.

	hr.	min.
1911 Foster, James (Oldham)	11	29
1933 Humphreys, John (Preston)	10	04
1934 Daly, Charles (Denton)	6	22
1955 Oldman, Fred (Huddersfield)	5	53
1958 Forsberg, Gerald (London)	5	19
1965 Lake, Geoffrey (Harrow)	5	17
1966 Gray, Elaine (St. Albans)	4	39
1967 Van Scheyndel, Jan (Neth)	4	36
1968 Van Scheyndel, Jan (Neth)	4	07

LONSBROUGH, Anita (Great Britain, 10 Aug. 1941–). Anita Lonsbrough's seven-year career (1958–64) brought seven gold, three silver and two bronze medals in major Games. She held the Olympic, European and Commonwealth breast-stroke titles at the same time and was a feared competitor throughout the swimming world.

Yet she turned to her medal-winning breast-stroke only nine months before competing in the 1958 Commonwealth Games in Cardiff where she won the 220 y. in 2:35·5 and a second gold in England's world record-breaking medley relay team, just two months after her first appearance for Britain. Before this, the Yorkshire girl had been a club standard free-styler of little consequence.

Her finest performance was in the 1960 Olympics in Rome where, in a brilliant tactical race, she took the 200 m. title in world record time (2:49·5). She beat German's Wiltrud Urselmann by half a second, having taken the lead only in the last few metres.

Miss Lonsbrough was the silver medallist in the European 200 m. championship in 1958 and a medley relay bronze medal-winner. Four years later, she completed her hat-trick of titles by winning the European championship in Leipzig, a silver in the 400 m. medley and a medley relay bronze. And in the Perth Commonwealth Games that year she retained her 220 y. title, won the new 110 y. breast-stroke and 440 y. medley events and a medley relay silver.

Anita, from Huddersfield, had to train mostly on her own. As a result she knew she had only herself to rely upon in her races. Finding morning racing difficult unless she got up hours before, she set her alarm for 4 a.m. in Rome so that she would be mentally and physically ready for the 10 a.m. heats. And she followed this pattern throughout her career.

As well as her medal triumphs, she broke four world breast-stroke records: 200 m. 2:50·3 (1959); 2:49·5 (1960); 220 y. 2:52·2 and 2:51·7 (1962). Then, having established herself without question as the world's No. 1, she returned successfully to free-style and also took up the difficult medley individual.

In addition to her five A.S.A. breast-stroke titles (220 y. 1958–62), she won the 440 y. medley (1963, '64), 220 y. free-style (1963) and was second in the 110 y. (1963) and 440 y. (1963/64). Her only disappointment was at never being allowed to swim in a free-style relay team in a major Games.

She ended her career after the Tokyo Olympics as British medley record holder (440 y. 5:36·8), with an M.B.E., having been voted 'Sportswoman of the Year' in two national polls in each of 1960 and '62 and the B.B.C. 'Sports Personality of the Year' in 1962. Anita is married to former British Olympic cyclist Hugh Porter, who won the world professional pursuit championship in 1968 and 1970.

LUDGROVE, Linda (Great Britain, 8 Sept. 1947–). The Commonwealth's top back-stroker at the 1962–66 Games, Linda Kay Ludgrove won five golds and a silver—and only Australia's great Dawn Fraser won more Commonwealth Games golds. At 15, in 1962, Linda took the 110 y. title in 1:11·1, having equalled her world record of 1:10·9 in a heat, the 220 y. in 2:35·2, equalling the world record she had set in a heat, and a silver in the medley relay. In Jamaica, in 1966, she retained her individual titles in 1:09·2, having set a Games record of 69·0 in a heat, and 2:28·5, again a world record. And she helped England to a world record-breaking win (4:40·6) in the medley relay. The Sports Writers' Association picked her as their top sportswoman of that year.

The South London blonde with the tremendous competitive spirit was nicknamed 'Little Linda' early on and it stuck with her throughout her six-year career. She was a medley relay bronze medallist at the 1962 European championships and four years later took the 100 m. back-stroke silver (68·9) and a second medley relay bronze.

She swam in the 1964 Olympics, but not in her best form and was only sixth in the 100 m. and was not picked for Britain's medley relay team. She broke

five individual world back-stroke marks
—110 y.: 1:10·9 and 1:09·5; 220 y.:
2:35·6, 2:35·2 and 2:38·5. Linda won
eight A.S.A. titles: 110 y. 1962, '63, '64,
'66, '67 and 220 y. 1964, '66, '67. Her
best 110 y. time was 68·7. a British
record, in Coventry in July 1967 when
Karen Muir (S.Africa), in beating her,
set a world record of 67·5.

LYONS, Nancy (Australia). Beatrice
Nancy Lyons was the silver medallist in
the 200 m. breast-stroke at the 1948
Olympics. Her 2:57·7, only 0·5 behind
the winner, Holland's Nel van Vliet,
made her favourite for the Commonwealth title in Auckland two years later.
But she had to settle for a silver again in
the 220 y. event (3:3·6), behind Scotland's Elenor Gordon, though she did win
a gold in Australia's medley relay team.

Nancy, from Queensland, was six
times Australian champion (1946–50 and
'52) and set seven National records:
100 m. 1:23·7 (which stood for six years),
110 y. 1:29·2 and 1:26·8 (seven years),
200 m. 3:04·8 in 1950 (her 1948 Olympic
time having not been ratified) and
2:27·7 in 1952; 220 y. 3:04·8, 2:59·4 (six
years).

M

McCLEMENTS, Lyn (Australia, 11 May 1951–). Shock winner of the 1968 Olympic 100 m. butterfly, Lynette McClements from Perth caused another sensation in 1970 by not qualifying for the Australian Commonwealth Games team. She was ruled out during the trials for an illegal leg kick, in which one foot dropped 9 inches below the other (instead of the foot movements being simultaneous and symmetrical). Lyn did this in the heats of the 100 and 200 m. butterfly and the Australian selectors decided they could not risk her being disqualified in Edinburgh and so did not choose her.

Yet in Mexico this typist, 5 ft. 10 in. and 10 st. 6 lb., who was only the sixth best swimmer on time before the Games, beat the might of America and the world record-holder Ada Kok (Neth). Lyn won in 65·5, which was 1·3 faster than her national record, three-tenths ahead of Ellie Daniels (USA) and with Miss Kok fourth. Lyn was only the thirteenth best in the 200 m. butterfly and failed by 7·1 sec. to qualify for the final but she helped the Australian team to silver medals in the medley relay.

McCORMICK, Pat (United States, 12 May 1930–). Double diving gold medallist at the 1952 Olympics, Pat McCormick, born Pat Keller, set herself a tough task in 1956 when she decided to try to get into the United States team and defend her titles in Melbourne only five months after the birth of her son. But this great competitor always rose to the big occasion. Coached by her airline pilot husband Glenn, she accomplished all she had set out to do. Her second double gold success—the only one in the diving history of the Olympics—came with her victories in the springboard by

16·47 points and the highboard by 3·19. This achievement earned her a place in the Swimming Hall of Fame, the first woman diver to be honoured.

Three times Pan American champion (highboard in 1951 and both titles in 1955), Mrs. McCormick kept fit for her Melbourne challenge before her son was born by swimming half a mile a day to within two days of his arrival. She won seventy-seven national championships and was named 'The Babe Zaharias Woman Athlete of the Year', 'The Helm's Hall North American Athlete of the Year', 'The Associated Press Woman Athlete of the Year' and 'The A.A.U.'s Sullivan Award Amateur Athlete of the Year'.

McGREGOR, Bobby (Great Britain, 3 Apr. 1944–). If nature ever designed a classic sprinter it was Robert Bilsland McGregor, from Falkirk, Scotland. Tall, broad shouldered, slim hipped, Bobby had all the natural advantages and ability to match. He became 100 m. champion of Europe in Utrecht in 1966 in one of the most astonishing races ever seen.

At the start, Russia's Leonid Ilichev wobbled and Horst Gregor of East Germany took a blatant flyer, while McGregor was left standing on his block, convinced the race would be called back. But, to the utter disbelief of everybody, the race went on. From a seemingly hopeless position, McGregor, unbelievably, was ahead at the turn and he went on to win by six-tenths in 53·7 from Ilychev.

There were long arguments about the amount of time McGregor had lost at the start—estimates ranged from 0·3 to 0·8. The largest would have put the Scot very close to the 52·9 world record of Alain Gottvalles of France.

But the real horror of that starting incident was that McGregor had never won a major title. He had been second to Canada's Dick Pound in the 1962 Commonwealth Games sprint . . . second, by one-tenth, to America's Don Schollander in the 1964 Olympics . . . and second to Mike Wenden of Australia in the 1966 Commonwealth Games.

McGregor, coached by his father David, a former British Olympic (1936) water-polo player, might well have won in Tokyo—the first Scot to do so in the pool—had he had Schollander's tremendous competitive experience. But it was not until he reached Japan, as a favourite that the Briton realized all the things other than just swimming that go to winning an Olympic title. He was wiser by the time of the 1968 Mexico Games— but his final university examinations in becoming an architect and unsympathetic handling by British team officials put paid to his medal hopes. He was, in fact, fourth in the 100 m. in 53·5, the same time as in 1964, and half a second behind bronze medallist Mark Spitz.

But in Europe McGregor was a towering swimmer. And in Britain and particularly Scotland he was a hero. He won the A.S.A. 110 y. title six times (1962–64 and 1966–68 . . . he did not swim in 1965) and the 220 y. title twice. He was second to Don Havens (USA) in the World Student Games 100 m. in 1967. He broke the world 110 y. record five times in three years, his final 53·5 (worth 53·2 for 100 m.) in 1966 being his best time. He was honoured with an M.B.E. for his swimming achievements.

McKECHNIE, Neil (Great Britain, 28 Apr. 1939–). Britain's fastest freestyler in the mid-1950s, Neil John McKechnie from Wallasey held all the English records from 100 y. to one mile from 1956–58. Most of these were set in his own home Guinea Gap pool, 25 y. of the fastest salt water anywhere in Britain. But McKechnie also proved his No. 1 place by winning eight A.S.A. titles in long course pools between 1955–

57, including the 110, 220, 440 and 880 y. in 1956, his best year, during which he set five of his six English marks.

In 1956 he swam in the Melbourne Olympics and was in Britain's sixth-placed free-style relay squad. At Guinea Gap, he set English records for 100 y. (51·8, also British record), 110 y. (57·8— British), 220 y. (2:08·0) and 440 y. (4:31·6—British). At Tynemouth (60 y.) he added the 880 y. record (10:12·9) to the mile mark (20:55·6) he had set the year before at Blackpool.

McKechnie swam for England at the 1958 Commonwealth Games (a bronze in the medley relay) and European championships. His best National championship winning times—all in 1956— were: 110 y. 58·9, 220 y. 2:11·3, 440 y. 4:45·8 and 880 y. 10:12·9.

McLACHLAN, Murray (South Africa). Winner of forty-five provincial and national campionships, 'Tich' McLachlan had considerable academic as well as swimming success. He obtained a Bachelor of Commerce degree at the University of Natal in Durban; a Rhodes scholarship to Wadham College, Oxford, and an English M.A. in Economics; and a third degree at Stanford University in the United States.

McLachlan's swimming forte was distance events and during his seven years at the top he dominated the South African scene. He won a bronze medal in the Commonwealth Games 1,650 y. in 1958 and placed fourth in the 440 y. He was sixth in the 400 and 1,500 m. in the 1960 Olympics, his times being inside the previous Games records. He won the World Student Games 1,500 m. in 1961 in record time and was second in the 400 m. He was second and third respectively in these events in the 1963 Student Games in Brazil.

During his years at Oxford, McLachlan played a considerable part in improving the standards of the University team and he led Oxford to victory in varsity matches.

MADISON, Helene (United States, 19 June 1913–Nov. 1970). Winner of the 100 and 400 m. at the 1932 Olympics in 66·8 (a world best long course time) and 5:28·5 (a world record) and anchor swimmer in the world record-breaking American relay team, Helene Madison, from Seattle, was the supreme free-styler of her era. In 1930–31 she broke the world record for every distance, with one exception—for 800 m. and techni-cally she should have been the first record-holder for this too.

The 880 y. for women came into the world record-book in 1919 (see EDERLE, GERTRUDE) but marks for the 15 ft. 4 in. shorter 800 m. (for men and women) were not accepted until the 1930s. On 6 July 1930, Helene, as the seventh record-breaker, set a world 880 y. mark of 11:41·2 in a 55 y. bath at Long Beach. On 23 August 1931, Yvonne Godard of France clocked 12:18·8 for 800 m. in a 500 m. Paris pool and this time was ratified by F.I.N.A. as the first world record for the distance. In fact, the American girl's 880 y. time was at least equal to 11:37·0 for metres which makes it all the more strange that her July 1930 time was not also accepted for metres.

The fifteen world record distances that fell to Miss Madison, five of them twice, in a space of sixteen months and thirteen days, were: 100 y. (60·8 and 60·0, the first level minute); 100 m. (68·0, 66·0); 200 m. (2:34·6); 220 y. (2:35·0, 2:34·8); 300 y. (3:41·6, 3:39·0); 300 m. (3:59·5); 400 m. (5:31·0); 440 y. (5:39·4, 5:31·0); 500 y. (6:16·4); 500 m. (7:12·0); 880 y. (11:41·2); 1,000 y. (13:23·6); 1,000 m. (14:44·8); 1,500 m. (23:17·2); 1,760 y. (24:34·6). Of these twenty marks, only her second 100y./100 m. successes were in the same swim and her 400 m. record was the time she clocked for the longer 440 y. No one, not even the great Dane, Ragnhild Hveger (see HVEGER, RAGN-HILD), has been the fastest in the world over the whole range from the shortest to the longest.

The speed of Helene's swimming is reflected by the years her records stood, particularly for the four longest events which she set in sixteen days in July 1931. It took nine years for her 1,000 y. and one mile marks to be bettered and five before her 1,000 and 1,500 m. marks disappeared.

Miss Madison won all four United States titles (100, 440, 880 and 1,760 y.) in 1930 and '31. After only three years at the top, but with so much to show for them, Helene Madison bowed out of swimming at the Los Angeles Olympics with her three gold medals and her twenty-first world record (5:28·5 for 400 m.) on 13 August 1932 at 19 years and 2 months young.

MAGIC MARKS. Swimming, like athletics with its four-minute mile, has magic marks that fire the imagination. Two of the modern era that will be long remembered were achieved by Australian girls, Dawn Fraser and Lorraine Crapp.

On 25 Aug. 1956 Miss Crapp took the world marks for 400 m. and 440 y. below the mythical five-minute barrier—and this sixteen years after Denmark's Ragnhild Hveger had come within one-tenth of five minutes. In one fabulous swim, the Sydney girl clocked 4:50·8 and 4:52·4 and on the way broke the world records for 200 m. and 220 y.

On 27 Oct. 1962 Miss Fraser swam 110 y. in 59·9, which was also a world record for the two feet shorter 100 m.

Johnny Weissmuller (USA) was the first man to break the minute for 100 m. (58·6), in Alameda on 9 July 1922. This improved the world record of 1920 Olympic champion Duke Kahanamoku by 1·8 sec. The powerful Weissmuller also was the first to swim 400 m. in under five minutes. He did this in the 25 y. Yale University pool on 6 Mar. 1923 when his 4:57·0 improved his own world mark by 9·6 seconds.

Don Schollander was the two minute-breaker. In Los Angeles on 27 July 1963, the fair-haired American clocked 1:58·8 for 200 m. to clip 1½ seconds from the three-month-old time of Australia's Bob Windle.

Of course, the longer the race, the greater the improvement. And minute-breaking has been a feature of the his-tory of swimming's longest Olympic event, the 1,500 m. In sixty-one years, seven minute barriers have been broken.

First under twenty-two minutes was Sweden's Arne Borg (21:35·3 on 8 July 1923) . . . under twenty-one minutes went Australia's Boy Charlton (20:06·6 on 7 July 1924). It was Arne Borg again for the first sub-twenty-minute mark (19:07·2 on 2 Sept. 1927) and that stood for eleven years until Japan's Tomikatsu Amano clocked 19:58·8 on 10 Aug. 1938.

After eighteen years and World War II, Murray Rose (Australia) returned 17:59·5—but it took only six more years for seventeen minutes to be broken, by America's Roy Saari (16:58·7 on 2 Sept. 1964). And on 23 Aug. 1970 John Kinsella (USA), then 17, sailed under sixteen minutes (15:57·1).

The women's assault on the 1,500 m. world record has been equally astonishing. Miss Hveger was the first girl under twenty-two and twenty-one minutes (21:45·7 in 1938 and 20:57·0 in 1941). Australia's Ilsa Konrads broke twenty minutes with 19:25·7 in 1959 and three years later America's Carolyn House returned 18:44·0 for the fourth minute-breaking performance in twenty-four years. And Debbie Meyer, in the second of her four world record swims over the distance, clocked 17:50·2 in 1967.

Tom Mann (USA) broke the minute for 100 m. back-stroke on the first leg of the Olympic relay in Tokyo in 1964 (59·5). The 100 m. butterfly minute went in 1960 when Lance Larson (USA) clocked 59·0.

American relay teams went through two barriers during the 1964 Games . . . under four minutes for 4 × 100 m. medley (Tom Mann, Bill Craig, Fred Schmidt and Steve Clarke) with 3:58·4 on 16 Oct. and under eight minutes for 4 × 200 m. free-style (Clarke, Saari, Gary Ilman and Schollander) with 7:52·1 on 18 Oct.

Other magic mark breakers were:

1902 Freddy Lane (Aus), 100 y. free-style under 1 min. (59·6)
1912 Percy Courtman (GB), 200 m. breast-stroke under 3 min. (2:56·6)
1934 Willy den Ouden (Neth), 100 y. free-style under 1 min. (59·8)
1935 Shozo Makino (Japan), 800 m. free-style under 10 min. (9:55·8)
1937 Jopie Waalberg (Neth), 200 m. breast-stroke under 3 min. (2:58·0)
1938 Al Vanderweghe (USA), 100 y. back-stroke under 1 min (59·4)
1944 Alan Ford (USA), 100 m. free-style under 50 sec. (49·7)
1947 Keith Carter (USA), 100 y. butterfly under 1 min. (59·4)—this was five years before butterfly was officially recognized.
1950 John Marshall (Aus), one mile under 20 min. (19:49·4)
1959 John Konrads (Aus), 800 m./880 y. under 9 min. (8:59·6)
1960 Lance Larson (USA), 100 m. butterfly under 1 min. (59·0)
1960 Jane Cederqvist (Swe), 800 m. under 10 min. (9:55·6)
1960 Anita Lonsbrough (GB), 200 m. breast-stroke (l/c) under 2:50·0 (2:49·5)
1961 Ted Stickles (USA), 400 m. and 440 y. medley under 5 min. (4:55·6/4:57·1)
1964 Jane Hughes (Can), 880 y. under 10 min. (9:57·1)
1965 Frank Wiegand (EGer), 220 y. free-style under 2 min. (1:59·9)

MARKOVITS, Kalman (Hungary, 26 Aug. 1931–). A descendant of a Hungarian count, Kalman Markovits won Olympic gold medals for water-polo in 1952 and '56 and a bronze in 1960. The world's best half-back of his era, Markovits was also in Hungary's European championship winning teams in 1954, '58 and '62. Former manager of a producers' co-operative, he became coach to the Hungarian water-polo team for the 1968 Mexico Games. His first wife was Katalin Szoke, Olympic and European 100 m. champion in 1952 and '54 respectively.

MARSHALL, John (Australia, 1930–57). John Marshall's rise to world class was quite phenomenal. He was runner-up in his first race, over 110 y. (1:19·0) in 1946, yet the next year, thanks to his first coach Tom Donnet, he won four Australian titles—220, 440, 880 and 1,650 y.

In 1948 he won the silver in the 1,500 m. and the bronze in the 400 m. at the London Olympics. Bob Kiphuth of Yale University and coach to the American team was so impressed with Marshall—'a potential world-beater' he called him —that he arranged for the Melbourne boy to study at Yale.

There Kiphuth transformed Marshall's technique so effectively that in 1950 and '51 the Australian broke nineteen world records, including 2:04·6 (200 m.), 2:05·5 (220 y.), 4:26·9 (400 m.), 4:36·4 to 4:28·1 (440 y., six marks in thirteen months), 5:12·0 (500 y.), 5:43·7 (500 m.), 9:37·5 (880 y.) and 19:49·4 (mile).

For all his record-breaking, the quiet modest Marshall was never able to emulate in an Olympics his promise of 1948. In 1952, his training hampered by business commitments, he was a bad last in the 1,500 m. final and failed to get through the semi-finals of the 400 m. For the 1956 Games in his home city, Marshall turned to the new butterfly style to win a place in the Australian team. His experiments were so successful that he came fifth in the 200 m. (2:27·2) at the age of 26. But the next year he was killed in a motor accident after a tyre of his car had burst.

MASTENBROEK, Rie (Netherlands). Hendrika Mastenbroek, whose first name in usual Dutch fashion was always abbrevitated to 'Rie', won three gold medals in the 1936 Olympics during her short and most successful swimming career. These were for the 100 m. in which she beat Jeannette Campbell (Arg) by 0·5 in 65·9, the 400 m. in which her 5:26·4 was 1·1 faster than Denmark's Ragnhild Hveger and the 4 × 100 m. relay. She missed a fourth gold in the 100 m. back-stroke by finishing 0·3 behind her team-mate Nina Senff.

Coached by the famous Dutchwoman Ma Braun, Rie trained in the Rotterdam canals for distance and in a 25 m. indoor baths for sprinting. She had a tremendous rise to fame, for in 1934, her first year outside Rotterdam regional competitions, she won the European 400 m. free-style and 100 m. back-stroke titles,

came second in the 100 m. and was a member of the Dutch winning relay squad.

Her seven world records—one for free-style and six for back-stroke—include 5:29·1 for 440 y. (1936), 1:15·8 (100 m. back-stroke), 2:49·6 (150 y. ba), 5:48·8 (400 m. ba). She was honoured by the Hall of Fame (1968) and now lives with her husband and three children in Amsterdam.

MATTHES, Roland (East Germany, 17 Nov. 1950–). The Rolls Royce of swimming is not an extravagant description of Matthes, who won both back-stroke titles at the 1968 Olympics and laid the groundwork for his team's silver medals in the medley relay. Every era has its 'greatest swimmer of all time', and the man-of-the-1970s nomination surely belongs to Matthes from Erfurt.

Slim and quiet, almost shy, out of the water, in it he is in a class of his own. He has a deceptively languid stroke with hidden power and when he accelerates he leaves everyone floundering. And so it was in the 200 m. final in Mexico. He was only third at half distance and at the last turn he was fifth. At exactly the right moment he speeded his stroke tempo just a fraction to glide ahead to win by one second, from Mitch Ivey (USA) in 2:09·6. He took the 100 m. by an even bigger margin, touching 1½ seconds ahead of Charles Hickcox (USA) in 58·7.

Matthes used eight to ten strokes less for each 50 m. lap than any of his rivals and though he admits he was worried about winning his Olympic titles, no one who watched from the bath-side had any doubt. His final Mexico effort was a world record 58·0 on the first leg of the medley relay.

He has a woman coach, Marlis Grohe, whom he respects tremendously and would also like to have her with him for his big races so that he doesn't need to worry. And Frau Grohe has trained her talented pupil to ten individual world records of astonishing excellence.

In three years (Sept. 1967–70) Matthes reduced his 100 m. time from 58·4 to

56·9. This latter performance, on the first leg of the medley relay at the Barcelona European championships, which enabled the East German team to break the world record, was a 0·9 improvement on his previous world mark. He also broke the 200 m. record five times, from 2:07·9 (8 Nov. 1967) to 2:06·1 (11 Sept. 1970).

His September 200 m. swim was in a heat of the European championship and, with one eye on the score-board clock, Matthes made it all look so easy that it came as a shock to realise it was another world record performance.

In Barcelona, Matthes—of course—won both the 100 and 200 m. back-stroke titles, though, for him, in slow times as he was saving his energies for relays. He was second in the 100 m. free-style (53·5) and won a medley relay gold and two bronzes in the free-style relays.

MEDICA, Jack (United States, 5 Oct. 1933–). Medica, from Seattle, Washington State, won the Olympic 400 m. gold and silvers in the 1,500 m. and relay at the 1936 Berlin Games. As a one-man team representing the University of Washington in the N.C.A.A. championships, he won three events (the maximum allowed) three times in a row to place his university third, behind the big squads from Michigan and Iowa, in the points-scoring table.

Winner of ten A.A.U. titles, Medica set eleven world records from 200 m. to one mile, of which his best times were: 2:07·2 (200 m., which stood for nine years), 2:07·9 (220 y.), 3:04·4 (300 y.), 3:21·6 (300 m.), 4:38·7 (400 m., unbroken for seven years), 4:40·8 (440 y.), 5:16·3 (500 y.), 5:57·8 (500 m.), 10:15·4 (880 y.), 1,000 y. (11:37·4), 20:58·8 (one mile, stood for eight years).

MEDLEY SWIMMING. Medley swimming, as the name suggests, is an event in which the competitor or team uses a variety of strokes in equal parts during the course of a race.

In medley relays the order of swimming is back-stroke, breast-stroke,

butterfly and free-style. In individual medley, to balance the load for the single swimmer, butterfly—the most tiring stroke—comes first followed by back-stroke, breast-stroke and free-style. In both events, and in the absence of technical rules covering front-crawl (see FREE-STYLE and FRONT-CRAWL), free-style is held to mean any stroke other than back-stroke, breast-stroke or butterfly and, therefore, is invariably front-crawl.

The Americans pioneered individual medley racing as the ultimate test of the complete swimmer in the 1930s, long before it became a world event. As a result, the swimmers of the United States have dominated the event and have won all the titles for men and women since medley individual was added to the Olympic programme in 1964. Medley individual world records have been recognized since 1952.

Medley relay swimming began earlier. The Commonwealth Games first included this event in the programme in 1934, the European championships in 1958 and the Olympic Games in 1960. World medley relay records were ratified from 1946. Prior to the separation of breast-stroke and butterfly in 1952 (see BREAST-STROKE and BUTTERFLY) medley events were for three strokes—back-stroke, breast-stroke and free-style—and teams of three.

MELVILLE CLARK, G. NATIONAL MEMORIAL TROPHY (England's 'Diving Club of the Year'). This trophy, presented in memory of Gordon Melville Clark, former national diving champion and chairman of the A.S.A. diving committee, is awarded each year to the English club (men's or women's or a section of a mixed club) scoring the most place points in Diving championships during the year. Winners:

1951–60 Highgate (men)
1961 Isleworth Penguins (women)
1962 Highgate (men)
1963 Highgate (men)—Isleworth Penguin (women) (tie)
1964–69 Highgate (men)
1970 Hillingdon (women)

EUROPEAN CHAMPIONSHIP WINNERS. The one that nearly got away and the triple winner. (*Above*) The start of the 100m free-style final in Utrecht in 1966 when Bobby McGregor (GB), in lane 5, was left on the block yet still managed to win the gold medal. (*Below*) Ian Black (GB), first in the 400 and 1,500m free-style and 200m butterfly at the 1958 championships in Budapest

GRINHAM, JUDY. Judy Grinham of Great Britain (centre) with her team-mate Margaret Edwards (left) and New Zealand's Phillipa Gould after the girls had finished in this order in the Commonwealth 110y. back-stroke in 1958

JARVIS, JOHN. Jarvis, from Leicester, with some of the 108 trophies he gained between 1897 and 1907

METROPOLITAN SWIMMING AS-SOCIATION. The Metropolitan Swimming Association, or, as it was known originally, the Associated Metropolitan Swimming Clubs and then the London Swimming Association, was founded on 7 Jan. 1869 following a swimming congress held at the German Gymnasium in King's Cross, London, under the presidency of Mr. E. G. Ravenstein.

This amalgamation of London clubs received a chorus of approval, but was given almost invisible active support. Its influence was purely local and its development hampered by lack of funds. Early in Feb. 1874 the title of the association was again changed to the Swimming Association of Great Britain, in order to include all the clubs in the country. In 1884, following a breakaway led by the Otter Club of London, a rival body, the Amateur Swimming Union, was set up. A desperate struggle for supremacy went on until 1886 when the S.A.G.B. and A.S.U. agreed to dissolve in order to found the Amateur Swimming Association (q.v.).

METRIC/LINEAR CONVERSIONS. Although almost all the world now measures in metres, there are many swimming baths, particularly in the United Kingdom, which are still linear in length. The simple conversion is that 100 m. is two feet shorter than 110 y. But the precise conversions, based on one inch equalling 2·54 cm., are:

91·44 m.	=	100 y.
100 m.	=	109 y. 1 ft. 1 in.
100·584 m.	=	110 y.
200 m.	=	218 y. 2 ft. 2 in.
201·168 m.	=	220 y.
400 m.	=	437 y. 1 ft. 4 in.
402·336 m.	=	440 y.
800 m.	=	874 y. 2 ft. 8 in.
804·672 m.	=	880 y.
1,500 m.	=	1,640 y. 1 ft. 3 in.
1,508,760 m.	=	1,650 y.
1,609·344 m.	=	1,760 y. (mile)

METRIC/LINEAR TIME CONVERSIONS. There are arbitrary international conventions for converting times for yards distances to those for the shorter metric distances and viceversa. In the list below, the first figure is for a man of good quality national standard and the second for a woman of similar stadard. However, the times of a man of world record calibre—i.e. like Debbie Meyer (USA) whose times are better than those of many men national champions—would convert more closely to the first figure while those for a man of world class could warrant an even smaller conversion time.

Style	Yards	Seconds — / +	Metres
Free-style	110	0·3 / 0·4	100
	220	0·7 / 0·8	200
	440	1·7 / 1·9	400
	880	3·5 / 4·0	800
	1,650	6·5 / 7·5	1,500
Back-stroke	110	0·4 / 0·5	100
	220	0·9 / 1·0	200
Breast-stroke	110	0·5 / 0·5	100
	220	1·0 / 1·1	200
Butterfly	110	0·4 / 0·5	100
	220	0·9 / 1·1	200
Individual medley	220	0·9 / 1·1	200
	440	1·9 / 2·1	400
Free-style relay	4 × 110	1·2 / 1·6	4 × 100
	4 × 220	2·8 / 3·2	4 × 200
Medley relay	4 × 110	1·6 / 1·9	4 × 110

MEYER, Debbie (United States, 14 Aug. 1952–). Typifying everything American in looks, personality and swimming, talented Deborah Meyer, from Sacramento, California, won three individual golds—the first competitor in the pool to do this at a single Games—at the 1968 Olympics. She took the new 200 m. title in 2:10·5, half a second ahead of 100 m. champion Jan Henne . . . the 400 m. in 4:31·8, with another team-mate Linda Gustavson (4:35·5) second . . . and she became the first 800 m. champion in 9:24·0, which was 11·7 faster than the third American runner-up Pam Kruse. And Debbie, of the Arden Hills Club, achieved all this despite being ill most of her time in Mexico with the inglorious local stomach infection.

If her Mexico racing was marvellous, the record-breaking performances of this girl who puts up man-style times have been breath-taking. In two years and five weeks (9 July 1967 to 17 Aug. 1969) Debbie set fifteen free-style world marks from 200 to 1,500 m. These included taking the 400 m., in four bites, from 4:32·6 to 4:24·5 (in thirteen months) ... the 800 m. from 9:35·8 to 9:10·4 ... and the 1,500 m. from 18:11·1 to 17:19·9 (nearly a minute off in two years)! People ask when will the swimming record-breaking stop. The answer is never while the Meyers of this world continue to appear.

As a comparison, her 4:24·5 would have beaten Australia's Murray Rose by 2·8 sec. for the gold in the 1956 Olympic 400 m. final. Debbie's world 1,500 mark (17:19·9) was 39·0 faster than Rose in winning the Melbourne title and only 0·3 slower than John Konrads' 1960 Olympic winning time.

Pan American 400 and 800 m. champion in 1967 (4:32·6 and 9:22·8) and chosen that year, by the Tass News Agency, as 'Woman Athlete of the Year', Debbie has also broken the world record for 200 m. (2:06·7). Coached by Sherman Chavoor, who believes in training his pupils for the longer distances first, then scaling down.

Miss Meyer won the United States 400 and 1,500 m. outdoor titles four successive years (1967–70) and the 400 m. medley in 1969. In August, 1970 she reduced her world mark for 400 m. freestyle to 4:24·3.

MIDLAND DISTRICT. The Amateur Swimming Association Midland District (founded in 1889) consists of the following counties: Beford, Cambridge, Hereford, Huntingdon, Leicester, Lincoln, Norfolk, Northampton, Rutland, Shropshire, Suffolk, Warwick, Worcester and parts of Berkshire, Buckinghamshire and Oxfordshire (north of latitude 51 degrees 37 minutes) and of Derbyshire and Staffordshire (south of latitude 53 degrees, except the city of Stoke-on-Trent.)

The Midlands have had three honorary secretaries who have served for more than twenty years—H. Thomsett (1892–1911), George Newton (1912–32) and C. W. 'Fritz' Plant (1933–54). There were only three honorary treasurers between 1894 and 1954—F. H. Thomas (1894–1911), C. N. Milner (1912–34) and Ken Martin (1935–54), who then held the honorary secretaryship 1955–59.

MILTON FAMILY, Freddie (Great Britain, 2 Oct. 1906–), **Irene Pirie** (Canada, 10 June 1914–), **Tony** (Great Britain, 22 Mar. 1938–). The Miltons, father, mother and son, all competed in the Olympic Games ... a rare hat-trick this in any sport and only one other family in swimming (see GYARMATI FAMILY) are known to have done it.

First to gain the honour was Irene Pirie, from Ontario, who was in the 1932 Canadian team whose relay squad came fourth, just behind bronze medallists Britain. Four years later, in Berlin, Frederick George Matt Milton was in the British water-polo team while Irene, who had married Freddie the previous summer, swam again for Canada and was in the relay team who placed fifth, this time just ahead of Britain. A further twenty-four years onwards, to 1960, and their son Hamilton Pirie Matt—better known as Tony—was in the British fourth-placed 4 × 200 m. relay team who broke the European record in Rome.

Freddie, of the Otter Club, swam internationally from 1929 to 1939, including two Commonwealth Games, winning a relay silver in Hamilton in 1930 ... where he met Irene, who was just 16. He won five A.S.A. titles—500 y. (1930), mile (1931, '32) and the long distance (1932, '33). The name Milton appeared again in the A.S.A. championship lists in 1963 when Tony won the long distance —and he won again in 1965, '66 plus the 880 y. (a title his father never gained) in 1964.

Irene Pirie was in Canada's silver medal winning relay team at the 1930 Commonwealth Games and took the 100 m. silver (63·6), a bronze in the 400 m. (5:54·4), plus a relay gold in the 1934 Games in London.

And to finish this family story, Irene's brother Bob, two years her junior, swam in the 1936 Olympics and also in the 1934 and 1938 Commonwealth Games, winning medals in the latter two. He was in the winning relay, second in the 1,500 y. and third in the 440 y. in London . . . and he won the 110 and 440 y. and was second in the 1,650 y. and freestyle and medley relays in Sydney.

MITCHELL, Stella (Great Britain, 21 July 1947–). Stella Marion Minter Mitchell succeeded gold-medal girl Anita Lonsbrough (see LONSBROUGH, ANITA) as Britain's No. 1 breast-stroke swimmer. Four times A.S.A. champion (1963–66), she twice broke Miss Lonsbrough's 220 y. world record (2:51·4 and 2:50·2 in September–October 1963) but never won a gold medal in a major Games.

The North London girl's best performance was fourth place in the 1964 Olympic 200 m. (2:49·0), 0·4 behind bronze medallist Babanina (USSR). On this occasion, she finished 0·6 ahead of her team-mate Jill Slattery. But, two years later, Jill won the 220 y. Commonwealth title in Kingston while Stella took the silver—though both had the same time (2:50·3). Two weeks later, Jill was third and Stella fifth in the European 200 m. in Utrecht. Miss Mitchell's best 200 m. time was 2:47·0 in 1964.

MONCKTON, John (Australia, 1939–). Silver medallist, behind his team-mate David Theile, in the 1956 Olympic 100 m. back-stroke (63·2), John Monckton, a carpenter from Sydney, also competed in the 1960 Games in Rome but only managed seventh place (64·1).

Between these Games, Monckton had his best year in 1958, when he won the Commonwealth 110 y. title in Cardiff (61·7), a second gold in the medley relay and set six world records in five weeks. On 15 Jan. he clocked 2:18·8 for 220 y. (also a 200 m. record)—15 Feb. 61·5 for 110 y. (also 100 m. mark) and 18 Feb. 2:18·4 (a 220 y. and 200 m. record).

His metric marks, set over the longer yards distances (equivalent to 61·0 and 2:17·5 for 100 and 200 m.) stood from one to three years, but his 110 y. time remained on the record book until 1967, when East Germany's great Roland Matthes (see MATTHES, ROLAND) clocked 60·1. And Monckton's Commonwealth winning time of that year (1958) was still the championship record in 1970 when the Games opened in Edinburgh. Monckton was Australian 110/220 y. back-stroke champion in 1957/58.

MORAS, Karen (Australia, 6 Jan. 1954–). A bronze medal in the 400 m. and fourth place in the 800 m. in the 1968 Olympics at 14 were the first successes of Karen Moras, who does not like training yet will do a 3½ hour work-out, starting at 5.30 a.m., before going to college.

One of six Moras children, all members of the Forbes and Ursula Carlile Swim School in Ryde, New South Wales, Karen started swimming at 7 and at 13 returned 4:41·0 for 400 m., a time that would have won the gold medal at the 1964 Olympics. One year later, in Mexico, she clocked 4:37·0 for third place and 9:38·6 for 800 m. in which she was fourth and missed the bronze by one-tenth.

Early in 1970, Karen twice beat America's triple Olympic gold medallist Debbie Meyer in Sydney and in the Australian championships she won three titles—the 400 m. in 4:26·3 (only 1·7 outside Miss Meyer's world mark) and 200 m. in 2:09·8, both Commonwealth records and then clocked 9:09·1 for 800 m. and her first world mark.

Miss Moras reduced her world 800 m. time to 9:02·4 in winning the first of her three titles in the 1970 Commonwealth Games. She finished 25·1 sec. ahead of her team-mate Helen Gray and would have beaten the combined efforts of any other two girls in the Games swimming 400 m. each.

She failed in her ambition to break the world 400 m. record in winning this title in Edinburgh (4:27·4) and in a solo attempt later she missed her target by three-tenths, but her 4:24·8 was the second fastest of all time. She also won the 200 m. and her 2:09·8 equalled her Commonwealth record.

MORTON, Lucy (Great Britain, 23 Feb. 1898–   ). The first British woman to win an individual Olympic swimming title was Lucy Morton of Blackpool, who took a surprise gold in the 200 m. breast-stroke in 1924 at the age of 26. She was only the second string as world record-holder Irene Gilbert was Britain's real hope.

Fate helped the Briton for Holland's Marie Baron, who had the fastest heat time (3:22·6) was disqualified for a faulty turn. America's Agnes Geraghty was ahead after 150 m., followed by Miss Morton and third string Gladys Carson. But over the last 50 m. Miss Morton fought ahead to win by 0·8 in 3:33·2, a Games record, with Miss Carson third (3:35·4) and Irene Gilbert (who had been ill) a shadow of her world record self fifth (3:38·0).

The north of England woman never held the world record for her Olympic gold medal distance though she twice set 200 y. figures—3:11·4 as the first holder in 1916 and 3:06·0 in 1920. She must have had a good chance of a gold in 1920 . . . but there were no breast-stroke events for women in the Antwerp Games.

Lucy also was a talented back-stroker —in the days of the old English double over-arm and frog leg-kick style—and was the first holder of the world record for 150 y. (2:17·0, 1916). She was the first A.S.A. champion for 150 y. back-stroke and 200 y. breast-stroke in 1920. Married in 1927, Mrs. Heaton, *née* Morton, taught swimming to Blackpool children for many years and has continued her interest in the sport as an official.

MUIR, Karen (South Africa, 16 Sept. 1952–). The youngest competitor in any sport to break a world record, Karen Yvette Muir was only 12 years, 10 months and 25 days young on 10 Aug. 1965 when she took seven-tenths off the 110 y. back-stroke time of Britain's

Linda Ludgrove. Karen's 68·7 in a heat of the A.S.A. junior championship at Blackpool compared most favourably with the world 100 m. record of America's Cathy Ferguson—67·7 (equal to 68·2 for 110 y.)—in winning the 1964 Olympic title. And the painfully shy, skinny South African, who had been brought to England 'for experience' and had no real idea of how to start or turn, showed this performance was no fluke by taking the final in 68·9.

Such exceptional talent deserved Olympic golds in Mexico. But South Africa were excluded from the 1968 Games where the back-stroke events were won by Americans: Kaye Hall in the 100 m. in 66·2 (breaking Karen's latest 100 m. mark by two-tenths, though the time was equivalent only to the Kimberley girl's 110 y. world mark of 66·7) and Pokey Watson in the 200 m. in 2:24·8 (against Karen's world record that year of 2:23·8). And with the expulsion of South Africa from the International Olympic Committee in May 1970 the chances of Karen Muir winning a major title are finished for ever.

She started swimming at 9. Two years later, few who watched this slip of a girl in the South African women's 110 y. free-style championship (she did not even do the standard time) would have imagined that within eighteen months her name would be a household word.

Karen has made many tours overseas, to Europe, the United States. Each time she has returned with fresh honours. She has been awarded the Helms Trophy for Africa and the South African President's Award of Merit. She has won twenty-two South African championships, for free-style and medley as well as back-stroke, holds fifteen national recores and three United States titles: 100 m. in 1968 and 200 m. in 1966 and '68.

MUNOZ, Felipe (Mexico, 3 Feb. 1951–). Mexico's only swimming champion in the history of the Olympics, the roof was almost exploded off his home Mexico City pool in 1968 when Felipe Munoz touched half a second ahead of the Russian favourite Vladimir Kosinski in the 200 m. breast-stroke. It was fortunate that the rest of the placings in this eight man final were clear cut and that the electrical timing and judging machine did not break down, for as Munoz finished every single Mexican at the poolside quit officiating and stood up and cheered.

Munoz, only the sixth fastest before the Games, was a national hero afterwards. He is known affectionately as 'Tibio' or 'luke-warm' because his father comes from Aguascalientes ('hot water') and his mother from the village of Rio Frio ('cold river'). But there was nothing tepid about his swimming that memorable October evening.

N

NEW ZEALAND AMATEUR SWIMMING ASSOCIATION.
Swimming on an organized basis in New Zealand began in 1880 when, on 11 Oct, at a meeting at the home of a Mr. Arthur Francis, the Christchurch Amateur Swimming Club was formed.

The N.Z.A.S.A.—after the English A.S.A., the second national governing body in the swimming world—was formally constituted on 4 Jan. 1890 through the efforts of Mr. Roland St. Clair. Rows between the North and South Islands led to the formation of a rival organization in the North Island, known as the New Zealand Amateur Swimming Association Registered. Peace was finally achieved on 21 Mar. 1904. There were eight affiliated clubs in 1892, though it is believed another eight were in existence. At the end of 1969, there were 200 clubs representing 25,800 members.

NEW ZEALAND CHAMPIONS.
New Zealand champions have been held since 1890 on a centralized basis . . . a practice not adopted in England until forty-five years later. The winners since 1946 are:

MEN

110 y. Free-style (instituted 1890)

1946*	Hatchwell, Bob	58·4
1947*	Hatchwell, Bob	55·2
1948*	Barry, Lyall	55·2
1949*	Ballantyne, Donald	1:00·2
1950*	Barry, Lyall	55·4
1951*	Keesing, Neil	59·0
1952*	Amos, Michael	56·4
1953*	Amos, Michael	57·0
1954*	Blackwood, Jim	58·2
1955*	Amos, Michael	55·6
1956*	Ramsey, Darryl	56·3
1957	Snoep, Otto	1:02·2
1958	Ramsey, Darryl	1:02·0
1959*	Dann, Graham	55·6
1960	Hatch, Peter	1:01·4
1961*	Hatch, Peter	52·6
1962	Hatch, Peter	59·0
1963	Hatch, Peter	57·8
1964	Hatch, Peter	58·7
1965	Walker, Robbie	57·6
1966	Walker, Robbie	58·1
1967	Smith, Glen	57·9
1968	O'Carroll, Paddy	56·7
1969	Curry, Ian	56·6
1970†	Borrie, Michael	55·6

* = 100 y.   † = 100 m.

220 y. Free-style (instituted 1892)

1946	Chambers, Noel	2:27·0
1947	Barry, Lyall	2:23·8
1948	Chambers, Noel	2:20·4
1949	Lucas, Buddy	2:27·2
1950	Amos, Michael	2:20·0
1951	Stanley, Jack	2:33·0
1952	Amos, Michael	2:26·0
1953	Hamilton, John	2:22·3
1954	Hamilton, John	2:22·9
1955	Hamilton, John	2:19·9
1956	Harker, Reg	2:21·6
1957	Lucas, Buddy	2:19·8
1958	McGuinness, John	2:20·3
1959	Smith, Bill	2:14·5
1960	Dann, Graham	2:18·6
1961	Hatch, Peter	2:15·8
1962	Hatch, Peter	2:13·7
1963	Dalton, Terry	2:09·5
1964	Walker, Robbie	2:10·2
1965	Walker, Robbie	2:07·1
1966	Walker, Robbie	2:09·8
1967	Campbell, Graham	2:10·8
1968	Smith, Glen	2:07·0
1969	Kindred, Alan	2:05·5
1970*	Borrie, Michael	2:01·8

* = 200 m.

440 y. Free-style (instituted 1890)

1946	Chambers, Noel	5:45·4
1947	Chambers, Colin	5:24·0

1948	Chambers, Noel	5:03·4
1949	Lucas, Buddy	5:20·0
1950	Lucas, Buddy	5:03·4
1951	Lucas, Buddy	5:03·2
1952	Jarvis, John	5:14·6
1953	Jarvis, John	5:08·2
1954	Hamilton, John	5:08·6
1955	Jarvis, John	5:00·1
1956	Flynn, John	5:04·4
1957	Lucas, Buddy	5:03·8
1958	McFadden, Colin	4:57·4
1959	McFadden, Colin	4:49·9
1960	Monteith, Graham	4:53·9
1961	Crowder, Brian	4:48·7
1962	Dalton, Terry	4:46·4
1963	Dalton, Terry	4:34·6
1964	Walker, Robbie	4:37·9
1965	Walker, Robbie	4:31·0
1966	Walker, Robbie	4:35·0
1967	Kindred, Alan	4:38·6
1968	Kindred, Alan	4:32·8
1969	Kindred, Alan	4:24·8
1970*	Kindred, Alan	4:26·5

* = 400 m.

1,650 y. Free-style (instituted 1953)

1953	Jarvis, John	20:43·7
1954	Hamilton, John	20:43·5
1955	Jarvis, John	20:04·7
1956	Flynn, John	20:13·8
1957	Lucas, Buddy	20:16·1
1958	McFadden, Colin	20:01·9
1959	McFadden, Colin	19:30·9
1960	Monteith, Graham	19:40·5
1961	Crowder, Brian	19:33·6
1962	Monteith, Graham	19:22·4
1963	Dalton, Terry	18:26·0
1964	Walker, Robbie	18:31·6
1965	Walker, Robbie	18:18·4
1966	Walker, Robbie	18:33·8
1967	Kindred, Alan	18:30·0
1968	Kindred, Alan	18:34·8
1969	Kindred, Alan	17:42·6
1970*	Treffers, Mark	17:24·5

* = 1,500 m.

110 y. Back-stroke (instituted 1938)

1946*	Cliff, Clive	1:06·6
1947*	Mathieson, Peter	1:06·2
1948*	Wilson, Trevor	1:05·8
1949*	Mathieson, Peter	1:07·0
1950*	Mathieson, Peter	1:07·6
1951*	Hurring, Lincoln	1:06·6
1952*	Hurring, Lincoln	1:03·6
1953*	Hurring, Lincoln	1:02·6

1954*	Hamilton, Neil	1:07·0
1955*	Hamilton, Neil	1:06·1
1956*	Tansley, Mark	1:05·8
1957	Tansley, Mark	1:11·0
1958	Tansley, Mark	1:11·2
1959*	Robertson, Bill	1:03·5
1960	Hurring, Lincoln	1:08·7
1961*	Robertson, Bill	1:01·1
1962	Robertson, Bill	1:08·6
1963	Robertson, Bill	1:07·2
1964	O'Carroll, Paddy	1:07·4
1965	O'Carroll, Paddy	1:06·8
1966	O'Carroll, Paddy	1:05·7
1967	O'Carroll, Paddy	1:05·3
1968	O'Carroll, Paddy	1:04·0
1969	O'Carroll, Paddy	1:05·4
1970†	Bond, Barnett	1:05·4

* = 100 y.   † = 100 m.

220 y. Back-stroke (instituted 1960)

1960	Robertson, Bill	2:31·6
1961	Robertson, Bill	2:27·5
1962	Robertson, Bill	2:28·7
1963	Robertson, Bill	2:26·0
1964	Seagar, Allan	2:26·4
1965	Seagar, Allan	2:22·3
1966	Seagar, Allan	2:23·8
1967	Brown, Hilton	2:24·1
1968	O'Carroll, Paddy	2:20·8
1969	Bond, Barnett	2:22·0
1970*	Bond, Barnett	2:19·5

* = 200 m.

110 y. Breast-stroke (instituted 1939)

1946*	Shanahan, John	1:14·4
1947*	Shanahan, John	1:12·2
1948*	Shanahan, John	1:10·0
1949*	Callan, Colin	1:14·8
1950*	Shanahan, John	1:10·0
1951*	Shaw, J.	1:15·0
1952*	Doms, John	1:14·0
1953*	Doms, John	1:13·6
1954*	Doms, John	1:12·0
1955*	Doms, John	1:11·9
1956*	Martlew, Garry	1:15·2
1957	Hilt, Con	1:19·8
1958	Hilt, Con	1:19·5
1959*	Hilt, Con	1:08·1
1960	Hilt, Con	1:18·5
1961*	Hilt, Con	1:09·1
1962	Graham, Tony	1:18·7
1963	Graham, Tony	1:15·6
1964	Ruzio-Saban, Gjoko	1:12·9
1965	Graham, Tony	1:12·0
1966	Graham, Tony	1:13·1

1967	Graham, Tony	1:12·9
1968	Johnstone, Ivan	1:14·0
1969	Graham, Tony	1:14·2
1970†	Graham, Tony	1:14·3

* = 100 y.   † = 100 m.

220 y. Breast-stroke (instituted 1906)

1946	Dowse, Desmond	3:06·4
1947	Shanahan, John	3:00·8
1948	Shanahan, John	2:58·0
1949	Callan, Colin	3:10·2
1950	Shanahan, John	2:58·0
1951	Dowse, Desmond	3:02·6
1952	Doms, John	2:58·6
1953	Doms, John	2:57·0
1954	Doms, John	2:57·6
1955	Doms, John	2:56·8
1956	McDonald, Ian	2:59·8
1957	Hilt, Con	2:57·2
1958	Brittendon, Garry	2:57·4
1959	Hilt, Con	2:48·2
1960	Hilt, Con	2:58·1
1961	Graham, Tony	2:48·5
1962	Graham, Tony	2:51·5
1963	Graham, Tony	2:45·2
1964	Ruzion-Saban, Gjoko	2:46·1
1965	Graham, Tony	2:38·4
1966	Graham, Tony	2:39·0
1967	Graham, Tony	2:42·4
1968	Graham, Tony	2:44·7
1969	Graham, Tony	2:43·3
1970*	Graham, Tony	2:42·9

* = 200 m.

110 y. Butterfly (instituted 1948)

1948*	Shanahan, John	1:08·6
1949*	Logan, Tom	1:30·0
1950*	Callan, Colin	1:09·4
1951*	Callan, Colin	1:11·0
1952*	Callan, Colin	1:09·4
1953*	Callan, Colin	1:10·3
1954*	Logan, Tom	1:10·8
1955*	Davies, John	1:06·4
1956*	Hilt, Con	1:06·3
1957	Hilt, Con	1:14·5
1958	Cruikshank, Dennis	1:12·0
1959*	Morse, Blake	1:03·1
1960	Hatch, Peter	1:09·5
1961*	Hatch, Peter	58·5
1962	Gerrard, David	1:04·8
1963	Gerrard, David	1:02·2
1964	Hatch, Peter	1:02·4
1965	Gerrard, David	1:01·8
1966	Gerrard, David	1:03·2
1967	Gerrard, David	1:02·3

1968	Gerrard, David	1:02·1
1969	Campbell, Graham	1:01·2
1970†	Campbell, Graham	1:01·1

* = 100 y.   † = 100 m.

220 y. Butterfly (instituted 1948)

1948	Shanahan, John	3:07·8
1949	Dowse, Desmond	No time
1950	Shanahan, John	2:57·6
1951	Callan, Colin	3:06·6
1952	Dowse, Desmond	3:04·0
1953	Dowse, Desmond	3:10·8
1954	Dowse, Desmond	3:08·7
1955	Hilt, Con	3:03·5
1956	Hilt, Con	3:01·0
1957	Hilt, Con	3:05·6
1958	Cruickshank, Dennis	2:53·4
1959	Hilt, Con	2:50·0
1960	Gerrard, David	2:39·5
1961	Gerrard, David	2:30·3
1962	Gerrard, David	2:26·4
1963	Gerrard, David	2:16·5
1964	Gerrard, David	2:18·2
1965	Gerrard, David	2:17·4
1966	Gerrard, David	2:19·3
1967	Gerrard, David	2:16·7
1968	Gerrard, David	2:19·0
1969	Gerrard, David	2:18·7
1970*	Barfoot, Alan	2:21·2

* = 200 m.

Individual medley (instituted 1947)

1947	Jarvis, J. (100 y.)	1:05·6
1948	Shanahan, J. (100 y.)	1:04·8
1949	Logan, T. (100 y.)	1:08·6
1950	Callan, C. (133⅓ y.)	2:03·8
1951	Branch, D. (133⅓ y.)	1:52·0
1952	Hurring, Lincoln (100 y.)	1:07·0
1953	Hurring, Lincoln (100 y.)	1:06·1
1954	Blackwood, J. (100 y.)	1:06·0
1955	Todd, J. (100 y.)	1:04·6
1956	Harker, R. (400 y.)	5:17·5
1957	Harker, R. (440 y.)	5:51·0
1958	Harker, R. (440 y.)	5:54·6
1959	McDonald, I. (400 y.)	5:24·9
1960	Hatch, P. (220 y.)	2:42·2
1961	Seagar, Allan (266⅔ y.)	3:10·0

220 y. Individual medley

1962	Seagar, Allan	2:24·7
1963	Seagar, Allan	2:23·3
1964	Seagar, Allan	2:23·8
1969	Bond, Barnett	2:25·2
1970*	Bond, Barnett	2:22·9

* = 200 m.

440 y. Individual medley

1962	Seagar, Allan	5:34·5
1963	Seagar, Allan	5:12·6
1964	Seagar, Allan	5·14:4
1965	Seagar, Allan	5:06·8
1966	Seagar, Allan	5:08·1
1967	Seagar, Allan	5:10·4
1968	Seagar, Allan	5:13·5
1969	Bond, Barnett	5:15·7
1970*	Bond, Barnett	5:05·7

* = 400 m.

WOMEN

110 y. Freestyle (instituted 1912)

1946*	Casey, Betty	1:09·8
1947*	Casey, Betty	1:07·0
1948*	Casey, Betty	1:04·8
1949*	Casey, Betty	1:04·8
1950*	Jacobi, Kristin	1:03·8
1951*	Jacobi, Kristin	1:06·4
1952*	Roe, Marion	1:05·2
1953*	Roe, Marion	1:03·8
1954*	Roe, Marion	1:03·6
1955*	Roe, Marion	59·8
1956*	Roe, Marion	59·4
1957	Hunter, Jennifer	1:09·4
1958	Hunter, Jennifer	1:07·7
1959*	Bell, Alison	1:03·2
1960	Bell, Alison	1:07·9
1961*	Moore, Lesley	1:02·4
1962	Moore, Lesley	1:07·5
1963	McMillan, Alison	1:05·7
1964	McMillan, Alison	1:05·6
1965	McMillan, Alison	1:06·0
1966	McMillan, Alison	1:07·6
1967	Hall, Koreen	1:06·8
1968	Wright, Judith	1:06·0
1969	Crawford, Felicity	1:04·4
1970†	Crawford, Felicity	1:04·2

* = 100 y.   † = 100 m.

220 y. Free-style (instituted 1924)

1946	Casey, Betty	2:49·6
1947	Casey, Betty	2:46·0
1948	Casey, Betty	2:44·8
1949	Casey, Betty	2:45·2
1950	Jacobi, Kristin	2:45·8
1951	Griffin, Winifred	2:43·4
1952	Menzies, Margaret	2:43·8
1953	Griffin, Winifred	2:36·0
1954	Roe, Marion	2:36·1
1955	Griffin, Winifred	2:30·4
1956	Roe, Marion	2:25·4

1957	Griffin, Winifred	2:31·6
1958	Bell, Alison	2:33·2
1959	Hunter, Jennifer	2:32·3
1960	Bell, Alison	2:30·6
1961	Moore, Lesley	2:30·3
1962	Mooré, Lesley	2:27·3
1963	Nicholson, Shirley	2:27·0
1964	McMillan, Alison	2:23·0
1965	McMillan, Alison	2:24·2
1966	Macrae, Margaret	2:25·7
1967	Amies, June	2:25·7
1968	Shipston, Tui	2:21·9
1969	Shipston, Tui	2:17·7
1970*	Wright, Judith	2:21·8

* = 200 m.

440 y. Free-style (instituted 1921)

1946	Casey, Betty	6:09·0
1947	Casey, Betty	6:01·2
1948	Holman, Maureen	5:54·8
1949	Casey, Betty	6:02·0
1950	McKenzie, Helen	5:51·4
1951	Griffin, Winifred	5:59·0
1952	Holman, Maureen	5:44 4
1953	Griffin, Winifred	5:34·2
1954	Griffin, Winifred	5:35·3
1955	Griffin, Winifred	5:22·3
1956	Roe, Marion	5:13·7
1957	Griffin, Winifred	5:29·4
1958	Bell, Alison	5:30·6
1959	Hunter, Jennifer	5:25·2
1960	Hunter, Jennifer	5:24·8
1961	Moore, Lesley	5:15·2
1962	Moore, Lesley	5:10·5
1963	Nicholson, Shirley	5:09·8
1964	Nicholson, Shirley	5:10·8
1965	McMillan, Alison	5:20·5
1966	Woonton, Suzanne	5:07·6
1967	Myers, Diane	5:06·7
1968	Shipston, Tui	4:59·1
1969	Shipston, Tui	4:53·1
1970*	Wright, Judith	4:53·0

* = 400 m.

880 y. Free-style (instituted 1967)

1967	Myers, Diane	10:45·3
1968	Shipston, Tui	10:33·0
1969	Shipston, Tui	10:11·6
1970*	Wright, Judith	9:55·1

* = 800 m.

110 y. Back-stroke (instituted 1929)

1946*	Lane, Ngaire	1:13·4
1947*	Lane, Ngaire	1:12·0
1948*	Lane, Ngaire	1:12·4

1949*	Lane, Ngaire	1:12·0
1950*	Stewart, Jean	1:13·6
1951*	Stewart, Jean	1:10·0
1952*	Stewart, Jean	1:08·8
1953*	Stewart, Jean	1:09·7
1954*	Stewart, Jean	1:13·0
1955*	Wilson, Moira	1:15·4
1956*	Stewart, Jean	1:09·1
1957	Gould, Phillipa	1:14·8
1958	Gould, Phillipa	1:13·8
1959*	Norman, Lynette	1:07·8
1960	Norman, Lynette	1:15·8
1961*	Norman, Lynette	1:06·9
1962	Macrae, Margaret	1:14·8
1963	Macrae, Margaret	1:15·2
1964	Macrae, Margaret	1:15·7
1965	Macrae, Margaret	1:14·7
1966	Macrae, Margaret	1:15·3
1967	Stirling, Glenda	1:13·1
1968	Stirling, Glenda	1:10·2
1969	Stirling, Glenda	1:12·9
1970†	Stirling, Glenda	1:10·5

* = 100 y.   † = 100 m.

220 y. Back-stroke (instituted 1938)

1946	Lane, Ngaire	3:00·6
1947	Lane, Ngaire	3:01·6
1948	Lane, Ngaire	3:03·0
1949	Lane, Ngaire	2:57·6
1950	Stewart, Jean	2:58·2
1951	Stewart, Jean	2:56·0
1952	Stewart, Jean	2:47·2
1953	Stewart, Jean	2:53·4
1954	Stewart, Jean	2:54·9
1955	Wilson, Moira	2:59·9
1956	Gould, Phillipa	2:44·3
1957	Gould, Phillipa	2:42·0
1958	Gould, Phillipa	2:43·0
1959	Norman, Lynette	2:42·2
1960	Norman, Lynette	2:44·0
1961	Norman, Lynette	2:42·5
1962	Macrae, Margaret	2:40·3
1963	Macrae, Margaret	2:41·6
1964	Macrae, Margaret	2:41·0
1965	Macrae, Margaret	2:41·1
1966	Macrae, Margaret	2:43·2
1967	Macrae, Margaret	2:38·9
1968	Stirling, Glenda	2:33·8
1969	Stirling, Glenda	2:34·4
1970*	Stirling, Glenda	2:32·7

* = 200 m.

110 y. Breast-stroke (instituted 1939)

| 1946* | Pasalich, Marie | 1:27·6 |
| 1947* | Smith, Helen | 1:26·4 |

1948*	Forsyth, Heather	1:23·8
1949*	Teague, Maureen	1:26·6
1950*	Sweeney, Margaret	1:25·6
1951*	Currie, Rae	1:27·4
1952*	Currie, Rae	1:26·0
1953*	Currie, Rae	1:25·0
1954*	Currie, Rae	1:22·9
1955*	Currie, Rae	1:23·1
1956*	Orbell, Lindley	1:22·4
1957	Sawyers, Kay	1:32·0
1958	Sawyers, Kay	1:28·3
1959*	Sawyers, Kay	1:19·0
1960	Sawyers, Kay	1:28·6
1961*	Sawyers, Kay	1:18·2
1962	Haddon, Vivien	1:22·5
1963	Haddon, Vivien	1:21·6
1964	Haddon, Vivien	1:24·8
1965	Jonas, Barbara	1:26·9
1966	Haddon, Vivien	1:25·2
1967	Deal, Christine	1:23·9
1968	McRae, Donna	1:22·4
1969	McRae, Donna	1:23·6
1970†	Hill, Margaret	1:23·4

* = 100 y.   † = 100 m.

220 y. Breast-stroke (instituted 1924)

1946	Pasalich, Marie	3:27·8
1947	Shaw, Nola	3:29·4
1948	Forsyth, Heather	3:23·2
1949	Sweeney, Margaret	3:24·6
1950	Forsyth, Heather	3:27·4
1951	Currie, Rae	3:22·4
1952	Currie, Rae	3:23·8
1953	Currie, Rae	3:18·4
1954	Currie, Rae	3:13·5
1955	Currie, Rae	3:14·1
1956	Orbell, Lindley	3:14·6
1957	Sawyers, Kay	3:17·8
1958	Sawyers, Kay	3:12·2
1959	Sawyers, Kay	3:07·1
1960	Sawyers, Kay	3:08·1
1961	Sawyers, Kay	3:05·0
1962	Haddon, Vivien	2:59·9
1963	Haddon, Vivien	2:56·3
1964	Haddon, Vivien	2:59·5
1965	Jonas, Barbara	3:06·4
1966	Haddon, Vivien	3:02·9
1967	Smith, Lesley	3:02·1
1968	Smith, Lesley	2:55·3
1969	Williams, Beth	2:57·6
1970*	Williams, Beth	2:59·0

* = 200 m.

110 y. Butterfly (instituted 1948)

| 1948* | Forsyth, Heather | 1:25·6 |

1949*	Bridson, Norma	1:27·8
1950*	Bridson, Norma	1:25·0
1951*	Bridson, Norma	1:25·8
1952*	Currie, Rae	1:28·2
1953*	Stewart, Jean	1:28·0
1954*	Cleaver, Judith	1:29·2
1955*	Currie, Rae	1:22·2
1956*	Orbell, Lindley	1:24·4
1957	Staveley, Tessa	1:22·8
1958	Staveley, Tessa	1:19·6
1959*	McCleary, Helen	1:08·6
1960	McCleary, Helen	1:15·4
1961*	Phillips, Marilyn	1:10·2
1962	Rogers, Helen	1:16·0
1963	Nicholson, Shirley	1:15·2
1964	Nicholson, Shirley	1:15·3
1965	Kerr, Heather	1:16·4
1966	Kerr, Heather	1:13·2
1967	Kerr, Heather	1:13·9
1968	Whittleston, Sandra	1:10·8
1969	Shipston, Tui	1:09·5
1970†	Whiting, Cathy	1:12·4

* = 100 y.   † = 100 m.

220 y. Butterfly (instituted 1966)

1966	Kerr, Heather	2:43·4
1967	Kerr, Heather	2:38·5
1968	Whittleston, Sandra	2:36·8
1969	Shipston, Tui	2:29·5
1970†	Williams, Beth	2:29·8

† = 200 m.

Individual medley (instituted 1947)

1947	Hobson, O. (100 y.)	1:21·4
1948	Bridson, Norma (100 y.)	1:14·0
1949	Bridson, Norma (100 y.)	1:16·8
1950	Bridson, Norma (133⅓ y.)	2:20·8
1951	Wilson, M. (133⅓ y.)	2:03·6
1952	Wilson, M. (100 y.)	1:13·8
1953	Wilson, M. (100 y.)	1:14·9
1954	Jones, B. (100 y.)	1:15·9
1955	Wilson, M. (100 y.)	1:16·4
1956	Duthie, J. (400 y.)	6:07·4
1957	Staveley, Tessa (440 y.)	6:44·0
1958	Staveley, Tessa (440 y.)	6:30·3
1959	Staveley, Tessa (400 y.)	5:35·5
1960	McCleary, Helen (220 y.)	2:55·2
1961	Phillips, M. (266⅔ y.)	3:40·8

220 y. Individual medley (instituted 1966)

1966	Macrae, Margaret	2:45·0
1967	Shipston, Tui	2:40·2
1968	Shipston, Tui	2:39·1
1969	Shipston, Tui	2:37·2
1970*	Hunter, Susan	2:38·4

* = 200 m.

440 y. Individual medley (instituted 1962)

1962	Rogers, Helen	6:13·7
1963	Nicholson, Shirley	6:12·5
1964	Nicholson, Shirley	6:07·6
1965	Macrae, Margaret	5:49·2
1966	Macrae, Margaret	5:51·7
1967	Shipston, Tui	5:40·2
1968	Shipston, Tui	5:35·4
1969	Shipston, Tui	5:28·7
1970*	Hunter, Susan	5:34·0

* = 400 m.

NORELIUS, Martha (United States, 2 Jan. 1909–55). The first woman to win the Olympic gold for the same event at successive Games—the 400 m. in 1924 at 15 and in 1928 (plus a relay gold that year). Born in Stockholm and raised in America, she was coached by her father Charles, who represented Sweden at the 1906 Interim Games, and later by L. de B. Handley.

Miss Norelius set seventeen world records between 28 Feb. 1926 and 27 Aug. 1928 of which the best times were: 200 m./220 y. 2:40·6, 400 m. 5:39·2, 880 y. 12:17·8 and 1,500 m. 23:44·6. After a seven-year reign as the queen of American swimming, she turned professional in 1929 following her suspension by the A.A.U. for swimming an exhibition in the same pool with professionals.

As a professional, she won the $10,000 ten-mile Wrigley Marathon in Toronto where she met and married Joe Wright, silver medal winner for Canada in the double sculls in the 1928 Olympics. The darling of the social set, Martha was considered to be the first woman to swim like the men, Her front crawl style was similar to Johnny Weissmuller's, with a high head position, arched back and heavy six-beat leg kick.

NORTH-EASTERN DISTRICT. The North-Eastern Counties A.S.A., founded in 1901, are responsible for the sport in the North of England, east of the Pennines. The bulk of the activities are carried out by two sub-associations, Yorkshire and the combined Northumberland and Durham.

Longest serving officer was Reggie

Pryde, honorary secretary from 1936–60, who followed H. Crapper (1914–35). In the financial field, W. H. Drake was honorary treasurer from 1920 to 1940 and Mark Latimer has held this office with a break in 1953, from 1947 to 1970.

NORTHERN DISTRICT. The Northern Counties A.S.A., founded in 1889, are responsible for the sport in the North of England, west of the Pennines for the following counties: Cheshire, Cumberland, Lancashire, Westmorland and the Isle of Man and of Derbyshire and Staffordshire (north of latitude 53 degrees) and also the city of Stoke-on-Trent.

In seventy-six years, from 1890–1965, there were only three honorary treasurers G. Marshall (1890–1918), Fred Isherwood (1919–45) and Harry Koskie (1946–65). The longest serving honorary secretary was F. R. Edwards (1895–1918). Later the brothers Hodgson, John (1930–43) and Dick (1944–45) held the secretaryship.

O

O'BRIEN, Ian (Australia, 3 Mar. 1947–   ). Olympic 200 m. breast-stroke champion in 1964 and four times champion of the Commonwealth—for the 110 and 220 y. breast-stroke in 1962 and '66, Ian O'Brien from Wellington, New South Wales, was a redoubtable competitor. He demonstrated this particularly in Jamaica in 1966 where he retained his Commonwealth titles in world record times though six weeks before the Games he was 30 lb. overweight and out of training.

O'Brien broke four world records: 110 y. (68·6 and 68·2), 200 m. (2:27·8, his Olympic winning time that stood for four years) and 220 y. (2:28·0, in Jamaica and worth 2:27·0 for 200 m. and so better than his metric record).

OLYMPIC GAMES. The earliest celebration of the ancient Olympic Games of which there is a record is that of July 776 B.C. The ancient Games were ended in A.D. 392 by the decree of the Roman Emperor Theodosius. The first Games of the modern era were organized in Greece, the home of the old Games, fifteen centuries later as a result of the idealism and energy of a Frenchman, Baron Pierre de Coubertin. Dates and venues:

OLYMPIC GAMES

No.	Venue	Dates
I	Athens, Greece	5 Apr.–15 Apr., 1896
II	Paris, France	14 May,–28 Oct., 1900
III	St. Louis, U.S.A.	1 July–28 Oct., 1904
IV	London, England	27 Apr.–29 Oct., 1908
V	Stockholm, Sweden	5 May–22 July, 1912
VI	Berlin, Germany	Not held, 1916
VII	Antwerp, Belgium	20 Apr.–12 Sept., 1920
VIII	Paris, France	3 May–27 July, 1924
IX	Amsterdam, Holland	28 July–12 Aug., 1928
X	Los Angeles, U.S.A.	31 July–7 Aug., 1932
XI	Berlin, Germany	2 Aug.–16 Aug., 1936
XII	Helsinki, Finland	Not held, 1940
XIII	No venue	Not held, 1944
XIV	London, England	29 July–14 Aug., 1948
XV	Helsinki, Finland	19 July–3 Aug., 1952
XVI	Melbourne, Australia	22 Nov.–8 Dec., 1956
XVII	Rome, Italy	25 Aug.–11 Sept., 1960
XVIII	Tokyo, Japan	10 Oct.–24 Oct., 1964
XIX	Mexico City, Mexico	12 Oct.–27 Oct., 1968
XX	Munich, West Germany	26 July–10 Aug., 1972

OLYMPIC GAMES CHAMPIONS. Swimming for men was included in the first Games of the modern era, in Athens in 1896. Two events for women—100 and 4 × 100 m. free-style—were added for Stockholm in 1912. For the Munich Olympics (1972) there are 12 individual swimming events and three relays for

125

men, 12 individual and two relays for women, highboard and springboard diving for men and women and water polo for men.

The only swimmer to win the same individual title at three successive Games is Dawn Fraser (Aus)—100 m. in 1956, 60 and 64. The first to win four golds at a single Games is Don Schollander (USA)—100, 400, 4 × 100 and 4 × 200 m. in 1964. Debbie Meyer (USA) was the first to take three individual titles at the same Games—200, 400 and 800 m. in 1968 (but the 200 and 800 m. were new events).

The technical conditions for the breast-stroke championships have varied according to the developments of the stroke (see BREAST-STROKE and BUTTER-FLY). In the lists of winners that follow:

The events in the Munich programme come first followed by obsolete championships.

Bu = won using over-water arm recovery before separation of breast-stroke and, butterfly on 1 Jan. 1954.

Uw = won swimming long distances under water—ruled out from 1 Jan. 1957.

MEN

100 m. Free-style

1896	Hajos, Alfred (Hun)	1:22·2
1904*	Halmay, Zoltan (Hun)	1:02·8
1908	Daniels, Charles (USA)	1:05·6
1912	Kahanamoku, Duke (USA)	1:03·4
1920	Kahanamoku, Duke (USA)	1:01·4
1924	Weissmuller, Johnny (USA)	59·0
1928	Weissmuller, Johnny (USA)	58·6
1932	Miyazaki, Yasuki (Jap)	58·2
1936	Csik, Ferenc (Hun)	57·6
1948	Ris, Wally (USA)	57·3
1952	Scholes, Clarke (USA)	57·4
1956	Henricks, Jon (Aus)	55·4
1960	Devitt, John (Aus)	55·2
1964	Schollander, Don (USA)	53·4
1968	Wenden, Mike (Aus)	52·2
	* 100 y.	

200 m. Free-style

1900	Lane, Freddy (Aus)	2:25·2
1904*	Daniels, Charles (USA)	2:44·2

1908–64	Event not held	
1968	Wenden, Mike (Aus)	1:55·2
	* = 220 y.	

400 m. Free-style

1904*	Daniels, Charles (USA)	6:16·2
1908	Taylor, Henry (GB)	5:36·8
1912	Hodgson, George (Can)	5:24·4
1920	Ross, Norman (USA)	5:26·8
1924	Weissmuller, Johnny (USA)	5:04·2
1928	Zorilla, Alberto (Arg)	5:01·6
1932	Crabbe, Buster (Clarence) (USA)	4:48·4
1936	Medica, Jack (USA)	4:44·5
1948	Smith, Bill (USA)	4:41·0
1952	Boiteux, Jean (Fra)	4:30·7
1956	Rose, Murray (Aus)	4:27·3
1960	Rose, Murray (Aus)	4:18·3
1964	Schollander, Don (USA)	4:12·2
1968	Burton, Mike (USA)	4:09·0
	* = 440 y.	

1,500 m. Free-style

1904*	Rausch, Emil (Ger)	27:18·2
1908	Taylor, Henry (GB)	22:48·4
1912	Hodgson, George (Can)	22:00·0
1920	Ross, Norman (USA)	22:23·2
1924	Charlton, Boy (Andrew) (Aus)	20:06·6
1928	Borg, Arne (Swe)	19:51·8
1932	Kitamura, Kusuo (Jap)	19:12·4
1936	Terada, Noboru (Jap)	19:13·7
1948	McLane, Jimmy (USA)	19:18·5
1952	Konno, Ford (USA)	18:30·0
1956	Rose, Murray (Aus)	17:58·9
1960	Konrads, John (Aus)	17:19·6
1964	Windle, Bobby (Aus)	17:01·7
1968	Burton, Mike (USA)	16:38·9
	* = One Mile (1,609 m.)	

100 m. Back-stroke

1904*	Brack, Walter (Ger)	1:16·8
1908	Bieberstein, Arno (Ger)	1:24·6
1912	Hebner, Harry (USA)	1:21·2
1920	Kealoha, Warren (USA)	1:15·2
1924	Kealoha, Warren (USA)	1:13·2
1928	Kojac, George (USA)	1:08·2
1932	Kiyokawa, Masaji (Jap)	1:08·6
1936	Kiefer, Adolph (USA)	1:05·9
1948	Stack, Allen (USA)	1:06·4
1952	Oyakawa, Yashinobu (USA)	1:05·7
1956	Theile, David (Aus)	1:02·2
1960	Theile, David (Aus)	1:01·9

| 1964 | Event not held | |
| 1968 | Matthes, Roland (EG) | 58·7 |

* = 100 y.

200 m. Back-stroke

1900	Hoppenberg, Ernst (Ger)	2:47·0
1904–60	Event not held	
1964	Graef, Jed (USA)	2:10·3
1968	Matthes, Roland (EG)	2:09·6

100 m. Breast-stroke

| 1968 | McKenzie, Don (USA) | 1:07·7 |

200 m. Breast-stroke

1908	Holman, Frederick (GB)	3:09·2
1912	Bathe, Walther (Ger)	3:01·8
1920	Malmroth, Hakan (Swe)	3:04·4
1924	Skelton, Robert (USA)	2:56·6
1928	Tsuruta, Yoshiyuki (Jap)	2:48·8
1932	Tsuruta, Yoshiyuki (Jap)	2:45·4
1936	Hamuro, Tetsou (Jap)	2:42·5
1948	Verdeur, Joe (USA)	Bu2:39·3
1952	Davies, John (Aus)	Bu2:34·4
1956	Furukawa, Masaru (Jap)	
		Uw2:34·7
1960	Mulliken, Bill (USA)	2:37·4
1964	O'Brien, Ian (Aus)	2:27·8
1968	Munoz, Felipe (Mex)	2:28·7

100 m. Butterfly

| 1968 | Russell, Doug (USA) | 55·9 |

200 m. Butterfly

1956	Yorzyk, Bill (USA)	2:19·3
1960	Troy, Mike (USA)	2:12·8
1964	Berry, Kevin (Aus)	2:06·6
1968	Robie, Carl (USA)	2:08·7

200 m. Individual medley

| 1968 | Hickcox, Charles (USA) | 2:12·0 |

400 m. Individual medley

| 1964 | Roth, Dick (USA) | 4:45·4 |
| 1968 | Hickcox, Charles (USA) | 4:48·4 |

4 × 100 m. Free-style relay

1964   United States   3:33·2
(Clark, Steve; Austin, Mike; Illman, Gary; Schollander, Don)
1968   United States   3:31·7
(Zorn, Zac; Rerych, Steve; Spitz, Mark; Walsh, Ken)

4 × 200 m. Free-style relay

1908   Great Britain   10:55·6
(Derbyshire, Rob; Radmilovic, Paul; Foster, Willie; Taylor, Henry)
1912   Australasia   10:11·2
(Healy, Cecil (Aus); Champion, Mal-

colm (NZ); Boardman, Leslie; Hardwick, Harold (Aus))
1920   United States   10:04·4
(McGillivray, Perry, Kealoha, Pua; Ross, Norman; Kahanamoku, Duke)
1924   United States   9:53·4
(O'Connor, Wallace; Glancy, Harry; Breyer, Ralph; Weissmuller, Johnny)
1928   United States   9:36·2
(Clapp, Austin; Laufer, Walter; Kojac, George; Weissmuller, Johnny)
1932   Japan   8:58·4
(Miyazaki, Yasuki; Yokoyama, Takashi; Yusa, Masanori; Toyoda, Hisakichi)
1936   Japan   8:51·5
(Yusa, Masanori; Sugiura, Shigeo; Arai, Shigeo; Taguchi, Masaharu)
1948   United States   8:46·0
(Ris, Wally; Wolf, Wallace; McLane, Jimmy; Smith, Bill)
1952   United States   8:31·1
(Moore, Wayne; Woolsey, Bill; Konno, Ford; McLane, Jimmy)
1956   Australia   8:23·6
(O'Halloran, Kevin; Devitt, John; Rose, Murray; Henricks, Jon)
1960   United States   8:10·2
(Harrison, George; Blick, Dick; Troy, Mike; Farrell, Jeff)
1964   United States   7:52·1
(Clark, Steve; Saari, Roy; Ilman, Gary; Schollander, Don)
1968   United States   7:52·3
(Nelson, John; Rerych, Steve; Spitz, Mark; Schollander, Don)

4 × 100 m. Medley relay

1960   United States   4:05·4
(McKinney, Frank; Hait, Paul; Larson, Lance; Farrell, Jeff)
1964   United States   3:58·4
(Mann, Tom; Craig, Bill; Schmidt, Fred; Clark, Steve)
1968   United States   3:54·9
(Hickcox, Charles; McKenzie, Don; Russell, Doug; Walsh, Ken)

Springboard diving

1904	Sheldon, George (USA)	12·66
1908	Zuerner Albert (Ger)	85·50
1912	Guenther, Paul (Ger)	79·23
1920	Kuehn, Louis (USA)	675·00
1924	White, Albert (USA)	696·40
1928	Desjardins, Pete (USA)	185·40

1932	Glitzen, Michael (USA)	161·38
1936	Degener, Dickie (USA)	163·57
1948	Harlan, Bruce (USA)	163·64
1952	Browning, Skippy (USA)	205·29
1956	Clotworthy, Bobby (USA)	159·56
1960	Tobian, Gary (USA)	170·00
1964	Sitzberger, Ken (USA)	159·90
1968	Wrightson, Bernie (USA)	170·15

Highboard diving

1912	Adlerz, Erik (Swe)	*73·94
1920	Pinkston, Clarence (USA)	*100·67
1924	White, Albert (USA)	*487·30
1928	Desjardins, Pete (USA)	98·74
1932	Smith, Harold 'Dutch' (USA)	124·80
1936	Wayne, Marshall (USA)	113·58
1948	Lee, Sammy (USA)	130·05
1952	Lee, Sammy (USA)	156·28
1956	Capilla, Joaquin (Mex)	152·44
1960	Webster, Robert (USA)	165·56
1964	Webster, Robert (USA)	148·58
1968	Dibiasi, Klaus (Ita)	164·18

* Known as 'fancy' high diving, a 'plain' diving event also being held

Water polo

1900 Great Britain (Manchester Osborne S.C.)
(Robertson, Arthur; Coe, Thomas; Robinson, Eric; Kemp, Peter; Wilkinson, George; Derbyshire, Rob; Lister, William)

1904 United States (New York AC)
(Van Cleef, George; Goodwin, Leo; Handley, Louis B. de; Hesser, David; Ruddy, Joseph; Steen, James; Bratton, David)

1908 Great Britain
(Smith, Charles; Nevinson, George; Cornet, George; Radmilovic, Paul; Wilkinson, George; Thould, Thomas; Forsyth Charles)

1912 Great Britain
(Smith, Charles; Cornet, George; Bugbee, Charles; Hill, Arthur; Wilkinson, George; Radmilovic, Paul; Bentham, Isaac)

1920 Great Britain
(Smith, Charles; Radmilovic, Paul; Bugbee, Charles; Purcell, Norman; Jones, Christopher; Peacock, William; Dean, William)

1924 France
(Dujardin, Paul; Padou, Henri; Rigal, George; Deborgie, Albert; Delberghe, Noel; Desmettre, Robert; Mayaud, Albert)

1928 Germany
(Rademacher, Erich; Gunst, Fritz; Cordes, Otto; Benecke, Emil; Rademacher, Joachim; Bahre, Karl; Amann, Max; Blank, Johannes; Protze, Karl-Heinz; Kuhne, Otto; Atmer, Heinrich)

1932 Hungary
(Brody, Gyorgy; Ivady, Sandor; Homonnai, Marton; Halasy, Oliver; Vertesy, Jozsef, Nemeth, Janos; Keseru II Alajos; Barta, Istvan; Sarkany, Miklos; Keseru I, Ferenc; Bozsi, Mihaly)

1936 Hungary
(Brody, Gyorgy; Hazai, Kalman; Homonnai, Marton; Halassy, Oliver; Brandi, Jeno; Nemeth, Janos; Bozsi, Mihaly; Molnar, Istvan; Kutasi, Gyorgy; Tarics, Sandor; Sarkany, Miklos)

1948 Italy
(Buonocore, Pasquale; Bulgarelli, Emilio; Rubini, Cesare; Ognio, Geminio; Arena, Ermenegildo; Ghira, Aldo; Pandolfini, Tullio; Maioni, Mario; Fabiano, Luigi; Pandolfini, Gianfranco; Toribolo, Alfredo)

1952 Hungary
(Jeney, Laszlo; Vizvary, Gyorgy; Gyarmati, Deszo; Karpati, Gyorgy; Antal, Robert; Fabian, Deszo; Szittya, Karoly; Lemhenyi, Deszo; Hasznos, Istvan; Martin, Miklos; Markovits, Kalman; Bolvari, Antal; Szivos, Istvan)

1956 Hungary
(Boros, Otto; Gyarmati, Dezso; Mayer, Mihaly; Markovits, Kalman; Bolvari, Antal; Sador, Ervin; Karpati, Gyorgy; Jeney, Laszlo; Hevesi, Istvan; Kanisza Tivadar; Szivos, Istvan)

1960 Italy
(Ambron, Amedeo; Bardi, Danio; D'Altrui, Giuseppe; Gionta, Salvatore; Lavoratori, Franco; Lonzi, Gianni; Manelli, Luigi; Parmegiani, Rosario; Pizzo Eraldo; Rossi, Dante; Spinelli, Brunello; Guerrini, Giancarlo)

KONRADS, JOHN AND ILSA. The Konrads, from Australia, the only brother and sister world record breakers

LONSBROUGH, ANITA. The unveiling in Huddersfield Town Hall of a plaque commemorating Anita Lonsbrough's achievements in winning Olympic, European and Commonwealth titles

MEYER, DEBBIE. The first swimmer to win three individual titles at the same Olympic Games—she took the 200, 400 and 800m titles in Mexico in 1968

MATTHES, ROLAND. The East German demonstrates the unusual back-stroke starting technique that sent him on the way to victory in the 100 and 200m events at the 1968 Olympics and 1970 European Championships and to ten world records

1964   Hungary
       (Ambrus, Miklos; Felkai, Laszlo;
       Konrad, Janos; Domotor, Zoltan;
       Kanizsa, Tivadar; Rusoran, Peter;
       Karpati, Gyorgy; Gyarmati, Deszo;
       Pocsik, Denes; Mayer, Mihaly; Bod-
       nar, Andra; Boros, Otto)
1968   Yugoslavia
       (Stipanic, Karlo; Trumbic, Ivo;
       Bonacic, Ozren; Marovic, Urcs;
       Lopanty, Ronald; Jankovic, Zorna;
       Poljak, Miroslav; Dabovic, Dejan;
       Perisic, Djordje; Sandic, Mirko;
       Hebel, Zoravko)

WOMEN

100 m. Free-style
1912	Durack, Fanny (Aus)	1:22·2
1920	Bleibtrey, Ethelda (USA)	1:13·6
1924	Lackie, Ethel (USA)	1:12·4
1928	Osipowich, Albina (USA)	1:11·0
1932	Madison, Helene (USA)	1:06·8
1936	Mastenbroek, Rie (Neth)	1:05·9
1948	Andersen, Greta (Den)	1:06·3
1952	Szoke, Katalin (Hun)	1:06·8
1956	Fraser, Dawn (Aus)	1:02·0
1960	Fraser, Dawn (Aus)	1:01·2
1964	Fraser, Dawn (Aus)	59·5
1968	Henne, Jan (USA)	1:00·0

200 m. Free-style
1968	Meyer, Debbie (USA)	2:10·5

400 m. Free-style
1924	Norelius, Martha (USA)	6:02·2
1928	Norelius, Martha (USA)	5:42·8
1932	Madison, Helene (USA)	5:28·5
1936	Mastenbroek, Rie (Neth)	5:26·4
1948	Curtis, Ann (USA)	5:17·8
1952	Gyenge, Valeria (Hun)	5:12·1
1956	Crapp, Lorraine (Aus)	4:54·6
1960	Von Saltza, Chris (USA)	4:50·6
1964	Duenkel, Ginny (USA)	4:43·3
1968	Meyer, Debbie (USA)	4:31·8

800 m. Free-style
1968	Meyer, Debbie (USA)	4:31·8

100 m. Back-stroke
1924	Bauer, Sybil (USA)	1:23·2
1928	Braun, Marie (Neth)	1:22·0
1932	Holm, Eleanor (USA)	1:19·4
1936	Senff, Nina (Neth)	1:18·9
1948	Harup, Karen (Den)	1:14·4
1952	Harrison, Joan (SAf)	1:14·3
1956	Grinham, Judy (GB)	1:12·9

1960	Burke, Lynn (USA)	1:09·3
1964	Ferguson, Cathie (USA)	1:07·7
1968	Hall, Kaye (USA)	1:06·2

200 m. Back-stroke
1968	Watson, L. 'Pokey' (USA)	2:24·8

100 m. Breast-stroke
1968	Bjedov, Djurdica (Yugo)	1:15·8

200 m. Breast-stroke
1924	Morton, Lucy (GB)	3:33·2
1928	Schrader, Hilde (Ger)	3:12·6
1932	Dennis, Clare (Aus)	3:06·3
1936	Maehata, Hideko (Jap)	3:03·6
1948	Van Vliet, Nel (Neth)	2:57·2
1952	Szekely, Eva (Hun)	Bu2:51·7
1956	Happe, Ursula (WGer)	2:53·1
1960	Lonsbrough, Anita (GB)	2:49·5
1964	Prosumenschikova, Galina (USSR)	2:46·4
1968	Wichman, Sharon (USA)	2:44·4

100 m. Butterfly
1956	Mann, Shelley (USA)	1:11·0
1960	Schuler, Carolyn (USA)	1:09·5
1964	Stouder, Sharon (USA)	1:04·7
1968	McClements, Lynn (Aus)	1:05·5

200m. Butterfly
1968	Kok, Ada (Neth)	2:24·7

200 m. Individual medley
1968	Kolb, Claudia (USA)	2:24·7

400 m. Individual medley
1964	De Varona, Donna (USA)	5:18·7
1968	Kolb, Claudia (USA)	5:08·5

4 × 100 m. Free-style relay
1912   Great Britain   5:52·8
       (Moore, Bella; Steer, Irene; Speirs,
       Annie; Fletcher, Jennie)
1920   United States   5:11·6
       (Bleibtrey, Ethelda; Schroth, Frances;
       Guest, Irene; Woodbridge, Margaret)
1924   United States   4:58·8
       (Ederle, Gertrude; Wehselau, Mar-
       lechen; Lackie, Ethel; Donelly,
       Euphrasia)
1928   United States   4:47·6
       (Lambert, Adelaide; Osipowich,
       Albina; Garatti, Eleanora; Norelius,
       Martha)
1932   United States   4:38·0
       (McKim, Josephine; Garatti-Saville,

I

Eleanor; Johns Helen; Madison, Helene)

1936 Netherlands   4:36·0
(Selbach, Jopie; Wagner, Catherina; Den Ouden, Willy; Mastenbroek, Rie)

1948 United States   4:29·2
(Corridon, Marie; Kalama, Thelma; Helser, Brenda; Curtis, Ann)

1952 Hungary   4:24·4
(Novak, Ilona; Temes, Judit; Novak, Eva; Szoke, Katalin)

1956 Australia   4:17·1
(Fraser, Dawn; Leech, Faith; Morgan, Sandra; Crapp, Lorraine)

1960 United States   4:08·9
(Spillane, Joan; Stobs, Shirley; Wood, Carolyn; Von Saltza, Chris)

1964 United States   4:03·8
(Stouder, Sharon; De Varona, Donna; Watson, Pokey; Ellis, Kathy)

1968 United States   4:02·5
(Barkman, Jane; Gustavson, Linda; Pedersen, Sue; Henne, Jan)

4 × 100 m. Medley relay
1960 United States   4:45·9
(Burke, Lynn; Kempner, Patty; Schuler, Carolyn; Von Saltza, Chris)

1964 United States   4:33·9
(Ferguson, Cathy; Goyette, Cynthia; Stouder, Sharon; Ellis, Kathy)

1968 United States   4:28·3
(Hall, Kaye; Ball, Catie; Daniels, Ellie; Pedersen, Sue)

Springboard diving
1920 Riggin, Aileen (USA)   539·90
1924 Becker, Elizabeth (USA)   474·50
1928 Meany, Helen (USA)   78·62
1932 Coleman, Georgia (USA)   78·52
1936 Gestring, Marjorie (USA)   89·27
1948 Draves, Vicky (USA)   108·74
1952 McCormick, Pat (USA)   147·30
1956 McCormick, Pat (USA)   142·36
1960 Kramer, Ingrid (EGer)   155·81
1964 Engel-Kramer, Ingrid
                          (EGer)   145·00
1968 Gossick, Sue (USA)   150·77

Highboard diving
1928 Becker-Pinkson, Elizabeth
                          (USA)   31·60
1932 Poynton, Dorothy (USA)   40·26
1936 Poynton-Hill, Dorothy
                          (USA)   33·93

1948 Draves, Vicki (USA)   68·87
1952 McCormick, Pat (USA)   79·37
1956 McCormick, Pat (USA)   84·85
1960 Kramer, Ingrid (EGer)   91·28
1964 Bush, Lesley (USA)   99·80
1968 Duchkova, Milena
                          (Czech)   109·59

Events no longer in the Olympic programme:

MEN

50 y. Free-style
1904 Halmay, Zoltan (Hun)   *28·0
* After swim-off with Scott Leary (USA)

500 m. Free-style
1896 Neumann, Paul (Aut)   8:12·6

880 y. Free-style
1904 Rausch, Emil (Ger)   13:11·4

1,000 m. Free-style
1900 Jarvis, John (GB)   13:40·0

1,200 m. Free-style
1896 Hajos, Alfred (Hun)   18:22·2

4,000 m. Free-style
1900 Jarvis, John (GB)   58:24·0

400 m. Breast-stroke
1904 Zacharias, Georg (Ger)   *7:23·6
1912 Bathe, Walther (Ger)   6:29·6
1920 Malmroth, Hakan (Swe)   6:31·8
* = 440 y.

100 m. For sailors (of ships anchored in the port of Pireus)
1896 Malokinis, Jean (Gre)   2:20·4

200 m. Obstacle swimming
1900 Lane, Freddy (Aus)   2:28·4

60 m. Under-water swimming
1900 De Vaudeville, Charles
                          (Fr)   1:53·4

Plunging
1904 Dickey, Paul (USA)   62′ 6″

4 × 50 y. Free-style relay
1904 New York A.C. (USA)*   2:04·6
(Ruddy, Joseph; Goodwin, Leon; Handley, Louis de B.; Daniels, Charles)
*The only Games when non-

OLYMPIC GAMES, DEVELOPMENT OF THE PROGRAMME: NUMBER OF EVENTS AT EACH GAMES

	1896	1900	1904	1908	1912	1920	1924	1928	1932	1936	1948	1952	1956	1960	1964	1968	1972
MEN																	
Free-style individual	3	3	6	3	3	3	3	3	3	3	3	3	3	3	3	4	4
Free-style relay	—	1	1	1	1	1	1	1	1	1	1	1	1	1	2	2	2
Back-stroke	—	1	1	1	1	1	1	1	1	1	1	1	1	1	1	2	2
Breast-stroke	—	—	1	1	2	2	1	1	1	1	1	1	1	1	1	2	2
Butterfly	—	—	—	—	—	—	—	—	—	—	—	—	1	1	1	2	2
Medley individual	—	—	—	—	—	—	—	—	—	—	—	—	—	—	1	2	2
Medley relay	—	—	—	—	—	—	—	—	—	—	—	—	—	1	1	1	1
Diving	—	—	2	2	3	3	3	2	2	2	2	2	2	2	2	2	2
Water-polo	—	1	1	1	1	1	1	1	1	1	1	1	1	1	1	1	1
Miscellaneous*	1	2	—	—	—	—	—	—	—	—	—	—	—	—	—	—	—
TOTAL	4	8	12	9	11	11	10	9	9	9	9	9	10	11	13	18	18
WOMEN																	
Free-style individual	—	—	—	—	1	2	2	2	2	2	2	2	2	2	2	4	4
Free-style relay	—	—	—	—	1	1	1	1	1	1	1	1	1	1	1	1	1
Back-stroke	—	—	—	—	—	—	1	1	1	1	1	1	1	1	1	2	2
Breat-stroke	—	—	—	—	—	—	1	1	1	1	1	1	1	1	1	2	2
Butterfly	—	—	—	—	—	—	—	—	—	—	—	—	1	1	1	2	2
Medley individual	—	—	—	—	—	—	—	—	—	—	—	—	—	—	1	2	2
Medley relay	—	—	—	—	—	—	—	—	—	—	—	—	—	1	1	1	1
Diving	—	—	—	—	1	2	2	2	2	2	2	2	2	2	2	2	2
TOTAL	—	—	—	—	3	5	7	7	7	7	7	7	8	9	10	16	16
GRAND TOTAL	4	9	12	9	14	16	17	16	16	16	16	16	18	20	23	34	34

* A race for sailors (1896), an obstacle race and plunging (1900).

national teams have been allowed to participate.

5 × 40 m. Free-style relay
1900   Germany   19 pts.
(Hoppenberg, Ernst; Hainle, Max; Von Petersdorff, Herbert; Schone, Max; Frey, Julius)

Plain high diving
1908   Johansson, Hjalmar (Swe)   83·75
1912   Adlerz, Erik (Swe)   40·00
1920   Wallman, Arvid (USA)   7 pts.
1924   Eve, Richmond (Aus)   160·00

WOMEN

Plain high diving
1912   Johansson, Greta (Swe)   39·90
1920   Fryland Clausen, Stefani
(Den)   34·60
1924   Smith, Caroline (USA)   166·00

INTERIM GAMES. After the failure of the 1904 Games in St. Louis, because of the thoughtless and incompetent arrangements by the American organizers and the very few visiting competitors, European Olympic leaders pressed for a sports festival for their athletes, most of whom had been unable to participate in the United States. Greece, the home of the Ancient Olympic Games and hosts to the first Games of the modern era in 1896, offered to stage such a meeting. In fact, their event in 1906, in Athens, proved as big a disappointment as St. Louis and attracted only a few national representatives. As a result, these Interim Games were refused recognition as an Olympiad, although F.I.N.A. list the 1906 winners among their Olympic roll of honour as follows:

100 m. Free-style
Daniels, Charles (USA)   1:13·0

400 m. Free-style
Scheff, Otto (Aut)   6:22·8

One mile
Taylor, Henry (GB)   28:28·0

1,000 m. Free-style relay
Hungary   17:16·2

Springboard diving
Walz, Gottlob (Ger)

OLYMPIC GAMES, DEVELOPMENT OF THE PROGRAMME. For details of events at each games see table on page 131.

OXFORD v. CAMBRIDGE, see VARSITY MATCH.

P

PAN AMERICAN GAMES. Instituted in 1951 as a multi-sports 'little Olympics', the Pan American Games has done a great deal to assist the development of swimming among the countries of North and South America so much dominated by the United States. Venues:

PAN AMERICAN GAMES

No.	Venue	Dates
I	Buenos Aires, Argentina	25 Feb.–8 Mar., 1951
II	Mexico City, Mexico	12 Mar.–26 Mar., 1955
III	Chicago, U.S.A.	27 Aug.–7 Sept., 1959
IV	Sao Paulo, Brazil	April, 1963
V	Winnipeg, Canada	22 July–5 Aug., 1967

PAN AMERICAN GAMES CHAMPIONS

MEN

100 m. Free-style

1951	Cleveland, Dick (USA)	58·9
1955	Scholes, Clarke (USA)	57·7
1959	Farrell, Jeff (USA)	56·3
1963	Clark, Steve (USA)	54·7
1967	Havens, Don (USA)	53·8

200 m. Free-style

1967	Schollander, Don (USA)	1:56·0

400 m. Free-style

1951	Okamoto, Tetsuo (Brazil)	4:52·4
1955	McLane, Jimmy (USA)	4:51·3
1959	Breen, George (USA)	4:31·4
1963	Saari, Roy (USA)	4:19·3
1967	Charlton, Greg (USA)	4:10·2

1,500 m. Free-style

1951	Okamoto, Tetsuo (Brazil)	19:23·3
1955	McLane, Jimmy (USA)	20:04·0
1959	Somers, Alan (USA)	17:53·2
1963	Saari, Roy (USA)	17:26·2
1967	Burton, Mike (USA)	16:44·4

100 m. Back-stroke

1951	Stack, Allen (USA)	1:08·0
1955	McKinney, Frank (USA)	1:07·1
1959	McKinney, Frank (USA)	1:03·6
1963	Bartsch, Edward (USA)	1:01·5
1967	Hickcox, Charles (USA)	1:01·2

200 m. Back-stroke

1967	Hutton, Ralph (Can)	2:12·5

100 m. Breast-stroke

1967	Fiolo, Jose (Braz)	1:07·5

200 m. Breast-stroke

1951	Dominguez, Hector (Arg)	2:43·8
1955	Dominguez, Hector (Arg)	2:46·9
1959	Mulliken, Bill (USA)	2:43·1
1963	Jastremski, Chet (USA)	2:35·4
1967	Fiolo, Jose (Braz)	2:30·4

100 m. Butterfly

1967	Spitz, Mark (USA)	56·3

200 m. Butterfly

1955	Rios, Eulalio (Mex)	2:39·8
1959	Gillanders, David (USA)	2:18·0
1963	Robie, Carl (USA)	2:11·3
1967	Spitz, Mark (USA)	2:06·4

200 m. Individual medley

1967	Russell, Doug (USA)	2:13·2

400 m. Individual medley

1967	Utley, Bill (USA)	4:48·1

4 × 100 m. Free-style relay

1967	United States	3:34·1

4 × 200 m. Free-style relay

1951	United States	9:06·0

1955	United States	9:00·0
1959	United States	8:22·7
1963	United States	8:16·9
1967	United States	8:00·5

3 × 100 m. Medley relay

| 1951 | United States | 3:16·9 |

4 × 100 m. Medley relay

1955	United States	4:29·1
1959	United States	4:14·9
1963	United States	4:05·6
1967	United States	3:59·3

Springboard diving

1951	Capilla, Joaquin (Mex)	201·716
1955	Capilla, Joaquin (Mex)	175·76
1959	Tobian, Gary (USA)	161·40
1963	Dinsley, Tom (Can)	154·40
1967	Wrightson, Bernie (USA)	166·95

Highboard diving

1951	Capilla, Joaquin (Mex)	159·966
1955	Capilla, Joaquin (Mex)	172·33
1959	Gaxiola, Alvaro (Mex)	168·77
1963	Webster, Robert (USA)	164·12
1967	Young, Win (USA)	154·93

WOMEN

100 m. Free-style

1951	Geary, Sharon (USA)	1:08·4
1955	Stewart, Helen (Can)	1:07·7
1959	Von Saltza, Chris (USA)	1:03·8
1963	Stickles, Terri (USA)	1:02·8
1967	Bricker, Erika (USA)	59·9

200 m. Free-style

1951	Schultz, Ana Maria (Arg)	2:32·4
1955	Werner, Wanda Lee (USA)	2:32·5
1959	Von Saltza, Chris (USA)	2:18·5
1963	Johnson, Robyn (USA)	2:17·5
1967	Kruse, Pam (USA)	2:11·9

400 m. Free-style

1951	Schultz, Ana Maria (Arg)	5:26·7
1955	Whittall, Beth (Can)	5:32·4
1959	Von Saltza, Chris (USA)	4:55·9
1963	Finneran, Sharon (USA)	4:52·7
1967	Meyer, Debbie (USA)	4:32·6

800 m. Free-style

| 1967 | Meyer, Debbie (USA) | 9:22·9 |

100 m. Back-stroke

1951	O'Brien, Maureen (USA)	1:18·5
1955	Fisher, Leonore (Can)	1:16·7
1959	Cone, Carin (USA)	1:12·2

| 1963 | Harmar, Nina (USA) | 1:11·5 |
| 1967 | Tanner, Elaine (Can) | 1:07·3 |

200 m. Back-stroke

| 1967 | Tanner, Elaine (Can) | 2:24·5 |

100 m. Breast-stroke

| 1967 | Ball, Catie (USA) | 1:14·8 |

200 m. Breast-stroke

1951	Turnbull, Dorothea (Arg)	3:08·4
1955	Elsenius, Mary Lou (USA)	3:08·4
1959	Warner, Ann (USA)	2:56·8
1963	Driscoll, Alice (USA)	2:56·2
1967	Ball, Catie (USA)	2:42·2

100 m. Butterfly

1955	Whittall, Beth (Can)	1:16·2
1959	Collins, Becky (USA)	1:09·5
1963	Ellis, Kathy (USA)	1:07·6
1967	Daniel, Ellie (USA)	1:05·2

200 m. Butterfly

| 1967 | Kolb, Claudia (USA) | 2:25·5 |

200 m. Individual medley

| 1967 | Kolb, Claudia (USA) | 2:26·1 |

400 m. Individual medley

| 1967 | Kolb, Claudia (USA) | 5:09·7 |

4 × 100 m. Free-style relay

1951	United States	4:37·1
1955	United States	4:31·8
1959	United States	4:17·5
1963	United States	4:15·7
1967	United States	4:04·6

3 × 100 m. Medley relay

| 1951 | United States | 3:49·3 |

4 × 100 m. Medley relay

1955	United States	5:11·6
1959	United States	4:44·6
1963	United States	4:49·1
1967	United States	4:30·0

Springboard diving

1951	Cunningham, Mary (USA)	131·93
1955	McCormick, Pat (USA)	142·42
1959	Pope, Paula Jean (USA)	139·23
1963	McAlister, Barbara (USA)	144·31
1967	Gossick, Sue (USA)	150·41

Highboard diving

1951	McCormick, Pat (USA)	65·716
1955	McCormick, Pat (USA)	92·05
1959	Pope, Paula Jean (USA)	97·13

1963   Cooper, Linda (USA)   100·35
1967   Bush, Lesley (USA)   108·20

PHELPS, Brian (Great Britain, 21 Apr.
1944–). Diving is not a sport for
records, yet the career of Brian Phelps
from East Ham is studded with them.
He was the youngest man to win a
European diving championship—at 14,
for highboard in 1958. He was the only
champion, swimmer or diver, to defend
a title four years later—and he won
again. He was the youngest man to
represent Britain and he has won more
gold medals (four) at the Commonwealth Games than any other diver, man
or woman.

Phelps, the perfectionist with the ideal
competitive temperament, was the first
British man in thirty-six years—and
only the second ever—to win an Olympic
diving medal. This was in 1960, when he
took the bronze on the highboard in
Rome. He dived also in the 1964 Olympics for sixth place.

His first appearance for Britain was
against Italy on 3 Aug. 1957—he was
then 13 years 3 months and 12 days old
and he had to learn two difficult voluntary dives in a hurry in order to compete.
The same year, he won the first of his
fourteen A.S.A. titles, the high plain.

The next year, although having hospital treatment for a badly strained
shoulder, he was second in the Commonwealth highboard for England, only 3·3
points behind Scotland's veteran Peter
Heatly. Six weeks later, Phelps was
champion of Europe, having beaten
men old enough to be his father and he
won by the tremendous margin of 7·17
points. This probably was his most
amazing achievement, for the contest
stretched over three rounds and two days
and the concentration and nerve of this
little boy, who watched every dive by
every one of his rivals, will always be
remembered by those who were in
Budapest.

It was harder in the 1962 Europeans
in Leipzig but Mr. Consistency Phelps
kept his highboard crown. But in 1966,
in Utrecht, after a row over judging, he
had to bow to Italy's Klaus Dibiasi, who

went on to become Olympic champion
in 1968.

Phelps appeared in three Commonwealth Games and in 1962 and '66
added four golds—for the springboard
and highboard diving doubles—to his
1958 silver. He was undefeated from the
highboard in Britain from 1958–66,
winning the A.S.A. title eight times (he
could not compete through injury in
1963). He was also springboard champion
1960–62 and took the plain diving in 1957
(at 13), 1960 and 1961.

PINKSTON, Clarence (United States,
2 Feb. 1900–65) and **BECKER, Betty** (6
Mar. 1903–). Husband and wife
Olympic champions, Clarence from
Wichita, Kansas, won the 1920 highboard title and was runner-up in the
springboard in Antwerp and four years
later won the two diving bronze medals.
He married Betty Becker from Philadelphia after her springboard gold and
highboard silver successes in the 1924
Paris Olympics and coached his wife to
her second Olympic crown, on the highboard, in 1928. Clarence was honoured
by the Hall of Fame in 1966 and Betty
a year later—a truly remarkable family
double.

PIRIE, Irene (Canada), see MILTON
FAMILY.

PLUNGING. A plunge is the shallow
dive used by competitors to start all
races except back-stroke (in which competitors start in the water). The perfect
starting dive requires the greatest
amount of forward momentum and the
minimum amount of submergence.

This principle is also important in
distance-plunging competitions which
were most popular in Britain until the
1940s because there were no age barriers
to hamper success. The competitor took
a standing plunge from a firm take-off,
then floated motionless, face down-
wards, until his breath gave out or 60
seconds had elapsed, whichever was the
shorter. No progressive actions were
allowed except the impetus from the
dive. Championships were decided on
the best distance of three attempts.

Plunging was held only once in the Olympics, in 1904, when America, with a preponderance of entries in all events, took all three medals. W. E. Dickey, the winner, plunged 62 ft. 6 in. which compared unfavourably with the 75 ft. 4 in. of John Jarvis in taking the A.S.A. title that year, but who did not go to Los Angeles.

PLUNGING, AMATEUR SWIMMING ASSOCIATION CHAMPIONS. A.S.A.

Plunging championships were instituted in 1883 and discontinued in 1947 after two breaks during World Wars I and II. Of the fifty-two championships held, Frank Parrington won eleven times between 1926 and 1939, W. Allason ten (1896–1922) and W. Taylor eight (1895–1906). The full list of champions is:

		ft.	in.
1883	Clarke T. H.	63	2
1884	Davenport, Horace	64	8
1885	Davenport, Horace	72	10½
1886	Davenport, Horace	67	11½
1887	Blake, G. A.	73	10½
1888	Blake, G. A.	71	3
1889	Blake, G. A.	73	5
1890	Blake, G. A.	69	3
1891	Blake, G. A.	67	3
1892	Wilson, H. A.	59	6
1893	Dadd, S. T.	64	3
1894	McHugh, J.	64	4
1895	Taylor, W.	65	3
1896	Allason, W.	73	4
1897	Allason, W.	68	11
1898	Taylor, W.	78	9
1899	Taylor, W.	73	9
1900	Taylor, W.	75	11
1901	Taylor, W.	78	0
1902	Allason, W.	73	10
1903	Taylor, W.	74	0
1904	Jarvis, John	75	4
1905	Taylor, W.	75	7
1906	Taylor, W.	82	7
1907	Allason, W.	75	10½
1908	Allason, W.	78	7

1909	Allason, W.	74	2¾
1910	Allason, W.	79	0
1911	Allason, W.	81	5
1912	Smith, W. H. M.	69	1½
1913	Davison, H.	73	3
1914–19	No events		
1920	Davison, H.	71	9
1921	Allason, W.	78	6
1922	Allason, W.	73	8¼
1923	Beaumont, Arthur	75	11
1924	Beaumont, Arthur	75	5
1925	Wilson, William	74	3½
1926	Parrington, Frank	85	6
1927	Parrington, Frank	80	9
1928	Parrington, Frank	81	0
1929	Parrington, Frank	85	4
1930	Beaumont, Arthur	85	10
1931	Beaumont, Arthur	85	9½
1932	Beaumont, Arthur	80	11
1933	Parrington, Frank	84	6
1934	Parrington, Frank	84	1½
1935	Parrington, Frank	84	0
1936	Parrington, Frank	80	6
1937	Parrington, Frank	80	7¼
1938	Parrington, Frank	81	7½
1939	Parrington, Frank	76	2½
1940–45	No events		
1946	Snow, J. C.	76	4½
1947	Discontinued		

POYNTON-HILL, Dorothy (United States, 17 July 1915–   ). Silver medallist for springboard diving in the 1928 Olympics—two weeks after her thirteenth birthday—Dorothy Poynton from Salt Lake City won the highboard gold in 1932 and retained her title (as Mrs. Poynton-Hill) in Berlin in 1936 when she also took the bronze medal from the springboard. A fair-haired glamour girl, she now teaches swimming and diving at her 'Dorothy Poynton' Aquatic Club in Los Angeles.

PROSUMENSCHIKOVA,   Galina (USSR). See Stepanova, Galina.

R

RADMILOVIC, Paul (Great Britain, 5 Mar. 1886–1968). The Olympic record of Paul (Paulo) Radmilovic is one of the most amazing in the history of organized swimming. He competed in five Olympic Games from 1908 to 1928 (London, Stockholm, Antwerp, Paris and Amsterdam) and in the 1906 Interim Games in Athens. And he won gold medals at three of them for swimming and waterpolo.

He was a member of the British waterpolo team who won in London in 1908 and captained the gold medal teams in 1912 and 1920. He was also in the winning 4 × 200 m. relay squad in 1908. Had the war not stopped the holding of the 1916 Games, Raddy, as he was best known, must have achieved a record number of appearances (and gold medals) in the pool.

Raddy, whose father was Greek and mother Irish, was in international swimming for thirty years—from the age of 16 to 45. He won nine A.S.A. championships from 100 y. to 5 miles and the span of his successes was remarkable. He took the sprint in 1909 in 61·0; the 440 y. in 1925 (5:41·2); the 880 y. in 1926 (11:57·4); one mile in 1925, '26, '27 (best time 24:27·0 in 1925 and '26); the long distance (five miles in the River Thames) in 1907 and 1925 and 1926 (best time 1 hr. 5:06·4 in 1925). There were twenty years between his first and last long distance victories and in 1926 he was 40.

His Welsh championship winning record was equally impressive. He won the 100 y. title fifteen times between 1901 and 1922 (with six races cancelled because of the war and W. J. Kimber winning in 1912). The 220 and 440 y. championships were not instituted until 1927, when Raddy was 41, yet he won the quarter in 1929 in a championships record of 5:43·2 that stood until 1938 He was the first winner of the 880 y. (1910) and won for the sixth time in 1929.

A scratch golfer, an outstanding footballer, Welshman Raddy, born in Cardiff but who lived most of his life in Weston-super-Mare, continued to swim for sheer pleasure almost until the day he died. At 78 he was still swimming a quarter-mile each day. He was honoured by the Hall of Fame in 1967.

RAE, Nan (Great Britain, 13 Jan. 1941–). Motherwell's Nan Rae was the first Briton to swim 400 m. long course in under five minutes. She did this in placing sixth in the 1960 Olympic final in 4:59·7 —only 1·2 behind fifth-placed Dawn Fraser (Australia), the 100 m. champion.

Two years earlier, Nan had come fifth in the Commonwealth 440 y. (5:15·2) and won a bronze medal in the European 400 m. (5:07·7). She won the A.S.A. 440 y. in 1961 (5:02·8) and seven Scottish titles—220 y. (1959–61), 440 y. (1958–61).

RATCLIFFE, Shelagh (Great Britain, 25 Jan. 1952–). Britain's best individual medley swimmer, Shelagh Ratcliffe from Everton (Liverpool), who was fifth in the 400 m. final at the 1968 Olympics, has suffered internationally from lack of British opposition. Had she been subjected to any sort of pressure at home, this stylish, talented swimmer, who practices Yoga like her father, certainly could have done even better than her 2:29·5 for 200 m. and 5:21·7 for 400 m. British records in April 1970. In fact, she won the A.S.A. 220 and 440 y. medley titles in 1967, '68 and '69 by at least four seconds in each of her six races. She also raced successfully on free-style, winning the A.S.A. 220 y. title in 1969 in 2:17·1.

Miss Ratcliffe won two medley medals at the 1970 Commonwealth Games. She was one tenth outside her British 200 m. record in winning a silver (2:29·6) but broke the British mark in coming third in the 400 m. in 5:17·9. Two weeks later. she set English records in easily retaining her A.S.A. 220 and 440 y. titles (2:30·7 and 5:19·1). And in September she was the only British double medallist, both bronzes, in the 200 and 400 m. medley in the European championships.

RAUSCH, Emil (Germany, 1881–14 Dec. 1954). The last man to win an Olympic gold medal swimming side-stroke, Rausch won the 880 and mile at the 1904 Games, in 13:11·4 and 26:18·2, and came third in the 220 y. He also won a silver medal in Germany's relay team at the 1906 Interim Games. He won national titles between 1900 and 1910 for distances from 100 to 7,500 m. and was awarded a gold honour medal for helping to promote life-saving in England.

RAWLS, Katherine (United States, 14 June 1918–). Probably the world's greatest all-round aquatic performer, Katherine Rawls was a fine diver— bronze medallist from the springboard at the 1932 Olympics (at 14) and again in 1936. She was a remarkable swimmer —a bronze medal in the American free-style relay squad in the 1936 Games was just one of her achievements. And had the medley individual event existed outside America in her days she must have been Olympic champion.

The oldest and best of the Rawls sisters from Fort Lauderdale—baby Peggy was in shows at 18 months, and there were Dorothy and Evelyn (who made United States national relay teams)—Katherine was a girl before her time. She twice won four titles at national championships—the first woman to do so. The first was in 1933 with the improbable combination of springboard diving, 200 m. breast-stroke, 880 y. free-style and 300 m.

medley (before the days of butterfly). She won thirty-three national titles— more than any other woman—in the days when there were only seven individual women's events, against the twelve of the modern era.

Katherine never held a world record, but she was undefeated in individual medley events for eight years (1932–39) and her performances were looked upon as world bests. World War II and a fascination for flying spelt the end of her pool career. She became one of the world's top women flyers and one of the original twenty-five glamorous women pilots who ferried planes to combat zones for the Air Transport Command.

RECORDS. There are records for all levels of swimming, from world and continental, national and area, junior and down to the youngest age groups (see AGE GROUP). There are Games and championship records, i.e., the best performances in competition during the Olympic, Commonwealth or Pan-American Games or the European championships. There are records for individual and relay events and for all recognized strokes and distances.

Generally, records are classified under the headings of long course (see LONG COURSE) and short course (SEE SHORT COURSE). At the upper echelon (World, European, Commonwealth, etc.) only long course metric records are recognized. At other levels there are usually short and long course lists.

In Britain, waiting to 'go metric' in 1971, the situation is more complex. British records are only long course for metric distances, though marks can be set in 55 y. baths with times for the longer yards distances (see METRIC/ LINEAR CONVERSIONS). For some obscure reason, there are no British short course marks, though every other major swimming nation in the world has both.

But England have two lists. One is for the best performances set in any appropriate length of bath. This list includes the traditional British distances of 100 y. free-style and 100 and 200 y. back-stroke, breast-stroke and butterfly, the international metric distances and also the multiples of 110y. (the linear equivalents of 100 m.). The second list is a long course one for both metric and linear distances.

It has been difficult for England (and for that matter Scotland, Wales) to make wholesale changes in record distances while so many different length pools—some built more than fifty years ago—still exist . . . for 25 y., 25 m., 30 y., 33½ y., 36⅔ y., 44 y., 50 m. and 55 y. But standardisation will come in time.

The world record list, which is the basis of all other records and ranking lists of importance, was cut to a tidy thirty-one events during the F.I.N.A. Congress at the 1968 Mexico Olympics to be operative from 1 Jan. 1969 as follows:

Men: 100, 200, 400, 800*, 1,500, 4 × 100 and 4 × 200 m. free-style, 100 and 200 m. back-stroke, breast-stroke and butterfly and 200, 400 and 4 × 100 m. medley = 16.

Women: 100, 200, 400, 800, 1,500*, and 4 × 100 m. free-style, 100 and 200 m. back-stroke, breast-stroke and butterfly and 200, 400 and 4 × 100 m. medley = 15.

* Not in the programme of the Olympic, Commonwealth or Pan-American Games or the European championships.

RELAY RACING. This is a team competition in which squads—normally four—race successively in order to produce an aggregate time. Relays are excellent tests of the strength of a country or a club.

At the take-over between swimmers 1 and 2, 2 and 3 and 3 and 4, the incoming racer must have touched the wall before the feet of the out-going team-mate have lost touch with the starting block. Failure to do this is described as a 'flyer' and results in disqualification. Only the first swimmer, who starts on the gun, can set an individual record in a relay.

Relay events were in the Olympics first in 1900 when there was a 5 × 200 m. free-style race for men which was won by Germany with Britain second. By the Games of 1908 the distance had become standardised at 4 × 200 m. And in 1912 a 4 × 100 m. event for women was included and it was won by Britain.

In 1960, 4 × 100 m. medley relays for men and women were added to the Olympic programme and in 1964 the men were given an additional free-style relay event, for 4 × 100 m. But before this there had been medley relay events in the Commonwealth Games (from 1934) and the European championships (1958).

Despite the early start of relay racing, it was not until 1932 that world relay records by national teams were recognized with the ratification of the Olympic winning times of Japan's men (4 × 200 m., 8:58·4) and America's women (4 × 100 m., 4:38·0).

REYNOLDS, Peter (Australia, 1947–). An Olympic medley relay bronze medallist in 1964, Peter Reynolds, from New South Wales, had his best year in 1966 when, in the Commonwealth Games in Jamaica, he won four gold medals.

Reynolds took the 220 y. back-stroke and 440 y. medley in world record times (2:12·0 and 4:50·8), the 110 y. back-stroke (62·4) and swam in Australia's 4 × 220 y. free-style team, who broke the world record (7:59·5) and became the first squad to break eight minutes. Reynolds would have won a record five golds in one Games had not the Australian team been disqualified for a 'flying' take-over in the 4 × 110 y. medley, having been inside the world record in touching first.

In his comparatively short time at the top, Reynolds (6 ft. 1 in. and 12 st. 6 lb.) won the Australian 110 and 220 y. backstroke and 440 y. medley titles three times each and the 220 y. medley twice, all between 1964–67. He also won the A.S.A. 220 y. backstroke and medley championships in 1967.

RIACH, Nancy (Great Britain 6 April 1927–15 Sept. 1947). Free-style champion Nancy Riach was stricken with poliomyelitis during the European championships of 1947 and died in Monte

Carlo. She was ill, though no one realized to what extent, as she swam, against doctor's orders, in what was to be her last race, a heat of the 100 m. free-style. A team-mate, convinced Nancy would not finish, walked up and down the bathside as the Scots girl raced. But Nancy did finish, in fourth place, then was rushed to hospital where she died the day after the championships ended.

A smiling, charming girl, from Motherwell, Nancy had a tremendous swimming future. She had won three A.S.A. titles in 1946, all by substantial margins—the 100 y. by 2·2 (63·0), 220 y. by 7·0 (2:36·0) and the 440 y. by 8·4 (5:50·0). And she had won the 100 y. again in 1947.

RICHARDS, Mike (Great Britain, 13 Sept. 1950–   ).

The year of 1970 was a much be-medalled one for Welshman Mike Richards from Newport who in two months won three golds, a silver and three bronzes. A promising, but nothing more, back-stroker in 1969, his trans-formation came after he became a student at Nottingham University and joined the Nottingham Northern club.

Richards opened with a shock gold in the 200 m. in the Edinburgh Common-wealth Games in a British record of 2:14·5 and followed with a silver in the 100 m. (61·7, again a British record). He also helped Wales to their first ever relay bronzes in the medley relay and the Principality's first victory over England.

In the A.S.A. championships he won the 110 and 220 y. titles (61·8 and 2:15·2. Welsh records) and then went on to the World Student Games in Turin where he came third in both the 100 and 200 m. events behind notable American swim-mers.

Then came the European champion-ships in Barcelona. And though the Welshman was not in the medals here, he broke his British record (61·6) in a heat of the 100 m. and reduced this to a Commonwealth record of 60·9 in coming fifth in the final. At this stage, not sur-prisingly, he ran out of steam and failed to qualify for the final of the 200 m.

RIGGIN, Aileen (United States, 2 May 1906–   ). Winner of the first Olympic springboard diving title for women, Aileen Riggin was a tiny child and had just passed her fourteenth birthday in 1920 when she beat her team-mate Helen Wainwright by 5·8 points for the gold medal. At the time, she was the youngest Olympic champion. America's Marjorie Gestring took Aileen's 'babe' record in 1936 when she also won the springboard title, three months before her fourteenth birthday (see GESTRING, MARJORIE).

Four years after this remarkable feat, Aileen became the only competitor in the history of the Games to win medals for swimming and diving . . . by coming third in the 100 m. back-stroke (1:28·2) as well as winning the silver for spring-board diving.

Aileen, born in Newport, Rhode Island, was high point woman for swim-ming and diving at a United States championships meeting, won three out-door and one indoor springboard titles and was a member of two teams who won American relay titles. She made the first under-water and slow-motion swim-ming and diving films for Grantland Rice in 1922 and '23.

She turned professional in 1926, toured the world, appeared in many Hollywood pictures, helped to coach and starred in Billy Rose's first Aqua-cade, at the 1937 Cleveland Exposition, and wrote articles for many of the prestige women's magazines. Now Mrs. Howard Soule, and still petite, Aileen lives in Honolulu.

RITTER, R. Max (Germany/United States, 1886–   ). The No. 1 citizen of world swimming, Richard Max Ritter has played a unique part in the develop-ment of the sport since the foundation of F.I.N.A. in 1908 (see FEDERATION INTER-NATIONALE DE NATATION AMATEUR). In fact, he is the only survivor of the inter-national delegates who attended the inaugural meeting in London in July of that year and the only person to have represented two countries at F.I.N.A. meetings.

Born in Magdeburg, the son of a well-to-do manufacturer, Ritter spent the years of 1905–09 in London, during which he swam for Germany in the 1908 Olympics, reaching the semi-finals of the back-stroke. He was the spokesman for Germany at the F.I.N.A. founding meeting and also swam for the country of his birth in the 1912 Olympics. Following high school, he had gone into the chemical business and after his spell in London his job took him to the United States. By 1916 he was an American citizen, building up a cloth dyeing and finishing company and becoming a millionaire.

But before leaving Germany, in 1904, he took his first step in swimming administration by founding the successful Hellas Club in his home town. In America, he became a member of the New York Athletic Club and continued to race and play polo. By 1936 he was the United States representative on the F.I.N.A. Bureau and in 1946 he took on the dual office of Hon. Secretary and Treasurer. The two-year financial stewardship of this astute business man resulted in a much improved F.I.N.A. bank balance. He continued as secretary until 1952, was elected president in 1960 and an honorary member in 1964.

He has pioneered—and often paid for out of his own pocket—many projects for the betterment of swimming, including the Ritter judging machine (development costs around $10,000), the first machine in swimming to record the finishing order of a race on a paper tape. Not surprisingly, Ritter was the first swimming administrator to be honoured by the Hall of Fame (1965).

ROBIE, Carl (United States, 12 May 1945–). At 23 and considered to be past his best, Robie rocked the swimming world by winning the 1968 Olympic 200 m. butterfly gold while his fancied team-mate Mark Spitz, the world record-holder, finished last in the final. Robie's victory in Mexico was carefully and quietly planned. Four years earlier, he had missed golds in Tokyo in two events —200 m. butterfly (2nd) and 400 m. m.

medley (4th)—having been the fastest qualifier for the final in each event. In 1968 he went for one event only and in a predicted American medal hat trick Robie had been put down for the bronze. He entered the final as an equal fourth fastest qualifier, but in the big race he was leading at 100 m. and he beat off the late challenge from Britain's Martyn Woodroffe to win by three-tenths in 2:08·7.

Robie played a part in two eras of top ranking swimming—an unusual achievement, particularly for an American. He broke his first world record on 19 Aug. 1961—200 m. butterfly in 2:12·6. He trimmed this to 2:12·4 and 2:10·8 in separate races on the same day, (11 Aug. 1962) and to 2:08·2 a year later. He won the Pan-American 200 m. butterfly title in 1963, but was not in the United States team to defend his crown four years later. Then he came back to his greatest triumph in Mexico.

ROMAIN, Roy (Great Britain, 27 July 1918–). Champion of Europe at 29 years old, the tall Royston Romain, using the over-water arm recovery, powered himself to a 1½ sec. victory over Hungary's Sandor Nemeth in the 200 m. breast-stroke (2:40·1) in Monte Carlo in 1947. Romain, of course, was a butter-flyer using the breast-stroke frog-like leg-kick in the days before the separation of the two strokes (see BREAST-STROKE and BUTTERFLY).

Romain, from Essex, was awarded the T. M. Yeaden Memorial Trophy as 'England's Swimmer of the Year' for that performance. At the 1948 London Olympics, Romain was again the best Briton but did not get past the semi-finals of the 200 m. breast-stroke. He swam in the 1950 Commonwealth Games, missing the 220 y. gold medal by one-tenth (2:54·2), but adding a relay gold, to his individual silver, in the 3 × 110 y. medley. Romain won the A.S.A. 200 y. breast-stroke titles in 1947, '48, '49.

ROSE, Murray (Australia, 1939–). British born Iain Murray Rose, who emigrated with his parents to Australia as a baby, became the youngest triple Olympic gold medallist in 1956 when he won the 400 and 1,500 m. and was a member of the Australian world record-breaking winning 4 × 200 m. squad. He made history again in 1960 when he became the first man to win a distance title, in this case the 400 m., at successive Games. With a silver in the 1,500 m. and a bronze in the free-style relay in Rome, Rose's Olympic medal tally was four golds, a silver and bronze.

Rose certainly would have swum in a third Olympics, in Tokyo in 1964, but for a row with officials of the Australian Swimming Union. They demanded that Rose return from the United States to take part in national trials and refused to pick him when he said he could not come. Rose's answer, in the months before the Games, was to break the world records for 880 y. and 1,500 m. And still Australia would not add him to the team.

He swam in only one Commonwealth Games, in 1962, when he won the 440 and 1,650 y. titles and two more golds in the free-style relays. His nine world records included three for 400 m. (first = 4:25·9 in 1957/last = 4:13·4 in 1962). 440 y. (4:27·1, 1957), 800 m. (8:51·3, 1962), 880 y. (9:34·2, 1956 and 8:55·5, 1964), 1,500 m. (17:59·5, Olympic winning time 1956, 17:01·8, 1964).

The Rose family came from Nairn in the Scottish Highlands and trace their origins back to Hugh de Ros, one of the early Scottish barons. Rose's ancestors fought for Bonnie Prince Charlie at Culloden in 1746 and the family have their own tartan, coat of arms and the motto 'Constant and True'.

In Australia, the family lived in Double Bay, a fashionable Sydney resort. But Murray finished his education at the University of Southern California where he graduated in drama and television in 1962. He was raised from birth on a diet which excluded meat, fish, poultry, refined flour and sugar. Wheatgerm, honey and seaweed were some of his substitute foods.

American coaches called Rose 'the greatest swimmer ever . . . greater even than Johnny Weissmuller'. He was awarded, by the American Amateur Athletic Union in 1962, a special trophy (given to only one other individual in history) for his major contribution to sport. The same year he received the Helms Foundation World Trophy. He has featured on a potage stamp issued by the Dominican Republic, been entertained on the royal yacht *Britannia* by the Queen and Prince Philip and, in 1965, was one of the first groups of swimmers to be honoured by the Hall of Fame.

ROTH, Dick (United States, 26 Sept. 1947–). Richard Roth's special claim to fame, in addition to winning the 400 m. medley at the 1964 Tokyo Olympics, was that he earned his gold medal in a world record 4:45·4 despite the fact that he had an appendix attack the night before his final. Told he must have an emergency operation, he said: 'Not until after the race'.

The winning time of Roth, from the amazingly-successful Santa Clara Swim Club, remained in the world record book for almost four years when Russia's Andrei Dunaev was able to trim one-tenth off the American's Tokyo mark.

Roth won six United States outdoor medley titles—the 200 m. (1963–65) in the days before world records were recognized for this distance and 400 m. (1964–66), but like so many talented American stars, he retired young, at 19, with perhaps his best swimming years ahead of him.

ROYAL LIFE SAVING SOCIETY. The R.L.S.S., at that time known as the Life Saving Society, was founded in 1891 and after one year the following aims and objects of the society were announced:

(a) To promote technical education in life saving and resuscitation of the apparently drowned.

(b) To stimulate public opinion in favour of general adoption of swimming and life saving as a branch of instruction in schools, colleges, etc.

(c) To encourage floating, diving,

plunging and such other swimming arts as would be of assistance to a person endeavouring to save life.

(d) To arrange and promote public lectures, demonstrations and competitions and to form classes of instruction, so as to bring about a widespread and thorough knowledge of the principles which underlie the art of natation.

These aims and objects still apply.

The first co-secretaries were Archibald Sinclair and William Henry (see HENRY, WILLIAM) and the ideology behind their pioneering work can be summarized in a paragraph out of the Life-Saving section of the *Badminton Book of Swimming* (c. 1894) by Henry and Sinclair:

'The ability to save life is the glorious privilege of a swimmer, and many are ever ready to risk their own lives in order to aid others in danger. That the ability ought to be cultivated is unquestionable, for the danger to the rescuer is thereby minimised and his chances of successfully rendering efficient aid increased.'

The headquarters of the R.L.S.S. are in London and there are four National Societies, with their own branches, who make up the Commonwealth Council. They are:

United Kingdom. More than forty branches in England, Scotland, Wales and Ireland plus overseas branches in Gibraltar, Hong Kong, Malta, Matabeleland, Rhodesia, Singapore and Zambia. Associated are honorary overseas representatives from Bahamas, Bermuda, Ceylon, Cyprus, Gambia, Gilbert and Ellice Island, H.M. Forces in Germany, India, Kenya, Mauritius, Nigeria, Pakistan, St. Helena, St. Lucia, Seychelles, Tanzania, Uganda.

Australia. Nine branches in New South Wales, Queensland, South Australia, Tasmania, Victoria, Western Australia, Fiji, Territory of Papua and New Guinea, Northern Territories.

Canada. Ten branches, Alberta, British Columbia, Manitoba, Nova Scotia, Ontario, Prince Edward Island, Quebec, Saskatchewan, New Brunswick, Newfoundland.

New Zealand. Fifteen branches in Auckland, Canturbury, Gisborne, Hawke's Bay, Manawatu, Marlborough, Nelson, Northland, Otago, South Auckland, Southland, Taranaki, Wanganui, Wellington, New Zealand Surf Life Saving Association. There are also Societies in Malaysia, Trinidad and Tobago and Jamaica.

An important aspect of the work of the R.L.S.S. is the long standing and very valuable and lucrative awards scheme. In the United Kingdom alone, there are almost twenty categories of awards, from Elementary to Distinction, for resuscitation and water safety. The annual number of individual awards obtained is now close to 450,000, and the total number of awards since 1891 is well in excess of seven million.

RYAN, Noel (Australia, 1912–69). Winner of four Commonwealth gold medals, Noel Ryan died doing what he liked most—swimming. He collapsed after competing in a half-mile race at Manly Beach, Sydney, age 57.

His Commonwealth victories were at the first Games in 1930, when he won the 400 y. in 4:39·8, seven sec. ahead of New Zealand's George Bridson and the 1,500 y. (18:55·4), again beating Bridson, this time by 45·6. In 1935, he beat England's Norman Wainwright, for the 440 y. gold (5:03·0) and Canada's Bob Pirie, with Wainwright third, in the 1,500 y. (18:25·4—30 sec. faster than in 1930). Only one man swimmer, Ian O'Brien, the Olympic breast-stroke champion (see O'BRIEN, IAN) had won more Commonwealth golds prior to 1970, when Mike Wenden (see WENDEN, MIKE) brought his tally to seven in Edinburgh.

Ryan won fifteen Australian titles and had his best times on his last victories: 100 y., 1934 (55·8); 220 y., 1931, '37 (2:18·2); 440 y. 1931, '33, '37 (5:00·2); 880 y., 1929, '31, '33, '34 (10:29·2); mile, 1928, '29, '31, '33, '34 (21:36·6).

S

SALTZA, Chris von (United States, 13 Jan. 1944–). Susan Christine von Saltza, who is still recognized as a baroness in the 'Who's Who' of Swedish nobility, was in 1957 the first star to spring from the then new American age-group programme, set up following the heavy United States defeats at the hands of Australia in the 1956 Melbourne Olympics.

The tangible proof of her talent, ability and willingness to work, are the three golds and a silver she won at the 1960 Rome Olympics in which she was first in the 400 m. (4:50·6) and America's world record-breaking medley and free-style relay teams and second (62·8), 1·6 behind Australia's Dawn Fraser in the 100 m.

Yet it was for back-stroke and not free-style that Chris won her first United States outdoor title, at 13, for 220 y. in 2:40·2 (1957). She won again in 1958, over 200 m. in a world record 2:37·4. On free-style, Chris was first in the 100 m.–110 y. 1958–60, 200 m./220 y. and 400 m./440 y. in 1959/60 . . . limited to three individual events at each meeting, she could not have won many more.

At the 1959 Pan-American Games, her medal haul was five golds for the 100 m. (63·8), 200 m. (2:18·5), 400 m. (4:55·9) and 4 × 100 m. free-style and medley relays. She broke about seventy-five American records for seventeen different distances on back-stroke, free-style and individual medley and the world 400 m. mark (4:44·5) in the 1960 United States Olympic trials.

Chris, whose Prussian forebears migrated to Sweden 700 years ago, and whose grandfather Count Philip came to the United States at the turn of the century, was a pupil of George Haines at Santa Clara, California. Haines first saw her as an untutored 11-year-old. He told her to kick a few lengths in a 20 y. pool until he could attend to her. A hundred and forty-four lengths later he remembered her . . . but Haines didn't forget Chris von Saltza again.

SCHOLLANDER, Don (United States, 30 Apr. 1946–). The first swimmer to win four golds at one Olympic Games, Donald Arthur Schollander looked and swam like a dream come true—fast, flat and with feeling. It was also so effortless, so beautiful that it was hard to realize he was going so fast.

His Games was Tokyo 1964 when he won the 100 m. by one-tenth from Britain's Bobby McGregor in 53·4, though Schollander had said: 'I'm not really a sprinter.' He took the 400 m. by 2·7 from East Germany's Frank Wiegand in a world record 4:12·2. Swimming even pace throughout, Schollander's first 200 m. was 2:05·7, he came back in 2:06·5 and his final 100 m. (61·7) was only 1·3 slower than his first . . . it was masterly.

Schollander won two relay golds in the 4 × 100 and 4 × 200 m. free-style. America broke world records both times and with 7:52·1 for the longer relay became the first nation to get inside the 8-minute barrier. Schollander's 'split' as an anchor man was 1:55·6, two seconds faster than the thirty-one other men in the race.

The free-style leg in the medley relay was decided by trial in Tokyo before the start of the Games and went to Steve Clark, who had not won a place in the USA team for the individual sprint. Clark had a 'split' of 52·4 in anchoring American to their third relay world record-breaking success.

A law student at Yale University,

Schollander, from Oregon, but who did most of his swimming with George Haines at Santa Clara, failed to qualify in the 1968 American trials for the right to defend his 100 and 400 m. titles in Mexico. Instead he earned his place in the 200 m.—which was last in the Olympic programme in 1900, though there was a 220 y. event in 1904—with a world record 1:54·3. And though Mike Wenden beat him for the gold (see WENDEN, MIKE) the Australian could not beat Schollander's world mark.

The 200 m. undoubtedly was Schollander's best distance. The 5 ft. 11 in. and 173 lb. student broke the world record for this eight times in five years . . . being the first to break the two-minute barrier with 1:58·8 on 27 July 1963, through to his 1:54·3 on 30 Aug. 1968. He also won the Pan-American 200 m. title in 1967 along with two more relay golds. The better of his two 400 m. world records was his Olympic winning 4:12·2 in 1964 and he was in eight world record-breaking American free-style relay teams though never in a medley squad that set a world time.

SCOTTISH AMATEUR SWIMMING ASSOCIATION. The early minutes of the S.A.S.A. have been lost, but it is agreed that the first meeting of club delegates was held in the Bible Society's Room, 5 St. Andrews Square, Edinburgh on 28 Jan. 1888. But there were clubs in Scotland long before this time. The records of Bon-Accord A.S.C. (Aberdeen), instituted on 26 Apr. 1862—and one of the world's longest surviving clubs—give proof that there were clubs in Aberdeen and other cities of Scotland before them, though these clubs do not exist today.

The first available information relating to an organized body is found in the minutes of the Edinburgh Carnegie Club, of 17 Sept. 1877, when Mr. W. Wilson of Glasgow—a noted swimming pioneer—invited the club to join the Association of Swimming Clubs of Scotland. On 17 Apr. 1886, a further letter resulted in the proposal that the

name of the Association should be the Scottish Amateur Swimming Association.

The longest serving officials of the S.A.S.A. are John Y. (Jock) Coutts of the Bon-Accord who became hon. secretary in 1946 and still held the office in 1970 and J. W. Williamson, hon. treasurer since 1955.

SCOTTISH CHAMPIONS

MEN

110 y. Free-style (instituted 1888 for 100 y.)

1946*	MacDonald, Ian	59·0
1947*	Harrop, Trevor	56·1
1948*	Harrop, Trevor	55·4
1949*	Wardrop, Jack	55·6
1950*	Wardrop, Jack	53·6
1951*	Wardrop, Jack	52·6
1952*	Wardrop, Jack	52·2
1953*	Welsh, Doug	54·0
1954*	Spence, Ian	55·0
1955*	Welsh, Doug	54·9
1956*	Murphy, Ron	55·0
1957*	Hill, Jimmy	54·7
1958*	Still, Athole	54·8
1959*	Black, Ian	52·0
1960*	Black, Ian	52·7
1961	McGregor, Bobby	59·2
1962	McGregor, Bobby	57·8
1963	McGregor, Bobby	57·5
1964	McGregor, Bobby	55·9
1965	Black, Gordon	57·9
1966	McGregor, Bobby	54·9
1967	McGregor, Bobby	54·4
1968	McGregor, Bobby	54·6
1969	MacGregor, Alastair	58·4
1970†	Shore, Martin	57·0

* = 100 y.   † = 100 m.

220 y. Free-style (instituted 1888)

1946	MacDonald, Ian	2:24·3
1947	MacDonald, Ian	2:22·2
1948	Wardrop, Jack	2:22·4
1949	Wardrop, Jack	2:24·2
1950	Wardrop, Jack	2:20·0
1951	Wardrop, Jack	2:17·2
1952	Wardrop, Jack	2:10·0
1953	Sreenan, Bob	2:19·4
1954	Still, Athole	2:16·4
1955	Baillie, Jack	2:20·8
1956	Baillie, Jack	2:18·2

K

1957	Murphy, Ron	2:15·0	1956	Sreenan, Bob	10:12·0
1958	Black, Ian	2:08·2	1957	Baillie, Jack	10:30·0
1959	Black, Ian	2:07·2	1958	Black, Ian	9:31·6
1960	Black, Ian	2:07·3	1959	Black, Ian	9:52·8
1961	Thomas, Frank	2:16·9	1960	Black, Ian	10:11·0
1962	Gallacher, Ian	2:16·0	1961	Sreenan, Bob	10:08·5
1963	McGregor, Bobby	2:12·4	1962	Sreenan, Bob	9:58·4
1964	McGregor, Bobby	2:09·8	1963	Wilson, Jim	10:20·6
1965	Black, Gordon	2:11·4	1964	Wilson, Jim	10:10·1
1966	McGregor, Bobby	2:06·1	1965	Galletly, Alex	9:49·5
1967	McGregor, Bobby	2:08·9	1966	Wilson, Jim	9:51·4
1968	McGregor, Bobby	2:06·5	1967	Wilson, Jim	9:47·8
1969	MacGregor, Alastair	2:11·4	1968	Henderson, Eric	9:47·0
1970*	Souter, Gordon	2:08·1	1969	Henderson, Eric	10:10·2
	* = 200 m.		1970*	Souter, Gordon	9:34·7
				* = 800 m.	

440 y. Free-style (instituted 1890)

1,650 y. Free-style

1946	Heatly, Peter	5:43·6	1964	Wilson, Jim	20:19·5
1947	Wardrop, Jack	5:15·9	1965	Galletly, Alex	19:21·6
1948	Wardrop, Jack	5:17·0	1966	Wilson, Jim	19:56·1
1949	Wardrop, Jack	5:12·9	1967	Henderson, Eric	18:50·4
1950	Wardrop, Jack	5:07·2	1968	Henderson, Eric	18:44·4
1951	Wardrop, Jack	4:55·9	1969	Henderson, Eric	19:01·7
1952	Wardrop, Jack	4:41·9	1970*	Devlin, Alex	18:37·8
1953	Sreenan, Bob	4:54·1		* = 1,500 m.	
1954	Sreenan, Bob	4:50·8			
1955	Sreenan, Bob	4:49·1			

110 y. Back-stroke (instituted 1913 for 100 y. In 1924 increased to 150 y.)

1956	Baillie, Jack	5:05·0	1946*	Harrop, Trevor	1:44·0
1957	Baillie, Jack	5:00·3	1947*	Wardrop, Bert	1:50·9
1958	Black, Ian	4:37·2	1948†	Wardrop, Bert	1:05·0
1959	Black, Ian	4:50·3	1949†	Wardrop, Bert	1:04·1
1960	Black, Ian	4:30·6	1950†	Wardrop, Bert	1:03·4
1961	Sreenan, Bob	4:50·8	1951†	Wardrop, Bert	1:03·2
1962	Gallacher, Ian	4:50·5	1952†	Wardrop, Bert	1:03·6
1963	Wilson, Jim	4:54·4	1953†	Burns, Ronnie	1:04·2
1964	Galletly, Alex	4:44·3	1954†	Robson, Tom	1:02·1
1965	Galletly, Alex	4:41·6	1955†	Burns, Ronnie	1:01·5
1966	Wilson, Jim	4:42·9	1956†	Burns, Ronnie	1:01·3
1967	Wilson, Jim	4:37·3	1957†	Robson, Tom	1:03·1
1968	McClatchey, John	4:37·0	1958†	Hill, Jimmy	1:03·2
1969	McClatchey, John	4:39·3	1959†	Hill, Jimmy	1:02·4
1970*	Souter, Gordon	4:32·8	1960†	Harrower, Andy	1:01·4
	* = 400 m.		1961	Not held	
			1962	Not held	

880 y. Free-style (instituted 1892)

1946	Heatly, Peter	11:50·0	1963	Littlejohn, Gary	1:07·9
1947	MacDonald, Ian	11:11·9	1964	Smart, Ian	1:06·5
1948	Wardrop, Jack	10:53·7	1965	Smart, Ian	1:07·0
1949	Wardrop, Jack	11:22·2	1966	Nelson, Casey	1:06·3
1950	Wardrop, Jack	11:29·2	1967	Smart, Ian	1:06·5
1951	Wardrop, Jack	10:08·0	1968	Smart, Ian	1:06·8
1952	Wardrop, Jack	9:57·3	1969	Simpson, Hammy	1:06·4
1953	Sreenan, Bob	10:32·4	1970‡	Simpson, Hammy	1:07·4
1954	Sreenan, Bob	10:06·7		* = 150 y. † = 100 y. ‡ = 100 m.	
1955	Sreenan, Bob	10:21·2			

220 y. Back-stroke (instituted 1961)

1961	Harrower, Andy	2:29·1
1962	Harrower, Andy	2:30·0
1963	Nelson, Casey	2:30·9
1964	Smart, Ian	2:26·5
1965	Smart, Ian	2:26·7
1966	Nelson, Casey	2:25·9
1967	Smart, Ian	2:25·8
1968	Smart, Ian	2:26·2
1969	Simpson, Hammy	2:25·2
1970*	Simpson, Hammy	2:25·0

* = 200 m.

110 y. Breast-stroke (instituted 1963)

1963	More, Ian	1:15·6
1964	More, Ian	1:14·3
1965	Young, Archie	1:17·6
1966	Leckie, Stuart	1:15·9
1967	Young, Archie	1:14·0
1968	Young, Archie	1:15·0
1969	Young, Archie	1:14·4
1970*	Wilkie, David	1:13·4

* = 100 m.

220 y. Breast-stroke (instituted 1913 for 200 y.)

1946*	Service, John	2:38·6
1947*	Service, John	2:34·0
1948*	Service, John	2:33·4
1949*	Calder, Ally	2:45·6
1950*	Service, John	2:42·0
1951*	Spence, Ian	Bu2:35·0
1952*	Spence, Ian	Bu2:35·4
1953*	Service, John	2:34·5
1954*	Service, John	2:29·8
1955*	Spence, Ian	2:37·7
1956*	Percy-Robb, Ian	2:31·0
1957*	Percy-Robb, Ian	2:29·6
1958*	Percy-Robb, Ian	2:36·0
1959*	MacTaggart, Jimmy	2:32·9
1960*	Crawford, Alastair	2:35·8
1961	Braund, R. W.	2:54·2
1962	Cowie, Cleave	2:45·8
1963	More, Ian	2:42·4
1964	More, Ian	2:44·8
1965	Leckie, Stuart	2:52·4
1966	Young, Archie	2:49·4
1967	Young, Archie	2:47·5
1968	Stirton, Gordon	2:52·8
1969	Stirton, Gordon	2:51·5
1970†	Wilkie, David	2:39·4

* = 200 y.   † = 200 m.

110 y. Butterfly (instituted 1963)

1963	McGregor, Bobby	1:03·5

1964	Harrower, Andy	1:02·9
1965	Henderson, Eric	1:02·7
1966	Henderson, Eric	1:02·6
1967	Brown, Downie	1:02·8
1968	Henderson, Eric	1:02·9
1969	Henderson, Eric	1:02·9
1970*	Henderson, Eric	1:01·5

* = 100 m.

220 y. Butterfly (instituted 1954 for 200 y.)

1954*	Smith, Hamilton	2:32·5
1955*	Smith, Hamilton	2:35·5
1956*	Smith, Hamilton	2:32·0
1957*	Smith, Hamilton	2:31·6
1958*	Black, Ian	2:09·9
1959*	Black, Ian	2:08·6
1960*	Black, Ian	2:09·7
1961	Blyth, Ian	2:27·2
1962	Blyth, Ian	2:25·9
1963	Harrower, Andy	2:31·0
1964	Henderson, Eric	2:21·9
1965	Henderson, Eric	2:17·7
1966	Henderson, Eric	2:23·4
1967	Henderson, Eric	2:22·7
1968	Henderson, Eric	2:20·4
1969	Henderson, Eric	2:18·7
1970†	Henderson, Eric	2:16·7

* = 200 y.   † = 200 m.

220 y. Individual medley (instituted 1968)

1968	Black, Gordon	2:28·4
1969	Henderson, Eric	2:29·0
1970*	MacGregor, Alastair	2:27·3

* = 200 m.

440 y. Medley (instituted 1952 for 300 y. and increased to 400 y. in 1956 after separation of breast-stroke and butterfly)

1952*	Spence, Ian	3:52·4
1953*	Cargill, T.	4:03·0
1954*	Spence, Ian	3:56·6
1955*	Spence, Ian	3:59·2
1956†	Spence, Ian	5:22·6
1957†	Black, Ian	4:59·0
1958†	Black, Ian	5:04·7
1959†	Black, Ian	4:48·6
1960†	Black, Ian	4:57·3
1961	Blyth, Ian	5:36·2
1962	Blyth, Ian	5:28·3
1963	Harrower, Andy	5:38·2
1964	Harrower, Andy	5:38·8
1965	Henderson, Eric	5:24·4
1966	Henderson, Eric	5:26·9

1967	Henderson, Eric	5:19·4
1968	Henderson, Eric	5:20·9
1969	Henderson, Eric	5:24·6
1970‡	Henderson, Eric	5:18·1

* = 300 y.   † = 400 y.   ‡ = 400 m.

Highboard diving (instituted 1947)

1947	Heatly, Peter
1948	No contest
1949	Heatly, Peter
1950	Heatly, Peter
1951	Heatly, Peter
1952	Berry, Geoff
1953	Heatly Peter
1954	Heatly, Peter
1955	Heatly Peter
1956	Heatly, Peter
1957	Heatly, Peter
1958	Heatly, Peter
1959	Davidson, Brian
1960	Davidson, Brian
1961	Davidson, Brian
1962	Davidson, Brian
1963	Davidson, Brian
1964	Davidson, Brian
1965	Campbell, Maurice
1966	Davidson, Brian
1967	Campbell, Maurice
1968	Campbell, Maurice
1969	Not held
1970	Campbell, Maurice

3 m. Springboard diving (instituted 1936)

1946	Heatly, Peter
1947	Heatly, Peter
1948	Heatly, Peter
1949	Heatly, Peter
1950	Heatly, Peter
1951	Heatly, Peter
1952	Berry, Geoff
1953	Heatly Peter
1954	Heatly, Peter
1955	Heatly, Peter
1956	Heatly, Peter
1957	Heatly, Peter
1958	Law, William
1959	Davidson, Brian
1960	Davidson, Brian
1961	Davidson, Brian
1962	Law, William
1963	Davidson, Brian
1964	Davidson, Brian
1965	Campbell, Maurice
1966	Davidson, Brian
1967	Davidson, Brian

1968	Campbell, Maurice
1969	Campbell, Maurice
1970	Campbell, Maurice

1 m. Springboard diving (instituted 1951)

1951	Heatly, Peter
1952	Heatly, Peter
1953	Heatly, Peter
1954	Heatly, Peter
1955	Heatly, Peter
1956	Heatly, Peter
1957	Law, William
1958	Law, William
1959	Davidson, Brian
1960	Law, William
1961	Davidson, Brian
1962	Davidson, Brian
1963	Davidson, Brian
1964	Law, William
1965	Campbell, Maurice
1966	Campbell, Maurice
1967	Davidson, Brian
1968	Campbell, Maurice
1969	Campbell, Maurice
1970	Campbell, Maurice

WOMEN

110 y. Free-style (instituted 1907 for 100 y.)

1946*	Munro, Margaret	1:05·4
1947*	Riach, Nancy	1:03·2
1948*	Gibson, Cathie	1:02·4
1949*	Turner, Elizabeth	1:03·5
1950*	Girvan, Margaret	1:05·4
1951*	Gibson, Cathie	1:02·8
1952*	Melville, Dorothy	1:04·2
1953*	Hogben, Frances	1:04·7
1954*	Gibson, Cathie	1:03·6
1955*	MacDonald, Flora	1:04·9
1956*	Girvan, Margaret	1:03·7
1957*	Girvan, Margaret	1:02·3
1958*	Harris, Christine	1:03·2
1959*	Rae, Nan	1:00·7
1960*	Harris, Christine	1:00·3
1961	Rae, Nan	1:06·2
1962	Watt, Sheila	1:09·0
1963	Nicol, Pat	1:07·6
1964	Stewart, Eleanor	1:07·1
1965	Kellock, Fiona	1:06·1
1966	Kellock, Fiona	1:05·2
1967	Kellock, Fiona	1:04·9
1968	Kellock, Fiona	1:04·4
1969	Brown, Moira	1:06·9

1970† Brown, Moira   1:04·6
       * = 100 y.   † = 100 m.

220 y. Free-style (instituted 1891 for 200 y.)

1946*	Gibson, Cathie	2:19·5
1947*	Gibson, Cathie	2:18·6
1948*	Gibson, Cathie	2:18·3
1949*	Gibson, Cathie	2:25·4
1950*	Girvan, Margaret	2:24·6
1951*	Gibson, Cathie	2:20·8
1952*	Gibson, Cathie	2:23·9
1953*	Melville, Dorothy	2:24·9
1954*	Girvan, Margaret	2:21·2
1955	Hogben, Frances	2:44·2
1956	Girvan, Margaret	2:38·6
1957	Girvan, Margaret	2:36·5
1958	Girvan, Margaret	2:36·0
1959	Rae, Nan	2:27·3
1960	Rae, Nan	2:27·7
1961	Rae, Nan	2:26·3
1962	Nicol, Pat	2:32·2
1963	Nicol, Pat	2:29·8
1964	Stewart, Eleanor	2:28·5
1965	Kellock, Fiona	2:26·9
1966	Kellock, Fiona	2:27·9
1967	Kellock, Fiona	2:25·2
1968	Kellock, Fiona	2:28·1
1969	Brown, Moira	2:28·8
1970†	Hogg (Davison), Sally	2:19·8

       * = 200 y.   † = 200 m.

440 y. Free-style (instituted 1931)

1946	Riach, Nancy	5:55·4
1947	Gibson, Cathie	5:29·2
1948	Gibson, Cathie	5:29·9
1949	Girvan, Margaret	5:45·7
1950	Girvan, Margaret	5:46·3
1951	Gibson, Cathie	5:38·6
1952	Melville, Dorothy	5:45·7
1953	Girvan, Margaret	5:41·5
1954	Girvan, Margaret	5:31·0
1955	Hogben, Frances	5:53·3
1956	Hogben, Frances	5:45·7
1957	Girvan, Margaret	5:30·4
1958	Rae, Nan	5:23·8
1959	Rae, Nan	5:06·6
1960	Rae, Nan	5:16·2
1961	Rae, Nan	5:10·5
1962	Watt, Sheila	5:28·8
1963	Nicol, Pat	5:29·8
1964	Nicol, Pat	5:13·2
1965	Kellock, Fiona	5:16·6
1966	Kellock, Fiona	5:15·0
1967	Kellock, Fiona	5:02·4

1968	Fenton, Margaret	5:17·4
1969	Fenton, Margaret	5:15·1
1970*	Mackie, Andrea	4:51·8

       * = 400 m.

880 y. Free-style (instituted 1967)

1967	Fenton, Margaret	10:45·5
1968	Fenton, Margaret	11:09·4
1969	Mackie, Andrea	11:01·1
1970*	Hogg (Davison), Sally	10:08·0

       * = 800 m.

110 y. Back-stroke (instituted 1924 for 150 y. Reduced to 100 y. 1948)

1946*	Gibson, Cathie	1:51·1
1947*	Gibson, Cathie	1:50·0
1948†	Gibson, Cathie	1:10·0
1949†	Girvan, Margaret	1:12·6
1950†	McDowall, Margaret	1:09·2
1951†	McDowall, Margaret	1:08·9
1952†	McDowall, Margaret	1:09·4
1953†	McDowall, Margaret	1:08·3
1954†	McDowall, Margaret	1:10·0
1955†	McDowall, Margaret	1:12·0
1956†	McDowall, Margaret	1:08·0
1957†	McDowall, Margaret	1:08·8
1958†	McDowall, Margaret	1:09·3
1959†	Johnston, Frances	1:12·8
1960†	Campbell, Louise	1:10·0
1961	Campbell, Louise	1:16·4
1962	Campbell, Louise	1:13·9
1963	Campbell, Louise	1:14·9
1964	Mays, Lorraine	1:16·1
1965	Robertson, Bobby	1:17·8
1966	Robertson, Bobby	1:14·0
1967	Robertson, Bobby	1:13·8
1968	Robertson, Bobby	1:15·5
1969	Armour, Linda	1:16·4
1970–	Armour, Linda	1:14 8

       * = 150 y.   † = 100 y.   ‡ = 100 m.

220 y. Back-stroke (instituted 1963)

1963	Campbell, Louise	2:42·4
1964	Mays, Lorraine	2:44·3
1965	Campbell, Louise	2:46·5
1966	Robertson, Bobby	2:39·9
1967	Robertson, Bobby	2:39·9
1968	Fenton, Margaret	2:42·7
1969	Armour, Linda	2:44·4
1970*	Armour, Linda	2:40 7

       * = 200 m.

110 y. Breast-stroke (instituted 1963)

1963	Baxter, Ann	1:23·9
1964	Baxter, Ann	1:20·7

1965	McLeod, Margaret	1:23·7
1966	Baxter, Ann	1:21·4
1967	Baxter, Ann	1:22·0
1968	McLeod, Margaret	1:25·3
1969	Stewart, Kathie	1:24·4
1970*	Wilson, Pam	1:21 8
	* = 100 m.	

220 y. Breast-stroke (instituted 1924 for 200 y.)

1946*	Bolton, Margaret	3:05·0
1947*	Gordon, Elenor	2:56·8
1948*	Gordon, Elenor	2:53·0
1949*	Gordon, Elenor	2:56·0
1950*	Gordon, Elenor	2:50·6
1951*	Gordon, Elenor	2:44·1
1952*	Gordon, Elenor	2:45·3
1953*	Gordon, Elenor	2:44·9
1954*	Gordon, Elenor	2:41·8
1955*	Gordon, Elenor	2:46·2
1956*	Gordon, Elenor	2:46·7
1957*	Gordon, Elenor	2:41·2
1958*	Turnbull, Alison	2:51·5
1959*	Turnbull, Alison	2:48·0
1960*	Turnbull, Alison	2:44·5
1961	Turnbull, Alison	2:58·0
1962	Turnbull, Alison	3:00·1
1963	Baxter, Ann	3:02·5
1964	Baxter, Ann	2:59·3
1965	Baxter, Ann	3:03·2
1966	Baxter, Ann	2:57·5
1967	Baxter, Ann	2:56·8
1968	Blyth, Ann	3:05·1
1969	Walker, Diane	3:08·1
1970†	Wilson, Pam	2:55 8
	* = 200 y. † = 200 m.	

110 y. Butterfly (instituted 1954 for 100 y.)

1954*	Laird, Heather	1:24·6
1955*	MacDonald, Flora	1:16·1
1956*	MacDonald, Flora	1:15·7
1957*	Watt, Sheila	1:09·8
1958*	Watt, Sheila	1:10·9
1959*	Watt, Sheila	1:06·7
1960*	Watt, Sheila	1:06·0
1961	Watt, Sheila	1:15·6
1962	Watt, Sheila	1:13·5
1963	Stewart, Eleanor	1:14·0
1964	Stewart, Eleanor	1:11·7
1965	Stewart, Eleanor	1:12·0
1966	Stewart, Eleanor	1:11·5
1967	Kellock, Fiona	1:14·7
1968	Brown, Moira	1:13·6
1969	Brown, Moira	1:16·4

1970†	Brown, Moira	1:10 7
	* = 100 y. † = 100 m.	

220 y. Butterfly (instituted 1963)

1963	Watt, Sheila	2:51·8
1964	Stewart, Eleanor	2:50·9
1965	Stewart, Eleanor	2:55·4
1966	Stewart, Eleanor	2:51·2
1967	McCallum, Margaret	2:54·7
1968	Brown, Moira	2:51·0
1969	Brown, Moira	2:52·2
1970*	Brown, Moira	2:38 1
	* = 200 m.	

220 y. Individual medley (instituted 1968)

1968	Fenton, Margaret	2:47·5
1969	Brown, Moira	2:45·5
1970*	Wilson, Pam	2:39·4
	* = 200 m.	

440 y. Individual medley (instituted 1952 for 300 y. and increased to 400 y. in 1956 after separation of breast-stroke and butterfly)

1952*	Taylor, J.	4:07·9
1953*	Taylor, J.	4:15·4
1954*	MacDonald, Flora	4:12·3
1955*	MacDonald, Flora	4:22·5
1956†	MacDonald, Flora	6:06·0
1957†	Watt, Sheila	5:42·6
1958†	Watt, Sheila	5:49·4
1959†	Mays, Karen	5:30·2
1960†	Mays, Karen	5:31·8
1961	Mays, Karen	6:07·0
1962	Watt, Sheila	6:09·5
1963	Mays, Karen	6:11·1
1964	Mays, Karen	6:07·3
1965	Stewart, Eleanor	6:08·9
1966	Stewart, Eleanor	6:03·2
1967	Fenton, Margaret	5:52·5
1968	Fenton, Margaret	6:07·0
1969	Fenton, Margaret	6:02·6
1970‡	Wilson, Pam	5:41·2
	* = 300 y. † = 400 y. ‡ = 400 m.	

Highboard diving (instituted 1950)

1950	Mitchell, Sheila
1951	Mitchell, Sheila
1952	Mitchell, Sheila
1953	Melville, Elsie
1954	Melville, Elsie
1955	Melville, Elsie
1956	Melville, Elsie
1957	Melville, Elsie
1958	No contest
1959	Melville, Elsie

1960 Melville, Elsie
1961 Melville, Elsie
1962 Melville, Elsie
1963 Melville, Elsie
1964 Rossi, Sylvia
1965–69 Events not held
1970 Graham, Carol

Springboard diving (instituted 1951)
1951 Marrian, Valerie
1952 Melville, Elsie
1953 Melville, Elsie
1954 Melville, Elsie
1955 Marrian, Valerie
1956 Melville, Elsie
1957 Melville, Elsie
1958 Marrian, Valerie
1959 Melville, Elsie
1960 Melville, Elsie
1961 Melville, Elsie
1962 Melville, Elsie
1963 Melville, Elsie
1964 Alston, M.
1965 Philip, Linda
1966 Melville, Elsie
1967 McCarroll, Anne
1968 McCarroll, Anne
1969 McCarroll, Anne
1970 McCarroll, Anne

1 m. Springboard diving (instituted 1950)
1950 Mitchell, Sheila
1951 Mitchell, Sheila
1952 Mitchell, Sheila
1953 Marrian, Valerie
1954 Melville, Elsie
1955 Melville, Elsie
1956 Melville, Elsie
1957 Melville, Elsie
1958 Marrian, Valerie
1959 Melville, Elsie
1960 Melville, Elsie
1961 Rossi, Sylvia
1962 Melville, Elsie
1963 Melville, Elsie
1964 Rollo, Joy
1965 Philip, Linda
1966 Philip, Linda
1967 Philip, Linda
1968 McCarroll, Anne
1969 McCarroll, Anne
1970 McCarroll, Anne

SEMI-FINALS. There was a time when semi-finals as well as heats and finals were the rule in swimming, irrespective of the number of competitors in the event. Nowadays, in events like the Olympics, it is the generally accepted practice to have semi-finals only for events for 100 metres and then only if there are more than thirty-two entires—requiring more than four heats in the eight-lane bath.

SHORT COURSE. The term 'short course' refers to any pool shorter than the international-size 50 m. The phrase has acquired special significance since 1 May 1957 when F.I.N.A. eliminated all 'short course' marks from their world record book (see LONG COURSE and WORLD RECORDS). However, many countries hold short course events, particularly in the winter and recognize short course national records. In short course races, competitors obtain a time advantage because of the extra turns (see TURNS).

SIX NATIONS CONTEST. The unofficial team championship of Western Europe, the Six-Nations contest was instituted in 1961 as a swimming spectacular for Eurovision. The countries concerned—Britain, France, Italy, Netherlands, Sweden and West Germany—enter teams of men and women, with one competitor or relay squad in each event. For men these are: 100, 400 and 4 × 200 m. free-style, 200 m. backstroke, breast-stroke and butterfly, 400 and 4 × 100 m. medley and springboard diving. The women have the same except that the free-style relay is 4 × 100 m. and the back-stroke and butterfly races are over 100 m.

Sweden were the first hosts and the first winners. West Germany, who tied with the Netherlands in 1962 (the only occasion there were joint winners), withdrew from their turn to organize the 1964 competition and it was cancelled. Britain won five of the first nine contests, including four successive times (1966–69). France are the only country never to have won. The results have been:
1961, Malmo, Sweden: 1. SWEDEN 93; 2. Britain 88; 3. West Germany and

Netherlands 85; 5. Italy 54; 6.
France 31.

1962, Rotterdam, Holland: 1. WEST
GERMANY AND NETHERLANDS 97;
3. Sweden 79; 4. Britain 76; 5.
France 47; 6. Italy 43.

1963, Blackpool, England: 1. BRITAIN
93; 2. Sweden and West Germany
90; 4. Netherlands 73; 5. Italy 52;
France 43.

1964, Due to be held in Germany, who
cancelled the event.

1965, Rome, Italy: 1. ITALY 92; 2.
Britain 91; 3. Sweden 86; 4. Netherlands 78; 5. West Germany 69;
6. France 66.

1966, Strasbourg, France: 1. BRITAIN
103; 2. Sweden 100; 3. West Germany 84; 4. France 78; 5. Netherlands 58; 6. Italy 54.

1967, Dortmund, Germany: 1. BRITAIN
107; 2. Sweden 90; 3. Netherlands
89; 4. France 85; 5. West Germany
80; 6. Italy 33.

1968, Stockholm, Sweden: 1. BRITAIN
104; 2. France 90; 3. Netherlands
87; 4. Sweden 82; 5. West Germany
77; 6. Italy 44.

1969, Blackpool, England: 1. BRITAIN
120; 2. West Germany 96; 3.
Sweden 82; 4. France 71; 5. Netherlands 60; 6. Italy 55.

1970, Bussum, Holland: 1. WEST
GERMANY 111; 2. Sweden 95; 3.
Britain 92; 4. Netherlands 70; 5.
France 60; 6. Italy 53.

SLADE, Betty (Great Britain, 18 June
1921–). European springboard diving
champion in 1938, Betty Joyce Slade,
from Ilford, Essex, was a tiny girl with
the flexible body of an acrobat who
fought like a giant at the Empire Pool,
Wembley, to win her gold. She dropped
an early dive, scoring only 2's and 3's
(out of 10), yet pulled back to win by
1·32 points from Germany's Gerda
Daumerlang.

She was ninth in the springboard at the
1936 Olympics but was not chosen for
the Commonwealth Games in Sydney
early in 1938, though she had twice won
(1936/37) the A.S.A. springboard title
and went on to win it twice more

(1938/39) and the highboard in 1939.
She turned professional and toured
Britain and many parts of the world
giving diving shows in swimming pools
and on the stage into a tank.

SLATTERY, Jill (Great Britain, 25 May
1945–). Joker Jill from Sheffield was
not as confident as her happy manner
suggested. The powerful breast-stroke of
this tall blonde, 5 ft. 10 in. and 10 st.
10 lb., won her many races but it was
not until after she had become Commonwealth 220 y. champion (2:50·3) and
European 200 m. bronze medallist
(2:47·9) in 1966 that she won the longer
distance breast-stroke title.

Her first A.S.A. victory was for 110 y.
in 1964 but she had to wait until 1967 to
take the 220 y., which she retained in
1968 before going to the Mexico Olympics as women's swimming team captain.
She was the only girl in the squad who
had also swum at the 1964 Games at
which she was fifth in the 200 m.

In Mexico she reached the semi-finals
of the 100 m. and was first reserve for
the final of the 200 m. Her best times
were 1:19·3 (110 y.) and 2:48·0 (220 y.).

SMITH, George (Canada, 20 Nov. 1949–
). The eldest of the six swimming
Smith family from Edmonton, Alberta,
George became the Commonwealth's
outstanding medley swimmer in 1969
when he set records of 2:13·4 and 4:48·0
for 200 and 400 m. respectively. And he
confirmed his place at the top by winning
these titles at the 1970 Commonwealth
Games in Edinburgh (2:13·7 and 4:48·9)
thanks to two brilliant and devastating
breast-stroke legs which carried him from
down the field into winning positions.

SOUTHERN DISTRICT. The Southern
Counties A.S.A. are the biggest of the
five English districts and take in the
whole of the Greater London area. Their
county associations are: Essex, Hamp-
shire, Hertfordshire, Kent, Middlesex,
Surrey and Sussex, parts of Berkshire,
Buckinghamshire and Oxfordshire
(south of latitude 51 degrees 37 minutes)
and the Channel Islands.

Notable Southern secretaries include Harold Fern (1905–21), Harry Rees (1922–36), Allen J. Perring (1937–52) and Alf Price (1958–   ). The South also claim Mrs. Alice M. Austin, hon. treasurer from 1937 to 1954, the only woman to have been a member of the A.S.A. Committee and President of the A.S.A. (1952).

SPEARHEAD PRINCIPLE. The spearhead or arrow formation is a fairly modern system, applied particularly to swimming, in which competitors qualifying for semi-finals or finals are placed in lanes according to the times they recorded in the heats or semi-finals.

In an eight-lane bath, the fastest competitor goes in lane 4, the second fastest in lane 5, and the others in order in lanes 3, 6, 2, 7, 1, 8. In a six-lane bath the order is lanes 3, 4, 2, 5, 1, 6. The reasons for this are two-fold—to give the best racers the opportunity to see each other and also to help the judges in their difficult job of visually deciding the order of finish. With the development of electrical timing and judging machines (see TIMING) the second reason is becoming less important.

Until the 1968 Olympics, the allocation of lanes for heats was not done on the spearhead principle. The lanes were drawn at random after the division of competitors into heats of equal standard; i.e. with each heat containing an equal number of fast and slow swimmers. For the 1972 Olympics, however, the spearhead principle will operate for heats, based on pre-Games times, as well as for semi-finals and finals.

SPITZ, Mark (United States, 10 Feb. 1950–   ). Brilliant yet nervy, talented but temperamental, Mark Spitz inappropriately from Modesto, California, tipped himself to win six gold medals at the 1968 Olympics. He finished with two, both for the free-style relays, but came away without any golds for his speciality, butterfly.

Spitz held the metric world butterfly records before the Games and after. But he lost the Olympic 100 m. to his team-mate Doug Russell by 0·5 in 56·4 (0·8 outisde the world mark); he was last from start to finish in the 200 m. (his 2:13·5 was 7·8 slower than his world record) and his defeat by Russell cost him the butterfly leg in the American winning medley relay squad.

The only event in which Spitz did better than expected was the 100 m. free-style. Third in the United States trials, he was second best American in the final, winning the bronze behind Wenden (Aus) and Ken Walsh (USA).

A member of the Santa Clara Club, Spitz broke seven world butterfly marks, of which his best times were 55·6 (100 m.), 56·3 (110 y.) and 2:05·7 (200 m.). He three times broke the 400 m. free-stule (best 4:07·7) and in 1969 equalled Don Schollander's 200 m. mark (1:54·3). Spitz won five gold medals at the 1967 Pan-American championships in Winnipeg—100 and 200 m. butterfly, 4 × 100 and 4 × 200 m. free-style relay and 4 × 100 m. medley relay—in what was his best concentrated swimming effort.

Spitz was at his most unpredictable during the 1970 USA outdoor championships in Los Angeles. He became the first man to break 52 sec. for 100 m. free-style (51·9) in a heat but was beaten into second place in the final though he kept his world record. He won the 200 m. free-style and 100 m. butterfly by substantial margins and broke his own world 200 m. butterfly record (2:05·4) in a heat. Once again, he was out-swum in the final—in fact, he came fourth. And the winner, Gary Hall, reduced the hours-old world mark of Spitz to 2:05·0

SPRINGBOARD DIVING. Springboards are 1 m. and 3 m. above the level of the water and there are often separate competitions for the two boards. In major competitions, the dives are almost always from the 3 m. board because of the higher tariff values.

The international test for men is five required dives, selected from five groups and six voluntary dives from five groups. The test for women is five required and five voluntary dives. In each case, the required dives, which may be performed in (a), (b) or (c) positions are forward dive, back dive, reverse dive, inward dive and forward dive half-twist.

In the Olympic Games and other major events there are preliminary and final rounds. The preliminary contest, in which all the competitors take part, consists of the five required dives and three voluntaries (men and five required and two voluntaries (women). The top twelve compete in the final round which consists of the last three voluntary dives. The winners, of course, are those with the highest scores for the whole test. (See DIVING.)

STARTS. A much neglected aspect of swimming, in Britain at any rate, is the art of starting. The speed with which a competitor can move from a static position on the bath-side (or in the water at the bath-end in the case of back-stroke) into flowing action can cut vital tenths of seconds off the total racing time.

The starting procedure in swimming is simple and false starts need not happen unless there is a deliberate effort on the part of competitors to steal a 'flyer'. For all events except back-stroke the start is from a dive. The competitors line up behind their starting blocks or line. If raised blocks are used—which may be from 0·5 to 0·75 m. above the water surface—on a signal from the referee the competitors step on to the back surface of the block and remain there. On the command from the starter of 'Take your marks', the competitors immediately step forward to the front of the block or line, bend forward into their pre-dive positions and remain stationary. When all competitors are still, the starter gives the starting signal (a shot, klaxon, whistle or voice command) and the race is off.

In back-stroke, the competitors line up in the water, facing the starting end, with their hands placed on the starting grips. Their feet, including the toes, must be under the surface of the water and standing in or on the gutter or bending the toes over the lip of the gutter is prohibited. On the 'Take your marks' command, the swimmers assume their push away position and their hands must not release the starting grip until the starting signal has been given.

The starter calls back the competitors at the first or second false start, i.e. if any competitor moves before his time. If there are a third or more false starts in the same heat, no matter if by the same or another swimmer, then the person making that false start is disqualified.

The most blantant occasion when the starter allowed a race to continue although a number of competitors had taken flyers was during the final of the European 100 m. free-style championship in Utrecht in 1966. It almost cost Britain's Bobby McGregor the gold medal (see McGREGOR, BOBBY and picture facing page 112).

STEPANOVA, Galina (USSR, 26 Nov. 1948–). Mrs. Stepanova, at that time known by her famous maiden name of Galina Prosumenschikova, was the only European to win a swimming gold medal at the 1964 Olympics. Six years later, and the mother of a year-old son, the brilliance of one of the worlds' most remarkable breast-stroke swimmers was undimmed at the European championships in Barcelona.

She won the 200 m. in Tokyo by 1·2 seconds from America's Claudia Kolb in 2:46·4 (an Olympic record) but the victory margin was unimportant for she looked a winner all the way. In Mexico four years later it was a different story for the heavy and powerful Miss P., who was affected more by the altitude than her lighter rivals. She lost the 100 m. title by one-tenth (1:15·9) to Djurdjica Bjedov (Yugo) and only fighting spirit enabled her to win the bronze for 200 m. by one-tenth, from her team-mate Alla Grebennikova. Galina collapsed after this race and was carried to the dressing-rooms by a small and most heroic Mexican.

Between these two Olympic appearances, the Muscovite won the 1966 European 200 m. title in a world record 2:40·8 —the most devastating of her four successive inroads into this world mark in two years and four months. Her first world mark was set in Britain, at Blackpool where her 2:47·7 for 220 y. was also a world best for 200 m. She broke the world record for 100 m. (1:15·7) in 1966.

By the time of the Barcelona championships, Catie Ball (USA) (see BALL CATIE) had taken the Russian's world records. But Mrs. Stepanova, much slimmer than in her maiden days, improved her personal bests despite the fact that she had only been back in training for six months.

She won the new 100 m. event by two metres in 1:15·6, having clocked 1:15·5 (one tenth outside her European record) in a heat. She retained her 200 m. title with 2:40·7, a European record and one tenth faster than her winning time in 1966, in beating her team-mate Alla Grebennikova by four metres. And it was her breast-stroke leg in the medley relay that enabled the Soviet Union to take the silver medals behind East Germany.

STEWARD, Natalie (Rhodesia–Great Britain, 30 Apr. 1943–). Mean, moody and magnificent, the description once given by publicists to an American film star, applied equally to South African-born Natalie Steward, of Rhodesia, who won her greatest glory while representing Britain.

She came to England with her South African mother, eighteen months before the 1960 Olympics, with the only aim of winning medals in Rome. And win she did. She was third in the 100 m. freestyle (63·1) and second in the 100 m. back-stroke (70·8)—an astonishing performance this, because before the Games, she had only the ninth best back-stroke time in the world that year. She also swam in Britain's free-style and medley relay teams, who reached the last eight.

Her eligibility to compete for Britain was through her English-born father, who, after years in Africa, became a Rhodesian citizen in 1958. She could have been considered by the country of her birth South Africa or her home land Rhodesia, for whom she swam in the 1958 Commonwealth Games in Cardiff, though without medal success.

During her two years in London, Natalie won six A.S.A. titles: free-style, 110/220 y. (1959/60), 440 y. (1959) and back-stroke, 110 y. (1960). She twice broke the world record for 110 y. back-stroke in 1960 (71·1 and 71·0) and also held the European 100 m. record (70·8). Then as suddenly as she had appeared on the scene, she returned to Rhodesia.

STEWART SISTERS (Canada), **Helen** (1939–) and **Mary** (1946–). The Stewart sisters, Helen and Mary, have a proud family swimming record. Helen first got the Stewart name into the medal lists at the 1954 Commonwealth Games in her home city of Vancouver where she won a silver in Canada's free-style relay team. A year later, she won the Pan-American 100 m. title (67·7) in Mexico City. In 1956 Helen clocked 57·6 for 100 y.—a world record, but one that was never claimed or ratified—and reached the semi-finals of the 100 m. at the Melbourne Olympics. Her last big swim occasion was, after her marriage, at the 1959 Pan-American Games in Chicago where she won a silver again in the free-style relay.

Mary, seven years younger and very much inspired by her sister, appeared on the international swimming scene at Chicago Pan-American's where she placed sixth in the 100 m. butterfly (1:22·2) at 13. A tiny 5 ft. 3 in. and 7 st. 12 lb. mermaid, Mary showed her power and potential at the 1960 Olympics by being a suprise finalist in the 100 m. free-style (65·5, 8th) having clocked 64·2 in a semi-final to rob Australia's famous Ilsa Konrads of a place in the last eight.

It was back to butterfly in 1961 and world records for 100 m. (68·8) and 110 y. (69·0) and election as Canada's 'Woman Athlete of the Year'—with 135 votes to the 94 of her nearest rival. She clipped the world marks to 67·3 in 1962 with her time over the longer 110 y. distance and at the Perth Commonwealth Games (1962) she won the 110 y. butterfly gold and a bronze in Canada's medley relay team.

At the 1963 Pan-American Games in Sao Paulo, Brazil, Mary missed putting her name two below Helen's in the list of 100 m. free-style winners. She was second, 0·5 behind Terri Stickles (USA) but her 63·3 was 4·4 faster than her sister's gold medal effort eight years earlier. Mary was second too in the 100 m. butterfly (68·9), won two more silvers in the relays and for good measure came sixth in the 100 m. back-stroke.

Mary, whose father William was born in Aberdeen and went to Canada in 1921, competed in the A.S.A. championships at Blackpool in 1963 and came first in the 110 y. butterfly. And she bowed out of swimming almost where she had begun—with eighth place in the 1964 Olympics—this time for butterfly and not free-style.

STIRLING, Glenda (New Zealand, 7 July 1952–). New Zealand have produced a number of world-class back-strokers—Jeanne Stewart, bronze medallist at the 1952 Olympics and world record-breaker Phillipa Gould (1957) are two. But the fastest girl of all, though at the end of 1969 she had not won a major Games medal or broken a world record, is Glenda Stirling from Auckland who was a finalist in the 1968 Mexico Olympic 100 m.

Glenda, New Zealand four times 100 m./110 y. champion (1967–70) and three times winner of the 200 m./220 y. (1968–70) placed high in world rankings in 1969. She was fourth best for 100 m. (67·2) and sixth for 200 m. (2:27·7)—times which were 4·8 and 11·2 faster than Phillpa's world marks of twelve years earlier.

Glenda was not in the medals at the 1970 Commonwealth Games but, after Edinburgh, she competed in the A.S.A. championships in Blackpool and won the 110 y. (68·7) and was second in the 220 y. (2:32·0) in NZ record times.

STOREY, Doris (Great Britain, 21 Dec. 1919–). The international career of Doris Storey, from the Montague Burton Club in Leeds, opened with a sixth place at the 1936 Olympics, at 16, and was closed by World War II at 19, after the Yorkshire girl had won two Common-

wealth golds, a European silver and four A.S.A. titles.

A powerful breast-stroke swimmer, she missed fourth place in the Berlin Olympics by only 0·3, clocking 3:09·7. Early in 1938, in Sydney, she took the Commonwealth 220 y. title in 3:06·6, 5½ seconds in front of South Africa's Carla Gerke and swam the breat-stroke leg in England's winning medley relay squad. That summer, in London, she faced Denmark's Inge Sorensen, who had won the bronze medal in the 1936 Olympics at 13, in the European 200 m. championship. And the Briton lost narrowly, by 0·6, in 3:06·0.

A.S.A. 200 y. champion 1936–39, Miss Storey was the first winner of the T. M. Yeaden Memorial Trophy, for 'England's Swimmer of the Year', in 1938.

STOUDER, Sharon (United States, 9 Nov. 1948–). Slim Sharon Stouder from Glendora, California, pulled off the shock victory of the 1964 Olympics in beating the hot favourite, Ada Kok of Holland, in the 100 m. butterfly. She won by 0·9 in 64·7, beating the Dutch girl's world record by 0·4. And though Miss Kok (see KOK, ADA), regained her world record with 64·5 the next year, Sharon's Olympic winning time was still the second fastest of all time as swimming moved into the 1970s.

The American, only 15, came close to a second, even more astonishing, victory in the 100 m. free-style. She chased Dawn Fraser (see FRASER, DAWN) to within four-tenths, and though the Australian achieved her historic third successive victory, Sharon, in clocking 59·9, became only the second woman in the world to break the minute. This talented 5 ft. 8 in. and 9 st. 9 lb. fair-haired schoolgirl added two more golds to her Tokyo tally in the free-style and medley relays.

A medley relay gold medallist—she swam the butterfly leg—in America's winning team at the 1963 Pan-American Games in Sao Paulo—Sharon won three titles at the 1964 United States outdoor championships. She took the 100 m. free-style (60·4), 100 m. butterfly (65·4) and broke her own world record in winning the 200 m. butterfly in 2:26·4.

SWIMMING

SWIMMING. The eight letters spelling 'Swimming' cover a wide range of aquatic activities. In the competitive sense, which is what this book is about, the word swimming includes not only speed racing, but also diving, water-polo, synchronized and long-distance swimming.

But water and the ability to swim have many other associations. There are recreational swimming (some call it bathing), water-skiing and sub-aqua diving. There are rowing, sailing and canoeing for which the ability to keep afloat is a prime safety requirement, though, unfortunately, all too many still go on the water without the insurance of being able to protect their lives should they unexpectedly go into the water.

In a world whose surface is two-thirds water, the importance of swimming cannot be over-emphasized. And the health-giving, recreational and life-saving aspects are as important as the glamour ones of competitions, records and medals.

America's noted coach Bob Kiphuth (see KIPHUTH, BOB) summed up the sport he loved like this: 'Swimming contributes to the physical and organic growth and development of the body, aids social development through intensive participation under leadership, helps the psychological development of children through the satisfaction of achievement and is a pleasurable leisure-time hobby.' And that, in fact, is what swimming is all about.

SYKES, Graham

SYKES, Graham (Great Britain, 20 July 1937–). Often captain of Britain's swimming team, Sykes nevertheless was a surprise winner of the Commonwealth 110 y. back-stroke title in 1962 at the age of 25. He came through in Perth by 0·9 sec. in 64·5 and also won a silver in the medley relay.

Sykes, from Coventry, had a long career (1956–62) at the top of British back-stroke rankings. He was sixth in the 1956 Olympic final (65·6) and won a bronze medal in England's medley team at the 1958 Commonwealth Games.

The European championships that year did not bring much personal success, though the fact that he achieved a swim-off for the last place in the back-stroke final—which he lost but which was held in between two of Ian Black's gold medal winning races (see BLACK, IAN) and gave valuable resting time to the Scot—was a piece of unintentional good team work.

Sykes missed the final of the 1960 Olympic 100 m. by one-tenth (64·7) and was first reserve for the final of the 200 m. at the 1962 European championships. Then, when it seemed he was too old to succeed, he won in Australia.

He was the first Englishman in eighteen years to win the A.S.A. (of England) back-stroke title and he retained it six successive times (a record)—110 y. 1956–60 and 220 y. 1961–62—Sykes held all the British records for his speciality from 1960 to 1964. His best times, all set in a 30 y. Coventry pool, were 56·4 (100 y.), 63·3 (110 y.), 2:06·9 (200 y.) and 2:21·4 (220 y.).

SYMONDS, Graham

SYMONDS, Graham (Great Britain, 21 Mar. 1937–). Silver medallist for 220 y. butterfly at the 1958 Commonwealth Games and European bronze medallist for 200 m. the same year—both events were won by Britain's Ian Black— Graham Symonds from Coventry began his swimming life as a free-styler, turned most successfully to butterfly and ended his career as a medleyist.

In the 1956 Olympics, Symonds, whose butterfly was at an experimental stage could do no better than 2:35·7 for 200 m. and did not qualify for the final. Two years later, he had improved his time to 2:25·5 for the four feet longer 220 y. in winning his Commonwealth silver in Cardiff.

Symonds was disciplined out of the 1960 Olympic Games team for leading a protest by swimmers against the arrangements made for them by officials. But he fought back into the British team for the 1962 European championships (400 m.

medley) though he was not chosen for the Commonwealth Games that year.

He won three A.S.A. titles—in 1954, 440 and 880 y. free-style (4:53·8 and 10:48·4) and 1955, 220 y. butterfly (2:36·3). He also was first in the butterfly in 1956, more than 10 seconds faster than his nearest rival, but was disqualified for a faulty turn, because his widespread arms caught in the narrow lane ropes.

SYNCHRONIZED SWIMMING. This

art form of swimming, ballet in the water, became recognized internationally in 1952. Although many countries organize national championships for synchronized swimming, it is the only one of the F.I.N.A. approved events which is not included in the Olympic programme.

Synchronized swimmers—almost always women—must have the speed of racers, the grace and acrobatic mobility of divers and a feeling for music. A competition consists of a stunt section and a free-routine section. It is very similar, in fact, to an ice-skating competition.

The stunts have tariff values similar to those for diving (see DIVING), and the points awards, after elimination of the highest and lowest, are multiplied by the tariff value (degree of difficulty) (see DIVING JUDGING). There are five stunt groups:

1. Ballet leg—in which one leg is extended vertically above the hip at some stage in the movement.
2. Dolphin head first—in which the body traverses as far as is possible the circumference of an imaginary circle about eight feet in diameter in a head first, backward rotating direction.
3. Dolphin foot first—similar to the

dolphin head first, but travelling in a foot first direction.
4. Somersault, front and back—in which the body rotates (somersaults) about a lateral axis.
5. Diverse—a miscellaneous section of movements.

The free-routine section, as in iceskating, is done to music. The competitors perform water-ballet 'dances' of their own arrangement incorporating any of the seventy-five listed stunts or strokes and/or parts thereof. In the freeroutines, competitors are restricted to five minutes, including a maximum of 20 sec. of deck movements before entry into the water.

The judging is in two parts. For the stunts the judges look for slow, high and controlled movements with each section of the stunt clearly defined and uniform in motion. For the routines, free rhythm brings in high marks. Points are awarded from 0–10, using $\frac{1}{2}$ points, on the following basis: Completely failed = 0; Unsatisfactory = $\frac{1}{2}$–$2\frac{1}{2}$; Deficient = 3–$4\frac{1}{2}$; Satisfactory = 5–$6\frac{1}{2}$; Good = 7–$8\frac{1}{2}$ and Very good = 9–10.

There are three competitive sections for solo, duet and team (four or more). Bigger teams get an advantage of half a point being added to their score for each additional member over four—but bigger teams have greater difficulty in obtaining perfect synchronization.

In competition, in the stunt section, plain dark costumes and white caps must be worn. For the free-routines, competitors may wear costumes, head-wear, etc., appropriate to the theme of their water dance.

SZEKELY, Eva (Hungary), see GYARMATI FAMILY.

T

TANNER, Elaine (Canada, 22 Feb. 1951–). Canada's 'Mighty Mouse', Elaine Tanner, 5 ft. 2 in. of power-packed versatility, was the most successful woman swimmer at the 1966 Commonwealth Games at 15. She won four golds and three silvers and broke two world records.

Her titles came in the 110 and 220 y. butterfly (66·8 and 2:29·9) and the 440 y. medley (5:26·3) and the 4 × 110 y. free-style, the Canadians setting a world record (4:10·8) in beating Australia by three-tenths. Elaine was second to England's Linda Ludgrove in both the 110 and 220 y. back-stroke and won her third silver in the medley relay (behind England's world record-breaking team).

In fact, her greatest successes were for back-stroke. She won the 100 and 200 m. on this style at the 1967 Pan-American Games in Winnipeg, both in world record times (67·3 and 2:24·4) and clipped her shorter distance mark to 67·1 on the first leg of the medley relay in which Canada came second to the United States. She was also second in the 100 m. butterfly and 4 × 100 m. free-style and fourth in the 100 m. free-style and 200 m. butterfly.

Elaine, from Vancouver, who spent some time in California with her English-born parents, made her final big-time appearance at the Mexico Olympics where she was second in both the 100 and 200 m. back-stroke and won a bronze in the free-style relay.

Her national championships successes were equally impressive. In 1965 she was the Canadian, American and British sprint butterfly champion. She took seventeen Canadian titles between 1965 and 1968, including four successive years for the 200 m./220 y. back-stroke and 100 m./110 y. butterfly. Her tally included the 440 y. free-style, sprint back-stroke and distance butterfly and both medleys.

Her best times—rankings in the Canada's top three of all-time—were for free-style 61·5 (100 m.), 2:14·8 (200 m.), 4:43·8 (400 m.) . . . for back-stroke 66·7 (100 m.) and 2:24·5 (200 m.) . . . for butterfly 65·4 (100 m.) and 2:29·9 (200 m.) . . . for medley 2:31·8 (200 m.) and 5:26·3 (400 m.).

TARIFF VALUES IN DIVING, see DIVING.

TAYLOR, Henry (Great Britain, 17 Mar. 1885–28 Feb. 1951). Happy Henry Taylor, from Oldham, Lancashire, was a swashbuckling athlete and the aquatic marvel of 1906–08. He won the mile and was second in the 400 m. at the Interim Games of 1906 in Athens. And he won the 400 and 1,500 m. at the 1908 London Olympics in world record times of 5:36·8 (7·4 ahead of Australia's Frank Beaurepaire) and 22:48·4 (beating his team-mate Syd Battersby by 2·8) as well as a gold in the free-style relay.

A member of the Hyde Seal Club, Taylor, an orphan ,was raised by his brother. He worked in the cotton mills and trained during his lunch break and in the evening in any water he could find —in canals, streams and in the baths on dirty-water (and cheaper) day. His one excursion into business—having mortgaged all his silver Cups to find the stake —was a failure and his last job was as a pool attendant at the Chadderton baths where he had done so much of his swimming in his youth as a 'boy who loved his swimming more than anything in his life'.

Taylor had won his Interim Games medals before he became champion of

England. He won fifteen A.S.A. titles: 440 y. (1906, '07), 500 y. (1906, '07, '08, '11), 880 y. (1906, '07, '11), one mile (1906, '07, '11) and long distance (1909, '12 and '20). This last success was at the age of 35, the year he also played water-polo for England. As well as his 1908 400 and 1,500 m. Olympic Games world records, which were the first for the dis-tances, Taylor was the first official holder of the 880 y. world mark. In 1969, the year of the centenary of the A.S.A., Taylor was honoured by the Hall of Fame.

TERRELL, Ray (Great Britain, 5 May, 1953–). In his first year as a senior swimmer, Terrell, from Southampton, had two surprise successes for England in the 1970 Commonwealth Games. Generally known as a free-style and medley man, Terrell came second in the 200 m. back-stroke (2:15·5) behind Mike Richards of Wales and won the silver again in the 400 m. medley (4:49·8), both English record times. Two weeks later, in the A.S.A. championships, he won his first National senior title, the 440 y. free-style (4:21·4—another En-glish record) and took second places, behind Martyn Woodroffe, in the 220 and 440 y. medley.

THEILE, David (Australia, 1938–). Twice winner of the Olympic 100 m. back stroke title (1956 and 1960), Dr. David Theile from Brisbane was a quiet, unobtrusive type except when he was actually swimming and then he was a danger man. His first victory, in Mel-bourne, was in a world record 62·2, one second ahead of his team-mate John Monckton. In Rome, having missed the 1958 Commonwealth Games and drop-ped a little out of the limelight, he came back to beat America's Frank McKinney for the individual gold by 0·2 and to win a silver in the new medley relay event.

Theile began competitive swimming at 9, won the Australian junior back-stroke title in 1954. The following year he took the men's 110 y. crown—his 67·4 taking 0·5 off Percy Oliver's national record set the year David was born. He kept the

title in 1956, rested from swimming during the first two years of his medical studies, then won again in 1959/60. Essentially a sprinter, Theile never won championsjips nor broke records for 200 m. or 220 y. But he took the Austra-lian 100 y. mark from 60·8 to 57·5 in two years and the 100 m. from 65·4—break-ing another 1938 record of Oliver—to 62·2.

Theile, a graduate of the University of Queensland and a Fellow of the Royal Australian College of Surgeons, was honoured by the Hall of Fame in 1968 during his time in London as a lecturer in surgery.

TIME CONVERSIONS, see METRIC/ LINEAR TIME CONVERSIONS.

TIMING. Until recent years, all swim-ming timing has been done by human watch-holders (time-keepers) holding precision stop-watches, graduated to one fifth or one-tenth—the latter being more common these days—of a second. Now, with the development of electrical timing machines, capable of recording times to one-thousandth of a second, the prob-lems of human judges sorting out ex-tremely close finishes with their vision obscured by the flurry of water have been largely eliminated.

A swimmer must be clocked by three manual time-keepers for a world record —and indeed for most national and other records—to be ratified. If at least two watches agree, then this is the accepted time. If all three differ, then the middle time is accepted.

With electrical timing, only one officially-approved machine, activated at the finish by the touch of the swim-mers on pads at the end of the bath, is required. And since 1970, F.I.N.A. rules lay down that automatic timing (and judging) equipment shall have precedence over the decisions of human timers (and judges).

Good time-keeping is all important in swimming, for progression from heats to semi-finals and to finals is determined by time and not by placings—except in the case of two swimmers achieving identical times in the same race being placed one ahead of the other by the judges (or judging machine).

TROY, Mike (United States, 3 Oct. 1940–   ). Pain was Mike Troy's watchword—he had it written in foot-high letters on the wall of his room at Indiana University, Indianapolis. And pain in training beyond what his body thought it could bear brought an improvement of 3·8 sec. in a year and the Olympic 200 m. butterfly title in a world record 2:12·8 at the 1960 Rome Games. His time was 7½ secs. better than Bill Yorzyk's gold medal effort at the 1956 Olympics, and Troy beat Australia's Neville Hayes by 1·8 with his American team-mate David Gillanders third (2:15·3).

The year before, Troy had come second in the Pan-American 200 m. butterfly (2:18·3), 0·3 behind Gillanders. And he won a gold in the medley relay.

Like so many American swimmers, Troy's time at the top was short—from 1958–60—during which he played havoc with the world record for his speciality 200 m. event. On 11 July 1959 he set two marks (2:19·0 and 2:16·4—the latter in winning the first of his two United States outdoor titles). The following summer he clipped back further with 2:13·4 (United States championship), 2:13·2 and his Rome record of 2:12·8. He also won the United States 100 m. title in 1958 (62·8).

TURNS. In swimming, there are rules to govern the way in which competitors turn for each of the four styles. They are:
Free-style—the touch on the wall can be made by any part of the body, a hand touch is not obligatory, and other than this the competitor can turn as he wants.
Back-stroke—the swimmer must remain on his back until his head, foremost hand or arm has touched the end of the course. He may turn beyond the vertical in executing the turn, but must have returned past the vertical on to his back before the feet leave the wall.
Breast-stroke—the touch (and finish) must be with both hands simultaneously on the same level and with the shoulders in the horizontal position and the swimmer must not do more than one leg kick and one arm pull before surfacing after the turn.
Butterfly—the touch is the same as for breast-stroke and the swimmer may take only one arm pull under the water before surfacing.
Medley individual—there is no specific international rule to cover turns in medley, but it is generally accepted that the swimmer goes into the turn and touch covered by the rules of the stroke he is using at that time, but comes out covered by the rule of the stroke he is about to start.

Good turns give a tremendous time advantage and it is for this reason that most record lists now distinguish between long course (50 m. pools) and short course (less than 50 m. and usually 25 m. pools) performances.

The time gain has been put at 0·7 sec. for each turn. Thus a 400 m. race in a 25 m. course has fifteen turns compared to the seven in a 50 m. pool, and a time advantage of 8×0.7 sec. $= 5.6$ sec.

TYERS, Jack (Great Britain). A prolific winner of A.S.A. championships, the career of Tyers, from Manchester Osborne Club (now defunct), was coming near its end as the first Olympic Games were held in Athens in 1896. But as one of the pioneers of England's early world swimming supremacy, the competitive record of this remarkable man is an important mile-stone in the history of swimming.

It is not known whether Tyers swam in Athens. The British Olympic Oassociation, founded in 1905, have no records of Britain's participation. Certainly there were British medal winning competitors in athletics, cycling, lawn tennis and weight-lifting. It seems likely that a swimming team did not compete, for otherwise Tyers surely must have been among the medal winners.

In 1896, he won the A.S.A. 100 y. title in 61·4 (equivalent at least to 68·0 for 100 m.) and 500 y. in 6:55·8 (worth about 7:36·0 for 500 m.). The swimming

L

in Athens took place in the Bay of Zea, near Piraeus where, it should be noted, Hungary's Alfred Hajos won the 100 m. in 1:22·2 and Paul Neumann (Austria) the 500 m. in 8:12·6. Perhaps a reader of this book may have the answer to this Olympic mystery . . .?

Tyers won twenty-nine A.S.A. championships between 1892 and 1897, including all seven free-style titles in 1893 and '94. In these six years he was undefeated over 100 and 220 y., his best winning times being 61·4 (1896) and 2:38·8 (1897) respectively. He won the 440 and 500 y. and mile four successive times (1893–96) and his fastest efforts were 6:08·8 (1895), 4:45·0 (1894) and 26:46·0 (1896). He took the 880 y. in 1893–95 (fastest 13:41·0, 1893) and the long distance twice (1893, '94). He also played water-polo in three winning England teams, against Scotland in 1893 and 1895, the latter occasion as captain, and against Ireland in 1895 when England scored 12 goals without conceding one.

U

UNITED STATES CHAMPIONS. The championships of the United States of America are organized by the national men's and women's swimming committees of the Amateur Athletic Union of the United States which controls altogether ten sports.

At the beginning, however, it was the New York Athletic Club who took the initiative. They organized a one mile championship in 1877 which was won by R. Weissenborn in 44:44¼. The event was held again in 1878, then there was nothing until 1883 when four races (100, 440 and 880 y. and mile) took place.

A platform diving championship for men was instituted in 1909 and was won in the first three years by George Gaidzik who had been joint third (with Waiz of Germany) and the best American diver at the 1908 London Olympics. Five championships for women were held in 1916—440 and 880 y., mile and long distance swimming and platform diving.

The United States racing season is now divided into winter (indoor) and summer (outdoor) halves. The winter championships, normally held short course in 25 y. baths in early April, have been one of the reasons why American starting and turning techniques are second to none. The summer championships, usually in August, used to be held in either 50 m. or 55 y. baths, but now are always metric, produce a high proportion of the world records set in any one year. The entry standards for both are high, but competitors of the right calibre from other countries are always welcome.

The winners of the summer championships since 1946 are:

MEN

100 m. Free-style

1946	Smith, Bill	59·0
1947	Ris, Wally	58·5
1948	Nugent, Robert	58·9
1949	Gibe, Robert	58·2
1950*	Cleveland, Dick	58·2
1951	Cleveland, Dick	58·2
1952*	Cleveland, Dick	58·4
1953	Cleveland, Dick	57·5
1954	Cleveland, Dick	57·5
1955	Gideonse, Hendrik	57·6
1956	Hanley, Richard	56·3
1957	Hanley, Richard	57·3
1958	Henricks, Jon (Aus)	55·8
1959	Farrell, Jeff	56·9
1960	Farrell, Jeff	54·8
1961	Clark, Steve	54·4
1962	Clark, Steve	54·4
1963	Clark, Steve	54·9
1964	Schollander, Don	54·0
1965	Roth, Donald	53·8
1966	Schollander, Don	53·5
1967	Schollander, Don	53·3
1968	Spitz, Mark	53·6
1969	Havens, Don	52·5
1970	Heckl, Frank	52·5
	* 110 y.	

200 m. Free-style

1946	Smith, Bill	2:14·4
1947	Smith, Bill	2:12·6
1948	Gilbert, Edward	2:16·9
1949	Hamaguchi, Yoshiro (Jap)	2:11·0
1950*	McLane, Jimmy	2:10·5
1951	Moore, Wayne	2:08·4
1952*	Woolsey, William	2:13·2
1953	Moore, Wayne	2:09·0
1954	Konno, Ford	2:10·6
1955	Woolsey, William	2:08·2
1956	Woolsey, William	2:06·6
1957	Hanley, Richard	2:08·4
1958	Henricks, Jon (Aus)	2:05·2
1959	Farrell, Jeff	2:06·9

1960	Farrell, Jeff	2:03·2		1957	Breen, George	18:17·9
1961	Yamanaka, Tsuyoshi (Jap)	2:00·4		1958	Rose, Murray (Aus)	18:06·4
1962	Schollander, Don	2:00·4		1959	Somers, Alan	17:51·3
1963	Schollander, Don	1:59·0		1960	Breen, George	17:33·5
1964	Schollander, Don	1:57·6		1961	Saari, Roy	17:29·8
1965	Ilman, Gary	1:59·0		1962	Rose, Murray (Aus)	17:16·7
1966	Schollander, Don	1:56·2		1963	Saari, Roy	17:34·6
1967	Schollander, Don	1:55·7		1964	Rose, Murray (Aus)	17:01·8
1968	Spitz, Mark	1:57·0		1965	Krause, Steve	16:58·6
1969	Fassnacht, Hans (WGer)	1:56·5		1966	Burton, Mike	16:41·6
1970	Spitz, Mark	1:54·6		1967	Burton, Mike	16:34·1
	* = 220 y.			1968	Burton, Mike	16:29·4
				1969	Burton, Mike	16:04·5

400 m. Free-style

				1970	Kinsella, John	15:57·1
1946	McLane, Jimmy	4:49·5			* = one mile	
1947	McLane, Jimmy	4:41·9				
1948	McLane, Jimmy	4:53·5		**100 m. Back-stroke**		
1949	Furuhashi, Hironoshin			1946	Holiday, Harry	1:08·0
	(Jap)	4:33·3		1947	Stack, Allen	1:07·8
1950*	Marshall, John (Aus)	4:39·3		1948	Stack, Allen	1:07·7
1951	Moore, Wayne	4:35·8		1949	Stack, Allen	1:07·1
1952*	Konno, Ford	4:48·0		1950*	Stack, Allen	1:08·2
1953	Konno, Ford	4:39·8		1951	Thomas, Jack	1:07·4
1954	Woolsey, William	4:43·3		1952*	Oyakawa, Yashinobu	1:05·7
1955	Konno, Ford	4:38·7		1953	Oyakawa, Yashinobu	1:06·8
1956	Breen, George	4:37·6		1954	Wiggins, Albert	1:07·2
1957	Breen, George	4:35·1		1955	Oyakawa, Yashinobu	1:05·3
1958	Rose, Murray (Aus)	4:24·5		1956	Oyakawa, Yashinobu	1:05·9
1959	Somers, Alan	4:30·6		1957	McKinney, Frank	1:04·5
1960	Somers, Alan	4:21·9		1958	McKinney, Frank	1:04·5
1961	Yamanaka, Tsuyoshi (Jap)	4:17·5		1959	McKinney, Frank	1:03·6
1962	Rose, Murray (Aus)	4:17·2		1960	Stock, Tom	1:02·9
1963	Schollander, Don	4:17·7		1961	Bennett, Robert	1:01·3
1964	Schollander, Don	4:12·7		1962	Stock, Tom	1:00·9
1965	Nelson, John	4:14·1		1963	McGeagh, Richard	1:01·7
1966	Schollander, Don	4:11·6		1964	McGeagh, Richard	1:01·6
1967	Charlton, Greg	4:09·8		1965	Mann, H. Thompson	1:00·5
1968	Hutton, Ralph (Can)	4:06·5		1966	Hickcox, Charles	1:01·0
1969	Fassnacht, Hans (WGer)	4:04·0		1967	Hickcox, Charles	59·7
1970	Kinsella, John	4:02·8		1968	Barbiere, Larry	1:00·9
	* = 440 y.			1969	Ivey, Mitch	1:00·2
				1970	Stamm, Mike	58·5

1,500 m. Free-style

					* = 110 y.	
1946	McLane, Jimmy	19:23·1				
1947	McLane, Jimmy	19:57·5		**200 m. Back-stroke**		
1948	Taylor, Jack	19:48·1		1953	Oyakawa, Yoshinobu	2:29·9
1949	Furuhashi, Hironoshin			1954	Wiggins, Albert	2:31·0
	(Jap)	18:29·9		1955	Oyakawa, Yoshinobu	2:26·1
1950*	Marshall, John (Aus)	20:08·6		1956	McKinney, Frank	2:24·5
1951	Konno, Ford	18:46·3		1957	McKinney, Frank	2:21·7
1952*	Konno, Ford	20:47·1		1958	McKinney, Frank	2:20·8
1953	Konno, Ford	19:20·0		1959	McKinney, Frank	2:17·9
1954	Konno, Ford	19:07·1		1960	Stock, Tom	2:16·0
1955	Onekea, George	18:52·3		1961	Stock, Tom	2:11·5
1956	Breen, George	18:27·6		1962	Stock, Tom	2:10·9

1963	Stock, Tom	2:12·4
1964	Bennett, Robert	2:15·7
1965	Mann, H. Thompson	2:12·4
1966	Hickcox, Charles	2:12·4
1967	Hickcox, Charles	2:12·3
1968	Horsley, Jack	2:12·2
1969	Hall, Gary	2:06·6
1970	Stamm, Mike	2:06·3

100 m. Breast-stroke

1952*	Holan, Jerry	Bu1:09·2
1953	Dudeck, John	Bu1:08·4
1954–55	Event not held	
1956	Hughes, Robert	1:11·2
1957	Hughes, Robert	1:12·1
1958	Sanguilly, Manuel (Cuba)	1:15·9
1959	Sanguilly, Manuel (Cuba)	1:14·6
1960	Jastremski, Chet	1:12·4
1961	Jastremski, Chet	1:07·5
1962	Jastremski, Chet	1:08·2
1963	Craig, William	1:10·2
1964	Jastremski, Chet	1:10·0
1965	Trethewey, Tom	1:08·3
1966	Merten, Ken	1:08·9
1967	Merten, Ken	1:08·7
1968	Dirksen, Mike	1:08·8
1969	Fiolo, Jose (Braz)	1:06·9
1970	Job, Brian	1:06·5
	* = 110 y.	

200 m. Breast-stroke

1946	Verdeur, Joe	Bu2:44·2
1947	Verdeur, Joe	Bu2:38·4
1948	Verdeur, Joe	Bu2:48·7
1949	Verdeur, Joe	Bu2:36·3
1950*	Brawner, Robert	Bu2:41·0
1951	Davies, John (Aus)	Bu2:35·8
1952*	Stassforth, Bowen	Bu2:34·7
1953	Hawkins, David (Aus)	Bu2:37·9
1954	Fadgen, Richard	2:49·5
1955	Mattson, Robert	2:46·8
1956	Fadgen, Richard	2:45·8
1957	Sanguilly, Manuel (Cuba)	2:44·0
1958	Rumpel, Norbert (WGer)	2:47·8
1959	Clark, Ronald	2:45·6
1960	Fogarasy, Peter	2:38·8
1961	Tremewan, Cary	2:36·0
1962	Jastremski, Chet	2:30·0
1963	Merten, Ken	2:34·5
1964	Jastremski, Chet/	
	Craig, William (tie)	2:31·8
1965	Jastremski, Chet	2:30·7
1966	Merten, Ken	2:31·2
1967	Merten, Ken	2:30·8
1968	Job, Brian	2:31·2

1969	Dirksen, Mike	2:26·9
1970	Job, Brian	2:23·5
	* = 220 y.	

100 m. Butterfly

1954	Fadgen, Richard	1:07·4
1955	Event not swum	
1956	Wiggins, Albert	1:04·2
1957	Wiggins, Albert	1:02·8
1958	Troy, Mike	1:02·8
1959	Larson, Lance	1:01·1
1960	Larson, Lance	58·7
1961	Schmidt, Fred	58·6
1962	Spencer, Edwin	58·9
1963	Richardson, Walter	58·8
1964	Richardson, Walter	57·5
1965	Nicolao, Luis (Arg)	57·8
1966	Spitz, Mark	58·1
1967	Spitz, Mark	56·7
1968	Spitz, Mark	57·0
1969	Russell, Douglas	56·0
1970	Spitz, Mark	56·1

200 m. Butterfly

1955	Yorzyk, Bill	2:29·1
1956	Yorzyk, Bill	2:24·3
1957	Yorzyk, Bill	2:22·0
1958	Yorzyk, Bill	2:22·5
1959	Troy, Mike	2:16·4
1960	Troy, Mike	2:13·4
1961	Robie, Carl	2:12·6
1962	Robie, Carl	2:10·8
1963	Robie, Carl	2:08·8
1964	Robie, Carl	2:09·2
1965	Robie, Carl	2:07·7
1966	Houser, Philip	2:09·9
1967	Spitz, Mark	2:06·4
1968	Robie, Carl	2:08·9
1969	Burton, Mike	2:06·5
1970	Hall, Gary	2:05·0

200 m. Individual medley

1959	Larson, Lance	2:24·7
1960	Stickles, Ted	2:22·1
1961	Stickles, Ted	2:15·9
1962	Stickles, Ted	2:16·2
1963	Roth, Dick	2:16·0
1964	Roth, Dick	2:15·5
1965	Roth, Dick	2:14·9
1966	Buckingham, Greg	2:12·4
1967	Buckingham, Greg	2:11·3
1968	Bello, Juan (Peru)	2:14·1
1969	Hall, Gary	2:09·6
1970	Hall, Gary	2:09·5

400 m. Individual medley

1946*	Holiday, Harry	3:58·8
1947*	Verdeur, Joe	3:59·2
1948*	Verdeur, Joe	4:00·0
1949*	Verdeur, Joe	3:53·7
1950†	Thomas, James	3:55·1
1951*	Jones, Burwell	3:52·3
1952†	Jones, Burwell	3:54·8
1953*	Jones, Burwell	3:46·2
1954	Jones, Burwell	5:29·0
1955	Harrison, George	5:23·3
1956	Yorzyk, Bill	5:19·0
1957	Heinrich, Gary	5:15·6
1958	Brunell, Frank	5:20·6
1959	Barton, William	5:14·6
1960	Rousanvelle, Dennis	5:04·5
1961	Stickles, Ted	4:55·6
1962	Stickles, Ted	4:51·5
1963	Stickles, Ted	4:55·0
1964	Roth, Dick	4:48·6
1965	Roth, Dick	4:49·2
1966	Roth, Dick	4:47·9
1967	Williams, Peter	4:50·8
1968	Hall, Gary	4:48·0
1969	Hall, Gary	4:33·9
1970	Hall, Gary	4:31·0

* = 300 m. † = 330 y.

WOMEN

100 m. Free-style

1946	Helser, Brenda	1:07·2
1947	Curtis, Ann	1:07·0
1948	Curtis, Ann	1:08·0
1949*	Kalama, Thelma	1:10·9
1950	Lavine, Jackie	1:10·0
1951	Geary, Sharon	1:07·6
1952	No championship meeting	
1953*	Roberts, Judy	1:07·9
1954	Alderson, Judy	1:06·1
1955	Werner, Wanda	1:06·1
1956*	Werner, Wanda	1:06·3
1957*	Fraser, Dawn (Aus)	1:03·9
1958	Von Saltza, Chris	1:03·5
1959*	Von Saltza, Chris	1:04·8
1960	Von Saltza, Chris	1:01·6
1961	Johnson, Robyn	1:03·2
1962	Johnson, Robyn	1:02·2
1963	Johnson, Robyn	1:01·5
1964	Stouder, Sharon	1:00·4
1965	Watson, L. 'Pokey'	1:00·7
1966	Watson, L. 'Pokey'	59·9
1967	Barkman, Janie	59·8
1968	Barkman, Janie	1:00·1
1969	Pedersen, Sue	59·7
1970	Schilling, Cindy	1:00·4

* = 110 y.

200 m. Free-style

1958	Botkin, Molly	2:23·2
1959*	Von Saltza, Chris	2:21·1
1960	Von Saltza, Chris	2:15·1
1961	House, Carolyn	2:18·9
1962	House, Carolyn	2:14·6
1963	Johnson, Robyn	2:15·6
1964	Hallock, Jeanne	2:13·3
1965	Randall, Martha	2:12·3
1966	Watson, L. 'Pokey'	2:10·5
1967	Kruse, Pam	2:09·7
1968	Wetzel, Eadie	2:08·8
1969	Pedersen, Sue	2:07·8
1970	Simmons, Ann	2:09·6

* = 200 y.

400 m. Free-style

1946	Curtis, Ann	5:26·7
1947	Curtis, Ann	5:21·5
1948	Curtis, Ann	5:26·5
1949*	Kalama, Thelma	5:41·2
1950	Kalama, Thelma	5:30·9
1951	Hobelmann, Barbara	5:21·6
1952	No championship meeting	
1953*	Meulenkamp, Delia	5:22·2
1954	Green, Carolyn	5:14·7
1955	Gray, 'Dougie'	5:16·1
1956*	Shriver, Marley	5:13·8
1957*	Crapp, Lorraine (Aus)	5:08·5
1958	Ruuska, Sylvia	5:04·1
1959*	Von Saltza, Chris	4:59·4
1960	Von Saltza, Chris	4:46·9
1961	House, Carolyn	4:52·5
1962	House, Carolyn	4:45·3
1963	Johnson, Robyn	4:46·8
1964	Ramenofsky, Marilyn	4:41·7
1965	Randall, Martha	4:39·2
1966	Randall, Martha	4:38·0
1967	Meyer, Debbie	4:29·0
1968	Meyer, Debbie	4:26·7
1969	Meyer, Debbie	4:26·4
1970	Meyer, Debbie	4:24·3

* = 440 y.

800 m. Free-style

1946	Curtis, Ann	11:26·3
1947	Curtis, Ann	11:21·8
1948	Curtis, Ann	11:37·2
1949*	Kleinschmidt, Catherine	11:48·1
1950	Green, Carolyn	11:28·3
1951	Green, Carolyn	11:15·5

1952	No championship meeting	
1953*	Green, Carolyn	11:15·2
1954	Green, Carolyn	10:49·9
1955	Green, Carolyn	10:45·3
1956*	Ruuska, Sylvia	10:54·5
1957*	Ruuska, Sylvia	10:45·8
1958	Event discontinued	
	* = 880 y.	

1,500 m. Free-style

1946	Curtis, Ann	22:08·1
1946	Sahner, Merilyn	22:23·1
1947	Mallory, Joan	22:58·4
1948*	Lutyens, Jean	24:34·5
1949	Hobelman, Barbara	22:25·7
1951	Green, Carolyn	21:48·3
1952	No championship meeting	
1953*	Green, Carolyn	23:03·4
1954	Green, Carolyn	21:08·5
1955	Green, Carolyn	21:15·4
1956†	Green, Carolyn	21:30·2
1957*	Murray, Carolyn	22:13·7
1958	Ruuska, Sylvia	20:34·6
1959*	Ruuska, Sylvia	21:38·9
1960	House, Carolyn	19:45·0
1961	House, Carolyn	19:46·3
1962	House, Carolyn	18:44·0
1963	Duenkel, Virginia	18:57·9
1964	Caretto, Patty	18:30·5
1965	Caretto, Patty	18:23·7
1966	Caretto, Patty	18:12·9
1967	Meyer, Debbie	17:50·2
1968	Meyer, Debbie	17:38·5
1969	Meyer, Debbie	17:19·9
1970	Meyer, Debbie	17:28·4
	* = one mile † = 1,650 y.	

100 m. Back-stroke

1946	Zimmerman, Suzanne	1:18·0
1947	Zimmerman, Suzanne	1:17·6
1948	Zimmerman, Suzanne	1:16·4
1949*	Jensen, Barbara	1:20·3
1950	O'Brien, Maureen	1:17·9
1951	Freeman, Mary	1:18·8
1952	No championship meeting	
1953*	Stark, Barbara	1:16·6
1954	Mann, Shelley	1:15·5
1955	Cone, Carin	1:15·6
1956*	Cone, Carin	1:14·5
1957*	Cone, Carin	1:13·6
1958	Cone, Carin	1:13·3
1959*	Cone, Carin	1:13·3
1960	Burke, Lynn	1:10·2
1961	Harmar, Nina	1:11·0
1962	De Varona, Donna	1:10·4

1963	Ferguson, Cathy	1:09·2
1964	Ferguson, Cathy	1:09·2
1965	Caron, Christine (Fra)	1:08·1
1966	Fairlie, Ann (SAf)	1:07·9
1967	Moore, Kendis	1:09·2
1968	Muir, Karen (SAf)	1:06·9
1969	Atwood, Sue	1:06·0
1970	Atwood, Sue	1:06·2
	* = 110 y.	

200 m. Back-stroke

1946	Zimmerman, Suzanne	2:48·7
1947	Zimmerman, Suzanne	2:49·0
1948	Zimmerman, Suzanne	2:48·3
1949*	Jensen, Barbara	2:54·9
1950	O'Brien, Maureen	2:51·2
1951	Freeman, Mary	2:49·8
1952	No championship meeting	
1953*	Stark Barbara	2:45·7
1954	Stark, Barbara	2:47·9
1955	Cone, Carin	2:45·6
1956*	Cone, Carin	2:43·8
1957*	Von Saltza, Chris	2:40·2
1958	Von Saltza, Chris	2:37·4
1959*	Cone, Carin	2:37·9
1960	Burke, Lynne	2:33·5
1961	Harmar, Nina	2:35·0
1962	Duenkel, Virginia	2:32·1
1963	Duenkel, Virginia	2:30·8
1964	Ferguson, Cathy	2:29·2
1965	Ferguson, Cathy/	
	Humbarger, Judy (tie)	2:28·0
1966	Muir, Karen (SAf)	2:26·4
1967	Moore, Kendis	2:28·1
1968	Muir, Karen (SAf)	2:24·3
1969	Atwood, Sue	2:21·5
1970	Atwood, Sue	2:22·0
	* = 220 y.	

100 m. Breast-stroke

1946	Wilson, Jeanne	1:26·2
1947	Van Vleit, Nel (Neth)	1:21·6
1948	Wilson, Jeanne	1:28·9
1949*	Pence, Carol	1:25·8
1950	Cornell, Judy	1:23·1
1951	Cornell, Judy	1:21·0
1952	No championship meeting	
1953*	Peters, Gail	Bu1:18·0
1954–55	Event not held	
1956*	Sears, Mary-Jane	1:22·7
1957*	Elsinius, Mary-Lou	1:24·9
1958	Ordogh, Susie (Hun)	1:23·8
1959*	Hargreaves, Marianne	1:22·4
1960	Warner, Ann	1:23·4
1961	Barnhard, Dale	1:22·6

1962	Urselmann, Wiltrud	
	(WGer)	1:20·6
1963	Dellekamp, Jean	1:20·7
1964	Kolb, Claudia	1:19·0
1965	Kolb, Claudia	1:17·1
1966	Ball, Catie	1:16·4
1967	Ball, Catie	1:14·6
1968	Ball, Catie	1:15·7
1969	Brecht, Kim	1:15·7
1970	Kurtz, Linda	1:16·7
	* = 110 y.	

200 m. Breast-stroke

1946	Merkie, Nancy	3:15·0
1947	Van Vliet, Nel (Neth)	2:58·6
1948	Wilson, Jeanne	3:17·7
1949*	Kawamoto, Evelyn	3:14·5
1950	Kawamoto, Evelyn/	
	Hulton, Marce (tie)	3:10·2
1951	Pence, Carol	3:09·2
1952	No championship meeting	
1953*	Peters, Gail	Bu3:01·1
1954	Sears, Mary-Jane	3:07·4
1955	Sears, Mary-Jane	3:01·4
1956*	Sears, Mary-Jane	2:59·0
1957*	Elsinius, Mary-Lou	3:04·8
1958	Ordogh, Susie (Hun)	2:58·6
1959*	Warner, Ann	3:02·4
1960	Warner, Ann	2:53·3
1961	Dellekamp, Jean	2:56·7
1962	Urselmann, Wiltrud	
	(WGer)	2:53·3
1963	Dellekamp, Jean	2:53·4
1964	Kolb, Claudia	2:49·8
1965	Kolb, Claudia/	
	Goyette, Cynthia (tie)	2:48·6
1966	Ball, Catie	2:44·4
1967	Ball, Catie	2:39·5
1968	Ball, Catie	2:40·9
1969	Brecht, Kim	2:45·4
1970	Clevenger, Claudia	2:46·7
	* = 220 y.	

100 m. Butterfly

1954	Mann, Shelley	1:17·0
1955	Mullen, Betty	1:15·0
1956*	Mann, Shelley	1:11·8
1957*	Ramey, Nancy	1:11·3
1958	Ramey, Nancy	1:10·3
1959*	Collins, Becky	1:11·2
1960	Collins, Becky	1:10·8
1961	Doerr, Susan	1:08·2
1962	Stewart, Mary (Can)	1:07·6
1963	Ellis, Kathy	1:06·5

1964	Stouder, Sharon	1:05·4
1965	Pitt, Susan	1:06·2
1966	Pitt, Susan	1:07·0
1967	Daniel, Ellie	1:05·7
1968	Daniel, Ellie	1:06·9
1969	Durkin, Virginia	1:05·9
1970	Jones, Alice	1:04·1
	* = 110 y.	

200 m. Butterfly

1956*	Mann, Shelley	2:44·4
1957*	Wilson, Jane	2:47·6
1958	Ruuska, Sylvia	2:43·6
1959*	Collins, Becky	2:37·0
1960	Collins, Becky	2:36·8
1961	Collins, Becky	2:32·8
1962	Finneran, Sharon	2:31·2
1963	Finneran, Sharon	2:31·8
1964	Stouder, Sharon	2:26·4
1965	Moore, Kendis	2:26·3
1966	Davis, Lee	2:27·2
1967	Hewitt, Toni	2:23·6
1968	Hewitt, Toni	2:24·2
1969	Colella, Lynn	2:21·6
1970	Jones, Alice	2:19·3
	* = 220 y.	

200 m. Individual medley

1961	De Varona, Donna	2:35·0
1962	De Varona, Donna	2:33·3
1963	De Varona, Donna	2:31·8
1964	De Varona, Donna	2:29·9
1965	Kolb, Claudia	2:30·8
1966	Kolb, Claudia	2:27·8
1967	Kolb, Claudia	2:25·0
1968	Kolb, Claudia	2:27·5
1969	Vidali, Lynn	2:26·2
1970	Vidali, Lynn	2:26·1

400 m. Individual medley

1946*	Merki, Nancy	4:29·9
1947*	Merki, Nancy	4:32·9
1948*	Jensen, Barbara	4:31·3
1949*	Kawamoto, Evelyn	4:27·5
1950*	Kawamoto, Evelyn	4:29·0
1951†	Kawamoto, Evelyn	4:33·0
1952	No championship meeting	
1953†	Peters, Gail	4:21·7
1954	Gillett, Marie	6:06·9
1955	Gillett, Marie	6:01·5
1956‡	Mann, Shelley	5:52·5
1957‡	Ruuska, Sylvia	5:49·5
1958	Ruuska, Sylvia	5:43·7
1959‡	Ruuska, Sylvia	5:40·2

1960	De Varona, Donna	5:36·5	1966	Kolb, Claudia	5:15·5
1961	De Varona, Donna	5:34·5	1967	Kolb, Claudia	5:08·2
1962	Finneran, Sharon	5:25·4	1968	Pedersen, Sue	5:10·3
1963	De Varona, Donna	5:24·5	1969	Meyer, Debbie	5:08·6
1964	De Varona, Donna	5:17·7	1970	Atwood, Sue	5:07·3
1965	Olcese, Mary-Ellen	5:19·6	* = 330 y. † = 300 m. ‡ = 440 y.		

V

VARONA, Donna de (United States, 26 Apr. 1947–). At 13, the youngest member of the American team at the 1960 Olympics, Donna Dee—as she was known—won two golds, for 400 m. medley and free-style relay, at the Tokyo Games four years later.

Her versatility was reflected in her almost complete dominance of the world 400 m. medley record list from 1960. She cut this time back from 5:35·5 to 5:14·9 in four years, her last mark in Aug. 1964 standing until 1967. She set her first world record only weeks before the Rome Olympics, and had the medley event been in the programme at that time Donna must have become the youngest Olympic swimming chapion.

One of the most photographed of American women athletes, dark-haired Donna was cover girl on *Life*, *Time*, *Saturday Evening Post* and twice on *Sports Illustrated*. She was also the first 'queen' of the Hall of Fame who honoured her beauty as well as her swimming talent in 1965. In 1964 Donna was voted America's outstanding woman athlete in any sport and she demonstrated her magnificent swimming talents in Australia, New Zealand, Germany, Japan, Netherlands, Peru, Brazil, England and Italy.

VARSITY MATCH. The meetings between Oxford and Cambridge—the longest-standing annual swimming fixture in the world—began in 1891 with a water-polo game between the two universities. Oxford won 4–1. The next year (1892) a swimming contest was added. And the two senior British universities have met at swimming and water-polo every year since, except during World Wars I and II. Of the 69 swimming matches to 1970, Cambridge have 44, Oxford 20 and 4 were drawn. In the 70 water-polo games, Cambridge have come out top in 34 to the 23 victories of Oxford and 13 drawn.

W

WAINWRIGHT, Kathy (Australia, 1949–). Miss Perpetual Motion Kathy Wainwright flew in and out of world swimming as quickly as her high speed arm action carried her to a gold in the Commonwealth 440 y. in 1966. In fact, the Jamaica Games was her only big event appearance, for she was not chosen for the 1964 Olympics and she had quit by the time of the Mexico Games.

Although her arms moved at a sprinter's rate, her best distances were from 400 m. upwards. Her winning time in Kingston, 4:38·8, was 6·6 faster than the six-year-old world record of her famous Australian predecessor Ilsa Konrads (see KONRADS) and she had already set a record of 4:39·6 in a heat (though apparently this was never claimed as a world record). Kathy was only 0·8 outside the world mark for 400 m. although she swam 7 ft. 8 in. further, and technically her converted time of 4:36·9 was 1·1 inside the metric mark of Martha Randall (USA).

Kathryn Knight Wainwright (5 ft. 4 in., 136 lb.), a bank officer in Sydney, won the Australian 440 y. title in 1966 (4:49·2), the year she also broke the world 880 y. record (9:50·3). She won the Australian 880 y. four times, 1964–67 and the 1,650 y. in 1966/67, setting a world record of 18:49·3 on the second occasion.

WAINWRIGHT, Norman (Great Britain, 4 July 1914–). Norman Wainwright, from Hanley, with Bobby Leivers from near-by Longton, dominated British free-style swimming in the 1930s (see LEIVERS, BOBBY). Their careers followed almost parallel courses.

Wainwright, five months older than Leivers, swam in the 400 and 1,500 m. at the 1932 and 1936 Olympics, but did not reach the first six on either occasion though he did swim in the sixth-placed relay team in Berlin. He won individual bronzes at the European championships of 1934 (1,500 m.) and 1938 (400 m.) and a third bronze for the relay in London on his second European appearance.

He also took part in two Commonwealth Games. In 1934 he was second in the 440 y. (5:07·8) and relay and third in the 1,500 y. (18:55·2). Four years later, he was third again in the long distance event, now increased to 1,650 y. (20:17·4) in which Leivers came first. Both men were in the winning English relay squad.

It coud be said the Leivers was fractionally more successful internationally. But Wainwright, undoubtedly, had the better of their private battle nationally. He won twenty-one A.S.A. titles—the 220 and 440 y. five times each (1935–39), the 880 y. and one mile five times each (1933–45, '37, '39) and the 500 y. once (1934, the last occasion the race was held). He received the Y. M. Yeaden Memorial Trophy as England's 'Swimmer of the Year' in 1939.

WARDROP TWINS, Jack and Bert (Great Britain, 26 May 1932–). John Caldwell Wardrop, called Jack and his ten-minutes younger brother Robert, called Bert, were probably the only twins to have swum in an Olympics (1952). Certainly Jack was the first British man to break a world record in forty years in 1954, when he cut 11·1 off the 400 y. medley mark (4:41·7) in the United States Indoor championships at Yale University. He went on to set four more world times, of which his first for 220 y. free-style (2:03·9) was never claimed on his behalf. But he took this and the record for 200 m. on 4 Mar. 1955 in clocking 2:03·4 for the longer yards distance. A month later, again in a United States Indoor meeting, he reduced his 400 y. medley time a further 4·8 to 4:36·9.

Jack competed in three Olympics. At 16 and still suffering from childhood asthma, he swam in the 1,500 m. at the 1948 London Games. It was only his second long distance race and he did not reach the final. In Helsinki, Jack was fifth in the 400 m. free-style (4:39·9) and Bert sixth in the 100 m. back-stroke (67·7).

The twin quit swimming early in 1956 and Jack told the British selectors that he would not be available for the Melbourne Olympics. But he was persuaded to come home in September from the University of Michigan, where he and Bert had been students for four years. And though he made it clear he would not be swimming fit until the Games at the end of November, he was chosen without a trial for his third Olympics to the considerable delight of the rest of the team.

Then the unsympathetic treatment by officials which had bedevilled him in Commonwealth Games and European championships, caused trouble again. He opted out of a pre-Olympic match with Hungary, with the permission of the Olympic team manager, was promptly dropped from the Melbourne team and only reinstated after a furious top-level Anglo-Scottish row.

The effect on Jack was devastating and he was nowhere near the form he had hoped for in Melbourne where he won his 400 m. free-style heat (4:39·8) but did not qualify for the final. Yet it was still worth having him there for his inspiration and expert coaching assistance.

The twins swam in the 1954 Commonwealth Games in Vancouver where Jack was second in the 440 y., Bert fifth in the back-stroke and both were in Scotland's 3 × 110 y. medley relay team who won the bronzes. They also competed in the European championships that year in Turin, but without medal success.

Jack won twelve A.S.A. titles in four years including all the free-style ones in 1952 (100, 220, 440, 880 y. and mile). He was as talented on back-stroke but, at 12, had tossed with Bert the styles they would swim and thus not have to race against each other. He won twenty-one Scottish titles between 1947–52, including the 440 y. six successive years (1947–52) and the 220 and 880 y. five times each (1948–52). When he left for America, he held all nine British free-style records from 100 y. to mile and was the first Briton to break the minute for 100 m. (59·3).

Bert won the A.S.A. 100 y. back-stroke in 1952 and was Scottish champion from 1947–52.

WATER-POLO. It is agreed the world over that Britian were the founders of the game of water-polo. Efforts were made from 1870 to draw up a code of rules for a game called at that time football-in-the-water, but it was not until 1885, after considerable pioneering work and pressure from Scotland and the clubs in the Midlands of England, that the Swimming Association of Great Britain, later to become the Amateur Swimming Association recognized the game as being under their jurisdiction.

Even then different and very primitive rules for play were used around the country. And some of them were odd indeed. There were no goal posts, a goal —called a 'touch down'—being scored by a swimmer placing the ball with both hands anywhere along the full width of the bath end or pontoon. And the goalkeeper—often there were two in the same team—used to stand out of the water and would jump on any players from the rival side who looked likely to score goals. This nearly resulted in a fatal accident in Portsmouth harbour where J. Mayger, later to become President of the Midland Counties A.S.A. (1892) got pushed under a pontoon during a desperate scrimmage—rugby-sounding language this—and was nearly insensible by the time he was found and rescued.

Scotland, whose William Wilson had drawn up a code of rules in 1877, were the first to use goal-posts (1879) which were similar to those used in football. And slowly a common set of rules, from trial and error, were formulated.

With all this pioneering work, it is not surprising that British teams dominated the early Olympic tournaments. Represented by the Manchester Osborne Club, Britain won the first water-polo golds at the 1900 Games in Paris. The 1904 tournament in St. Louis was contested by club teams from the United States and was won by the New York Ahtletic Club. Britain were successful again in 1908, 1912 and 1920 and it was not until 1924 in Paris, the scene of their first world victory, that they had to bow to Hungary 6–7 in the first round after three periods of extra time. The Magyars in their turn were beaten by Belgium who lost to France who won the tournament. Hungary were second to Germany in 1928 and then went on to win five of the next seven Olympic competitions (1932, '36, '52, '56, '64), coming second in 1948 and third in 1960 when Italy were the winners. Hungary were third again in 1968 when Yogoslavia and Russia finished ahead of them. (See OLYMPIC GAMES CHAMPIONS).

WATER-POLO, AMATEUR SWIMMING ASSOCIATION CLUB CHAMPIONS. This, the first water-polo championship in the world, was instituted in 1888. Entries were meagre at the beginning because of the expense of travelling around the country for matches. The Midlands club Burton, one of the first to adopt the new ball games (1877) as a club pastime, won three of the first four championships (1888, '89, '91) and were beaten finalists in 1890.

The reign of the Manchester Osborne Club began in 1894 and they were decisive winners through to 1901, except in 1900 when the entire club team were busy representing Britain and winning the first Olympic water-polo championship in Paris. Soon after this the club was disbanded, the members moving either to Wigan or Hyde Seal. These two clubs continued to dominate English water-polo until World War I.

Plaistow United had a long run of victories, winning eight times in eleven years (1928–31, 1935–38), during which time, also representing Essex, they won the county title (see later) seven times (1931, 1933–38).

1888	Burton beat Otter	3–0
1889	Burton beat Amateur	2–0
1890	Hanley beat Burton	6–0
1891	Burton beat Nautilus	3–2
1892	Nautilus beat Hanley	3–2
1893	Tunbridge Wells beat Hanley	3–1
1894	Osborne beat Leicester	8–2
1895	Osborne beat Leicester	8–1
1896	Osborne beat Leicester	3–0
1897	Osborne beat People's Palace	9–2
1898	Osborne beat People's Palace	3–2
1899	Osborne beat St. Helens	5–1
1900	Leicester beat Hyde Seal	2–1
1901	Osborne beat Worthing	6–2
1902	Wigan beat Leicester	5–2
1903	Hyde Seal beat St. Helens	4–2
1904	Hyde Seal beat Wigan	4–2
1905	Hyde Seal beat Weston-super-Mare	4–2
1906	Weston-super-Mare beat Polytechnic	6–4
1907	Weston-super-Mare beat Wigan	3–2
1908	Hyde Seal beat Polytechnic	5–2
1909	Wigan beat Polytechnic	4–3
1910	Wigan beat Polytechnic	3–2
1911	Hyde Seal beat Wigan	7–6
1912	Hyde Seal beat Hornsey	8–2
1913	Hyde Seal beat Wigan	4–1
1914	Weston-super-Mare, Sheffield, Hyde Seal and Burslem—semi-finalists (event abandoned owing to War)	
1915–19	Not held	
1920	Hyde Seal beat Hammersmith	10–1
1921	Weston-super-Mare beat Hyde Seal	11–10
1922	Walsall beat Weston-super-Mare	6–5
1923	Blackburn beat Avondale	8–1
1924	Hyde Seal beat Weston-super-Mare	8–1
1924	Hyde Seal beat Weston-super-Mare	7–5
1925	Weston-super-Mare beat Hyde Seal	6–1

1926	Penguin beat Weston-super-Mare	4–2
1927	Penguin beat Harpurhey	4–3
1928	Plaistow beat Walsall	5–3
1929	Plaistow beat Harpurhey	4–3
1930	Plaistow beat Harpurhey	8–2
1931	Plaistow beat Liverpool Police	7–3
1932	Penguin beat Coventry	5–4
1933	Coventry beat Cheltenham	6–5
1934	Oldham Police beat Plaistow	5–4
1935	Plaistow beat Hyde Seal	5–2
1936	Plaistow beat Oldham Police	4–0
1937	Plaistow beat Polytechnic	7–4
1938	Plaistow beat Otter	5–1
1939	Sheffield Police, Bradford, Avondale, Oldham Police semi-finalists, (event abandoned owing to War).	
1940–45	Not held	
1946	Avondale beat Bradford D	8–5
1947	Penguin beat Otter	2–1
1948	Plaistow beat Bradford D	9–6
1949	Motherwell beat Bradford	8–3
1950	Motherwell beat Plaistow	7–6
1951	Penguin beat Motherwell	5–3
1952	Penguin beat Cheltenham	7–5
1953	Plaistow beat Motherwell	6–2
1954	Plaistow beat Cheltenham	6–5
1955	Cheltenham beat Plaistow	6–2
1956	Polytechnic beat Cheltenham	9–5
1957	Polytechnic beat Cheltenham	5–3
1958	Cheltenham beat Polytechnic	7–5
1959	Cheltenham beat Polytechnic	6–5
1960	Polytechnic beat Otter	10–3
1961	Birkenhead beat Penguin	8–7
1962	Cheltenham beat Sheffield	9–5
1963	Polytechnic beat Sheffield	6–2
1964	Otter beat Walsall	6–5
1965	Penguin beat Cheltenham	6–5
1966	Birkenhead beat Sutton and Cheam	4–3
1967	Walsall beat Birkenhead	9–7
1968	Cheltenham beat Sutton and Cheam	10–5
1969	Polytechnic beat Everton	6–4
1970	Polytechnic beat Birkenhead	11–4

WATER-POLO, AMATEUR SWIMMING ASSOCIATION COUNTY CHAMPIONS. The County championship was instituted in 1896. The early rounds were played on a regional basis,

but despite this the North of England dominated the competition, claiming one of the teams in the final right through to 1923. Lancashire won the first eight championships and thirteen in all up to World War I.

This regional system, that had kept Cheshire out of the final in the years when Lancashire were the top northern county, bedevilled the championship until 1965. Middlesex, Surrey and Essex, for a long time three of the best county sides, were all too often in the same subdivision of the southern group and only one could go forward.

The system from 1965 provides for the top seven teams to be seeded and exempted from preliminary rounds. They, with the winner of the qualifying competition, are drawn into groups of four, playing all-against-all tournaments at centralized venues, the top two teams going forward to a final league of four.

The results of the finals since 1896 are:

1896	Lancashire beat Middlesex	4–1
1897	Lancashire beat Staffordshire	9–2
1898	Lancashire beat Leicestershire	3–2
1899	Lancashire beat Middlesex	4–2
1900	Lancashire beat Middlesex	3–1
1901	Lancashire (Surrey scratched after draw)	2–2
1902	Lancashire beat Surrey	6–2
1903	Lancashire beat Middlesex	7–1
1904	Middlesex beat Lancashire	3–2
1905	Cheshire beat Middlesex	5–1
1906	Lancashire beat Middlesex	11–7
1907	Lancashire beat Somerset	4–2
1908	Middlesex beat Lancashire	7–5
1909	Lancashire beat Somerset	6–1
1910	Lancashire beat Somerset	6–3
1911	Middlesex beat Cheshire	5–4
1912	Lancashire beat Middlesex	1–0
1913	Cheshire beat Middlesex	5–4
1914	Cheshire and Surrey finalists (event abandoned owing to war)	
1915–19	Not held	
1920	Lancashire beat Surrey	4–1
1921	Surrey beat Lancashire	7–1
1922	Cheshire beat Somerset	7–3
1923	Middlesex beat Lancashire	4–2
1924	Staffordshire beat Somerset	5–1
1925	Lancashire beat Middlesex	8–3

1926	Middlesex beat Lancashire	9–5
1927	Middlesex beat Lancashire	5–4
1928	Lancashire beat Essex	2–1
1929	Middlesex beat Lancashire	6–3
1930	Middlesex beat Lancashire	8–4
1931	Essex beat Warwickshire	9–1
1932	Middlesex beat Yorkshire	6–2
1933	Essex beat Gloucestershire	4–2
1934	Essex beat Cheshire	9–2
1935	Essex beat Lancashire	5–0
1936	Essex beat Lancashire	2–1
1937	Essex beat Yorkshire	9–5
1938	Essex beat Gloucestershire	8–1
1939	Essex and Yorkshire finalists, event abandoned because of the war	
1940–45	Not held	
1946	Somerset beat Yorkshire	6–5
1947	Middlesex beat Yorkshire	7–6
1948	Surrey beat Lancashire	4–3
1949	Surrey beat Lancashire	6–5
1950	Lancashire beat Glamorgan	5–4
1951	Lancashire beat Essex	5–4
1952	Gloucestershire beat Middlesex	7–6
1953	Essex beat Gloucestershire	8–7
1954	Cheshire beat Gloucestershire	9–5
1955	Gloucestershire beat Cheshire	7–4
1956	Middlesex beat Gloucestershire	7–5
1957	Middlesex beat Gloucestershire	6–5
1958	Gloucestershire beat Middlesex	5–4
1959	Gloucestershire beat Cheshire	8–5
1960	Surrey beat Cheshire	9–7
1961	Gloucestershire beat Middlesex	8–6
1962	Surrey beat Middlesex	6–3
1963	Cheshire beat Gloucestershire	6–3
1964	Gloucestershire beat Middlesex	4–2
1965	*Surrey, runners-up Gloucestershire	
1966	*Gloucestershire, runners-up Warwickshire	
1967	*Surrey, runners-up Staffordshire	
1968	*Middlesex, runners-up Gloucestershire	
1969	*Surrey, runners-up Middlesex	

1970 *Middlesex, runners-up Warwickshire

* Chapionship decided on a four-team final, each team playing all others on a league basis.

WATER-POLO, HOME INTER-NATIONAL MATCHES. The first known international water-polo match of any kind was played between England and Scotland at the Kensington baths, London, on 28 July 1890. There was no conformity of rules and as England were the hosts, the match was contested under their rules which permitted 'ducking'. The Englishmen, although heavier and speedier were sadly lacking in skill and strategy and the Scots, who concentrated on playing the ball not the man, won easily, 4–0 The teams on that historic occasion were: Scotland—C. W. Donald (Edinburgh University), goal; G. S. Bryson (Dennistoun) and S. D. Cawood (Victoria), backs; A. Strauss (Southern), captain, half-back; J. Bissland (Leander), A. Whyte (Victoria) and S. Capie (Dennistoun), forwards. England—F. Browne (Burton-on-Trent), goal; W. G. Carrey (Amateur) and H. F. Clark (Stroud Green), backs; J. F. Genders (Nautilus), half-back; J. Finegan (Liverpool Sefton) and W. Henry (Zephyr) (see HENRY WILLIAM,) and J. I. Mayger (Burton-on-Trent), captain, forwards.

England and Scotland played annually until 1901 while Ireland, who lost their first game with England (1895, 0–12) and Wales, who were defeated by Scotland in 1897 (3–2) were also producing teams. By 1906 a home international programme had been devised in which each of the four teams played each other on a two-year cycle. Except during war years; this system continued until 1962 when the home international tournament at a centralized venue was instituted (see end of results).

England v. Scotland

1890	Scotland	London	4–0
1891	Scotland	Glasgow	2–0
1892	England	Liverpool	4–0
1893	England	Glasgow	3–0

1894	England	Nottingham	4–1
1895	England	Edinburgh	3–0
1896	England	London	4–2
1897	Scotland	Edinburgh	2–1
1898	England	Liverpool	8–3
1899	England	Aberdeen	5–1
1900	England	Leicester	5–0
1901	England	Glasgow	7–0
1906	England	Glasgow	5–1
1908	England	Bradford	9–0
1910	England	Hamilton	3–1
1912	England	Weston-super-	
		Mare	4–0
1920	England	Paisley	7–3
1922	England	Blackburn	12–1
1924	England	Glasgow	5–4
1926	England	Birmingham	7–3
1928	England	Dundee	6–1
1930	England	Great Yarmouth	9–0
1932	England	Prestwick	5–1
1934	England	Hastings	6–0
1936	England	Portobello	8–1
1938	England	Leeds	6–2
1948	England	Aberdeen	6–2
1950	England	Exmouth	10–0
1952	England	Kilmarnock	6–3
1954	England	Morecambe	7–2
1956	England	Coatbridge	9–2
1958	England	Morecambe	7–2

England v. Ireland

1895	England	London	12–0
1898	England	Dublin	7–0
1899	England	London	12–0
1900	England	Belfast	5–0
1901	England	Radcliffe	8–0
1902	England	Dublin	6–1
1903	England	Swindon	6–0
1904	England	Belfast	10–1
1906	England	Leicester	2–1
1908	England	Cork	10–0
1910	England	Weston-super-	
		Mare	7–1
1912	England	Belfast	6–4
1920	England	Newcastle	11–0
1922	England	Belfast	6–4
1924	England	Cheltenham	8–2
1926	England	Dublin	9–3
1928	England	Birmingham	7–0
1930	England	Dublin	6–3
1932	England	Coventry	11–1
1934	England	Bangor Co.	
		Down	7–2
1936	England	Uxbridge	11–1

1938	England	Dublin	6–1
1948	England	Skegness	9–3
1950	England	Dublin	19–3
1952	England	Tynemouth	13–1
1954	England	Cork	9–1
1956	England	Morecambe	6–0
1958	England	Bangor Co.	
		Down	10–5
1960	Cancelled		
1961	England	Morecambe	16–7

England v. Wales

1898	England	Newport	4–0
1899	England	Warrington	8–1
1900	England	Penarth	7–3
1901	England	Leicester	7–0
1902	England	Newport	8–0
1903	England	Weston-super-	
		Mare	10–1
1904	England	Penarth	5–2
1905	Draw	Bradford	3–3
1907	England	Swansea	7–1
1909	England	Ilfracombe	16–0
1911	England	Penarth	9–1
1913	England	Brighton	8–1
1921	England	Newport	12–3
1923	England	Great Yarmouth	4–1
1925	England	Penarth	9–3
1927	England	Croydon	6–3
1929	England	Newport	8–0
1931	England	Barking	14–2
1933	England	Newport	9–2
1935	England	Luton	6–0
1937	England	Cardiff	13–3
1947	England	Wallasey	4–1
1949	England	Barry	4–1
1951	England	Exmouth	13–1
1953	England	Barry	11–1
1955	England	Morecambe	10–1
1957	England	Newport	6–3
1959	England	Morecambe	16–2
1961	England	Newport	14–2

Scotland v. Ireland

1898	Scotland	Glasgow	9–3
1899	Scotland	Belfast	4–1
1900	Scotland	Alloa	6–1
1901	Scotland	Dublin	4–3
1902	Scotland	Aberdeen	4–1
1905	Ireland	Belfast	4–3
1907	Scotland	Dunfermline	3–0
1909	Ireland	Carrickfergus	5–1
1911	Scotland	Paisley	9–2
1913	Scotland	Dublin	4–3
1921	Scotland	Paisley	6–2

OLYMPIC GAMES. (*Above*) The first Olympic women's relay champion team, the British squad, at the 1912 Games in Stockholm. The swimmers were (left to right) Bella Moore, Jennie Fletcher—who also won the individual 100m bronze, Annie Speirs and Irene Steer. In the centre is the chaperone Miss Jarvis, a sister of Olympic champion John Jarvis. (*Below*) The pool built specially for the 1964 Olympic Games in Tokyo

PHELPS, BRIAN. Britain's greatest male diver, shown in a back dive with
pike, was only 14 in 1958 when he won his first major title, the European
highboard crown in Budapest

1923	Ireland	Belfast	4–2
1925	Scotland	Paisley	4–2
1927	Ireland	Belfast	6–1
1929	Scotland	Dumbarton	2–0
1931	Ireland	Portrush	6–2
1933	Scotland	Prestwick	6–1
1935	Scotland	Dublin	6–2
1937	Scotland	Portobello	5–3
1939	Scotland	Bangor Co. Down	7–2
1947	Scotland	Dublin	5–2
1949	Scotland	Aberdeen	7–1
1951	Scotland	Cork	9–3
1953	Scotland	Cumnock	8–3
1955	Scotland	Bangor Co. Down	5–4
1957	Scotland	Leith	14–4
1959	Ireland	Dublin	7–5

Scotland v. Wales

1897	Scotland	Newport	3–2
1898	Draw	Aberdeen	0–0
1899	Wales	Penarth	6–4
1900	Scotland	Edinburgh	1–0
1901	Scotland	Swansea	7–3
1906	Wales	Penarth	9–1
1908	Scotland	Leith	3–2
1910	Draw	Newport	2–2
1912	Scotland	Paisley	5–1
1920	Wales	Penarth	6–5
1922	Scotland	Paisley	8–0
1924	Wales	Llandaff	6–5
1926	Scotland	Paisley	4–2
1928	Wales	Newport	9–4
1930	Scotland	Paisley	5–2
1932	Draw	Cardiff	1–1
1934	Scotland	Troon	3–2
1936	Scotland	Llandridod	7–3
1938	Scotland	Portobello	9–3
1948	Wales	Barry	5–3
1950	Scotland	Paisley	9–3
1952	Scotland	Barry	7–3
1954	Scotland	Coatbridge	5–4
1956	Wales	Rhyl	8–1
1958	Scotland	Leith	6–3
1960	Scotland	Rhyl	7–3

In 1962, the format of the home international water-polo matches was changed to an annual four-country competition on an all-play-all league basis. England won on each occasion up to 1970, except in 1967 when they did not participate in protest over the Welsh choice of venue (Maindee bath, Newport) which did not conform to the con-

ditions of the tournament as regards the depth of water.

1962	England	Cumnock	6 pts
	(beat Ireland	8–3)	
	(beat Scotland	11–5)	
	(beat Wales	6–0)	
1963	England	Newport	6 pts
	(beat Ireland	12–5)	
	(beat Scotland	6–3)	
	(beat Wales	21–5)	
1964	England	Dublin	6 pts
	(beat Ireland	5–3)	
	(beat Scotland	5–2)	
	(beat Wales	12–0)	
1965	England	London	6 pts
	(beat Ireland	5–2)	
	(beat Scotland	4–1)	
	(beat Wales	7–0)	
1966	England	Portobello	6 pts
	(beat Ireland	5–4)	
	(beat Scotland	10–5)	
	(beat Wales	5–3)	
1967	Wales	Newport	4 pts
	(beat Ireland	9–6)	
	(beat Scotland	5–3)	
	(England did not compete)		
1968	England	Dublin	6 pts
	(beat Ireland	5–4)	
	(beat Scotland	)	
	(beat Wales	)	
1969	England	Exmouth	6 pts
	(beat Ireland	6–5)	
	(beat Scotland	7–4)	
	(beat Wales	11–7)	
1970	England	Burntisland	6 pts
	(beat Ireland	8–5)	
	(beat Scotland	4–2)	
	(beat Wales	10–5)	

WATER-POLO RULES. For many years, the pattern set by Britain in the early days, with teams of seven playing in positions similar to those in Association Football, was followed internationally. The players were not allowed to move once the referee's whistle had been blown for an infringement until the free throw had been taken. This static play eventually detracted from the excitement and popularity of the game.

The rules were changed after the 1948 Olympics to allow free movement after the whistle, except for the player taking the throw, and this revived interest in

M

water-polo. But the rule whereby a major offender or offenders could be ordered from the water until a goal had been scored—which at the 1936 Olympics had resulted in a large part of one match being contested between one team with three players and a goal-leeper left in the water and the other with two players and a goal-keeper—remained in the laws.

The most significant rule changes came in the 1960s. In 1966 a system of penalty points for major fouls was devised by which a free throw and a penalty point was given against the offending team but the offender was not ordered out of the water. After a side had received three penalty points against them, a penalty shot at goal was awarded to the other side. The weakness of this idea was demonstrated in the final of the Olympic tournament in 1968 when, at the end of full time in the match between Yugoslavia and Russia a total of 73 penalty points had been awarded—the teams, in fact, having played for them as the easiest way to score goals.

As a result, in 1969, the International Water-Polo Committee faced up to the fact that they could not avoid penalizing seriously offending teams by making them have to play a man short—which generally meant a goal for the other side —for some part of a match. Thus, for a major foul, the offender is now ordered from the water for one minute or until a goal is scored. And any player having three penalty points marked against him is out of the match for good though a substitute may replace him after the one-minute suspension (or a goal). In order to do away with gamesmanship, the I.W.P.C. also decided that any team having possession of the ball for more than 45 sec. without shooting should concede a free throw to the other side.

It had become an Olympic rule that a team in the Games might enter eleven playes and pick from these seven to play in any particular match in the tournament. In 1961, it was decided that a team would consist of seven players plus four reserves who could be substituted during a single match.

The playing time up to 1952 was two halves of seven minutes each way with time taken out for all stoppages. In 1953 this was extended to ten minutes each and in 1961 varied to four quarters of five minutes each of actual play.

WATSON, Lynn (Australia, 22 Nov. 1952–   ). A medley relay silver medallist, at 15, in the 1968 Olympic Games, Lynn Watson, from Western Australia, won four gold medals at the 1970 Commonwealth Games.

She took the 100 and 200 m. backstroke, setting a Commonwealth record in the latter of 2:22·9. She broke her own Australian 100 m. record for the fourth time during the Games with 66·8 to send her team on the way to victory in the 4 × 100 m. medley relay and had the best split (60·6) in Australia's winning free-style relay squad. Her back-stroke performances showed considerable improvement on her 69·1 and 2:29·5 in coming sixth and fourth respectively in the individual events in the Mexico Olympics.

WATSON, Pokey (United States, 11 July 1950–   ). Christened Lillian Debra, but known the swimming world over by the unflattering nickname of 'Pokey', Miss Watson was one of only three girl swimmers in the American team at the Mexico Olympics who competed in the 1964 Games in Tokyo.

Her first Olympic appearance was at 14 and she won a free-style relay gold. Then it was the 1967 Pan-American Games and a bronze in the 100 m. free-style (61·5) and fourth in the 200 m. (2:19·1). With three United States free-style outdoor titles to her credit—100 m. in 1956 (60·7) and '66 (59·9) and the 200 m. in 1966 (2:10·5, a world record that stood for exactly a year)—it was slightly surprising to see her in Mexico in the 200 m. back-stroke. She had never won a United States outdoor back-stroke title, though she was second behind Karen Muir in 1968 when the South African, whose country had been excluded from the 1968 Olympics, broke the world 200 m. record with 2:24·3 (see MUIR, KAREN).

But Pokey, born in Mineloa, New York but living in California and a member of the Santa Clara Club, knew what she was about in Mexico. And she won the gold (2:48·8) by the handsome margin of 2·6 from Canada's Elaine Tanner, having been 1·3 down at half distance.

WEBB, Captain Matthew (Great Britain, 19 June 1848–83). Captain Matthew Webb earned his place in immortality on 25 Aug. 1875 when, after 21 hrs. and 45 min. in the water, he stepped on to the Calais beach as the first to swim across the English Channel. It took until 1923 for another man (London's Tom Burgess) to emulate this heroic feat and until 1934 before Webb's time was beaten (by Ted Temme of England).

Webb left from Admiralty Pier, Dover, at 12.55 on 24 Aug., 3¼ hr. before high water, on a 15 ft. 10 in. tide. In the first 1¾ hr., he was swept 1½ miles to the west of his direct route to France. In the next 5¼ hr., he was swept 8½ miles on an eastern drift, parallel with the distant French coast. Between 20.00 on the Tuesday and 03.00 on the Wednesday morning, Webb again was taken 2½ miles west of his course. Then seven hours in a north-east stream drifted him 7¼ miles to the east and closer and closer to France. It took him ¾ hr. in slack water under Calais Pier to finish.

The shortest distance from England to France (Dover to Cap Gris Nez) is 17¾ nautical miles and Dover to Calais is 21¼ miles. Webb, who swam through three tides, plus 1¾ hours in a south-west stream at the start and about ¾ hour in slack water at the finish, actually swam 39½ miles.

Webb, 5 ft. 8 in. and 14½ st., was rubbed with porpoise oil before the start and for the first 15 hr. the weather was splendid, the sea, 65°, smooth as glass, the sun obscured by a haze during the day, and a three-quarter moon to light his way at night.

The worst time was from 3 a.m. on 25 Aug. when drowsiness had to be over-come and the water was rough. At this time, Webb was only 4½ miles off Cap Gris Nez, but had not the strength then to fight the N.E. stream and strike directly for land. Had he been able to go forward he could have landed between 07.00 and 08.00. As it was, he finally landed in Calais at 10.40.

Webb, fortified by beer, brandy and beef tea, swam very high on the water on his breast, with slow and steady arm strokes and powerful leg action, averaging about twenty cycles a minute. He was accompanied by a lugger and two rowing boats and a posse of journalists, who were undisputed witnesses to the veracity of his feat.

Born at Irongate, near Dawley in Shropshire, Webb learned to swim at seven and while on the Conway training ship had been awarded the Albert Medal for saving a comrade from drowning. He had a good breat-stroke, but was not a fast swimmer, even measured against those days, and he had spent a seafaring life for some years before his Channel success, which was, in fact, his second attempt. On 12 Aug. 1875 he swam for seven hours but had drifted so far off course that he retired.

Eight years after his epic achievement, in an attempt to bolster lagging attendances at his vaudeville act, he tried for immortality a second time by swimming across the rapids just above Niagara Falls. But this 'impossible' feat proved indeed to be impossible and Webb was drowned. He is buried at Niagara Falls, Ontario, Canada, but Captain Matthew Webb will for ever be remembered.

WEISSMULLER, Johnny (United States, 2 June 1904–). A Tarzan of swimming indeed was Johnny Weissmuller, who was voted 'The Greatest Swimmer of the half century' by 250 sports writers in 1950. He won five Olympic gold medals and a bronze, broke twenty-four world records and is reputed never to have lost in ten years of amateur competition in races from 50 to 880 y.

His high-riding stroke, with its pull-and-push arm stroke, independent head

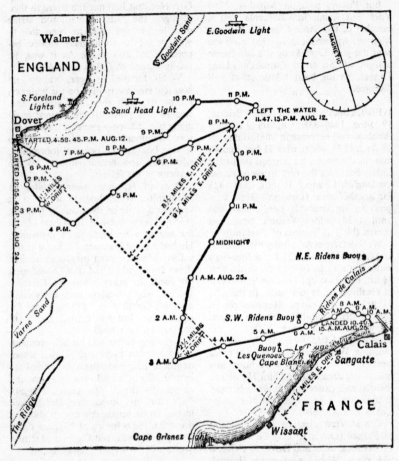

Map showing the routes of Captain Matthew Webb's Channel swims in August 1875. His first, unsuccessful, attempt started on the afternoon of 12 Aug. and was abandoned 6 hr. 48 min. 30 sec. later, after Webb had covered 13½ miles but had drifted 9¼ miles off his course. His second, successful, attempt began just before 1 p.m. on 24 Aug. and finished 21 hr. 44 min. 35 sec. after he had entered the water at Dover as he stepped on to French soil, under Calais Pier, on 25 Aug. The dotted line shows the shortest route as the crow might fly. (This map originally appeared in the *Field* but is reproduced from the Badminton Book of Swimming 1894).

turning action for breathing and deep
flutter leg-kick, was revolutionary and
had a tremendous influence on the
development of the crawl throughout the
world.

Weissmuller won the 100 and 400 m.
free-style at the 1924 Games in Olympic
records of 59·0 and 5:04·2, a third gold
in the 4 × 200 m. relay and a bronze in
water-polo. In Amsterdam in 1928, he
retained his sprint title, again in a Games
record (59·6) and won his fifth Olympic
gold in the relay.

Johnny's first world records were set
on 25 Mar. 1922, when he was 17, for
300 y. and 300 m. (3:16·6 and 3:35·2) and
his next, on 20 Apr. of that year, was for
150 y. back-stroke (1:45·4). But of his
records for all eleven free-style distances
on the books in his time, his best remembered and admired achievement were his
51·0 for 100 y. (his fifth successive mark
on 5 Apr. 1927, which stood for seventeen years; 58·6 for 100 m. on 9 July
1922—the first man to break the minute
and he did it in a 100 y.-long pool—and
his subsequent 57·4 for 100 m. (25 m.
pool) on 17 Feb. 1924 which stood for
ten years.

But there were many more Weissmuller world marks that took nearly a
decade to be bettered . . . his 2:08·0 for
200 m. in Apr. 1927, which improved his
own five-year-old record by 7·6 sec. (and
was set on the same day he clocked 51·0
for 100 y.) stood for seven years . . . so
did his 220 y. time of 2:09·0, set during
the same swim . . . and so, too, did his
300 m. mark. And it took a man as great
as Arne Borg of Sweden to trim Weissmuller's 4:57·0 (the first man under five
minutes) for 400 m. and 440 y. and his
5:47·6 and 6:24·2 for 500 y. and 500 m.
Johnny got back the 440 y. record from
Borg on 25 Aug. 1927. It was to be his
last world mark. He clocked 4:52·0,
racing in a 110 y. pool in Honolulu, and
though the time did not break Borg's
metric mark of 4:50·3 (25 y. bath) it was
equivalently much faster. In fact, it was
worth 4:47·3 for 400 m. in a 50 m. pool,
whereas Borg's time was equal to 4:57·3
over a 50 m. course. Weissmuller's 440 y.
time was not bettered for six years. When

he was 36, Johnny, who was born in
Windsor, Conn., swam 100 y. in 48·5 as
a professional in Bill Rose's World Fair
Aquacade.

Invited to take a screen test for the
film part of Tarzan, Weissmuller said
'no thanks'. Bribed with promises that
he could meet Greta Garbo and lunch
with Clark Gable, Johnny agreed. There
were 150 husky young men trying out
also, and after his test the disinterested
Johnny took off for Oregon and his job
as a swim-suit salesman. That he got the
part is film history—but it nearly lost
him his name. The producer, obviously
not a sports fan, said: 'Johnny Weissmuller, that's too long, it won't go on
the posters, we'll have to change it."
Then somebody told him just who
Weissmuller was! And the swimming
Tarzan was born.

**WELSH AMATEUR SWIMMING
ASSOCIATION.** The W.A.S.A. was
founded in 1896 in Cardiff, where an
indoor bath, the first in Wales, had been
built that year. Before this there had
been active clubs in Newport, Swansea
and at Penarth, who had been playing
water-polo for a number of years. But it
was the energetic Cardiff club who had
the drive to form a national association.

The first secretary was Jack Coppock,
the second eldest of nine water-polo-
playing brothers. Seven Coppocks used
to make up a team and the other two
played for the opposition—who usually
lost. Between the two world wards,
R. P. Green served as honorary secretary for twenty-one years. The present
secretary, Wilf Hooper of Newport, has
served almost as long.

WELSH CHAMPIONS. The first
Welsh championship was held in 1897—
100 y. free-style for men. In the early
days, this title was almost exclusively the
property of Paul Radmilovic (see
RADMILOVIC, PAUL) who won it fifteen
times between 1901 and 1922. With the
races from 1914–19 (5) cancelled because
of the war, this left one year (1912) when
'Raddy' did not win in more than two

decades. A 100 y. free-style for women was instituted in 1905, four years after England held their first women's championship.

Since 1953, the majority of the Welsh championships have been held at centralized venues as follows:

Year	Venue	Bath length
1953	Maindee	33⅓ y.
1954	Bargoed	33⅓ y.
1955	Barry	50 y.
1956	Tenby	50 y.
1957	Pwllheli	55 y.
1958	Cardiff*	55 y.
1959	Cardiff*	55 y.
1960	Maindee	33⅓ y.
1961	Rhyl	110 y.
1962	Neath	36⅔ y.
1963	Maindee	33⅓ y.
1964	Cardiff*	55 y.
1965	Afan Lido	55 y.
1966	Ebbw Vale	36⅔ y.
1967	Afan Lido	55 y.
1968	Afan Lido	55 y.
1969	Afan Lido	55 y.
1970	Maindee	33⅓ y.

* Wales Empire Pool

The winners, since 1946, are:

MEN

110 y. Free-style (instituted 1897)

1946*	Huxtable, Graham	1:00·0
1947*	Webb, Roy	58·0
1948*	Mail, Arthur	1:00·8
1949*	Webb, Roy	58·2
1950*	Casa-Grande, Roger	58·0
1951*	Casa-Grande, Roger	56·4
1952*	Casa-Grande, Roger	58·2
1953*	Casa-Grande, Roger	57·7
1954*	Newman, Bernard	54·5
1955*	Newman, Bernard	54·3
1956*	Newman, Bernard	58·6
1957	Edwards, Mike	1:04·3
1958	Newman, Bernard	1:02·8
1959	Hansard, Chris	1:02·8
1960*	Hansard, Chris	55·5
1961	Morgan, Glyn	1:02·5
1962	Hansard, Chris	1:02·7
1963*	Hansard, Chris	53·5
1964	Lewis, Alun	59·3
1965	Lewis, Alun	58·9
1966	Jones, Roddy	57·5
1967	Ross, Keith	59·7
1968	Moran, Kevin	59·0
1969	Woodroffe, Martyn	56·6
1970*	Sheard, David	53·5

* = 100 y.

220 y. Free-style (instituted 1927)

1946	Bates, Harry	2:24·8
1947	Summers, Tony/Webb, Roy	2:33·4
1948	Summers, Tony	2:24·4
1949	Summers, Tony	2:37·7
1950	Casa-Grande, Roger	2:26·2
1951	Williams, Eugene	2:22·5
1952	Williams, Eugene	2:29·1
1953	Casa-Grande, Roger	2:25·9
1954	Stevens, Alban	2:28·6
1955	Newman, Bernard	2:20·6
1956	Newman, Bernard	2:33·2
1957	Edwards, Mike	2:22·1
1958	Edwards, Mike	2:20·9
1959	Jenkins, Brian	2:18·2
1960	Flook, Brian	2:23·0
1961	Flook, Brian	2:25·2
1962	Lewis, Alun	2:21·8
1963	Jones, Roddy	2:19·0
1964	Lewis, Alun	2:15·7
1965	Lewis, Alun	2:13·5
1966	Moran, Kevin	2:10·9
1967	Moran, Kevin	2:13·8
1968	Moran, Kevin	2:11·0
1969	Woodroffe, Martyn	2:05·1
1970	Maher, Sean	2:10·4

440 y. Free-style (instituted 1927)

1946	Bates, Harry	5:24·8
1947	Summers, Tony	No time
1948	Geary, S.	No time
1949	Williams, Eugene	5:44·0
1950	Williams, Eugene	5:25·6
1951	Williams, Eugene	5:06·3
1952	Casa-Grande, Roger	5:18·4
1953	Williams, Eugene	5:20·2
1954	Stevens, Alban	5:32·8
1955	Thomas, C.	5:46·6
1956	Morgan Glyn	5:32·8
1957	Edwards, Mike	5:10·0
1958	Edwards, Mike	5:04·8
1959	Jenkins, Brian	4:56·5
1960	Flook, Brian	5:01·4
1961	Flook, Brian	5:20·0
1962	Flook, Brian	5:04·9
1963	Flook, Brian	5:04·4
1964	Lewis, Alun	4:55·7
1965	Lewis, Gethin	4:47·3
1966	Lewis, Gethin	4:50·4
1967	Lewis, Gethin	4:45·2

1968	Woodroffe, Martyn	4:39·9
1969	Woodroffe, Martyn	4:23·2
1970	Maher, Sean	4:40·5

880 y. Free-style (instituted 1910)

1946	Lewis, Trevor	No time
1947	Mail, Arthur	No time
1948	Mail, Arthur	No time
1949	Not held	
1950	Davies, Ken	No time
1951	Casa-Grande, Roger	12:16·9
1952	Casa-Grande, Roger	11:46·2
1953	Casa-Grande, Roger	11:57·0
1954	Landey, R.	15:07·4
1955	Bebell, D.	13:34·0
1956	Morgan, Glyn	12:25·2
1957	Morgan, Glyn	11:55·0
1958	Flook, Brian	11:25·0
1959	Flook, Brian	10:50·4
1960	Flook, Brian	11:10·0
1961	Flook, Brian	10:29·1
1962	Wooding, Trevor	10:53·2
1963	Flook, Brian	11:06·0
1964	Lewis, Gethin	10:29·5
1965	Lewis, Gethin	10:28·5
1966	Elliott, Terry	10:54·9
1967	Jones, Larry	10:03·5
1968	Jones, Larry	10:00·0
1969	Maher, Sean	9:48·0
1970	Maher, Sean	9:48·9

One mile (instituted 1925)

1946	Mail, Arthur	No time
1947	Summers, Tony	No time
1948	Summers, Tony	No time
1949	Not held	
1950	Not held	
1951	Williams, Eugene	25:00·0
1952	Casa-Grande, Roger	23:22·5
1953	Casa-Grande, Roger	24:43·0
1954	Mutch, Alf	32:27·5
1955	Thomas, C.	25:08·0
1956	Morgan, Glyn	23:51·5
1957	Flook, Brian	25:54·0
1958	Flook, Brian	22:36·0
1959	Flook, Brian	22:40·0
1960	Flook, Brian	22:17·0
1961	Flook, Brian	23:11·6
1962	Flook, Brian	22:42·7
1963	Flook, Brian	22:41·6
1964	Lewis, Gethin	21:35·1
1965	Williams, Peter	21:22·6
1966	Lewis, Gethin	20:55·8
1967	Jones, Larry	20:26·2
1968	Jones, Larry	21:25·8

| 1969 | Maher, Sean | 20:35·3 |
| 1970 | Maher, Sean | 19:51·5 |

110 y. Back-stroke (instituted 1924 for 100 y.)

1946*	Brockway, John	1:04·8
1947*	Summers, Tony	1:03·8
1948*	Brockway, John	1:02·2
1949*	Brockway, John	1:02·0
1950*	Brockway, John	1:01·5
1951*	Stevens, Alban	1:04·6
1952*	Stevens, Alban	1:07·4
1953*	Brockway, John	1:02·7
1954*	Stevens, Alban	1:07·6
1955*	Brockway, John	1:01·0
1956*	Brockway, John	1:07·9
1957	Stevens, Alban	1:12·4
1958	Brockway, John	1:01·1
1959	Birchenhough, Ian	1:11·9
1960*	Jones, Roddy	1:01·0
1961	Stevens, Alban	1:12·8
1962	Jones, Roddy	1:08·8
1963*	Jones, Roddy	1:00·8
1964	Wooding, Trevor	1:07·1
1965	Jones, Roddy	1:05·1
1966	Jones, Roddy	1:05·4
1967	Richards, Mike	1:06·0
1968	Richards, Mike	1:03·5
1969	Richards, Mike	1:05·2
1970*	Richards, Mike	57·3

* = 100 y.

220 y. Back-stroke (instituted 1962)

1962	Jones, Roddy	2:28·6
1963*	Jones, Roddy	2:13·5
1964	Jones, Roddy	2:28·7
1965	Thwaites, Geoff	2:29·3
1966	Jones, Roddy	2:26·0
1967	Jones, Roddy	2:23·5
1968	Richards, Mike	2:18·7
1969	Richards, Mike	2:24·6
1970*	Roberts, Keith	2:08·5

* = 200 y.

110 y. Breast-stroke (instituted 1966)

1966	Tiffany, Trevor	1:14·0
1967	Davies, Keith	1:16·2
1968	Woodroffe, Martyn	1:15·4
1969	Carty, Mark	1:13·2
1970*	Carty, Mark	1:04·0

* = 100 y.

220 y. Breast-stroke (instituted 1924 for 200 y.)

| 1946* | Langley, Bill | 3:01·0 |

1947*	Williams, John	2:57·6
1948*	Davies, Brian	2:49·8
1949*	Williams, John	2:52·8
1950*	Davies, Graham	2:51·0
1951*	Dudley, Terry	2:44·6
1952*	Read, John	2:46·3
1953*	Read, John	2:41·8
1954*	Read, John	2:43·5
1955*	Beavan, John	2:44·1
1956*	Beavan, John	2:43·2
1957	Beavan, John	2:58·2
1958	Beavan, John	2:50·4
1959	Cooke-Davies, Terry	2:51·7
1960	Beavan, John	2:49·0
1961	Beavan, John	2:59·6
1962	Beavan, John	2:47·6
1963*	Jenkins, Hugh	2:30·9
1964	Jenkins, Hugh	2:51·2
1965	Jenkins, Hugh	2:51·7
1966	Davies, Keith	2:49·6
1967	Davies, Keith	2:48·8
1968	Morgan, Trevor	2:48·2
1969	Morgan, Trevor	2:46·4
1970*	Johnson, Nigel	2:23·2

* = 200 y.

110 y. Butterfly (instituted 1966)

1966	Woodroffe, Martyn	1:03·0
1967	Woodroffe, Martyn	1:01·2
1968	Woodroffe, Martyn	59·8
1969	Woodroffe, Martyn	59·1
1970*	Godfrey, Peter	56·1

* = 100 y.

220 y. Butterfly (instituted 1953 for 200 y.)

1953*	Dudley, Terry	2:39·4
1954*	Read, John	2:46·2
1955*	Taylor, Gareth	3:01·9
1956*	Read, John	2:52·4
1957	Evans, Richard	3:00·5
1958	Evans, Richard	2:50·6
1959	Hewitt, John	2:52·0
1960	O'Brien, M.	2:45·6
1961	Harber, Mike	3:01·5
1962	Jenkins, Brian	2:22·3
1963*	Jenkins, Brian	2:03·9
1964	Williams, G.	2:41·0
1965	Woodroffe, Martyn	2:30·7
1966	Woodroffe, Martyn	2:22·4
1967	Woodroffe, Martyn	2:18·0
1968	Woodroffe, Martyn	2:12·5
1969	Woodroffe, Martyn	2:14·2
1970*	Maher, Sean	2:10·6

* = 200 y.

Individual medley (instituted 1954, various distances)

1954*	Stevens, Alban	1:43·8
1955†	Stevens, Alban	2:33·1
1956†	Newman, Bernard	2:43·4
1957‡	Stevens, Alban	2:53·4
1958‡	Stevens, Alban	2:49·9
1959‡	Evans, Richard	2:46·9
1960*	Stevens, Alban	1:33·6
1961†	Stevens, Alban	2:16·0
1962§	Jones, Roddy	1:38·5
1963*	Jones, Roddy	1:27·4
1964†	Jones, Roddy	2:38·1
1965†	Thwaites, Geoff	2:31·8

* = 133⅓ y.   † = 200 y.
‡ = 220 y.   § = 136⅔ y.

220 y. Individual medley (instituted 1969)

1969	Woodroffe, Martyn	2:23·8
1970*	Maher, Sean	2:59·7

* = 266⅔ y.

440 y. Individual medley (instituted 1966)

1966	Woodroffe, Martyn	5:17·2
1967	Woodroffe, Martyn	5:14·0
1968	Woodroffe, Martyn	4:59·4
1969	Woodroffe, Martyn	5:09·0
1970*	Maher, Sean	4:38·4

* = 400 y.

WOMEN

110 y. Free-style (instituted 1905 for 100 y.)

1946*	Grande, Mary	1:09·6
1947*	Linton, Pip	1:06·4
1948*	Linton, Pip	1:06·0
1949*	Linton, Pip	1:05·4
1950*	Linton, Pip	1:03·1
1951*	Linton, Pip	1:03·4
1952*	Linton, Pip	1:04·5
1953*	Linton, Pip	1:04·7
1954*	Dallimore, Vida	1:06·2
1955*	Linton, Pip	1:05·2
1956*	Francis, Geraldine	1:10·6
1957	Hooper, Jocelyn	1:12·2
1958	Hooper, Jocelyn	1:10·3
1959	Hooper, Jocelyn	1:09·5
1960*	Redwood, Sidney	1:01·0
1961	Hooper, Jocelyn	1:11·6
1962	Hooper, Jocelyn	1:10·7
1963*	Phillips, Glenda	1:01·2
1964	Hooper, Jocelyn	1:10·5
1965	Phillips, Glenda	1:08·1
1966	Phillips, Glenda	1:07·0
1967	Phillips, Glenda	1:07·1

1968	Wheeler, Anne	1:06·2
1969	Wheeler, Anne	1:06·7
1970*	Davies, Christine	57·9
	* = 100 y.	

220 y. Free-style (instituted 1927)

1946	James, S.	3:09·0
1947	Linton, Pip	2:42·5
1948	Dowsell, Margaret	3:11·0
1949	Linton, Pip	2:45·7
1950	Linton, Pip	2:47·4
1951	Linton, Pip	2:41·9
1952	Linton, Pip	2:48·2
1953	Linton, Pip	2:41·6
1954	Dallimore, Vida	2:56·0
1955	Linton, Pip	2:42·1
1956	Francis, Gerladine	2:54·4
1957	Francis, Geraldine/Hooper,	
	Jocelyn	2:41·1
1958	Hooper, Jocelyn	2:37·7
1959	Hooper, Jocelyn	2:37·4
1960	Hooper, Jocelyn	2:38·2
1961	Hooper, Jocelyn	2:42·9
1962	Hooper, Jocelyn	2:41·2
1963	Phillips, Glenda	2:31·9
1964	Phillips, Glenda	2:30·5
1965	Phillips, Glenda	2:29·6
1966	Phillips, Glenda	2:28·1
1967	Phillips, Glenda	2:28·9
1968	Bowen, Bernadette	2:29·9
1969	Bowen, Bernadette	2:28·0
1970	Hurn, Sally	2:27·4

440 y. Free-style (instituted 1927)

1946	Westacott, Marion	7:00·0
1947	Linton, Pip	6:02·0
1948	Linton, Pip	No time
1949	Linton, Pip	6:30·4
1950	Linton, Pip	5:50·1
1951	Linton, Pip	5:49·8
1952	Linton, Pip	6:07·6
1953	Linton, Pip	5:47·7
1954	Dallimore, Vida	5:56·4
1955	Linton, Pip	5:48·2
1956	Francis, Geraldine	6:34·6
1957	Francis, Geraldine	6:07·7
1958	Francis, Geraldine	5:49·4
1959	Francis, Geraldine	5:35·8
1960	Francis, Geraldine	5:40·5
1961	Hooper, Jocelyn	5:56·5
1962	Hooper, Jocelyn	5:41·3
1963	Hooper, Jocelyn	5:40·4
1964	Bowen, Bernadette	5:39·3
1965	Mitrenko, Susan	5:40·4
1966	Phillips, Glenda	5:14·1

1967	Bowen, Bernadette	5:27·3
1968	Bowen, Bernadette	5:17·4
1969	Bowen, Bernadette	5:12·6
1970	Jones, Sue	5:17·8

880 y. Free-style (instituted 1937)

1946	Westacott, Marion	No time
1947–49	Not held	
1950	Dowsell, Margaret	No time
1951	Dallimore, Vida	No time
1952	Not held	
1953*	Dallimore, Vida	12:50·7
1954	Jones, F.	19:12·3
1955	Hughes, Christine	13:49·1
1956*	Francis, Geraldine	13:53·0
1957	Francis, Geraldine	12:18·0
1958	Francis, Geraldine	12:09·0
1959	Hooper, Jocelyn	13:14·5
1960	Hooper, Jocelyn	12:37·4
1961*	Hooper, Jocelyn	12:19·0
1962	Hooper, Jocelyn	11:55·8
1963	Hooper, Jocelyn	11:44·4
1964	Bowen, Bernadette	12:17·4
1965	Phillips, Glenda	10:48·4
1966	Phillips, Glenda	11:03·5
1967	Bowen, Bernadette	11:41·8
1968	Bowen, Bernadette	11:19·6
1969	Jones, Sue	10:41·3
1970	Jones, Sue	10:35·2
	* = open water	

One mile (instituted 1925)

1946	Vittle, Pat	No time
1947	No result available	
1948	Dowsell, Margaret	No time
1949	Not held	
1950	No result available	
1951	Dallimore, Vida	No time
1952	No result available	
1953	Dallimore, Vida	26:37·1
1954	Not held	
1955	Hughes, Christine	27:36·3
1956	Francis, Geraldine	27:48·5
1957*	Francis, Geraldine	27:46·0
1958*	Francis, Geraldine	30:12·0
1959	Hooper, Jocelyn	26:59·1
1960	Francis, Geraldine	24:48·8
1961	Hooper, Jocelyn	25:55·1
1962	Hooper, Jocelyn	24:55·8
1963	Bowen, Bernadette	24:56·2
1964	Bowen, Bernadette	25:01·5
1965	Phillips, Glenda	22:15·1
1966	Bowen, Bernadette	24:18·6
1967	Bowen, Bernadette	24:26·6
1968	Bowen, Bernadette	23:19·1

1969	Bowen, Bernadette	23:06·5
1970	Jones, Sue	22:15·8
	* = open water	

110 y. Back-stroke (instituted 1925 for 100 y.)

1946*	Vittle, Pat	1:15·0
1947*	Vittle, Pat	No time
1948*	Vittle, Pat	No time
1949*	Daymond, Rosina	1:17·0
1950*	Seaborne, Shirley	1:17·0
1951*	Daymond, Rosina	1:13·8
1952*	Crossman, Judy	1:16·5
1953*	Crosswaite (Daymond), Rosina	1:16·4
1954*	Dallimore, Vida	1:18·8
1955*	Dewar, Lesley	1:14·8
1956*	Davies, Diane	1:17·3
1957	Davies, Diane	1:24·4
1958	Dixon, Joyce	1:22·7
1959	Dixon, Joyce	1:20·4
1960*	Dixon, Joyce	1:08·2
1961	Dixon, Joyce	1:21·1
1962	Ford, Carol	1:18·4
1963*	Ford, Carol	1:08·2
1964	Lawson, Janice	1:18·6
1965	Lawson, Janice	1:19·6
1966	Lawson, Janice	1:19·5
1967	Lawson, Janice	1:17·9
1968	Lawson, Janice	1:16·6
1969	Lawson, Janice	1:15·1
1970*	Williams, Avis	1:07·0
	* = 100 y.	

220 y. Back-stroke (instituted 1966)

1966	Lawson, Janice	2:52·0
1967	Lawson, Janice	2:49·1
1968	Lawson, Janice	2:52·1
1969	Lawson, Janice	2:48·7
1970*	Hiron, Carol	2:27·6
	* = 200 y.	

110 y. Breast-stroke (instituted 1966)

1966	Willett, Yvonne	1:22·4
1967	Bevan, Julie	1:22·9
1968	Davies, Christine	1:25·2
1969	Davies, Christine	1:26·4
1970*	Wells, Pat	1:12·6
	* = 100 y.	

220 y. Breast-stroke (instituted 1925 for 200 y.)

1946*	Wade, Pat	3:04·0
1947*	Wade, Pat	3:20·0
1948*	Dowsell, Margaret	3:00·2
1949*	Dowsell, Margaret	3:05·8

1950*	Dowsell, Margaret	3:02·0
1951*	Libby, Diana	3:00·6
1952	Lewis, Margaret	2:57·4
1953*	Lewis, Margaret	3:00·3
1954*	Lewis, Margaret	2:58·0
1955*	Libby, Diana	2:55·0
1956*	Libby, Diana	3:02·5
1957	Howells, Gillian	3:15·3
1958	Howells, Gillian	3:05·5
1959	Shaddick, Cynthia	3:05·5
1960	Shaddick Cynthia	3:02·8
1961	Shaddick, Cynthia	3:14·2
1962	Shaddick, Cynthia	3:04·3
1963*	Lemare, Janet	2:48·9
1964	Phillips, Kathryn	3:09·1
1965	Edwards, Ceinwen	3:03·6
1966	Willett, Yvonne	3:00·1
1967	Bevan, Julie	2:59·3
1968	Edwards, Ceinwen	3:00·3
1969	Edwards, Ceinwen	3:01·1
1970*	Davies, Christine	2:37·5
	* = 200 y.	

110 y. Butterfly (instituted 1954)

1954*	Lewis, Margaret	1:20·1
1955*	Lewis, Margaret	1:21·5
1956*	Phillips, J.	1:30·7
1957	Francis, Geraldine	1:28·4
1958	Francis, Geraldine	1:23·9
1959	Francis, Geraldine	1:24·0
1960*	Howells, Gillian	1:13·0
1961	Howells, Gillian	1:17·5
1962	Phillips, Glenda	1:12·7
1963*	Phillips, Glenda	1:07·2
1964	Hooper, Jocelyn	1:24·4
1965	Phillips, Glenda	1:12·7
1966	Phillips, Glenda	1:12·7
1967	Phillips, Glenda	1:12·0
1968	Phillips, Glenda	1:12·8
1969	Adams (Phillips), Glenda	1:11·0
1970*	Davies, Christine	1:08·0
	* = 100 y.	

220 y. Butterfly (instituted 1969)

1969	Adams (Phillips), Glenda	2:48·0
1970*	Bull, Frances	2:39·8
	* = 200 y.	

Individual medley (instituted 1954, various distances)

1954*	Dallimore, Vida	1:48·6
1955†	Lewis Margaret	2:59·0
1956†	Davies, Diane	3:08·0
1957‡	Francis, Geraldine	3:03·9
1958‡	Francis, Geraldine	3:01·0

1959‡	Hooper, Jocelyn	3:03·1
1960*	Hooper, Jocelyn	1:40·1
1961†	Hooper, Jocelyn	2:21·4
1962§	Phillips, Glenda	1:44·9
1963*	Phillips, Glenda	1:34·6
1964‡	Hooper, Jocelyn	2:57·7
1965‡	Phillips, Glenda	2:46·4

    * = 133⅓ y.   † = 200 y.
    ‡ = 220 y.   § = 136⅔ y.

220 y. Individual medley (instituted 1969)

| 1969 | Comins, Jackie | 2:45·9 |
| 1970* | Davies, Christine | 3:20·5 |

    * = 266⅔ y.

440 y. Individual medley (instituted 1966)

1966	Phillips, Glenda	5:56·5
1967	Phillips, Glenda	5:55·7
1968	Phillips, Glenda	5:59·0
1969	Comins, Jackie	5:58·5
1970*	Evans, Janet	5:44·0

    * = 400 y.

WELSH, Charmian (Great Britain, 17 May 1937–   ). This tall girl from Durham burst on to the diving scene at 15, in the Olympics of 1952 when she came fifth in the sprinboard diving. Two years later, she was fourth in the Commonwealth Games in Vancouver and sixth in the European championships. Her 1956 Olympic appearance was less successful for she did not make the last eight in either the springboard or highboard events. But in 1958, in Cardiff, she won both Commonwealth diving titles.

Charmian won fifteen A.S.A. championships: highboard 1955–58, springboard 1953/54, plain diving 1953, '56, '57 and 1 m. springboard six times, 1952–56 and 1958.

WENDEN, Michael (Australia, 17 Nov. 1949–   ). Australia's 'Swimming Machine' Mike Wenden does not so much swim as attack the water, but he slaughtered the might of America in the 1968 Olympics in winning the 100 and 200 m. In the sprint, he beat Ken Walsh by six-tenths in 52·2, a world record. His victim in the 200 m. was the 1964 quadruple gold medal winner Don Schollander. Six-tenths was the victory margin again, with Wenden clocking 1:55·2.

Wenden versus Schollander was a battle of the extremes—a contrast of the classic against the unorthodox. The sandy-haired Australian was the rough-stroking, tough, animated windmill. The sleek, gold-haired American the immaculate, effortless, flowing stylist. In the end, Wenden using ten to fifteen strokes more per length than his rival, was just too strong.

For all that Wenden's stroke looked wrong on the surface, underwater, where it counted, his command of the alien element, the power of his pull and the co-ordination of his arm cycle made him 100 per cent effective. And his preparations for Mexico were almost super-human. He covered between 12,000 to 15,000 m. a day—distances no sprinter had ever done before. And the effect could be seen in the fitness of his body, 12 st. but without an ounce of excess weight.

The Australian's Mexico haul also included a silver and a bronze in the 4 × 200 and 4 × 100 m. relays in which his last leg 'splits' were 1:54·3 and 51·7. There was no medal from the medley relay, but Wenden's anchor leg was covered in an amazing 51·4, worth probably under 52·0 from a standing start.

For his Mexico achievements Wenden received the M.B.E.

Wenden first came to world notice during the 1966 Commonwealth Games in Jamaica where he beat Scotland's Bobby McGregor in the 110 y. (54·0) and broke the world 220 y. record (1:57·3) on the first leg of the 4 × 220 y. relay. A third gold came in the 4 × 110 y. relay but the Australians were disqualified in the medley relay for a flying take-over having won in a world record 4:03·5. Later that week they made a solo record attempt and thanks to Wenden's last leg in 52·5 were successful with 4:03·2.

The Sydney boy started serious swimming at 12, broke his first records at 13—New South Wales under 14 marks for 100, 200 and 400 m. In 1966 he broke the Australian junior 100 and 200 m. marks in the same swim—a most unusual achievement—and became the first junior to win the senior 100 m. title.

Not in the superb condition, because of studies, that had brought his Mexico successes, Wenden was still too good for the rest of the Commonwealth's free-stylers in the 1970 Games in Edinburgh. He retained the sprint title (53·1), won the new 200 m. event (1:56·7) and anchored Australia to victory in both free-style relays to bring his Commonwealth gold medal tally to seven, the highest number ever to have been won by a single competitor in the swimming.

WESTERN DISTRICT. The Western Counties A.S.A. are the smallest of the English districts and consists of Cornwall, Devon, Dorset, Gloucestershire, Somerset and Wiltshire—a geographical area in the toe of England which makes it very difficult to administer.

Edgar Jordan of Gloucester served the West for forty-five years, as honorary secreatry from 1907–30 and then as honorary treasurer from 1931–51. The present secretary, Bill Tiver has held office since 1956.

WETZKO, Gabriele (East Germany, 28 Aug. 1954–). An Olympic silver medallist at 14, in the 4 × 100 m. free-style, fourth in the 200 m. (2:12·3) and fifth in the 400 m. (4:40·2) at the 1968 Olympics, Gabriele, from Leipzig, became the first European woman to swim 100 m. in under a minute (59·6) in Budapest on 23 Aug. 1969.

In that year she also set European records for 200 m. (2:08·9) and 400 m. (4:36·1), was a member of the East German squad who broke the world mark for 4 × 100 m. medley and won the 100 and 400 m. European Youth titles.

Tall (1 m. 64 cm.) and slim, Wetzko belies her build in the water where she shows tremendous power and speed. In the European championships of 1970 she won the 100 and 200 m. free-style titles and was the architect of East Germany's victories in the free-style and medley relays. She equalled, for the second time, her European record (59·6)

in winning the sprint and clipped this time to 59·3, the fastest time in the world in 1970, on the first leg of the free-style relay. She also broke her own European 200 m. record with 2:08·2.

But her finest performance was her anchor leg in the medley relay in which she turned a 3·7 sec. deficit behind the Soviet Union into a 1·2 sec. world record breaking victory (4:00·8) with a split of 58·2. Even allowing for the advantage of a flying take-over (about 0·5 sec.) this was equivalently inside the 58·9 world record of Australia's Dawn Fraser (see FRASER, DAWN).

WHITE, Belle (Great Britain, 1 Sept. 1894–). The honour of being the first Briton to win an Olympic diving medal is just one of the achievements of Isabella Mary White, of London who, among other feats, was also the first British diver to win a European championship. The fact that fifteen years divided these successes is some indication of Belle's tremendous courage, talent and ability.

Belle had been diving for eight years before women's events were included in the Olympic programme in 1912. She had trained carefully for her big occasion, even going to Sweden to practice on their fine wooden highboards the year before the Games. And her reward in Stockholm was the bronze medal.

In 1927, just before her thirty-third birthday, she won the European high-board title in Bologna with 36·04 points. Between these two successes, she had competed in the Olympics of 1920 (4th) and 1924 (6th). And she made her fourth Olympic appearance in 1928 but did not reach the last six.

A good swimmer as well as a diver, she won the Swedish 'Magistern' in 1911 which was a test of both swimming and diving. There were no A.S.A. diving championships then—in fact, the first one was not until 1924 for highboard, which Belle won and went on doing so until 1929. She was also the first winner, in 1916, of the Ladies Plain Diving Bath championship organized by the Amateur Diving Association (later to become part of the A.S.A.) and she won this nine times.

Her only local highboard facility in the early days was in the men's pool at the Highgate Ponds to which women were admitted, as a concession, on one day a week. Much of her training for her competitions from 33-foot boards, was done from tiny platforms attached to unsteady ladders, rising from the end of seaside piers at Brighton and Clacton! Still enthusiastic, still interested, Belle stayed on in her sport as an official and committee-woman.

WIEGAND, Frank t(East Germany, 15 Mar. 1943–). Voted 'Swimmer of the Championships' at the 1966 Europeans in Utrecht, Frank Wiegand set a world mark for 400 m. free-style (4:11·1) and European figures for 400 m. medley (4:47·9) in winning these titles and he added a third gold and two silvers in East German relay teams.

But the best season for this soldier from Rostock was 1964 when he was second by 2·7 to Don Schollander in the Olympic 400 m. free-style in 4:14·9 and was a member of the combined East/West German team who won the silvers in the 4 × 100 and 4 × 200 m. free-style relays.

Wiegand swam in three Olympics—as a relay man (medalless) in 1960, and for relays again in 1968 when his team won the silvers in the medley. He was also a medallist in the 1962 European championships—400 m. free-style (3rd), 4 × 100 m. medley (1st) and 4 × 200 m. free-style (3rd).

His best times for free-style were: 53·7 (100 m.); 1:57·8 (200 m.); 4:11·1 400 m.); 9:03·8 (800 m.) and for medley: 2:13·5 (200 m.) and 4:47·9 (400 m.). All but his 100 m. were world marks.

WILKINSON, Diana (Great Britain, 17 Mar. 1944–). The youngest at the time ever to swim for Britain, Diana Wilkinson was only 13 years, 3 months and 4 days in 1957 when she competed against Germany in Liverpool. And three months later she had become the youngest

winner of the A.S.A. women's 110 y. title (65·7).

Swimming was wonderful for this curly-haired little girl from Stockport who was always laughing at that time. It was only later in her ten-year international career, when too much had been asked of her, that she experienced the anguish of defeat. Her biggest disappointment was the 1962 European championships. She was European record-holder for 100 m. (62·4 for the longer 110 y.). In the Leipzig final, three girls touched in a line, Heidi Pechstein East Germany was given the verdict—though a great number of experienced officials were convinced the British girl was first—and the time was 63·3.

Diana's great year was 1958 when she swam in the Commonwealth Games in Cardiff and anchored England's medley relay team to victory. Her last-leg free-style rival was Olympic champion Dawn Fraser—and Diana's three team-mates, Judy Grinham, Anita Lonsbrough and Christine Gosden knew they would have to swim their hearts out to give their 14-year-old last girl the big lead to withstand the challenge of the Australian. They did, and Diana swam one second faster than she had ever done before to touch 1·1 ahead. England's 4:54·0 was not only a world record for the yards distance but also for 4 × 100 m.

Good team girl Diana won ten major Games medals, five each in European championships (1958/62) and Commonwealth Games (1958/62/66) . . . but except for that 100 m. individual silver in 1962, all the rest were for relays. She swam in the 1960 Olympics, but did not get through her heat of the 100 m. and her chances at the 1964 Tokyo Games were ruined before she left Britain by a badly administered injection which made one arm almost useless.

She was the first British girl to swim 100 y. in under a minute (9 Aug. 1957—57·3) for which she was elected England's 'Swimmer of the Year'. She was also the *Daily Express* 'Sportswoman of the Year' in 1957—at 13. Diana won seven A.S.A. titles: 110 y. (1957, 1961–64) and 220 y. (1961/62). A number of times she swam in British teams with her brother Chris, who in 1961–62 won the A.S.A. 220 y. breast-stroke title.

WILLIAMS, Esther (United States). Esther Williams, from Los Angeles, might have been an Olympic swimming champion. Instead she became an aquatic film star. American 100 m. free-style champion in 1939 (69·0), Esth'ers Olympic hopes were blasted by World War II. So she was one of seventy-five girls who auditioned for the female lead opposite Johnny Weissmuller in the 1940 San Francisco World's Fair Aquacade. Johnny wanted someone tall, picked Esther from the crowd and that was the end of her amateur swimming career and the start of her movie fame.

WINDEATT, Graham (Australia, 1954–). Commonwealth 1,500 m. record-holder (16:23·1) before the 1970 Games, Windeatt, from the Don Talbot squad at Auburn, Sydney, concentrated on winning this event in Edinburgh. And win he did, by 10·7 sec. from his team-mate Max Tavasci. His 16:23·8, was 0·8 outside his six month old record but he had the satisfaction of breaking the Commonwealth 800 m. mark on the way (8:36·2).

WINDLE, Bob (Australia, 7 Nov. 1944–). A relay reserve at 15, Olympic 1,500 m. champion four years later and a double relay medallist four years after, that is Robert George Windle's proud achievement.

Windle's victory in Tokyo was something of a surprise for his pre-Games times did not challenge those of his American rivals. But, on the day, he was too good for everyone and he proved it with his Games record of 17:01·7 and victory by 1·3 sec. And to show his versatility, he also won a bronze medal in Australia's 4 × 100 m. free-style relay squad.

In Mexico Windle's fine competitive temperament enabled him to rise to the occasion and come sixth in the 200 m. and help Australia to the silver medals in the 4 × 200 m. and bronzes in the 4 × 100 m. free-style relays, with personal 'splits' of 1:59·7 and 53·7.

Between these three Olympics, Windle from Sydney swam successfully in two Commonwealth Games. In 1962, he was third in the 440 y. (4:23·1), second in the 1,650 y. (17:44·5) and first with the 4 × 220 y. relay squad. In 1966, he won the 440 y. (4:15·0) and got two more golds in the 4 × 110 and 4 × 220 y. relays.

Although his big successes were for the longer distances, his only world records were for 200 m. (2:00·3, 1963) and 220 y. (2:01·1, 1964). He won eleven Australian titles: 100 m./220 y. and 400 m./440 y. (1962–64), 880 y. (1963) and 1,500 m./1,650 y. (1961–64).

WOLSTENHOLME, Celia (Great Britain, 18 May 1915–). Commonwealth 200 y. breast-stroke champion in 1930 (2:54·8), Celia Wolstenholme from Manchester was not the favourite for the European 200 m. crown the following year—her team-mate and fellow-Mancunian Margery Hinton (see HINTON, MARGERY) having broken the world record only five week before the championships opened in Magdeburg. But it was second string Celia who won in 3:16·2 with Margery third. Miss Hinton got her revenge in the Olympics of 1932 when she came fourth (3:11·7) while Miss Wolstenholme (3:24·5) did not qualify for the final.

Celia broke world records for 200 y. (2:56·0 and 2:54·6) and 400 m. (6:41·4) breast-stroke, all in 1930—the year she won her only A.S.A. breast-stroke title. Her younger sister Beatrice (Beatie) won two bronze medals for free-style in 1934 —in relays at the Commonwealth Games and European championships— and four A.S.A. free-style titles: 220 y. (1933) and 440 y. (1933–35).

WOODROFFE, Martyn (Great Britain, 8 Sept. 1950–). Dour determination, talent and hard training took Martyn John Woodroffe from Cardiff, the best swimmer to come out of Wales since Paul Radmilovic (see RADMILOVIC,

PAUL), to the silver medal spot in the 200 m. butterfly (2:09·0) at the 1968 Olympics—the only Briton to win a swimming medal in Mexico.

But Woodroffe's swimming talents are not confined to his Olympic medal style. In 1969 he was the fastest Briton at the A.S.A. championships for eight of the thirteen events: free-style—220 y. 2:01·5, 440 y. 4:19·6 (British record 400 m.), 880 y. 9:05·4; 1,650 y. 17:34·0; butter-fly—110 y. 59·2, 220 y. 2:09·9; medley—220 y. 2:17·6 and 440 y. 4:55·1. That year also he won the international invi-tation 200 m. butterfly in Santa Clara, California, in a European record of 2:07·8 and set British marks for 100 m. butterfly (58·8) and 400 m. medley (4:49·5) plus a 200 m. medley mark (2:17·1) in Wurtzburg.

Sadly, 1970 proved to be a disappoint-ing year for the Welshman. He lost the Commonwealth 200 m. butterfly title by 0·1 (2:09·1), was only third in the 200 m. medley—though his 2:16·6 was a British record—and was out of the medals in the 100 m. butterfly and 400 m. medley. His only consolation in Edinburgh was that the Welsh team, thanks to his butterfly leg, took the bronze medals in the medley relay and for the first time ever beat England.

He retained his 110 and 220 y. butter-fly and 220 and 440 y. medley crowns in the A.S.A. championships but was beaten by Ray Terrell (see TERRELL, RAY) in the 440 y. free-style. Then, as an ex-cellent captain, for the first time, of the British team he had a disasterous ap-pearance in the European championships. And on the way home from Barcelona, Woodroffe announced his retirement from swimming only five days after his 20th birthday.

WORLD RECORDS. After sixty years of chopping and changing, a single, tidy list of world records became established in 1968 (operative from 1 Jan. 1969) when F.I.N.A. settled for thirty-one metric distances and long-course (see LONG COURSE) times only for their record book. Thus sixteen events for men and fifteen for women emerged from the 105 distances which had been in and out of the list since official world records were first recognized in 1908.

Of the records of the modern era, eight for men (100, 200, 400, 1,500 m. free-style, 100 and 200 m. back-stroke and 100 and 200 m. breast-stroke) and one for women (100 m. free-style) were among the original list of 1908 when F.I.N.A. ratified not only the best of that year but also certain authenticated times set previously. At that time, world records for distances under 800 m. could be set in pools of any length over 25 y., and it was possible for times to be taken mid-course not just at the bath end.

The first cutting back of record dis-tances was in 1948 when out went the little-raced 300 y., 300 m., 1,000 y. 1,000 m. free-style, 400 m. back-stroke and 400 and 500 m. breast-stroke. Four years later saw the elimination of 500 y. and 500 m. free-style, 150 y. back-stroke and, with the separation of breast-stroke and butterfly (to give four styles of swim-ming), the 3 × 100 y. and m. medley relays.

The traditional English linear distances (100, 200, 400 y. and mile) went out on 1 May 1957, being replaced by multiples of 110 y. (the 1 ft. 11 in. longer linear equivalent of metric distance). At this time, F.I.N.A. also decided that only long course performances would be accepted for all distances. Finally, during the 1968 Olympics, with even Britain moving towards metric measure-ment, all the yards records were thrown out.

In the building up of world record lists, there have been a number of anomalies. Early record retrospective ratification of records was not consis-tent. Freddy Lane (Aus) see LANE, FREDDY) was the first man to swim 100 y. in under a minute (Oct. 1902—59·6) but this was not ratified although his 2:28·6 for 220 y. the same year (appear-ing wrongly in the F.I.N.A. handbook as 1903) was. And although Lane's 220 y. time was immeasurably faster than the 2:31·6 for the shorter 200 m. by Otto Scheff (Austria) on 11 Nov. 1908, it is Scheff and not Lane who appears as the first 200 m. world-record-holder. In fact, it was not until Mar. 1911 that America's Charles Daniels (see DANIELS, CHARLES) swam 200 m. (2:25·4) faster than Lane's nine-year-old 220 y. time.

There were wonderful performances by Barney Kieran (see KIERAN, BARNEY) between 1904–06, which were Australian records but only one was accepted by F.I.N.A. as a world mark. Later, in Aug. 1931, when Yvonne Godard (France) was credited with the first world record for 800 m. (12:18·8), officials overlooked the year-old ratified 880 y. mark (11:41·2) by Helene Madison (USA) (see MADISON, HELENE) which was equivalently 41·8 sec. better. In the early days, too, the system of claiming records was not as efficient as it is to-day and many world record breaking performances do not appear simply because no claims were put in for them.

In order that a world record can be ratified by F.I.N.A., the following conditions must be observed by the swimmer or team:

1. The swim must be made in still water either in a scratch competition or in an individual race against time held in public and announced by advertisement at least three clear days in advance.
2. No pacemaking is permitted nor any device or plan used which has this effect.
3. There shall be three time-keepers. If at least two times are the same, this shall be accepted. If all three times are different, the middle one shall be accepted. If electrical timing is used, this shall have precedence over any human time-keepers.

In the following lists, the eras when 'short course' and 'long course only' records were ratified are separated by dotted lines. There is a third division in the breast-stroke lists indicating those marks which were set when underwater swimming was permitted. Tables showing the ins and outs of the various world record distances are on pages 218–221.

* = set in a bath shorter than 50 m.

MEN

100 m. Free-style

1:05·8*	Halmay, Zoltan (Hun)	Vienna	3 Dec. 1905
1:02·8*	Daniels, Charles (USA)	New York	15 Apr. 1910
1:02·4*	Bretting, Kurt (Ger)	Brussels	6 Apr. 1912
1:01·6	Kahanamoku, Duke (USA)	Hamburg	20 July 1912
1:01·4	Kahanamoku, Duke (USA)	New York	9 Aug. 1918
1:00·4	Kahanamoku, Duke (USA)	Antwerp	24 Aug. 1920
58·6	Weissmuller, Johnny (USA)	Alameda	9 July 1922
57·4*	Weissmuller, Johnny (USA)	Miami	17 Feb. 1924
56·8*	Fick, Peter (USA)	New Haven	2 Mar. 1934
56·6*	Fick, Peter (USA)	New Haven	5 Mar. 1935
56·4*	Fick, Peter (USA)	New Haven	11 Feb. 1936
55·9*	Ford, Alan (USA)	New Haven	13 Apr. 1944
55·8*	Jany, Alex (Fra)	Mentone	15 Sept. 1947
55·4*	Ford, Alan (USA)	New Haven	29 June 1948
54·8*	Cleveland, Dick (USA)	New Haven	1 Apr. 1954
55·4	Henricks, Jon (Aus)	Melbourne	30 Nov. 1956
55·2y	Devitt, John (Aus)	Sydney	19 Jan. 1957
54·6	Devitt, John (Aus)	Brisbane	28 Jan. 1957
54·4	Clark, Steve (USA)	Los Angeles	18 Aug. 1961
53·6	Dos Santos, Manuel (Braz)	Rio de Janeiro	20 Sept. 1961
52·9	Gottvalles, Alain (Fra)	Budapest	13 Sept. 1964
52·6	Walsh, Ken (USA)	Winnipeg	27 July 1967
52·6	Zorn, Zac (USA)	Long Beach	2 Sept. 1968

UNITED STATES CHAMPIONS. In the 1968 Olympic Games Gary Hall (*top*) was runner-up to Charles Hickcox (*middle*) in the 400m medley. Hickcox also won the 200m medley. Mike Burton (*bottom*) was first in the 400 and 1,500m free-style

(*Left*) WEISSMULLER, JOHNNY.
Weismuller (right), winner of
five Olympic gold meals, with
Australia's 'Boy' Charlton, the
1,500m champion, at the 1924
Games in Paris

(*Below*) WENDEN, MICHAEL.
Wenden with his Australian
team-mate Karen Moras at the
1970 Commonwealth Games

| 52·2 | Wenden, Mike (Aus) | Mexico City | 19 Oct. 1968 |
| 51·9 | Spitz, Mark (USA) | Los Angeles | 23 Aug. 1970 |

200 m. Free-style

2:31·6*	Scheff, Otto (Aut)	Vienna	11 Nov. 1908
2:30·0*	Beaurepaire, Frank (Aus)	Exeter	9 Sept. 1910
2:25·4*	Daniels, Charles (USA)	Pittsburg	28 Mar. 1911
2:21·6*	Ross, Norman (USA)	San Francisco	24 Nov. 1916
2:15·6*	Weissmuller, Johnny (USA)	Honolulu	26 May 1922
2:08·0*	Weissmuller, Johnny (USA)	AnnArbor	5 Apr. 1927
2:07·2*	Medica, Jack (USA)	Chicago	12 Apr. 1935
2:06·2*	Smith, Bill (USA)	Columbus	12 Feb. 1944
2:05·4*	Jany, Alex (Fra)	Marseille	20 Sept. 1946
2:04·6*	Marshall, John (Aus)	New Haven	31 Mar. 1950
2:03·9*	Konno, Ford (USA)	Columbus	27 Feb. 1954
2:03·4*	Wardrop, Jack (GB)	Columbus	4 Mar. 1955
2:01·5*	Hanley, Dick (USA)	Minneapolis	8 Mar. 1957
2:04·8y	Konrads, John (Aus)	Sydney	18 Jan. 1958
2:03·2y	Konrads, John (Aus)	Sydney	5 Mar. 1958
2:03·0	Yamanaka, Tsuyoshi (Jap)	Osaka	22 Aug. 1958
2:02·2y	Konrads, John (Aus)	Sydney	16 Jan. 1959
2:01·5	Yamanaka, Tsuyoshi (Jap)	Osaka	26 July 1959
2:01·2	Yamanaka, Tsuyoshi (Jap)	Osaka	24 June 1961
2:01·1	Yamanaka, Tsuyoshi (Jap)	Tokyo	6 Aug. 1961
2:00·4	Yamanaka, Tsuyoshi (Jap)	Los Angeles	20 Aug. 1961
2:00·3	Windle, Bob (Aus)	Tokyo	21 Apr. 1963
1:58·8	Schollander, Don (USA)	Los Angeles	27 July 1963
1:58·5	Schollander, Don (USA)	Tokyo	17 Aug. 1963
1:58·4	Schollander, Don (USA)	Osaka	24 Aug. 1963
1:58·2	Klein, Hans-Joachim (WGer)	Dortmund	24 May 1964
1:57·6	Schollander, Don (USA)	Los Altos	1 Aug. 1964
1:57·2	Schollander, Don (USA)	Los Angeles	29 July 1966
1:56·2	Schollander, Don (USA)	Lincoln	19 Aug. 1966
1:56·0	Schollander, Don (USA)	Winnipeg	29 July 1967
1:55·7	Schollander, Don (USA)	Oak Park	12 Aug. 1967
1:54·3	Schollander, Don (USA)	Long Beach	30 Aug. 1968
1:54·3	Spitz, Mark (USA)	Santa Clara	12 July 1969

400 m. Free-style

5:36·8	Taylor, Henry (Eng)	London	16 July 1908
5:35·8*	Battersby, Syd (Eng)	London	21 Sept. 1911
5:29·0*	Kenyery, Alajos (Hun)	Magdeburg	21 Apr. 1912
5:28·4*	Las Torres, Béla (Hun)	Budapest	5 June 1912
5:24·4	Hodgson, George (Can)	Stockholm	13 July 1912
5:21·6*	Hatfield, Jack (Eng)	London	26 Sept. 1912
5:14·6*	Ross, Norman (USA)	Los Angeles	9 Oct. 1919
5:14·4*	Ross, Norman (USA)	Brighton Beach	25 Sept. 1921
5:11·8*	Borg, Arne (Swe)	Stockholm	9 Apr. 1922
5:06·6	Weissmuller, Johnny (USA)	Honolulu	22 June 1922
4:57·0*	Weissmuller, Johnny (USA)	New Haven	6 Mar. 1923
4:54·7*	Borg, Arne (Swe)	Stockholm	9 Dec. 1924
4:50·3*	Borg, Arne (Swe)	Stockholm	11 Sept. 1925
4:47·0*	Taris, Jean (Fra)	Paris	16 Apr. 1931
4:46·4	Makino, Shozo (Jap)	Tokyo	14 Aug. 1933

N

4:38·7*	Medica, Jack (USA)	Honolulu	30 Aug. 1934
4:38·5*	Smith, Bill (USA)	Honolulu	13 May 1941
4:35·2	Jany, Alex (Fra)	Monte Carlo	12 Sept. 1947
4:34·6	Furuhashi, Hironashin (Jap)	Tokyo	24 July 1949
4:33·3	Furuhashi, Hironashin (Jap)	Los Angeles	18 Aug. 1949
4:33·1*	Marshall, John (Aus)	New Haven	11 Mar. 1950
4:29·5*	Marshall, John (Aus)	New Haven	1 Apr. 1950
4:26·9*	Marshall, John (Aus)	New Haven	24 Mar. 1951
4:26·7*	Konno, Ford (USA)	New Haven	3 Apr. 1954
4:25·9	Rose, Murray (Aus)	Sydney	12 Jan. 1957

4:27·0	Rose, Murray (Aus)	Melbourne	27 Oct. 1956
4:25·9y	Konrads, John (Aus)	Sydney	15 Jan. 1958
4:21·8y	Konrads, John (Aus)	Melbourne	18 Feb. 1958
4:19·0y	Konrads, John (Aus)	Sydney	7 Feb. 1959
4:16·6	Yamanaka, Tsuyoshi (Jap)	Osaka	26 July 1959
4:15·9y	Konrads, John (Aus)	Sydney	23 Feb. 1960
4:13·4	Rose, Murray (Aus)	Chicago	17 Aug. 1962
4:12·7	Schollander, Don (USA)	Los Altos	31 July 1964
4:12·2	Schollander, Don (USA)	Tokyo	15 Oct. 1964
4:11·8	Nelson, John (USA)	Lincoln	18 Aug. 1966
4:11·6	Schollander, Don (USA)	Lincoln	18 Aug. 1966
4:11·1	Wiegand, Frank (EGer)	Utrecht	25 Aug. 1966
4:10·6	Spitz, Mark (USA)	Heywood	25 June 1967
4:10·6	Mosconi, Alain (Fra)	Monaco	2 July 1967
4:09·2	Mosconi, Alain (Fra)	Monaco	4 July 1967
4:08·8	Spitz, Mark (USA)	Santa Clara	7 July 1967
4:08·2	Charlton, Greg (USA)	Tokyo	28 Aug. 1967
4:07·7	Spitz, Mark (USA)	Heywood	23 June 1968
4:06·5	Hutton, Ralph (Can)	Lincoln	1 Aug. 1968
4:04·0	Fassnacht, Hans (WGer)	Louisville	14 Aug. 1969
4:02·8	Kinsella, John (USA)	Los Angeles	20 Aug. 1970
4:02·6	Larsson, Gunnar (Swe)	Barcelona	7 Sept. 1970

800 m. Free-style

10:19·6	Taris, Jean (Fra)	Paris	30 May 1930
10:17·2	Taris, Jean (Fra)	Cannes	9 June 1931
10:16·6	Makino, Shozo (Jap)	Osaka	30 Aug. 1931
10:15·6	Taris, Jean (Fra)	Cannes	21 June 1932
10:08·6	Makino, Shozo (Jap)	Tokyo	25 June 1933
10:01·2	Makino, Shozo (Jap)	Tokyo	16 Sept. 1934
9:55·8	Makino, Shozo (Jap)	Tokyo	15 Sept. 1935
9:50·9	Smith, Bill (USA)	Honolulu	24 July 1941
9:45·6	Furuhashi, Hironashin (Jap)	Tokyo	26 June 1949
9:45·0	Hashizume, Shiro (Jap)	Los Angeles	16 Aug. 1949
9:40·7	Furuhashi, Hironashin (Jap)	Los Angeles	16 Aug. 1949
9:35·5	Furuhashi, Hironashin (Jap)	Los Angeles	19 Aug. 1949
9:30·7	Konno, Ford (USA)	Honolulu	7 July 1951
9:15·7	Breen, George (USA)	New Haven	27 Oct. 1956
9:17·7y	Konrads, John (Aus)	Sydney	11 Jan. 1958
9:14·5y	Konrads, John (Aus)	Melbourne	22 Feb. 1958
8:59·6y	Konrads, John (Aus)	Sydney	10 Jan. 1959
8:51·5	Rose, Murray (Aus)	Los Altos	26 Aug. 1962
8:47·4	Belits-Geiman, Semyon (USSR)	Kharkov	3 Aug. 1966

8:47·3	Bennett, John (Aus)	Sydney	16 Jan. 1967
8:46·8	Mosconi, Alain (Fra)	Monaco	5 July 1967
8:42·0	Luyce, Francis (Fra)	Dinard	21 July 1967
8:34·3	Burton, Mike (USA)	Long Beach	3 Sept. 1968
8:28·8	Burton, Mike (USA)	Louisville	17 Aug. 1969

Note: Prior to 1930 the equivalent world record was for 880 y. (804·672 m.), a distance not recognized after 31 Dec. 1948. For continuity, however, 880 y. records set before 1930 are listed below:

880 y. Free-style (804·672 m.)

11:25·4	Taylor, Henry (Eng)	Runcorn	21 July 1906
11:24·2	Ross, Norman (USA)	Sydney	10 Jan. 1920
11:05·2	Charlton, Boy (Aus)	Sydney	13 Jan. 1923
10:51·8	Charlton, Boy (Aus)	Sydney	19 Jan. 1924
10:43·6	Borg, Arne (Swe)	Honolulu	11 Apr. 1924
10:37·4	Borg, Arne (Swe)	Harnus	25 Aug. 1925
10:32·0	Charlton, Boy (Aus)	Sydney	8 Jan. 1927
10:22·2	Weissmuller, Johnny (USA)	Honolulu	27 July 1927
10:20·4	Crabbe, Buster (USA)	Long Beach	7 July 1930

The 880 y. was broken 11 more times to stand finally at 8:55·5 to Rose, Murray (Aus) before being discontinued on 31 Dec. 1968.

1,500 m. Free-style

22:48·4	Taylor, Henry (Eng)	London	25 July 1908
22:00·0	Hodgson, George (Can)	Stockholm	10 July 1912
21:35·3	Borg, Arne (Swe)	Gothenburg	8 July 1923
21:15·0	Borg, Arne (Swe)	Sydney	30 Jan. 1924
21:11·4	Borg, Arne (Swe)	Paris	13 July 1924
20:06·6	Charlton, Boy (Aus)	Paris	15 July 1924
20:04·4	Borg, Arne (Swe)	Budapest	18 Aug. 1926
19:07·2	Borg, Arne (Swe)	Bologna	2 Sept. 1927
18:58·8	Amano, Tomikatsu (Jap)	Tokyo	10 Aug. 1938
18:35·7	Hashizume, Shiro (Jap)	Los Angeles	16 Aug. 1949
18:19·0	Furuhashi, Hironashin (Jap)	Los Angeles	16 Aug. 1949
18:05·9	Breen, George (USA)	New Haven	3 May 1956
17:59·5	Rose, Murray (Aus)	Melbourne	30 Oct. 1956
17:52·9	Breen George (USA)	Melbourne	5 Dec. 1956
17:28·7y	Konrads, John (Aus)	Melbourne	22 Feb. 1958
17:11·0y	Konrads, John (Aus)	Sydney	27 Feb. 1960
17:05·5	Saari, Roy (USA)	Tokyo	17 Aug. 1963
17:01·8	Rose, Murray (Aus)	Los Altos	2 Aug. 1964
16:58·7	Saari, Roy (USA)	New York	2 Sept. 1964
16:58·6	Krause, Steve (USA)	Maumee	15 Aug. 1965
16:41·6	Burton, Mike (USA)	Lincoln	21 Aug. 1966
16:34·1	Burton, Mike (USA)	Oak Park	13 Aug. 1967
16:28·1	Echevarria, Guillermo (Mex)	Santa Clara	7 July 1968
16:08·5	Burton, Mike (USA)	Long Beach	3 Sept. 1968
16:04·5	Burton, Mike (USA)	Louisville	17 Aug. 1969
15:57·1	Kinsella, John (USA)	Los Angeles	23 Aug. 1970

100 m. Back-stroke

1:20·8*	Wechesser, Maurice (Belg)	Schaerbeck	2 Oct. 1910
1:18·8*	Baronyi, Andras (Hun)	Budapest	17 July 1911
1:18·4*	Schiele, Oskar (Ger)	Brussels	6 Apr. 1912
1:15·6*	Fahr, Otto (Ger)	Magdeburg	29 Apr. 1912

1:14·8	Kealoha, Warren (USA)	Antwerp	22 Aug. 1920
1:12·6*	Kealoha, Warren (USA)	Honolulu	17 Oct. 1922
1:12·4	Kealoha, Warren (USA)	Honolulu	13 Apr. 1924
1:11·4*	Kealoha, Warren (USA)	Honolulu	19 June 1926
1:11·2	Laufer, Walter (USA)	Berlin	20 June 1926
1:10·2*	House, P. A. (USA)	New Haven	22 Mar. 1927
1:09·0	Kojac, George (USA)	Detroit	23 June 1928
1:08·2	Kojac, George (USA)	Amsterdam	9 Aug. 1928
1:07·4*	Vandeweghe, Albert (USA)	Honolulu	23 July 1934
1:07·0*	Kiefer, Adolph (USA)	Berlin	20 Oct. 1935
1:06·2*	Kiefer, Adolph (USA)	Krefeld	22 Oct. 1935
1:04·9*	Kiefer, Adolph (USA)	Breslau	9 Nov. 1935
1:04·8*	Kiefer, Adolph (USA)	Detroit	18 Jan. 1936
1:04·0*	Stack, Allen (USA)	New Haven	23 June 1948
1:03·6*	Stack, Allen (USA)	New Haven	4 Feb. 1949
1:03·3*	Bozon, Gilbert (Fra)	Troyes	26 Dec. 1952
1:02·8*	Oyakawa, Yoshinobu (USA)	New Haven	1 Apr. 1954
1:02·1*	Bozon, Gilbert (Fra)	Troyes	27 Feb. 1955

1:02·2	Theile, David (Aus)	Melbourne	6 Dec. 1956
1:01·5y	Monckton, John (Aus)	Melbourne	15 Feb. 1958
1:01·3	Bennett, Bob (USA)	Los Angeles	19 Aug. 1961
1:01·0	Stock, Tom (USA)	Cuyahoga Falls	11 Aug. 1962
1:00·9	Stock, Tom (USA)	Cuyahoga Falls	12 Aug. 1962
1:00·8	Kuppers, Ernst-Joachim (WGer)	Dortmund	28 Aug. 1964
1:00·0	Mann, Tom (USA)	New York	3 Sept. 1964
59·6	Mann, Tom (USA)	Tokyo	16 Oct. 1964
59·5	Russell, Doug (USA)	Tokyo	28 Aug. 1967
59·3	Hickcox, Charles (USA)	Tokyo	28 Aug. 1967
59·1	Hickcox, Charles (USA)	Tokyo	31 Aug. 1967
58·4	Matthes, Roland (EGer)	Leipzig	21 Sept. 1967
58·0	Matthes, Roland (EGer)	Mexico City	26 Oct. 1968
57·8	Matthes, Roland (EGer)	Wurzburg	23 Aug. 1969
56·9	Matthes, Roland (EGer)	Barcelona	8 Sept. 1970

200 m. Back-stroke

3:04·4	Schiele, Oskar (Ger)	Charlottenburg	27 June 1909
2:59·8*	Arnold, Georg (Ger)	Magdeburg	3 Jan. 1910
2:56·4*	Weckesser, Maurice (Belg)	Schaerbeck	18 Oct. 1910
2:50·6*	Pentz, Hermann (Ger)	Magdeburg	11 Mar. 1911
2:48·4*	Fahr, Otto (Ger)	Magdeburg	3 April 1912
2:47·1	Laufer, Walter (USA)	Bremen	24 June 1926
2:44·9	Laufer, Walter (USA)	Nurnberg	11 July 1926
2:38·8*	Laufer, Walter (USA)	Magdeburg	13 July 1926
2:37·8	Irie, Toshio (Jap)	Tamagawa	14 Oct. 1928
2:32·2*	Kojac, George (USA)	New Haven	16 June 1930
2:27·8*	Vandeweghe, Albert (USA)	Honolulu	30 Aug. 1934
2:24·0*	Kiefer, Adolph (USA)	Chicago	11 Apr. 1935
2:23·0*	Kiefer, Adolph (USA)	Honolulu	23 May 1941
2:22·9*	Holiday, Harry (USA)	Detroit	18 May 1943
2:19·3*	Kiefer, Adolph (USA)	Annapolis	4 Mar. 1944
2:18·5*	Stack Allen (USA)	New Haven	4 May 1949
2:18·3*	Bozon, Gilbert (Fra)	Algiers	26 June 1953

2:18·8y	Monckton, John (Aus)	Sydney	15 Jan. 1958
2:18·4y	Monckton, John (Aus)	Melbourne	18 Feb. 1958
2:17·9	McKinney, Frank (USA)	Los Altos	12 July 1959
2:17·8	McKinney, Frank (USA)	Osaka	25 July 1959
2:17·6	Bittick, Charles (USA)	Los Angeles	26 June 1960
2:16·0	Stock, Tom (USA)	Toledo	24 July 1960
2:13·2	Stock, Tom (USA)	Chicago	2 July 1961
2:11·5	Stock, Tom (USA)	Los Angeles	20 Aug. 1961
2:10·9	Stock, Tom (USA)	Cuyahoga Falls	10 Aug. 1962
2:10·3	Graef, Jed (USA)	Tokyo	13 Oct. 1964
2:09·4	Hickcox, Charles (USA)	Tokyo	29 Aug. 1967
2:07·9	Matthes, Roland (EGer)	Leipzig	8 Nov. 1967
2:07·5	Matthes, Roland (EGer)	Leipzig	14 Aug. 1968
2:07·4	Matthes, Roland (EGer)	Santa Clara	12 July 1969
2:06·6	Hall, Gary (USA)	Louisville	14 Aug. 1969
2:06·4	Matthes, Roland (EGer)	Berlin	29 Aug. 1969
2:06·3	Stamm, Mike (USA)	Los Angeles	20 Aug. 1970
2:06·1	Matthes, Roland (EGer)	Barcelona	11 Sept. 1970

100 m. Breast-stroke

1:24·0*	Baronyi, Andras (Hun)	Vienna	17 Nov. 1907
1:22·6*	Courbet, Felicien (Belg)	Brussels	30 Sept. 1909
1:21·8*	Goldi, Odon (Hun)	Budapest	12 June 1910
1:18·4*	Bathe, Walther (Ger)	Magdeburg	2 Oct. 1910
1:17·8*	Bathe, Walther (Ger)	Budapest	18 Dec. 1910
1:16·8*	Lutzow, Wilhelm (Ger)	Magdeburg	24 May 1921
1:16·2*	Sipos, Márton (Hun)	Budapest	24 Sept. 1922
1:15·9*	Rademacher, Erich (Ger)	Leipzig	5 Apr. 1925
1:15·6*	Faust, Heinz (Ger)	Strasbourg	5 Dec. 1926
1:14·0*	Spence, Walter (USA)	New York	28 Oct. 1927
1:13·6*	Cartonnet, Jacques (Fra)	Paris	20 May 1932
1:13·0*	Cartonnet, Jacques (Fra)	Paris	8 Feb. 1933
1:12·4*	Cartonnet, Jacques (Fra)	Paris	4 Feb. 1933
1:10·8*	Higgins, John (USA)	New Haven	Bu22 Feb. 1935
1:10·0*	Higgins, John (USA)	New Haven	Bu3 Mar. 1936
1:09·8*	Cartonnet, Jacques (Fra)	Toulouse	Bu6 Aug. 1937
1:09·5*	Balke, Joachim (Ger)	Bremen	Bu12 Nov. 1938
1:07·3*	Hough, Dick (USA)	New Haven	Bu15 Apr. 1939
1:07·2*	Meshkov, Leonid (USSR)	Moscow	Bu20 Dec. 1949
1:07·0*	Meshkov, Leonid (USSR)	Minsk	Bu23 Feb. 1950
1:06·8*	Meshkov, Leonid (USSR)	Moscow	Bu17 Apr. 1950
1:06·6*	Meshkov, Leonid (USSR)	Moscow	Bu7 Jan. 1951
1:06·5*	Meshkov, Leonid (USSR)	Moscow	Bu5 May 1951
1:05·8*	Klein, Herbert (Ger)	Nordeney	Bu17 Feb. 1952

1:11·9*	Minashkin, Vladimir (USSR)	Leningrad	Uw11 Feb. 1953
1:11·2*	Minashkin, Vladimir (USSR)	Leningrad	Uw23 Feb. 1953
1:10·9*	Petrusewicz, Marek (Pol)	Wroclaw	Uw18 Oct. 1953
1:10·5*	Minashkin, Vladimir (USSR)	Stockholm	Uw24 Feb. 1954
1:09·8*	Petrusewicz. Marek (Pol)	Wroclaw	Uw23 May 1954
1:08·2*	Furukawa, Masaru (Jap)	Tokyo	Uw1 Oct. 1955

| 1:12·7 | Svozil, Viteslav (Czech) | Piestany | 1 May 1957 |
| 1:11·6 | Lieh-Yung, Chi (China) | Canton | 1 May 1957 |

1:11·5	Minashkin, Vladimir (USSR)	Leipzig	15 Sept. 1957
1:11·4	Kolesnikov, Leonid (USSR)	Moscow	5 May 1961
1:11·1	Jastremski, Chet (USA)	Chicago	2 July 1961
1:10·8	Tittes, Gunter (EGer)	Berlin	5 July 1961
1:10·7	Jastremski, Chet (USA)	Tokyo	28 July 1961
1:10·0	Jastremski, Chet (USA)	Tokyo	30 July 1961
1:09·5	Jastremski, Chet (USA)	Osaka	3 Aug. 1961
1:07·8	Jastremski, Chet (USA)	Los Angeles	20 Aug. 1961
1:07·5	Jastremski, Chet (USA)	Los Angeles	20 Aug. 1961
1:07·4	Prokopenko, Georgy (USSR)	Baku	26 Mar. 1964
1:06·9	Prokopenko, Georgy (USSR)	Moscow	3 Sept. 1964
1:06·7	Kosinsky, Vladimir (USSR)	Leningrad	8 Nov. 1967
1:06·4	Fiolo, Jose (Braz)	Rio de Janeiro	19 Feb. 1968
1:06·2	Pankin, Nicolai (USSR)	Moscow	18 Apr. 1969
1:05·8	Pankin, Nicolai (USSR)	Magdeburg	20 Apr. 1969

200 m. Breast-stroke

3:09·2	Holman, Frederick (Eng)	London	18 Aug. 1908
3:08·3*	Andersson, Robert (Swe)	Stockholm	18 Apr. 1909
3:00·8*	Courbet, Felicien (Belg)	Schaerbeck	2 Oct. 1910
2:56·6*	Courtman, Percy (Eng)	Garston	28 July 1914
2:54·4*	Rademacher, Erich (Ger)	Amsterdam	12 Nov. 1922
2:52·6*	Skelton, Robert (USA)	Milwaukee	21 Mar. 1924
2:50·4*	Rademacher, Erich (Ger)	Magdeburg	7 Apr. 1924
2:48·0*	Rademacher, Erich (Ger)	Brussels	11 Mar. 1927
2:45·0*	Tsuruta, Yoshiyuki (Jap)	Kyoto	27 July 1929
2:44·6*	Spence, Lionel (USA)	Chicago	2 Apr. 1931
2:44·0*	Spence, Lionel (USA)	New Haven	1 Apr. 1932
2:42·6*	Cartonnet, Jacques (Fra)	Paris	8 Feb. 1933
2:42·4*	Sietas, Erwin (Ger)	Dusseldorf	16 Mar. 1935
2:39·6*	Cartonnet, Jacques (Fra)	Paris	4 May 1935
2:37·2*	Kasley, Jack (USA)	New Haven	Bu28 Mar. 1936
2:36·8*	Nakache, Alfred (Fra)	Marseilles	Bu6 July 1941
2:35·6*	Verdeur, Joe (USA)	Bainbridge	Bu5 Apr. 1946
2:35·0*	Verdeur, Joe (USA)	New Haven	Bu15 Feb. 1947
2:32·0*	Verdeur, Joe (USA)	New Haven	Bu14 Feb. 1948
2:30·5*	Verdeur, Joe (USA)	New Haven	Bu2 Apr. 1948
2:30·0*	Verdeur, Joe (USA)	New Haven	Bu28 June 1948
2:28·3*	Verdeur, Joe (USA)	New Haven	Bu31 Mar. 1950
2:27·3*	Klein, Herbert (Ger)	Munich	Bu9 June 1951

2:37·4*	Gleie, Knud (Den)	Copenhagen	14 Feb. 1953
2:36·6*	Furukawa Masaru (Jap)	Tokyo	Uw10 Apr. 1954
2:35·4*	Furukawa, Masaru (Jap)	Tokyo	Uw10 Apr. 1954
2:35·2*	Tanaka, Mamoru (Jap)	Tokyo	Uw17 Sept. 1954
2:33·7	Furukawa, Masaru (Jap)	Tokyo	Uw5 Aug. 1955
2:31·0*	Furukawa, Masaru (Jap)	Tokyo	Uw1 Oct. 1955

2:36·5y	Gathercole, Terry (Aus)	Townsville	28 June 1958
2:33·6	Jastremski, Chet (USA)	Tokyo	28 July 1961
2:29·6	Jastremski, Chet (USA)	Los Angeles	19 Aug. 1961
2:28·2	Jastremski, Chet (USA)	New York	30 Aug. 1964
2:27·8	O'Brien, Ian (Aus)	Tokyo	15 Oct. 1964
2:27·4	Kosinsky, Vladimir (USSR)	Kalev	3 Apr. 1968

2:26·5	Pankin, Nicolai (USSR)	Minsk	22 Mar. 1969
2:25·4	Pankin, Nicolai (USSR)	Magdeburg	19 Apr. 1969
2:23·5	Job, Brian (USA)	Los Angeles	22 Aug. 1970

100 m. Butterfly

1:04·3*	Tumpek, Gyorgy (Hun)	Budapest	31 May 1953
1:03·7*	Tumpek, Gyorgy (Hun)	Budapest	8 May 1954
1:02·3	Tumpek, Gyorgy (Hun)	Budapest	1 Aug. 1954
1:02·1*	Tumpek, Gyorgy (Hun)	Szehesfehervar	20 Nov. 1954
1:02·0*	Tumpek, Gyorgy (Hun)	Budapest	21 Dec. 1954
1:01·5*	Wiggins, Albert (USA)	New Haven	2 Apr. 1955

1:03·4	Tumpek, Gyorgy (Hun)	Budapest	26 May 1957
1:01·5	Ishimoto, Takashi (Jap)	Kurume	16 June 1957
1:01·3	Ishimoto, Takashi (Jap)	Tokyo	7 July 1957
1:01·2	Ishimoto, Takashi (Jap)	Tokyo	6 Sept. 1957
1:01·0	Ishimoto, Takashi (Jap)	Kochi	14 Sept. 1958
1:00·1	Ishimoto, Takashi (Jap)	Los Angeles	29 June 1958
59·0	Larson, Lance (USA)	Los Angeles	26 June 1960
58·7	Larson, Lance (USA)	Toledo	24 July 1960
58·6	Schmidt, Fred (USA)	Los Angeles	20 Aug. 1961
58·4	Nicolao, Luis (Arg)	Rio de Janeiro	24 Apr. 1962
57·0	Nicolao, Luis (Arg)	Rio de Janeiro	27 Apr. 1962
56·3	Spitz, Mark (USA)	Winnipeg	31 July 1967
56·3	Russell, Doug (USA)	Tokyo	29 Aug. 1967
55·7	Spitz, Mark (USA)	Berlin	7 Oct. 1967
55·6	Spitz, Mark (USA)	Long Beach	30 Aug. 1968

200 m. Butterfly

2:21·6*	Nagasawa, Jiro (Jap)	Tokyo	17 Sept. 1954
2:20·8*	Ishimoto, Takashi (Jap)	Tokyo	1 Oct. 1955
2:19·3*	Nagasawa, Jiro (Jap)	New Haven	14 Mar. 1956
2:16·7*	Yorzyk, Bill (USA)	Winchendon	14 Apr. 1956

2:19·0	Troy, Mike (USA)	Los Altos	11 July 1959
2:16·4	Troy, Mike (USA)	Los Altos	11 July 1959
2:15·0	Troy, Mike (USA)	Evansville	10 July 1960
2:13·4	Troy, Mike (USA)	Toledo	23 July 1960
2:13·2	Troy, Mike (USA)	Detroit	4 Aug. 1960
2:12·8	Troy, Mike (USA)	Rome	2 Sept. 1960
2:12·6	Robie, Carl (USA)	Los Angeles	19 Aug. 1961
2:12·5y	Berry, Kevin (Aus)	Melbourne	20 Feb. 1962
2:12·4	Robie, Carl (USA)	Cuyahoga Falls	11 Aug. 1962
2:10·8	Robie, Carl (USA)	Cuyahoga Falls	11 Aug. 1962
2:09·7y	Berry, Kevin (Aus)	Melbourne	23 Oct. 1962
2:08·4y	Berry, Kevin (Aus)	Sydney	12 Jan. 1963
2:08·2	Robie, Carl (USA)	Tokyo	18 Aug. 1963
2:06·9	Berry, Kevin (Aus)	Sydney	29 Feb. 1964
2:06·6	Berry, Kevin (Aus)	Tokyo	18 Oct. 1964
2:06·4	Spitz, Mark (USA)	Winnipeg	26 July 1967
2:06·4	Spitz, Mark (USA)	Oak Park	12 Aug. 1967
2:06·0	Ferris, John (USA)	Tokyo	30 Aug. 1967
2:05·7	Spitz, Mark (USA)	Berlin	8 Oct. 1967
2:05·4	Spitz, Mark (USA)	Los Angeles	22 Aug. 1970
2:05·0	Hall, Gary (USA)	Los Angeles	22 Aug. 1970

200 m. Individual Medley

2:12·4	Buckingham, Greg (USA)	Lincoln	21 Aug. 1966
2:11·3	Buckingham, Greg (USA)	Oak Park	23 Aug. 1967
2:10·6	Hickcox, Charles (USA)	Long Beach	31 Aug. 1968
2:09·6	Hall, Gary (USA)	Louisville	17 Aug. 1969
2:09·5	Hall, Gary (USA)	Los Angeles	23 Aug. 1970
2:09·3	Larsson, Gunnar (Swe)	Barcelona	12 Sept. 1970

400 m. Individual medley

5:48·5	O'Neill, Frank (Aus)	Sydney	17 Jan. 1953
5:43·0	O'Neill, Frank (Aus)	Sydney	24 Feb. 1953
5:38·7*	Kettesy, Gusztáv (Hun)	Budapest	24 Apr. 1953
5:35·6*	Lucien, Maurice (Fra)	Troyes	24 Apr. 1953
5:32·1	Kettesy, Gusztáv (Hun)	Budapest	26 July 1953
5:31·0*	Andsberg, Jan (Swe)	Lund	29 Oct. 1953
5:27·3*	Lucien, Maurice (Fra)	Reims	18 Mar. 1954
5:18·3*	Spengler, Alfred (EGer)	Dresden	22 Apr. 1954
5:15·4*	Stroujanov, Vladimir (USSR)	Minsk	2 Oct. 1954
5:09·4*	Androssov, Gennadi (USSR)	Lvov	10 Mar. 1957
5:08·3*	Stroujanov, Vladimir (USSR)	Moscow	17 Mar. 1957

5:12·9	Stroujanov, Vladimir (USSR)	Moscow	20 Oct. 1957
5:08·8y	Black, Ian (GB)	Cardiff	6 June 1959
5:07·8	Harrison, George (USA)	Los Angeles	24 June 1960
5:05·3	Harrison, George (USA)	Los Angeles	24 June 1960
5:04·5	Rounsavelle, Dennis (USA)	Toledo	22 July 1960
5:04·3	Stickles, Ted (USA)	Chicago	1 July 1961
4:55·6	Stickles, Ted (USA)	Los Angeles	18 Aug. 1961
4:53·8	Hetz, Gerhard (WGer)	Moscow	24 May 1962
4:51·4	Stickles, Ted (USA)	Chicago	30 June 1962
4:51·0y	Stickles, Ted (USA)	Louisville	12 July 1962
4:50·2	Hetz, Gerhard (WGer)	Tokyo	12 Oct. 1963
4:48·6	Roth, Dick (USA)	Los Altos	31 July 1964
4:45·4	Roth, Dick (USA)	Tokyo	14 Oct. 1964
4:45·3	Dunaev, Andrei (USSR)	Tallinen	3 Apr. 1968
4:45·1	Buckingham, Greg (USA)	Santa Clara	6 July 1968
4:43·4	Hall, Gary (USA)	Los Angeles	20 July 1968
4:39·0	Hickcox, Charles (USA)	Long Beach	30 Aug. 1968
4:38·7	Hall, Gary (USA)	Santa Clara	11 July 1969
4:33·9	Hall, Gary (USA)	Louisville	15 Aug. 1969
4:31·0	Hall, Gary (USA)	Los Angeles	21 Aug. 1970

4 × 100 m. Free-style relay

4:10·2	Budapest University, Hungary	Budapest	26 June 1937
	(Kiss, Zoltan; Dienes, Gyula; Lengyel, Arpad; Csik, Ferenc)		
4:06·6	Hungary	Budapest	15 Aug. 1937
	(Zolyomi, Gyula; Korosi, Istvan; Grof, Odon; Csik, Ferenc)		
4:03·6*	Bremischer, Germany	Bremen	5 Mar. 1938
	(Heibel, Hermann; Freese, Hans; Askamp, Edward; Fischer, Helmuth)		
4:02·4*	City of Berlin, Germany	Copenhagen	1 Apr. 1938
	(Wille, Otto; Birr, Werner; Plath, Werner; Eckenbrecher, Kurt von)		
4:02·0*	Hungary	Budapest	14 July 1938
	(Zolyomi, Gyula; Csik, Ferenc; Korosi, Istvan; Grof, Odon)		
3:59·2	United States	Berlin	20 Aug. 1938
	(Hirose, T.; Jaretz, O.; Wolf, Paul; Fick, Peter)		

3:54·4*	Yale University, United States	New Haven	8 Mar. 1940
	(Sanburn, W.; Pope, E.; Duncan, R.; Johnson, H.)		
3:50·8*	Yale University, United States	New Haven	18 Mar. 1942
	(Johnson, H.; Kelly, R.; Pope, E.; Lilley, F.)		
3:48·6*	New Haven S.C., United States	New Haven	29 June 1948
	(Ford, Alan; Hueber, E.; Dooley, F.; Johnson, H.)		
3:47·9*	Yale University, United States	New Haven	19 Mar. 1951
	(Thoman, Dick; Sheff, D.; Farnsworth, W.; Reid, R.)		
3:46·8	Japan	Tokyo	6 Aug. 1955
	(Susuki, Hiroshi; Tani, A.; Goto, Toro; Koga, M.)		

- -

3:46·3	Australia	Brisbane	3 May 1958
	(Chapman, Gary; Konrads, John; Shipton, Geoff; Devitt, John)		
3:44·4	United States	Tokyo	21 July 1959
	(Follett, Ed.; Larson, Lance; Farrell, Jeff; Alkire, Joe)		
3:42·5	France	Thionville	10 Aug. 1962
	(Gottvalles, Alain; Gropaiz, Gerard; Curtillet, Jean-Pierre; Christophe, Robert)		
3:39·9	Santa Clara S.C., United States	Los Altos	4 July 1963
	(Clark, Steve; Schoenmann, N.; Schollander, Don; Townsend, Ed)		
3:36·1	United States	Tokyo	18 Aug. 1963
	(Clark, Steve; McDonough, R.; Ilman, Gary; Townsend, Ed)		
3:33·2	United States	Tokyo	14 Oct. 1964
	(Clark, Steve; Austin, Mike; Ilman, Gary; Schollander, Don)		
3:32·6	United States	Tokyo	28 Aug. 1967
	(Walsh, Ken; Zorn, Zac; Havens, Don; Charlton, Greg)		
3:32·5	United States	Long Beach	3 Sept. 1968
	(Zorn, Zac, Rerych, Steve, Walsh, Ken; Schollander, Don)		
3:31·7	United States	Mexico City	17 Oct. 1968
	(Zorn, Zac; Rerych, Steve; Spitz, Mark; Walsh, Ken)		
3:28·8	Los Angeles S.C. United States	Los Angeles	23 Aug. 1970
	(Havens, Don; Weston, Mike; Frawley, Bill; Heckl, Frank		

4 × 200 m. Free-style relay

8:58·4	Japan	Los Angeles	9 Aug. 1932
	(Miyazaki Yasuji; Yokoyama, Takashi; Yusa, Masanori; Toyoda, Hisakichi)		
8:52·2	Japan	Tokyo	19 Aug. 1935
	(Yusa, Masanori; Makino, Shozo; Isiharada, S.; Negami, H.)		
8:51·5	Japan	Berlin	11 Aug. 1936
	(Yusa, Masanori; Sugiura, Shigeo; Arai, Shigeo; Taguchi, Masaharu)		
8:46·0	United States	London	3 Aug. 1948
	(Ris, Wally; Wolf, Wallace; McLane, Jimmy; Smith, Bill)		
8:45·4	Tokyo SC, Japan	Los Angeles	18 Aug. 1949
	(Hamaguchi, Yoshihiro; Maruyama, S.; Murayama, S; Furuhashi, Hironashin)		
8:43·2*	Yale University, United States	New Haven	24 Feb. 1950
	(Farnsworth, W.; Munson, L.; Blum, J.; Reid, R.)		
8:40·6*	Tokyo S.C., Japan	Marilaia	2 Apr. 1950
	(Hamaguchi, Yoshihiro; Murayama, S.; Hashizume, Shiro; Furuhashi, Hironashin)		
8:33·0*	France	Marseilles	2 Aug. 1951
	(Bernardo, Joseph; Blioch, Willy; Boiteux, Jean; Jany, Alex)		
8:29·4*	Yale University, United States	New Haven	16 Feb. 1952
	(Moore, Wayne; McLane, Jimmy; Sheff, D.; Thoman, Dick)		

| 8:24·5* | U.S.S.R. | Moscow | 4 Nov. 1956 |

(Nikitin, Boris; Strujanov, Vladimir; Nikolaev, Gennadi; Sorokin, Vitali)

| 8:23·6 | Australia | Melbourne | 3 Dec. 1956 |

(O'Halloran, Kevin; Devitt, John; Rose, Murray; Henricks, Jon)

| 8:21·6 | Japan | Tokyo | 22 July 1959 |

(Umenoto, T.; Fujimoto, Tatsuo; Fukui, Makoto; Yamanaka, Tsuyoshi)

| 8:18·7 | Japan | Osaka | 26 July 1959 |

(Yamanaka, Ysuyoshi; Fukui, Makoto; Kenjo, K.; Fujimoto, Tatsuo)

| 8:17·0 | Indianapolis A.C., United States | Toledo | 23 July 1960 |

(Sintz, Peter; Breen, George; Somers, Alan; Troy, Mike)

| 8:16·6y | Australia | Townsville | 6 Aug. 1960 |

(Henricks, Jon; Dickson, David; Konrads, John; Rose, Murray)

| 8:10·2 | United States | Rome | 1 Sept. 1960 |

(Harrison, George; Blick, Dick; Troy, Mike; Farrell, Jeff)

| 8:09·8 | Japan | Tokyo | 21 Apr. 1963 |

(Fujimoto, Tatsuo; Yamanaka, Tsuyoshi; Okabe, Y.; Fukui, Makoto)

| 8:07·6 | Santa Clara S,C., United States | Illinois | 10 Aug. 1963 |

(Townsend, Ed; Wall, Mike; Clark, Steve; Schollander, Don)

| 8:03·7 | United States | Tokyo | 19 Aug. 1963 |

(Schollander, Don; McDonough, R.; Townsend, Ed; Saari, Roy)

| 8:01·8 | United States | Los Angeles | 28 Sept. 1964 |

(Mettler, W.; Wall, Mike; Lyons, Dick; Schollander, Don)

| 7:52·1 | United States | Tokyo | 18 Oct. 1964 |

(Clark, Steve; Saari, Roy; Ilman, Gary; Schollander, Don)

| 7:52·1 | Santa Clara S.C., United States | Oak Park | 12 Aug. 1967 |

(Ilman, Gary; Wall, Mike; Spitz, Mark; Schollander, Don)

| 7:50·8 | Australia | Edinburgh | 24 July 1970 |

(Rogers, Greg; Devenish, Bill; White, Graham; Wenden, Mike)

| 7:48·0 | United States | Tokyo | 28 Aug. 1970 |

(Kinsella, John; McBreen, Tim; Hall, Gary; Lambert, Mark)

4 × 100 m. Medley relay

| 4:39·2* | S.K. Poseidon, Sweden | Halsingborg | 22 Feb. 1953 |

(Hellsing, Gustaf; Brock, Lennart; Dahl, Roy; Westesson, Hakan)

| 4:32·2* | France | Charleroi | 22 Mar. 1953 |

(Bozon, Gilbert; Dumesnil, Pierre; Lucien, Maurice; Jany, Alex)

| 4:31·5* | Racing Club de France (France) | Troyes | 1 Apr. 1953 |

(Violas, A.; Dumesnil, Pierre; Arene, Julian; Eminente, Aldo)

| 4:30·8* | Sweden | Lund | 17 Apr. 1953 |

(Hellsing, Gustaf; Brock, Lennart; Larsson, Goran; Ostrand, Per-Ola)

| 4:27·8* | Sweden | Boras | 24 Apr. 1953 |

(Hellsing, Gustaf; Brock, Lennart; Larsson, Goran; Ostrand, Per-Ola)

| 4:24·8* | U.S.S.R. | Moscow | 13 May 1953 |

(Lopatine, V.; Minaschkin, Vladimir; Skriptschenkov, P.; Balandin, Lev)

| 4:21·3* | U.S.S.R. | Moscow | 26 Jan. 1954 |

(Soloviev, V.; Minaschkin, Vladimir; Skriptschenkov, P.; Balandin Lev)

| 4:14·8* | U.S.S.R. | Moscow | 14 Aug. 1956 |

(Kuvaldin, G.; Minaschkin, Vladimir; Stroujanov, Vladimir; Balandin, Lev)

4:17·8	Japan	Tokyo	7 Sept. 1957
	(Tomita, Kazuo; Furukawa, Masaru; Ishimoto, Takashi; Ishihara, K.)		
4:17·2	Japan	Tokyo	28 May 1958
	(Hase, K.; Furukawa, Masaru, Ishimoto, Takashi, Koga M)		
4:14·2y	Australia	Cardiff	25 July 1958
	(Monckton, John; Gathercole, Terry; Wilkinson, Brian; Devitt, John)		
4:10·4	Australia	Osaka	22 Aug. 1958
	(Monckton, John; Gathercole, Terry; Wilkinson, Brian; Devitt, John)		
4:09·2	Indianapolis A.C. United States	Toledo	24 July 1960
	(McKinney, Frank; Jastremski, Chet; Troy, Mike; Sintz, Peter)		
4:08·2	United States	Rome	27 Aug. 1960
	(Bennett, Bob; Hait, Paul; Gillanders, David; Clark, Steve)		
4:05·4	United States	Rome	1 Sept. 1960
	McKinney, Frank; Hait, Paul; Larson, Lance; Farrell, Jeff)		
4:03·0	Indianapolis A.C., United States	Los Angeles	20 Aug. 1961
	(Stock, Tom; Jastremski, Chet; Schulhof, Larry; Sintz, Peter)		
4:01·6	Indianapolis A.C., United States	Cuyahoga Falls	12 Aug. 1962
	(Stock, Tom; Jastremski, Chet; Schmidt, Fred; Sintz, Peter)		
4:00·1	United States	Osaka	24 Aug. 1963
	(McGeagh, Dick; Craig, Bill; Richardson, W.; Clark, Steve)		
3:58·4	United States	Tokyo	16 Oct. 1964
	(Mann, Tom; Craig, Bill; Schmidt, Fred; Clark, Steve)		
3:57·2	National University Team, United States	Tokyo	31 Aug. 1967
	(Hickcox, Charles; Merten, Ken; Russell, Doug; Walsh, Ken)		
3:56·5	East Germany	Leipzig	7 Nov. 1967
	(Matthes, Roland; Henninger, Egon; Gregor, Horst; Wiegand, Frank)		
3:54·9	United States	Mexico City	26 Oct. 1968
	(Hickcox, Charles; McKenzie, Don; Russell, Doug; Walsh, Ken)		
3:54·4	East Germany	Barcelona	8 Sept. 1970
	(Matthes, Roland; Katzur, Klaus; Poser, Udo; Unger, Lutz)		

WOMEN

100 m. Free-style

1:35·0*	Gerstung, Martha (Ger)	Magdeburg	18 Oct. 1908
1:26·6*	Guttenstein, C. (Belg)	Schaerbeck	2 Oct. 1910
1:24·6*	Curwen, Daisy (Eng)	Liverpool	29 Sept. 1911
1:20·6*	Curwen, Daisy (Eng)	Birkenhead	10 June 1912
1:19·8	Durack, Fanny (Aus)	Stockholm	9 July 1912
1:18·8	Durack, Fanny (Aus)	Hamburg	21 July 1912
1:16·2	Durack, Fanny (Aus)	Sydney	6 Feb. 1915
1:13·6	Bleibtrey, Ethelda (USA)	Antwerp	25 Aug 1920
1:12·8	Ederle, Gertrude (USA)	Newark	30 June 1923
1:12·2	Wehselau, Mariechen (USA)	Paris	19 July 1924
1:10·0*	Lackie, Ethel (USA)	Toledo	28 Jan. 1926
1:09·8	Garratti, Eleanora (USA)	Honolulu	7 Aug. 1929
1:09·4	Osipowich, Albina (USA)	San Francisco	25 Aug. 1929
1:08·0*	Madison, Helene (USA)	Miami Beach	14 Mar. 1930
1:06·6*	Madison, Helene (USA)	Boston	20 Apr. 1931
1:06·0*	Den Ouden, Willy (Neth)	Antwerp	9 July 1933
1:05·4*	Den Ouden, Willy (Neth)	Amsterdam	24 Feb. 1934
1:04·8*	Den Ouden, Willy (Neth)	Rotterdam	15 Apr. 1934
1:04·6*	Den Ouden, Willy (Neth)	Amsterdam	27 Feb. 1936
1:04·5	Fraser, Dawn (Aus)	Sydney	21 Feb. 1956
1:04·2*	Gastelaars, Cockie (Neth)	Amsterdam	3 Mar. 1956

1:04·0*	Gastelaars, Cockie (Neth)	Schiedam	14 Apr. 1956
1:03·3	Fraser, Dawn (Aus)	Townsville	25 Aug. 1956
1:03·2	Crapp, Lorraine (Aus)	Sydney	20 Oct. 1956
1:02·4	Crapp, Lorraine (Aus)	Melbourne	25 Oct. 1956
1:02·0	Fraser, Dawn (Aus)	Melbourne	1 Dec. 1956
1:01·5y	Fraser, Dawn (Aus)	Melbourne	18 Feb. 1958
1:01·4y	Fraser, Dawn (Aus)	Cardiff	21 July 1958
1:01·2	Fraser, Dawn (Aus)	Schiedam	10 Aug. 1958
1:00·2y	Fraser, Dawn (Aus)	Sydney	23 Feb. 1960
1:00·0y	Fraser, Dawn (Aus)	Melbourne	23 Oct. 1962
59·9y	Fraser, Dawn (Aus)	Melbourne	27 Oct. 1962
59·5y	Fraser, Dawn (Aus)	Perth	24 Nov. 1962
58·9	Fraser, Dawn (Aus)	Sydney	29 Feb. 1964

200 m. Free-style

2:56·4	Dorfner, O. (USA)	Alameda	21 July 1918
2:47·6*	Boyle, C. (USA)	New Brighton	25 Aug. 1921
2:45·2*	Ederle, Gertrude (USA)	Brooklyn	4 Apr. 1923
2:40·6*	Norelius, Martha (USA)	Miami	28 Feb. 1926
2:34·6*	Madison, Helene (USA)	St. Augustine	6 Mar. 1930
2:28·6*	Den Ouden, Willy (Neth	Rotterdam	3 May 1933
2:25·3*	Den Ouden, Willy (Neth)	Copenhagen	8 Sept. 1935
2:24·6*	Van Veen, Rie (Neth)	Rotterdam	26 Feb. 1938
2:21·7*	Hveger, Ragnild (Den)	Aarhus	11 Sept. 1938
2:20·7	Fraser, Dawn (Aus)	Sydney	25 Feb. 1956
2:19·3	Crapp, Lorraine (Aus)	Townsville	25 Aug. 1956
2:18·5	Crapp, Lorraine (Aus)	Sydney	20 Oct. 1956
2:17·7y	Fraser, Dawn (Aus)	Adelaide	10 Feb. 1958
2:14·7y	Fraser, Dawn (Aus)	Melbourne	22 Feb. 1958
2:11·6y	Fraser, Dawn (Aus)	Sydney	27 Feb. 1960
2:10·5	Watson, Pokey (USA)	Lincoln	19 Aug. 1966
2:09·7	Kruse, Pam (USA)	Philadelphia	19 Aug. 1967
2:09·5	Pedersen, Sue (USA)	Santa Clara	6 July 1968
2:08·8	Wetzel, Eadie (USA)	Lincoln	2 Aug. 1968
2:06·7	Meyer, Debbie (USA)	Los Angeles	24 Aug. 1968

400 m. Free-style

6:30·2	Bleibtrey, Ethelda (USA)	New York	16 Aug. 1919
6:16·6*	James, Hilda (Eng)	Leeds	29 July 1921
5:53·2	Ederle, Gertrude (USA)	Indianapolis	4 Aug. 1922
5:51·4	Norelius, Martha (USA)	Coral Gables	23 Jan. 1927
5:49·6	Norelius, Martha (USA)	New York	30 June 1928
5:42·8	Norelius, Martha (USA)	Amsterdam	6 Aug. 1928
5:39·2*	Norelius, Martha (USA)	Vienna	27 Aug. 1928
5:31·0*	Madison, Helene (USA)	Seattle	3 Feb. 1931
5:28·5	Madison, Helene (USA)	Los Angeles	13 Aug. 1932
5:16·0*	Den Ouden, Willy (Neth)	Rotterdam	12 July 1934
5:14·2*	Hveger, Ragnild (Den)	Copenhagen	10 Feb. 1937
5:14·0*	Hveger, Ragnild (Den)	Gand	3 Oct. 1937
5:12·4*	Hveger, Ragnild (Den)	Magdeburg	14 Nov. 1937
5:11·0*	Hveger, Ragnild (Den)	Copenhagen	12 Dec. 1937
5:08·2*	Hveger, Ragnild (Den)	Copenhagen	16 Jan. 1938
5:06·1*	Hveger, Ragnild (Den)	Copenhagen	1 Aug. 1938

5:05·4*	Hveger, Ragnild (Den)	Svendborg	8 Sept. 1940
5:00·1*	Hveger, Ragnild (Den)	Copenhagen	15 Sept. 1940
4:50·8	Crapp, Lorraine (Aus)	Townsville	25 Aug. 1956
4:47·2	Crapp, Lorraine (Aus)	Sydney	20 Oct. 1956
4:45·4y	Konrads, Ilsa (Aus)	Sydney	9 Jan. 1960
4:44·5	Von Saltza, Chris (USA)	Detroit	5 Aug. 1960
4:42·0	Ramenofsky, Marilyn (USA)	Los Altos	11 July 1964
4:41·7	Ramenofsky, Marilyn (USA)	Los Altos	1 Aug. 1964
4:39·5	Ramenofsky, Marilyn (USA)	New York	31 Aug. 1964
4:39·2	Randall, Martha (USA)	Maumee	14 Aug. 1965
4:38·0	Randall, Martha (USA)	Monaco	26 Aug. 1965
4:36·8	Kruse, Pam (USA)	Ft. Lauderdale	30 June 1967
4:36·4	Kruse, Pam (USA)	Santa Clara	7 July 1967
4:32·6	Meyer, Debbie (USA)	Winnipeg	27 July 1967
4:29·0	Meyer, Debbie (USA)	Philadelphia	18 Aug. 1967
4:26·7	Meyer, Debbie (USA)	Lincoln	1 Aug. 1968
4:24·5	Meyer, Debbie (USA)	Los Angeles	25 Aug. 1968
4:24·3	Meyer, Debbie (USA)	Los Angeles	20 Aug. 1970

800 m. Free-style

12:18·8	Godard, Yvonne (Fra)	Paris	23 Aug. 1931
11:44·3	Knight, Laura (USA)	Jones Beach	23 July 1933
11:34·4	Knight, Laura (USA)	Manhattan Beach	21 July 1935
11:11·7	Hveger, Ragnild (Den)	Copenhagen	3 July 1936
10:52·5	Hveger, Ragnild (Den)	Copenhagen	13 Aug. 1941
10:42·4	Gyenge, Valeria (Hun)	Budapest	28 June 1953
10:30·9	Crapp, Lorraine (Aus)	Sydney	14 Jan. 1956
10:17·7y	Konrads, Ilsa (Aus)	Sydney	9 Jan. 1958
10:16·2y	Konrads, Ilsa (Aus)	Melbourne	20 Feb. 1958
10:11·8y	Konrads, Ilsa (Aus)	Townsville	13 June 1958
10:11·4y	Konrads, Ilsa (Aus)	Hobart	19 Feb. 1959
9:55·6	Cederqvist, Jane (Swe)	Uppsala	17 Aug. 1960
9:51·6	House, Carolyn (USA)	Los Altos	26 Aug. 1962
9:47·3	Caretto, Patty (USA)	Los Altos	30 July 1964
9:36·9	Finneran, Sharon (USA)	Los Angeles	28 Sept. 1964
9:35·8	Meyer, Debbie (USA)	Santa Clara	9 July 1967
9:22·9	Meyer, Debbie (USA)	Winnipeg	29 July 1967
9:19·0	Meyer, Debbie (USA)	Los Angeles	21 July 1968
9:17·8	Meyer, Debbie (USA)	Lincoln	4 Aug. 1968
9:10·4	Meyer, Debbie (USA)	Los Angeles	28 Aug. 1968
9:09·1	Moras, Karen (Aus)	Sydney	1 Mar. 1970
9:02·4	Moras, Karen (Aus)	Edinburgh	18 July 1970

1,500 m. Free-style

25:06·6	Wainwright, Helen (USA)	Manhattan Beach	19 Aug. 1922
24:07·6	McGary, E. (USA)	Coral Gables	31 Dec. 1925
24:00·2	Mayne, Edith (Eng)	Exmouth	15 Sept. 1926
23:44·6	Norelius, Martha (USA)	Massapaqua	28 July 1927
23:17·2	Madison, Helene (USA)	New York	15 July 1931
22:36·7	Frederiksen, G. (Den)	Copenhagen	26 June 1936
21:45·7	Hveger, Ragnild (Den)	Helsingor	3 July 1938
21:10·1	Hveger, Ragnild (Den)	Helsingor	11 Aug. 1940
20:57·0	Hveger, Ragnild (Den)	Copenhagen	20 Aug. 1941

| 20:46·5 | De Nijs, Lenie (Neth) | Utrecht | 23 July 1955 |
| 20:22·8 | Koster, Jans (Neth) | Utrecht | 21 Aug. 1956 |

20:03·1	Koster, Jans (Neth)	Hilversum	27 July 1957
19:25·7y	Konrads, Ilsa (Aus)	Sydney	14 Jan. 1959
19:23·6	Cederqvist, Jane (Swe)	Uppsala	8 Sept. 1960
19:02·8	Rylander, Margareta (Swe)	Uppsala	27 June 1961
18:44·0	House, Carolyn (USA)	Chicago	16 Aug. 1962
18:30·5	Caretto, Patty (USA)	Los Altos	30 July 1964
18:23·7	Caretto, Patty (USA)	Los Altos	12 Aug. 1965
18:12·9	Caretto, Patty (USA)	Lincoln	21 Aug. 1966
18:11·1	Meyer, Debbie (USA)	Santa Clara	9 July 1967
17:50·2	Meyer, Debbie (USA)	Philadelphia	20 Aug. 1967
17:31·2	Meyer, Debbie (USA)	Los Angeles	21 July 1968
17:19·9	Meyer, Debbie (USA)	Louisville	17 Aug. 1969

100 m. Back-stroke

1:36·7	Hart, Doris (Eng)	Gothenburg	6 July 1923
1:35·0	Mullerova, J. (Czech)	Prague	29 July 1923
1:26·6	Bauer, Sybil (USA)	Newark	8 Aug. 1923
1:22·4*	Bauer, Sybil (USA)	Miami	6 Jan. 1924
1:22·0*	Van Den Turk, Willy (Neth)	Rotterdam	10 July 1927
1:21·6	Braun, Marie (Neth)	Amsterdam	11 Aug. 1928
1:21·4*	Braun, Marie (Neth)	Brussels	20 Apr. 1929
1:21·0*	Braun, Marie (Neth)	Gravenhage	27 Nov. 1929
1:20·6*	Mealing, Bonnie (Aus)	Sydney	27 Feb. 1930
1:18·6*	Harding, Phyllis (GB)	Wallasey	30 May 1932
1:18·2	Holm, Eleanor (USA)	Jones Beach	16 July 1932
1:16·8*	Mastenbroek, Rie (Neth)	Dusseldorf	25 Nov. 1934
1:16·3	Holm, Eleanor (USA)	Chicago	15 Jan. 1935
1:15·8*	Mastenbroek, Rie (Neth)	Amsterdam	27 Feb. 1936
1:15·7*	Senff, Nina (Neth)	Copenhagen	8 Sept. 1936
1:15·4*	Senff, Nina (Neth)	Copenhagen	10 Sept. 1936
1:13·6*	Senff, Nina (Neth)	Dusseldorf	25 Oct. 1936
1:13·5*	Kint, Cor (Neth)	Copenhagen	1 Nov. 1938
1:13·2*	Van Feggelen, Iet (Neth)	Amsterdam	10 Nov. 1938
1:13·0*	Van Feggelen, Iet (Neth)	Gravenhage	12 Nov. 1938
1:12·9*	Van Feggelen, Iet (Neth)	Antwerp	26 Nov. 1938
1:10·9*	Kint, Cor (Neth)	Rotterdam	22 Sept. 1939

1:12·9	Grinham, Judy (GB)	Melbourne	5 Dec. 1956
1:12·5y	Gould, Phillipa (NZ)	Auckland	12 Mar. 1958
1:12·4y	Edwards, Margaret (GB)	Cardiff	19 Apr. 1958
1:12·3	Van Velsen, Ria (Neth)	Nijmegen	20 July 1958
1:11·9y	Grinham, Judy (GB)	Cardiff	23 July 1958
1:11·7	Van Velsen, Ria (Neth)	Waalwijk	26 July 1959
1:11·4	Cone, Carin (USA)	Chicago	6 Sept. 1959
1:11·0	Van Velsen, Ria (Neth)	Leipzig	12 June 1960
1:10·9	Van Velsen, Ria (Neth)	Maastricht	10 July 1960
1:10·1	Burke, Lynn (USA)	Indianapolis	17 July 1960
1:10·0	Burke, Lynn (USA)	Detroit	4 Aug. 1960
1:09·2	Burke, Lynn (USA)	Detroit	5 Aug. 1960
1:09·0	Burke, Lynn (USA)	Rome	2 Sept. 1960
1:08·9	De Varona, Donna (USA)	Los Angeles	28 July 1963

1:08·6	Caron, Christine (Fra)	Paris	14 June 1964
1:08·3	Duenkel, Ginny (USA)	Los Angeles	28 Sept. 1964
1:07·7	Ferguson, Cathy (USA)	Tokyo	14 Oct. 1964
1:07·4	Fairlie, Ann (SAf)	Beziers	23 July 1966
1:07·3	Tanner, Elaine (Can)	Winnipeg	27 July 1967
1:07·1	Tanner, Elaine (Can)	Winnipeg	30 July 1967
1:06·7	Muir, Karen (SAf)	Kimberley	30 Jan. 1968
1:06·4	Muir, Karen (SAf)	Paris	6 Apr. 1968
1:06·2	Hall, Kaye (USA)	Mexico City	23 Oct. 1968
1:05·6	Muir, Karen (SAf)	Utrecht	6 July 1969

200 m. Back-stroke

3:06·8*	Bauer, Sybil (USA)	Brighton Beach	4 July 1922
3:03·8*	Bauer, Sybil (USA)	Miami	9 Feb. 1924
2:59·2*	Braun, Marie (Neth)	Brussels	24 Nov. 1928
2:58·8*	Holm, Eleanor (USA)	Buffalo	1 Feb. 1930
2:58·2*	Holm, Eleanor (USA)	New York	1 Mar. 1930
2:50·4*	Harding, Phyllis (Eng)	Wallasey	19 Sept. 1932
2:49·6*	Mastenbroek, Rie (Neth)	Amsterdam	20 Jan. 1935
2:48·7*	Holm, Eleanor (USA)	Toledo	3 Mar. 1936
2:44·6*	Senff, Nina (Neth)	Amsterdam	2 Feb. 1937
2:41·3*	Hveger, Ragnild (Den)	Aarhus	14 Feb. 1937
2:41·0*	Kint, Cor (Neth)	Aarhus	17 Apr. 1938
2:40·6*	Van Feggelen, Iet (Neth)	Dusseldorf	26 Oct. 1938
2:39·0*	Van Feggelen, Iet (Neth)	Amsterdam	18 Dec. 1938
2:38·8*	Kint, Cor (Neth)	Rotterdam	29 Nov. 1939
2:35·3*	Wielema, Geertje (Neth)	Hilversum	2 Apr. 1950

2:39·9y	Gould, Philippa (NZ)	Auckland	16 Jan. 1957
2:38·5y	De Nijs, Lenie (Neth)	Blackpool	17 May 1957
2:37·4	Von Saltza, Chris (USA)	Topeka	1 Aug. 1958
2:37·1	Tanaka, Satoko (Jap)	Tokyo	12 July 1959
2:34·8	Tanaka, Satoko (Jap)	Tokyo	2 Apr. 1960
2:33·5	Burke, Lynn (USA)	Indianapolis	15 July 1960
2:33·3	Tanaka, Satoko (Jap)	Tokyo	23 July 1960
2:33·2	Tanaka, Satoko (Jap)	Tokyo	30 July 1961
2:32·1	Tanaka, Satoko (Jap)	Beppu	3 June 1962
2:31·6	Tanaka, Satoko (Jap)	Osaka	29 July 1962
2:29·6y	Tanaka, Satoko (Jap)	Sydney	10 Feb. 1963
2:28·9y	Tanaka, Satoko (Jap)	Perth	18 Feb. 1963
2:28·5y	Tanaka, Satoko (Jap)	Perth	21 Feb. 1963
2:28·2	Tanaka, Satoko (Jap)	Tokyo	4 Aug. 1963
2:27·4	Ferguson, Cathy (USA)	Los Angeles	28 Sept. 1964
2:27·1	Muir, Karen (SAf)	Beziers	25 July 1966
2:26·4	Muir, Karen (SAf)	Lincoln	18 Aug. 1966
2:24·4	Tanner, Elaine (Can)	Winnipeg	26 July 1967
2:24·1y	Muir, Karen (SAf)	Kimberley	29 Jan. 1968
2:23·8	Muir, Karen (SAf)	Los Angeles	21 July 1968
2:21·5	Atwood, Susie (USA)	Louisville	14 Aug. 1969

100 m. Breast-stroke

1:37·6*	Van Den Bogaert, E. (Belg)	Brussels	22 July 1921
1:33·4*	Hart, Doris (Eng)	Aldershot	23 Aug. 1922
1:31·8*	Gilbert, Irene (Eng)	Rotherham	30 Oct. 1924
1:29·0*	Huneus, Erno (Ger)	Aachen	4 Oct. 1925

1:28·8*	Geraghty, Agnes (USA)	St. Augustine	13 Feb. 1926
1:26·3*	Muhe, Lotte (Ger)	Magdeburg	9 June 1928
1:26·2*	Jacobsen, Else (Den)	Copenhagen	10 Apr. 1932
1:26·0*	Jacobsen, Else (Den)	Stockholm	11 May 1932
1:24·6*	Dennis, Clare (Aus)	Unley	14 Feb. 1933
1:24·5*	Holzner, Johanna (Ger)	Copenhagen	15 Jan. 1935
1:23·4*	Holzner, Johanna (Ger)	Halle	16 Feb. 1936
1:22·8*	Christensen, V. (Den)	Dusseldorf	8 Mar. 1936
1:20·2*	Holzner, Johanna (Ger)	Plauen	13 Mar. 1936
1:19·8*	Grass, Gisela (Ger)	Leipzig	9 May 1943
1:19·4*	Van Vliet, Nel (Neth)	Alost	29 July 1946
1:19·0*	Van Vliet, Nel (Neth)	Den Haag	1 Aug. 1946
1:18·2*	Van Vliet, Nel (Neth)	Arnhem	28 Apr. 1947
1:17·4*	Vallerey, Gisele (Fra)	Casablanca	Bu23 Apr. 1950
1:16·9*	Szekely, Eva (Hun)	Moscow	Bu9 May 1951

1:20·3	Beyer, Karin (EGer)	Berlin	20 July 1958
1:19·6	Beyer, Karin (EGer)	Leipzig	12 Sept. 1958
1:19·1	Urselmann, Wiltrud (WGer)	Zurich	12 Mar. 1960
1:19·0	Kuper, Ursela (EGer)	Leipzig	14 July 1960
1:18·2	Gobel, Barbara (EGer)	Rostock	1 July 1961
1:17·9	Kolb, Claudia (USA)	Los Angeles	11 July 1964
1:17·2	Babanina, Svetlana (USSR)	Moscow	3 Sept. 1964
1:16·5	Babanina, Svetlana (USSR)	Tashkent	11 May 1965
1:15·7	Prosumenschikova, Galina (USSR)	Lenin	17 July 1966
1:15·6	Ball, Catie (USA)	Ft. Lauderdale	28 Dec. 1966
1:15·6	Ball, Catie (USA)	Santa Clara	7 July 1967
1:14·8	Ball, Catie (USA)	Winnipeg	31 July 1967
1:14·6	Ball, Catie (USA)	Philadelphia	19 Aug. 1967
1:14·2	Ball, Catie (USA)	Los Angeles	25 Aug. 1968

200 m. Breast-stroke

3:38·2	Van Den Bogaert, E. (Belg)	Antwerp	7 Aug. 1921
3:34·6*	Van Den Bogaert, E. (Belg)	Brussels	6 May 1922
3:31·4*	Van Den Bogaert, E. (Belg)	Antwerp	4 Oct. 1922
3:20·4*	Gilbert, Irene (Eng)	Rotherham	18 June 1923
3:20·2*	Murray, Erna (Ger)	Leipzig	5 Apr. 1925
3:19·1*	Hazelius, B. (Swe)	Stockholm	11 Aug. 1926
3:18·4*	Baron, Marie (Neth)	Brussels	24 Oct. 1926
3:16·6	Jacobsen, Else (Den)	Oslo	20 Aug. 1927
3:15·8*	Muhe, Lotte (Ger)	Magdeburg	15 Apr. 1928
3:12·8*	Baron, Marie (Neth)	Rotterdam	22 Apr. 1928
3:11·2	Muhe, Lotte (Ger)	Berlin	15 July 1928
3:10·6*	Hinton, Margery (Eng)	Manchester	20 July 1931
3:08·4*	Dennis, Clare (Aus)	Sydney	18 Jan. 1932
3:08·2*	Rocke, Lisa (Ger)	Leipzig	21 Apr. 1932
3:03·4*	Jacobsen, Else (Den)	Stockholm	11 May 1932
3:00·4*	Maehata, Hideko (Jap)	Tokyo	30 Sept. 1933
3:00·2*	Waalberg, Jopie (Neth)	Amsterdam	11 May 1937
2:58·0*	Waalberg, Jopie (Neth)	Zaandyk	27 June 1937
2:56·9*	Waalberg, Jopie (Neth)	Gand	2 Oct. 1937
2:56·0*	Lenk, Maria (Braz)	Rio de Janeiro	8 Nov. 1939
2:52·6*	Van Vliet, Nel (Neth)	Bilthoven	17 Aug. 1946
2:51·9*	Van Vliet, Nel (Neth)	Amsterdam	29 Mar. 1947

2:49·2*	Van Vliet, Nel (Neth)	Hilversum	20 July 1947
2:48·8*	Novak, Eva (Hun)	Szekesfehervar	21 Oct. 1950
2:48·5*	Novak, Eva (Hun)	Moscow	5 May 1951

| 2:46·4* | Den Haan, Ada (Neth) | Naarden | 13 Nov. 1956 |

2:52·5y	Den Haan, Ada (Neth)	Blackpool	18 May 1957
2:51·9	Den Haan, Ada (Neth)	Rhenen	3 Aug. 1957
2:51·3	Den Haan, Ada (Neth)	Rhenen	4 Aug. 1957
2:50·3	Lonsbrough, Anita (GB)	Waalwijk	25 July 1959
2:50·2	Urselmann, Wiltrud (WGer)	Aachen	6 June 1960
2:49·5	Lonsbrough, Anita (GB)	Rome	27 Aug. 1960
2:48·0	Beyer, Karin (EGer)	Budapest	5 Aug. 1961
2:47·7y	Prosumenschikova, Galina (USSR)	Blackpool	11 Apr. 1964
2:45·4	Prosumenschikova, Galina (USSR)	Berlin	17 May 1964
2:45·3	Prosumenschikova, Galina (USSR)	Groningen	12 Sept. 1965
2:40·8	Prosumenschikova, Galina (USSR)	Utrecht	22 Aug. 1966
2:40·5	Ball, Catie (USA)	Santa Clara	9 July 1967
2:39·5	Ball, Catie (USA)	Philadelphia	20 Aug. 1967
2:38·5	Ball, Catie (USA)	Los Angeles	26 Aug. 1968

100 m. Butterfly

1:16·6	Langenau, Jutta (EGer)	Turin	31 Aug. 1954
1:14·0*	Mann, Shelley (USA)	Richmond	4 Sept. 1954
1:13·8*	Kok, Mary (Neth)	Alkmaar	16 Apr. 1955
1:13·7*	Voorbij, Atie (Neth)	Naarden	14 July 1955
1:13·2*	Voorbij, Atie (Neth)	Algiers	28 Aug. 1955
1:13·1*	Voorbij, Atie (Neth)	Vlaardingen	21 Sept. 1955
1:11·9*	Voorbij, Atie (Neth)	Velsen	5 Feb. 1956
1:11·8*	Mann, Shelley (USA)	Tyler	7 July 1956
1:10·5*	Voorbij, Atie (Neth)	Hilversum	12 Nov. 1956

1:10·5	Voorbij, Atie (Neth)	Rhenen	4 Aug. 1957
1:09·6	Ramey, Nancy (USA)	Los Angeles	28 June 1958
1:09·1	Ramey, Nancy (USA)	Chicago	2 Sept. 1959
1:08·9	Andrew, Jan (Aus)	Tokyo	2 Apr. 1961
1:08·8	Stewart, Mary (Can)	Philadelphia	12 Aug. 1961
1:08·2	Doerr, Susan (USA)	Philadelphia	12 Aug. 1961
1:07·8	Doerr, Susan (USA)	Philadelphia	2 Aug. 1962
1:07·3y	Stewart, Mary (Can)	Vancouver	28 July 1962
1:06·5	Ellis, Kathy (USA)	N. Carolina	16 Aug. 1963
1:06·1	Kok, Ada (Neth)	Soestduinen	1 Sept. 1963
1:05·4	Stouder, Sharon (USA)	Los Altos	1 Aug. 1964
1:05·1y	Kok, Ada (Neth)	Blackpool	30 May 1964
1:04·7	Stouder, Sharon (USA)	Tokyo	16 Oct. 1964
1:04·5	Kok, Ada (Neth)	Budapest	14 Aug. 1965
1:04·1	Jones, Alice (USA)	Los Angeles	20 Aug. 1970

200 m. Butterfly

| 2:42·3* | Lagerberg, Tineke (Neth) | Naarden | 12 Dec. 1956 |
| 2:38·1* | Lagerberg, Tineke (Neth) | Naarden | 19 Mar. 1957 |

2:40·5	Ramey, Nancy (USA)	Los Angeles	29 June 1958
2:38·9	Lagerberg, Tineke (Neth)	Naarden	13 Sept. 1958
2:37·0y	Collins, Becky (USA)	Redding	19 July 1959

o

2:34·4	Heemskerk, Marianne (Neth)	Leipzig	12 June 1960
2:32·8	Collins, Becky (USA)	Philadelphia	13 Aug. 1961
2:31·2	Finneran, Sharon (USA)	Chicago	19 Aug. 1962
2:30·7	Finneran, Sharon (USA)	Los Altos	25 Aug. 1962
2:29·1	Pitt, Sue (USA)	Philadelphia	27 July 1963
2:28·1	Stouder, Sharon (USA)	Los Angeles	12 July 1964
2:26·4	Stouder, Sharon (USA)	Los Altos	2 Aug. 1964
2:26·3	Moore, Kendis (USA)	Maumee	15 Aug. 1965
2:25·8	Kok, Ada (Neth)	De Vleit	21 Aug. 1965
2:25·3	Kok, Ada (Neth)	Groningen	12 Sept. 1965
2:22·5	Kok, Ada (Neth)	Groningen	2 Aug. 1967
2:21·0y	Kok, Ada (Neth)	Blackpool	25 Aug. 1967
2:20·7	Moe Karen (USA)	Santa Clara	11 July 1970
2:19·3	Jones, Alice (USA)	Los Angeles	22 Aug. 1970

200 m. Individual medley

2:27·8	Kolb, Claudia (USA)	Lincoln	21 Aug. 1966
2:27·5	Kolb, Claudia (USA)	Santa Clara	8 July 1967
2:26·1	Kolb, Claudia (USA)	Winnipeg	30 July 1967
2:25·0	Kolb, Claudia (USA)	Philadelphia	18 Aug. 1967
2:23·5	Kolb, Claudia (USA)	Los Angeles	25 Aug. 1968

400 m. Individual medley

5:50·4*	Szekely, Eva (Hun)	Budapest	10 Apr. 1953
5:47·3*	Kok, Mary (Neth)	Hilversum	28 Mar. 1955
5:40·8*	Szekely, Eva (Hun)	Budapest	13 July 1955
5:38·9*	Kok, Mary (Neth)	Hilversum	2 Dec. 1956

5:46·6	Ruuska, Sylvia (USA)	Los Angeles	27 June 1958
5:43·7	Ruuska, Sylvia (USA)	Topeko	1 Aug. 1958
5:41·1y	Ruuska, Sylvia (USA)	Melbourne	24 Feb. 1959
5:40·2y	Ruuska, Sylvia (USA)	Redding	17 July 1959
5:36·5	De Varona, Donna (USA)	Indianapolis	15 July 1960
5:34·5	De Varona, Donna (USA)	Philadelphia	11 Aug. 1961
5:29·7	De Varona, Donna (USA)	Los Altos	2 June 1962
5:27·4	Finneran, Sharon (USA)	Osaka	26 July 1962
5:24·7	De Varona, Donna (USA)	Osaka	26 July 1962
5:21·9	Finneran, Sharon (USA)	Osaka	28 July 1962
5:16·5	De Varona, Donna (USA)	Lima	10 Mar. 1964
5:14·9	De Varona, Donna (USA)	New York	30 Aug. 1964
5:11·7	Kolb, Claudia (USA)	Santa Clara	9 July 1967
5:09·7	Kolb, Claudia (USA)	Winnipeg	1 Aug. 1967
5:08·2	Kolb, Claudia (USA)	Philadelphia	19 Aug. 1967
5:04·7	Kolb, Claudia (USA)	Los Angeles	24 Aug. 1968

4 × 100 m. Free-style relay

| 4:38·0 | United States | Los Angeles | 12 Aug. 1932 |

(McKim, Josephine; Johns, Helen; Garatti-Saville, Eleanor; Madison, Helene)

| 4:33·3* | Netherlands | Rotterdam | 14 Apr. 1934 |

(Selbach, Jopie; Timmermans, Annie; Mastenbroek, Rie; Den Ouden, Willy)

| 4:32·8* | Netherlands | Rotterdam | 24 May 1936 |

(Selbach, Jopie; Mastenbroek, Rie; Wagner, Catherina; Den Ouden, Willy)

4:29·7*   Denmark   Copenhagen   8 Feb. 1938
          (Svendsen, E.; Kraft, Gunvor; Ove-Petersen, Birte; Hveger, Ragnhild)
4:27·6*   Denmark   Copenhagen   7 Aug. 1938
          (Arndt, Eva; Kraft, Gunvor; Ove-Petersen, Birte; Hveger, Ragnhild)
4:27·2*   Hungary   Moscow   27 Apr. 1952
          (Littomeriszky, Maria; Novak, Eva; Szekely, Eva; Szoke, Katalin)
4:24·4   Hungary   Helsinki   1 Aug. 1952
          (Novak, Ilona; Temes, Judith; Novak, Eva; Szoke, Katalin)
4:22·3   Australia   Sydney   20 Oct. 1956
          (Crapp, Lorraine; Fraser, Dawn; Gibson, Margaret; Jackson, Barbara)
4:19·7   Australia   Melbourne   25 Oct. 1956
          (Crapp, Lorraine; Fraser, Dawn; Leech, Faith; Gibson, Margaret)
4:17·1   Australia   Melbourne   6 Dec. 1956
          (Fraser, Dawn; Leech, Faith; Morgan, Sandra; Crapp, Lorraine)
- -
4:16·2y   Australia   Townsville   6 Aug. 1960
          (Fraser, Dawn; Colquhoun, Alva; Konrads, Ilsa; Crapp, Lorraine)
4:08·9   United States   Rome   3 Sept. 1960
          (Spillane, Joan; Stobs, Shirley; Wood, Carolyn; Von Saltza, Chris)
4:08·5   Santa Clara S.C., United States Los Altos   31 July 1964
          (Stickles, Terri; De Varona, Donna; Watson, Pokey; Haroun, Judy)
4:07·6   United States   Los Angeles   28 Sept. 1964
          (Allsup, Lynn; Seidel, Kathy; Bricker, Eleanor; Stickles, Terri)
4:03·8   United States   Tokyo   15 Oct. 1964
          (Stouder, Sharon; De Varona, Donna; Watson, Pokey; Ellis, Kathy)
4:03·5   Santa Clara S.C., United States Philadelphia   19 Aug. 1967
          (Gustavson, Linda; Ryan, Nancy; Fritz, L.; Watson, Pokey)
4:01·1   Santa Clara S.C., United States Santa Clara   6 July 1968
          (Gustavson, Linda; Watson, Pokey; Carpinelli, Pam; Henne, Jan)
4:00·8   East Germany   Barcelona   11 Sept. 1970
          (Wetzko, Gabriele; Komor, Iris; Sehmisch, Elke; Schulze, Carola)

4 × 100 m. Medley relay
5:10·8   Hungary   Budapest   24 July 1953
          (Hunyadfi, Magda; Killermann, Klara; Szekely, Eva; Gyenge, Valeria)
5:09·2   Hungary   Bucarest   10 Aug. 1953
          (Hunyadfi, Magda; Killermann, Klara; Szekely, Eva; Gyenge, Valeria)
5:07·8   Hungary   Budapest   3 Aug. 1954
          (Temes, Judit; Killermann, Klara; Littomeritzky, Maria; Szoke,
          Katalin)
5:06·2*   France   Marseilles   16 Aug. 1954
          (Andre, Marie-Helene; Derommeleere, Francoise; Lusien, Odette;
          Arene, Josette)
5:02·1*   Netherlands   Rotterdam   27 Nov. 1954
          (De Korte, Joke; Bruins, Rika; Kok, Mary; Wielema, Geertje)
5:00·1   Netherlands   Paris   17 July 1955
          (Van Alphen, Jopie; Bruins, Rika; Voorbij, Atie; Balkenende, Hetty)
4:57·8   Hungary   Budapest   3 Sept. 1955
          (Pajor, Eva; Szekely, Eva; Szekely, Rypsyma; Szoke, Katalin)
4:54·3*   De Robben S.C., Netherlands   Hilversum   19 Nov. 1956
          (De Nijs, Lenie; Kroon, Rita; Voorbij, Atie; Kraan, Greetje)
4:53·1*   Netherlands   Zwolle   8 Dec. 1956
          (De Korte, Joke; Den Haan, Ada; Lagerberg, Tineke; Gastelaars,
          Cocky)
- -

| 4:57·0y | Netherlands | Blackpool | 18 May 1957 |

(Kraan, Greetje; Den Haan, Ada; Voorbij, Atie; Gastelaars, Cocky)

4:54·0y England   Cardiff   25 July 1958
(Grinham, Judy; Lonsbrough, Anita; Gosden, Chris; Wilkinson, Diana)

4:52·9 Netherlands   Budapest   5 Sept. 1958
(De Nijs, Lenie; Den Haan, Ada; Voorbij, Atie; Gastelaars, Cocky)

4:51·5 Netherlands   Waalwijk   26 July 1959
(Van Velsen, Ria; Den Haan, Ada; Lagerberg, Tineke; Gastelaars, Cocky)

4:44·6 United States   Chicago   6 Sept. 1959
(Cone, Carin; Bancroft, Ann; Collins, Becky; Von Saltza, Chris)

4:41·1 United States   Rome   2 Sept. 1960
(Burke, Lynn; Kempner, Patty; Schuler, Carolyn; Von Saltza, Chris)

4:40·1 East Germany   Leipzig   23 Aug. 1962
(Schmidt, Ingrid; Gobel, Barbara; Noack, Uta; Pechstein, Heidi)

4:38·1 Santa Clara S.C., United States Los Altos   4 July 1964
(Haroun, Judy; Kolb, Claudia; De Varona, Donna; Watson, Pokey)

4:34·6 United States   Los Angeles   28 Sept. 1964
(Ferguson, Cathy; Goyette, Cynthia; Ellis, Kathy; Randall, Martha)

4:33·9 United States   Tokyo   18 Oct. 1964
(Ferguson, Cathy; Goyette, Cynthia; Stouder, Sharon; Ellis, Kathy)

4:30·0 United States   Winnipeg   30 July 1967
(Moore, Kendis; Ball, Catie; Daniel, Ellie; Fordyce, Wendy)

4:28·1 United States   Colorado Springs   14 Sept. 1968
(Hall, Kaye; Ball, Catie; Daniel, Ellie; Pedersen, Sue)

4:27·4 United States   Tokyo   1 Sept. 1970
(Atwood, Sue; Brecht, Kim; Jones, Alice; Schilling, Cindy)

Obsolete World Records (last date for recognition in brackets after event)

MEN

100 y. Free-style (1 May 1957)

| 55·4* | Daniels, Charles (USA) | 1907 | First |
| 48·9* | Moore, Robin (USA) | 1956 | Last |

110 y. Free-style (31 Dec. 1968)

| 55·2 | Devitt, John (Aus) | 1957 | First |
| 53·5 | McGregor, Bobby (GB) | 1966 | Last |

220 y. Free-style (31 Dec. 1968)

| 2:28·6* | Lane, Freddy (Aus) | 1902 | First |
| 1:57·0 | Schollander, Don (USA) | 1966 | Last |

300 y. Free-style (31 Dec. 1948)

| 3:31·4* | Battersby, Syd (Eng) | 1909 | First |
| 3:03·0* | Jany, Alex (Fra) | 1948 | Last |

300 m. Free-style (31 Dec. 1948)

| 3:57·6* | Daniels, Charles (USA) | 1910 | First |
| 3:21·0 | Jany, Alex (Fra) | 1947 | Last |

440 y. Free-style (31 Dec. 1968)

| 5:26·4* | Battersby, Syd (Eng) | 1908 | First |
| 4:12·2 | Charlton, Greg (USA) | 1966 | Last |

500 y. Free-style (31 Dec. 1952)

6:07·2*	Kieran, Barney (Aus)	1905	First
5:12·0*	Marshall, John (Aus)	1950	Last

500 m. Free-style (31 Dec. 1952)

7:06·4*	Scheff, Otto (Aut)	1906	First
5:43·7*	Marshall, John (Aus)	1951	Last

880 y. Free-style (31 Dec. 1968)

11:25·4	Taylor, Henry (Eng)	1906	First
8:55·5	Rose, Murray (Aus)	1964	Last

1,000 y. Free-style (31 Dec. 1948)

13:34·8	Billington, David (Eng)	1905	First
11:37·4	Medica, Jack (USA)	1933	Last

1,000 m. Free-style (31 Dec. 1948)

15:50·8	Scheff, Otto (Aut)	1908	First
12:33·8	Amamo, Tomikatsu (Jap)	1938	Last

1,650 y. Free-style (31 Dec. 1968)

17:28·7	Konrads, John (Aus)	1958	First
17:11·0	Konrads, John (Aus)	1960	Last

1,760 y. Free-style (1 May 1957)

25:24·4	Scheff, Otto (Aut)	1908	First
19:40·4	Breen, George (USA)	1956	Last

100 y. Back-stroke (1 May 1957)

59·4*	Vanderweghe, Albert (USA)	1939	First
55·7*	Oyakawa, Yoshinobu (USA)	1954	Last

110 y. Back-stroke (31 Dec. 1968)

1:01·5	Monckton, John (Aus)	1958	First
1:00·1	Matthes, Roland (EGer)	1967	Last

150 y. Back-stroke (31 Dec. 1952)

1:57·6*	Unwin, Fred (Eng)	1909	First
1:29·9*	Stack, Allen (USA)	1949	Last

220 y. Back-stroke (31 Dec. 1968)

2:18·8	Monckton, John (Aus)	1958	First
2:12·0	Reynolds, Peter (Aus)	1966	Last

400 m. Back-stroke (31 Dec. 1948)

6:46·0*	Meyboom, H. (Belg)	1910	First
5:03·9*	Stack, Allen (USA)	1948	Last

100 y. Breast-stroke (1 May 1957)

1:02·1*	Skinner, J. (USA)	1939	First
1:00·4*	Hughes, R. (USA)	1956	Last

110 y. Breast-stroke (31 Dec. 1968)

1:13·5	Gathercole, Terry (Aus)	1958	First
1:08·2	O'Brien, Ian (Aus)	1966	Last

200 y. Breast-stroke (31 Dec. 1952)

2:41·8*	Baronyi, Andras (Hun)	1908	First
2:12·9*	Davies, John (Aus)	Bu1952	Last

220 y. Breast-stroke (31 December 1968)

2:38·8*	Gleie, Knud (Den)	1953	First
2:28·0	O'Brien, Ian (Aus)	1966	Last

400 m. Breast-stroke (31 Dec. 1948)

6:53·4	Zacharias, Georg (Ger)	1907	First
5:40·2*	Bonte, Bjorn (Neth)	1948	Last

500 m. Breast-stroke (31 Dec. 1948)

8:30·6	Zacharias, Georg (Ger)	1904	First
7:10·6*	Bonte, Bjorn (Neth)	1948	Last

100 y. Butterfly (1 May 1957)

57·3*	Baarcke, Larry (USA)	1954	First
54·3*	Wiggins, Albert (USA)	1957	Last

110 y. Butterfly (31 Dec. 1968)

1:03·8	Wilkinson, Brian (Aus)	1958	First
56·3	Spitz, Mark (USA)	1967	Last

220 y. Butterfly (31 Dec. 1968)

2:26·1*	Drake, Phil (USA)	1955	First
2:08·4	Berry, Kevin (Aus)	1963	Last

220 y. Individual medley (31 Dec. 1968)

2:14·0	(Standard time never achieved)	1964

400 y. Individual medley (1 May 1957)

4:52·8*	Jones, Burwell (USA)	1953	First
4:36·9*	Wardrop, Jack (GB)	1955	Last

440 y. Individual medley (31 Dec. 1968)

5:08·8	Black, Ian (GB)	1959	First
4:46·8	Holthaus, Michael (WGer)	1968	Last

4 × 100 y. Free-style relay (1 May 1957)

3:31·4*	Michigan Univ. (USA)	1937	First
3:18·3*	Yale Univ. (USA)	1957	Last

4 × 110 y. Free-style relay (31 Dec. 1968)

3:47·3	Australia	1958	First
3:35·6	Australia	1966	Last

4 × 200 y. Free-style relay (1 May 1957)

8:38·8	Yale Univ. (USA)	1934	First
7:39·9*	Yale Univ. (USA)	1953	Last

4 × 220 y. Free-style relay (31 Dec. 1968)

8:24·5	Australia	1958	First
7:59·5	Australia	1966	Last

3 × 100 y. Medley relay (31 Dec. 1952)

2:57·6*	Yale Univ. (USA)	1946	First
2:47·1*	Ohio State Univ. (USA)	1952	Last

3 × 100 m. Medley relay (31 Dec. 1952)

3:20·7	Ohio State Univ. (USA)	1946	First
3:07·0*	New Haven S.C. (USA)	1952	Last

4 × 110 y. Medley relay (31 Dec. 1968)

4:19·4	Australia	1958	First
4:03·2	Australia	1966	Last

WOMEN

100 y. Free-style (1 May 1957)

1:13·6*	Fletcher, Jennie (Eng)	1909	First
56·9	Fraser, Dawn (Aus)	1956	Last

110 y. Free-style (31 Dec. 1968)

1:02·4	Fraser, Dawn (Aus)	1958	First
59·5	Fraser, Dawn (Aus)	1962	Last

220 y. Free-style (31 Dec. 1968)

2:56·0*	Durack, Fanny (Aus)	1915	First
2:11·6	Fraser, Dawn (Aus)	1960	Last

300 y. Free-style (31 Dec. 1948)

4:33·2*	Neave, Vera (Eng)	1911	First
3:25·6*	Hveger, Ragnhild (Den)	1938	Last

300 m. Free-style (31 Dec. 1948)

5:57·6*	Zahoure, Berta (Aut)	1910	First
3:42·5*	Hveger, Ragnhild (Den)	1940	Last

440 y. Free-style (31 Dec. 1968)

6:30·2	Bleibtrey, Ethelda (USA)	1919	First
4:38·8	Wainwright, Kathy (Aus)	1966	Last

500 y. Free-style (31 Dec. 1952)

7:32·4	Durack, Fanny (Aus)	1915	First
5:53·0*	Hveger, Ragnhild (Den)	1942	Last

500 m. Free-style (31 Dec. 1952)

7:22·2	Ederle, Gertrude (USA)	1922	First
6:27·4*	Hveger, Ragnhild (Den)	1940	Last

880 y. Free-style (31 Dec. 1968)

13:19·0	Ederle, Gertrude (USA)	1919	First
9:44·1	Meyer, Debbie (USA)	1967	Last

1,000 y. Free-style (31 Dec. 1948)

14:58·4	Wainwright, Helen (USA)	1922	First
12:36·0	Hveger, Ragnhild (Den)	1938	Last

1,000 m. Free-style (31 Dec. 1948)

15:49·6	Mayne, Edith (Eng)	1926	First
13:54·4	Hveger, Ragnhild (Den)	1941	Last

1,650 y. Free-style (31 Dec. 1968)

19:25·7	Konrads, Ilsa (Aus)	1959	First
18:47·8	Coughlan, Angela (Can)	1968	Last

1,760 y. Free-style (1 May 1957)

26:08·0	Durack, Fanny (Aus)	1914	First
22:05·5	De Nijs, Lenie (Neth)	1955	Last

100 y. Back-stroke (1 May 1957)

1:05·1*	Kint, Cor (Neth)	1939	First
1:03·8*	Cone, Carin (USA)	1957	Last

110 y. Back-stroke (31 Dec. 1968)

1:13·5	Edwards, Margaret (GB)	1957	First
1:06·7	Muir, Karen (SAf)	1968	Last

150 y. Back-stroke (31 Dec. 1952)

2:17·0*	Morton, Lucy (GB)	1916	First
1:40·4*	Wielema, Geertje (Neth)	1951	Last

220 y. Back-stroke (31 Dec. 1968)

2:39·9	Gould, Philippa (NZ)	1957	First
2:24·1	Muir, Karen (SAf)	1968	Last

400 m. Back-stroke (31 Dec. 1948)

6:24·8*	Bauer, Sybil (USA)	1922	First
5:38·2*	Hveger, Ragnhild (Den)	1941	Last

100 y. Breast-stroke (1 May 1957)

1:16·6*	Dillard, J. (USA)	1939	First
1:09·2*	Van Vliet, Nel (Neth)	1947	Last

110 y. Breast-stroke (31 Dec. 1968)

1:21·2	Lassig, Rose (Aus)	1960	First
1:17·0	Ball, Catie (USA)	1967	Last

200 y. Breast-stroke (31 Dec. 1952)

3:11·4*	Morton, Lucy (Eng)	1916	First
2:34·0*	Novak, Eva (Hun)	1950	Last

220 y. Breast-stroke (31 Dec. 1968)

2:52·5	Den Haan, Ada (Neth)	1957	First
2:46·9	Ball, Catie (USA)	1967	Last

400 m. Breast-stroke (31 Dec. 1948)

7:42·2*	Van Den Bogaert, E. (Belg)	1922	First
5:58·6*	Van Vliet, Nel (Neth)	1947	Last

500 m. Breast-stroke (31 Dec. 1948)

10:33·2	Welch, D. (Aus)	1930	First
7:41·0*	Van Vliet, Nel (Neth)	1946	Last

100 y. Butterfly (1 May 1957)

1:06·3*	Mann, Shelley (USA)	1954	First
1:01·9*	Ramey, Nancy (USA)	1957	Last

110 y. Butterfly (31 Dec. 1968)

1:11·3	Ramey, Nancy (USA)	1957	First
1:05·1	Kok, Ada (Neth)	1964	Last

220 y. Butterfly (31 Dec. 1968)

2:44·4*	Mann, Shelley (USA)	1956	First
2:21·0	Kok, Ada (Neth)	1967	Last

220 y. Individual medley (31 Dec. 1968)

2:29·0	(Standard time never achieved)	1964

400 y. Individual medley (1 May 1957)

5:10·5*	Kok, Mary (Neth)	1955	First
5:08·0*	Ruuska, Sylvia (USA)	1957	Last

440 y. Individual medley (31 Dec. 1968)

5:41·1	Ruuska, Sylvia (USA)	1959	First
5:25·1	Olcese, Mary-Ellen (USA)	1965	Last

4 × 100 y. Free-style relay (1 May 1957)

4:08·1*	Denmark	1939	First
3:56·8*	Lafayette S.C. (USA)	1956	Last

4 × 110 y. Free-style relay (31 Dec. 1968)

4:18·9	Australia	1958	First
4:10·8	Canada	1966	Last

3 × 100 y. Medley relay (31 Dec. 1952)

3:26·6*	Denmark	1947	First
3:18·1*	Lafayette S.C. (USA)	1952	Last

3 × 100 m. Medley relay (31 Dec. 1952)

3:46·3*	Netherlands	1946	First
3:35·9*	Netherlands	1950	Last

4 × 100 y. Medley relay (1 May 1957)

4:43·4*	Lafayette S.C. (USA)	1954	First
4:23·0*	Walter Reed S.C. (USA)	1956	Last

4 × 110 y. Medley relay (31 Dec. 1968)

4:57·0	Netherlands	1957	First
4:37·4	United States	1967	Last

WORLD RECORDS DEVELOP-MENT. Since 1 January, 1969, a simple list, of metric distances only, has been recognised for world record purposes. But the complicated evolution of the world record book in the previous 60 years is illustrated in the following pages (218–221).

The significant years have been:

1908—when the F.I.N.A. was founded and established the first official list of world records during the Olympic Games in London. At this time F.I.N.A. accepted certain authenticated marks set before this date.

1957—when, from 1 May, all 100 y. and multiples of 100 y. distances were discontinued and the linear equivalents of the metric distances (110 y. and multiples) were introduced. From this date, also, world records had to be set in 50 m. or 55 y. baths; i.e.: long course.

1969—when, from 1 January, all yards distances were discontinued.

In reading the tables, it should be noted that:

E = the year in which the first record to be ratified was set and is not necessarily the year when the record came on the books.

D = the year when the distance was discontinued.

Normally, changes in the world record distances are made during an Olympic Games, to be operative from the next 1 Jan. In some cases a minimum standard was set before a record could be approved . . . and some retrospective performances were accepted for new distances.

World Records Development

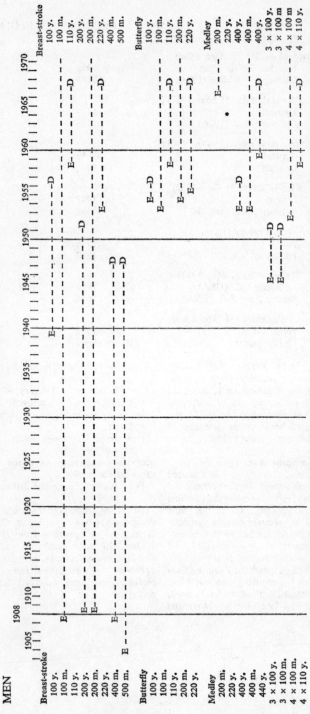

* Record distance established 1 Jan. 1965 with minimum standard time for ratification of 2:14·0. Event discontinued 31 Dec. 1968 without any swimmer having achieved this time (although 200 m. performances had been well within the standard).

World Records Development

MEN   1908

Free-style		Free-style
100 y.		100 y.
100 m.		100 m.
110 y.		110 y.
200 m.		200 m.
220 y.		220 y.
300 y.		300 y.
300 m.		300 m.
400 m.		400 m.
440 y.		440 y.
500 y.		500 y.
500 m.		500 m.
800 m.		800 m.
880 y.		880 y.
1,000 y.		1,000 y.
1,000 m.		1,000 m.
1,500 m.		1,500 m.
1,650 y.		1,650 y.
1,760 y.		1,760 y.
4 × 100 y.		4 × 100 y.
4 × 100 m.		4 × 100 m.
4 × 110 y.		4 × 110 y.
4 × 200 y.		4 × 200 y.
4 × 200 m.		4 × 200 m.
4 × 220 y.		4 × 220 y.

Back-stroke		Back-stroke
100 y.		100 y.
100 m.		100 m.
110 y.		110 y.
150 y.		150 y.
200 m.		200 m.
220 y.		220 y.
400 m.		400 m.

Years: 1905 1910 1915 1920 1925 1930 1935 1940 1945 1950 1955 1960 1965 1970

World Records Development

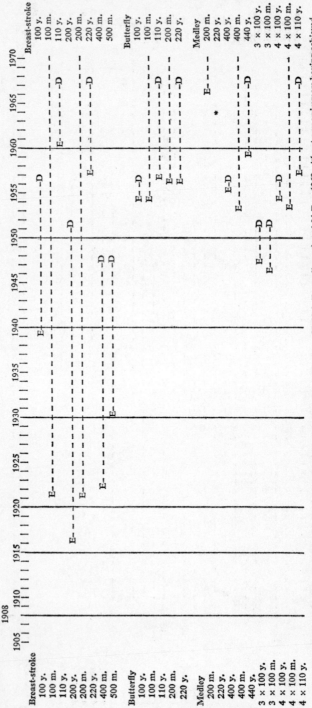

* Record distance established 1 Jan. 1965 with minimum standard time for ratification of 2:29·0. Event discontinued 31 Dec. 1968 without any swimmers having achieved the time (although 200 m. performances had been well within the standard).

World Records Development

WOMEN

Free-style
100 y.
100 m.
110 y.
200 m.
220 y.
300 y.
300 m.
400 m.
440 y.
500 y.
500 m.
800 m.
880 y.
1,000 y.
1,000 m.
1,500 m.
1,650 y.
1,760 y.
4 × 100 y.
4 × 100m.
4 × 110 y.

Back-stroke
100 y.
100 m.
110 y.
150 y.
200 m.
220 y.
400 m.

1905 1908 1910 1915 1920 1925 1930 1935 1940 1945 1950 1955 1960 1965 1970

Y

YEADEN, T. M. MEMORIAL TROPHY (England's 'Swimmer of the Year'. This trophy was presented to the A.S.A. by the five district associations to perpetuate the memory of T. M. Yeaden, honorary secretary of the A.S.A. from 1913–20, honorary treasurer 1921–36 and president in 1924, who died on 17 Jan. 1937. It has been awarded since 1938 to the English swimmer whose performance is judged the best of the year. Winners:

1938 Storey, Doris (Montague Burton)
1939 Wainwright, Norman (Hanley)
1940–46 Not awarded
1947 Romain, Roy (King's College, London)
1948 Hale, Jack (Hull Kingston)
1949 Wellington, Margaret (Beckenham L.)
1950 Wilkinson, Daphne (Sparkhill)
1951 Wilkinson, Daphne (Woolwich)
1952 Wilkinson, Daphne (Woolwich)
1953 Preece, Lillian (Wallasey)
1954 Symons, Pat (Northumberland)
1955 Symonds, Graham (Coventry)
1956 Grinham, Judy (Hampstead L.)
1957 Wilkinson, Diana (Stockport)
1958 Grinham, Judy (Hampstead L.)
1959 Lonsbrough, Anita (Huddersfield)
1960 Lonsbrough, Anita (Huddersfield)
1961 Wilkinson, Chris (Stockport)
1962 Ludgrove, Linda (St. James's L.)
1963 Mitchell, Stella (Hampstead L.)
1964 Mitchell, Stella (Hampstead L.)
1965 Long, Elizabeth (Ilford)
1966 Kimber, Alan (Southampton)
1967 Williams, Sue (Exeter)
1968 Jackson, Alex (Peel, I.o.M.)
1969 Terrell, Ray (Southampton)
1970 Harrison, Dorothy (Hartlepool)

INDEX

For names with the prefix of de, den, van, van den, von, etc., the entry appears under the initial of the main surname.

P